JOURNAL OF
A RESIDENCE ON A
GEORGIAN PLANTATION

FRANCES ANNE KEMBLE

After a drawing by the French portrait and landscape painter Jean Gigoux. Reproduced from a lithograph by courtesy of the Folger Shakespeare Library, Washington, D.C.

JOURNAL
of a Residence on a
GEORGIAN
PLANTATION
in 1838–1839
by Frances Anne Kemble

EDITED
WITH AN INTRODUCTION
BY JOHN A. SCOTT

Brown Thrasher Books
THE UNIVERSITY OF GEORGIA PRESS
ATHENS

Published in 1984 by the
University of Georgia Press, Athens, Georgia 30602
© 1961 by Alfred A. Knopf, Inc.
Foreword to the Brown Thrasher edition © 1984 by John A. Scott
All rights reserved
Printed in the United States of America

Library of Congress Cataloging in Publication Data
Kemble, Fanny, 1809–1893.
Journal of a residence on a Georgian plantation in
1838–1839.
"Brown thrasher books."
Reprint. Originally published: New York: Knopf, 1961.
Includes bibliographical references and index.
1. Slavery—Georgia—History—19th century. 2. Plan-
tation life—Georgia—History—19th century. 3. Georgia—
Social life and customs. 4. Kemble, Fanny, 1809–1893.
5. Plantation owners' wives—Georgia—Biography.
I. Scott, John Anthony, 1916– . II. Title.
E445.G3K46 1984   975.8′03′0924   83-24106
ISBN 0-8203-0707-6 (pbk.)

For ELIZABETH *and* WENDY

General Table of Contents

Illustration and Maps

Foreword to the
Brown Thrasher Edition

I N 1961, as part of the commemoration of the Civil War cen-
tennial, Alfred A. Knopf published the first modern edition
of Frances Anne Kemble's *Journal of a Residence on a Georgian
Plantation in 1838–1839*. New American Library made this edition available in paperback in 1975. In one form or the other the
Journal became accessible to a wide audience. Thousands of high
school and college students read it in their classes. Teachers and
writers both of black history and of women's history discovered
the *Journal* as a resource, as did actresses and students of drama.
It became a guide for archaeologists working in the field.

In the early 1980s the 1961 edition of the *Journal* went out of
print in both hardcover and paperback forms. The new Brown
Thrasher edition is welcome because it continues to make Kemble's classic available to a readership that has a growing awareness of its value. The *Journal* is one of those relatively rare books,
as one reviewer remarked in 1961, "that should never have gone
out of print in the first place, and should never be allowed to go
out of print again."

In her book Fanny Kemble tried to give a truthful account of
the life experience of enslaved people, voiceless and anonymous.

At the outset she proudly acknowledged her bias against human slavery. "I am," she wrote, "an Englishwoman in whom the absence of such a prejudice would be disgraceful" (p. 11). But Kemble did not believe that bias, in and of itself, takes from a person the ability to observe the world accurately and to record such observations objectively. "I feel very sure," she told her friend Elizabeth Dwight Sedgwick, "that you may rely upon the carefulness of my observation, and the accuracy of my report, of every detail of the working of the thing that comes under my notice" (p. 11).

This attitude is striking in its modernity. Today we too begin to reject the dogma that writers, teachers, and historians ought to cultivate "value-free" attitudes. Does the fact that a doctor loathes disease disqualify him from diagnosing illness and recording pathology? Does the fact that a person thinks of war as the ultimate obscenity disqualify him from recording the history of war and trying to lay bare its causes? In the words quoted above, Fanny Kemble was insisting that there is no necessary incompatibility between a commitment to ethical or social values and a commitment to truth.

Indeed, Kemble embodied in her own person passionate morality, brilliant powers of memory and of observation, and considerable talent as writer and recorder. Both as factual truth and as a vision of the tragic world which engulfed an entire people, her work has stood the test of time.

The 1961 edition of the *Journal* was a first contribution to the verification of a work that had been dismissed for a century as the libelous product of bias and a malicious spirit. Archival research turned up much information about the Butler family and the Butler plantations, and this was supplemented by field studies. Butler Island and St. Simons Island were subjected to scrutiny with the help of recent aerial photographs and also of nineteenth-century maps. Butler Island, for example, when viewed from ground level, seemed no more than a trackless wilderness of grass and swamp. Photographs and maps—with the help of a magnifying glass—revealed the remains of three slave "settlements," or villages, in the locations that Fanny Kemble had described. Kemble, again, gave a moving description of a "people's burial ground" in her chapter on "Shadrach's Death and Funeral." In 1960 no trace of this burial ground remained. But Alvin Cannon, a Georgia conservationist then residing on Butler Island, made careful probes which revealed the location and the extent of it. Many slaves were given Christian burial there during antebellum days, but the ground remained unmarked for more than a century.

Most of this new information was incorporated into maps prepared especially for the 1961 edition. Examination of the aerial surveys, too, dissipated a number of minor mysteries. Kemble, for example, makes several references in the *Journal* to a desolate penal settlement on Little St. Simons Island where rebellious slaves, both men and women, were sent—a sort of tiny Devil's Island where even the toughest spirits, forced to work long, hard, and lonely days in the rice swamps, might be broken. This penal settlement, Kemble asserted, was called "Five Pound." Why? The appropriateness of the name became clear from a glance at the aerial map. A strip of cultivation lay along the western edge of that swampy wilderness; it was marked by the faint signs of ruined dikes that had once divided the area into five fields, or "pounds." *

The findings of the 1961 edition were further amplified when archaeological investigation of the Sea Island coast was launched during the early 1970s. Excavations at Butler Island and Hampton Point were carried out under the direction of Professor Charles H. Fairbanks of the University of Florida. Fairbanks and his students contributed a wealth of new information about the Butler plantation. Enriching the picture that Fanny Kemble had painted, they also corrected it in minor details. Kemble, for example, had as-

* "A place of confinement, as a prison for criminals or debtors." Webster's *New International Dictionary*. Springfield, Mass., 1943. 2d edition.

serted that Butler slaves were not allowed the use of firearms (p. 276). St. Simons Island excavations turned up the remains of a hunting weapon buried in the soil where a slave cabin had once stood. The gun had probably been issued to a slave driver for the purpose of shooting game.

The 1970s witnessed not only the beginning of archaeological investigation of the slavery past but also important contributions in the publication of archival sources. During the 1930s Federal Works Project writers and Fisk University researchers took down from the lips of aged survivors over two thousand accounts of the slavery experience. Until recently this unique body of evidence— most of it in the Library of Congress in typescript form—was available to only a limited number of students. But much of it was published between 1972 and 1977. Historians began to undertake serious analysis and evaluation of this huge new literary contribution by slaves themselves to the story of their enslavement.

A composite picture of slavery as experienced by the slaves themselves emerges. Slavery was a complex institution with a variety of living patterns that reflected varying environmental conditions throughout the South. But in its broad outlines this picture substantiates the central features of Kemble's work. One of her most forceful generalizations, for example, was the statement that slavery, in its essence, was characterized by "the most disgusting struggle which is going on the whole time, on the one hand to inflict, and on the other to evade oppression and injustice" (p. 86). This "disgusting" reality of struggle, of a hundred different kinds and in a hundred different forms, permeates much of the literature created both by slaves and ex-slaves themselves. Over the years this "disgusting reality" has on the whole not received from historians the attention which it perhaps merits. Yet this concept of struggle as Kemble witnessed it and expressed it opens up, even today, new perspectives for the treatment of black history under slavery and for the restoration to that history of the human identity and human dignity that has so long been withheld from it.

Kemble's achievement may still be contemplated with a sense of awe. In December 1838, when she left New England for the South, she was just twenty-nine years of age. Yet she plumbed the meaning of human bondage and set forth what she had learned in language of evocative beauty.

The 1961 edition of Kemble's *Journal* appeared when the civil rights movement was rising into flood. Struggles against state-enforced segregation in schools, parks, libraries, theaters, restaurants, buses, and trains were beginning to rock the South. The sit-in movement had been launched in North Carolina in 1960; 1961 was the year of the Freedom Rides, and many new battles lay ahead. Birmingham (1963), the Mississippi Freedom Summer (1964), and Selma (1965) are the best remembered.

It was clear enough that the struggle to do away with segregation was linked with democracy, human dignity, and human freedom. But what relationship, if any, did the civil rights movement have to slavery itself and to the antislavery struggles of an earlier time? This question is far from academic; what may be involved here is the status and meaning of the Thirteenth Amendment in our own time. The answer to this question might conceivably shape the political perspectives of millions as well as the conduct of federal and state governments themselves.

Many people, and this includes historians, have for years held the belief that the Civil War and the Thirteenth Amendment laid the ax to the system of slavery and swept it away.* Historian C. Vann Woodward gave a fresh formulation to this position in a series of lectures delivered at the University of Virginia in 1954 and subsequently published under the title *The Strange Career of Jim Crow*. Segregation, said Woodward, was indeed "a capitulation to racism," but it had little or no connection with slavery.

* A classic and highly influential statement of this position was provided by Justice Joseph Philo Bradley in the Supreme Court majority opinion in *The Civil Rights Cases* 109 U.S. 3 (1883).

What he termed "genuine segregation" was uniquely the product of the 1890s and succeeding years. This interpretation of segregation as a social institution with only the shallowest of legal and social roots in the slavery past has continued to dominate historical thinking until this day.

Woodward's position conflicts directly with the picture of a rigidly segregated slavery society conveyed by Kemble in her *Journal*. The word *segregate* is defined in Webster's *International Dictionary* as follows: "to separate or cut off from others or from the general mass or main body." The essential feature of the concept, evidently, is the *isolation* of a group from the general mass or the mainstream. Such isolation is voluntarily accepted or voluntarily imposed in the case of the religious; otherwise segregation is forcibly imposed and forcibly maintained by outer constraints. Such forcible segregation, if words mean anything, was the fate of countless slaves on the large Southern plantations. These people were isolated from the ambient world; they were powerless to mingle with that world or to enter the mainstream of American life. The Sea Island society that Kemble so vividly described is indeed a picture of an almost totally segregated society. It is true that the slaves came into daily contact with a handful of whites (masters, overseers, traders, doctors). But this contact in no way lessened the reality of segregation—on the contrary, the principal role of the whites was to maintain and enforce the continued isolation of the black people from the outside American world. This racial segregation is all the more noteworthy in that it was totally the antithesis of prevailing social patterns of American life during the nineteenth century. Dozens of travelers and observers testified that even in the antebellum period Americans had to be considered, among civilized peoples, as the most mobile on earth. The white population moved about with a speed and an ease that was a constant source of surprise to foreign observers.

Kemble did not view the segregation of the Sea Island slaves as unique. She visited other plantations on the mainland and described them, many years later, as "like so many fortresses, approachable for 'observers' only at the owners' will" (p. 355). In a number of brilliant passages Kemble portrayed segregation as a dominant and all-engulfing reality in the slave's experience. Note, for example, the following:

> We skirted the plantation burial ground, and a dismal place it looked; the cattle trampling over it in every direction, except where Mr. King [the overseer] had had an enclosure put up round the graves of two white men who worked on the estate. . . . by virtue of their white skins, their resting place was protected from the hoofs of the cattle, while the parents and children, wives, husbands, brothers and sisters, of the poor slaves, sleeping beside them, might see the graves of those they loved trampled upon and browsed over, desecrated and defiled, from morning til night. There is something intolerably cruel in this disdainful denial of a common humanity pursuing these wretches even when they are hid beneath the earth. (pp. 307–8).

Kemble saw segregation as part of the very essence of slavery. The conclusion of the Civil War witnessed a bitter assault upon it in various parts of the South, but these campaigns did not survive the end of Reconstruction. By the end of the century segregation had triumphed once more, but in a different form. After 1890 it would be carefully defined by state law and enforced by the power of the state itself, not, as previously, by private owners.* Another generation, a hundred years later, would be faced with the painful and bloody task of demolition.

There is already an impressive literature on the history of the

---

* The leading role of the private owner in enforcing the segregation of his slaves, and in keeping them upon the plantation received indispensable support from state authorities in the form of the militia patrols. The basic similarities between the two systems of segregation, and also the important differences, especially in legal form, await investigation.

civil rights movement. But a fruitful appraisal of the meaning of this movement must await further analysis of the relationship between slavery and segregation. It will then be possible to place the movement in perspective as an antislavery struggle and to restore to it the full historical dimension which gives it significance. In this ongoing work Frances Anne Kemble's *Journal* will doubtless continue to be an indispensable source.

JOHN ANTHONY SCOTT

School of Law, Rutgers University
January 1984

Editor's Introduction

FRANCES ANNE KEMBLE recorded her stay in the Georgia Sea Islands twenty-two years before the outbreak of the Civil War; her book was the product of the fierce debate over slavery that exercised the minds of men and women on both sides of the Atlantic in the years following the end of the American Revolution. Published in the same year that the slaves were emancipated, her work was designed to contribute to the understanding of the historic struggle then being waged within the United States, to discourage British intervention in that struggle, and to spur the North to victory. Passionate in its denunciation of oppression, the *Journal of a Residence on a Georgian Plantation* painted a picture of slavery so brutal in its realism that it was unacceptable to Victorian society. Although the *Journal* enjoyed an intensive wartime fame, it was soon forgotten by the general public and soon out of print. For nearly a hundred years it has led a twilight existence in the secondhand book stores and in the footnotes of professional historians. In this respect it stands in sharp contrast to the contemporary work of Harriet Beecher Stowe. *Uncle Tom's Cabin* has never, since its first publication in 1852, been out of print nor lost its hold upon the public's attention.

Neither as literary work nor as social study has the *Journal* merited the oblivion that has fallen upon it. It is written by one of the most gifted women that the nineteenth century produced, and it affords insight into the life and mind of a great artist. As intense study of the ante-bellum South, it provides a fitting complement to Olmsted's classic account, *The Cotton Kingdom*. Olmsted's observations of the South were the product of a fourteen-month sojourn in which the author made three extended trips and covered many thousand miles. Kemble's picture, on the other hand, was based upon a stay of three and one half months on two small islands at the mouth of the Altamaha River. Her observations were made within an area no more than sixteen miles square, at the heart of one of the South's most important and productive cotton-, rice-, and sugar-producing zones, the home of a number of its most influential ruling families.

EARLY YEARS IN ENGLAND

Frances Anne Kemble[1] was born in London, England, on November 27, 1809, the third child of Charles Kemble and Marie Thérèse De Camp. The Kembles were England's most celebrated family of actors. Fanny's grandfather Roger had been a strolling player, and eight of his twelve children achieved varying degrees of success as actors or theatrical managers. Fanny's aunt Sarah was the incomparable Mrs. Siddons, the country's leading Shakespearian actress from 1782 until her retirement in 1812; her uncle, John Philip, was a famous actor, and manager in turn of the Drury Lane and Covent Garden theaters practically without intermission from 1788 until 1817; her father, Charles, achieved a high reputation in the performance of Shakespearian roles.

Fanny grew up largely under the care of an aunt, Adelaide

---

[1] The most useful published source for the early years of Fanny Kemble's life is her own *Records of a Girlhood* (London: 1878). Subsequent references are to the New York edition, which appeared in 1879.

("Dall") De Camp. As far as education was concerned, family tradition and the home were doubtless the most important factors, but the child was sent on two separate occasions to school in France. The first of these experiences, at an elementary school in Boulogne, does not appear to have left particularly agreeable memories: in later life Fanny recalled with pleasure the joy of release from this institution, "the disbanded freedom of the sunny afternoon, spent in gathering wild flowers along the pretty, secluded valley of the Liane, through which no iron road then bore its thundering freight." [2]

The second visit to France was to prove a more significant experience and to produce a more lasting impression. In her twelfth year Fanny, running wild at home and fast becoming an unmanageable child, was sent away to Paris; and here she was exposed to influences that were to have a lifelong effect upon her thought and literary style. She acquired an intimate knowledge of the Bible, became fluent in French, and began to read Byron, whose poetry she described as affecting her "like an evil potion taken into my blood." Scott became her literary companion. With transports of delight she immersed herself in "those enchanting and admirable works, that deserve nothing less than love in return for the healthful delight they have bestowed." [3] At this time the young girl herself began to write. She thus embarked upon the intense literary activity that was to continue throughout her life in the form of plays, poetry, letters, journals, and memoirs, and that entitles her to be considered one of the grandest and most articulate Victorian women of letters.

Fanny's Italian master was the exile Biagoli. She recalled with affection her tutor's "high forehead, from which his hair fell back in a long grizzled curtain, his wild, melancholy eyes, and the severe and sad expression of his face." She revered him for introducing her to "the divine Italian language" and to the *Divina Commedia* at one and the same time. The impact upon her of Dante is worthy

[2] *Records of a Girlhood*, 30.   [3] Ibid., 58.

of our attention, for Dante's influence is evident in the *Journal of a Residence on a Georgian Plantation.* Of his great poem she said:

> I have forgotten my Italian grammar, rules of syntax and rules of prosody alike, but I read and re-read the *Divina Commedia* with ever increasing amazement and admiration. Setting aside its weightier claims to the high place it holds among the finest achievements of human genius, I know of no poem in any language in which so many single lines and detached passages can be found of equally descriptive force, picturesque beauty, and delightful melody of sound.[4]

Fanny stayed in Paris for three years. School routine was enlivened by visits from her father, whom she adored, and by vacations with family friends. Upon her return home she again fell into the carefree life of a passionate young Romantic—reading the German poets, scribbling verses with effervescent abandon, wandering as a child of nature through the woods and over the moors and heaths around her parents' summer cottage in Surrey.[5] Three more years thus passed in which the adolescent girl was left pretty much to herself. "I think," she recalled later, "my education had come nearly to a standstill at this period, for, with the exception of these physical exercises and certain hours of pianoforte practicing and singing lessons, I was left very much to the irregular and unsystematic reading which I selected for myself."[6]

In these years Fanny pondered the problem of a career. How was a girl, who aspired before everything else to independence of mind and body, in no haste to marry, with a deep sense of her own literary mission—how was such a girl to support herself? If writing was too uncertain to be the source of a steady income, might not

[4] Ibid., 59.
[5] She described this country, characteristically, as "a region of light, sandy soil, hiding its agricultural poverty under a royal mantle of golden gorse and purple heather, and with large tracts of blue aromatic pinewood . . . [from which] the eye sweeps to the downs above the Sussex cliffs and the glint of the narrow seas," ibid., 74.
[6] Ibid., 85–6.

the stage provide a woman with the means both to support herself and to carry on her beloved literary pursuits? With such thoughts in mind, Fanny went off for a year, in 1828, to visit her cousin, Mrs. Harry Siddons, in Edinburgh; and for awhile the delicious life of carefree youth was resumed. This time, when she returned home, Fanny found the family fortunes were approaching a crisis for the resolution of which her help was urgently needed. A decision about her career could no longer be postponed.

This crisis was bound up with Covent Garden Theater, which Charles Kemble had been managing since 1822, and which constituted the sole source of the family income. Legitimate drama in London had been dominated, since the early eighteenth century, by two groups operating under Royal Patents which conferred upon them the monopoly of providing this form of entertainment. One of these "Patent Theaters" was Drury Lane; the other, Covent Garden.[7] The latter from 1803 to 1817 was under the management of Fanny's uncle, John Philip Kemble. He strove against discouraging odds to make the business pay—jealousies of rivals, a disastrous fire, personal antagonisms, heavy overhead and debt charges, and public resentment at high admission prices. But all of this proved too much for John Philip. He threw in the sponge, made over his share in Covent Garden to Charles, and retired to Lausanne. Poor Charles was an elegant actor and a devoted father, but he knew nothing of management. By 1829 a long and back-breaking struggle began to assume ominous proportions. Distraint warrants for unpaid rates and taxes were issued, and one autumn day Marie Thérèse came in in tears, with the news that the theater was covered with bills of sale, and that the end had come.

Fanny's enthusiasm for the stage had evaporated during the year she was in Scotland. Covent Garden, "my father's disastrous property, to which his life was being sacrificed," appeared more and

[7] The interrelationships between the Kemble family and the Patent Theater are dealt with in Henry Gibbs: *Affectionately Yours, Fanny* (London: 1946).

more odious to her. She knew nothing of Shakespeare [8] and had received no dramatic training, but at her mother's prompting she learned a passage from *Romeo and Juliet* by heart and recited it to her parents. Charles and Marie Thérèse made the difficult decision to give the Shakespearian stage a new leading lady. On October 5, 1829, one of the finest actresses that England has produced made her reluctant debut as Juliet, with a supporting cast that included Charles Kemble as Mercutio.[9]

Overnight Fanny became the idol of the theatergoing public. Society opened its doors to her. Hostesses clamored to receive her, prime ministers accompanied her upon her morning rides. For two and a half crowded years she played before enraptured audiences in London and in the provinces. Charles Kemble began to pay off debts. Yet, for all this, the respite was only temporary: debts still went on piling up. The great political crisis through which the country was passing in 1830 to 1832 thinned houses, and an outbreak of cholera completed what politics had begun. In March 1832, Charles was forced to cut his ties with Covent Garden and to abandon "the crumbling fabric we have spent having and living, body, substance, and all but soul. . . ." He and his daughter would go to "that dreadful America" for a two years' tour in a further effort to recoup the family fortunes. After the summer tour of 1832, Charles and Fanny Kemble, accompanied by Aunt Dall, set sail for America on August 1 and arrived in New York on September 3.

AMERICAN TOUR AND MARRIAGE

The Kemble's American tour opened on September 17, 1832, at the Park Theater in New York. Their appearance marked something of an epoch in the history of the American theater. "The

[8] *Records of a Girlhood,* 169.
[9] "He was," wrote Fanny, "one of the best Romeos, and incomparably the best Mercutio, that ever trod the English stage," ibid., 194.

reputation of the family," writes one authority, "might have been amply sustained by the acting of Charles Kemble; but Fanny Kemble was to New York something of a divine manifestation. . . ." [1] This father-daughter partnership graced the American stage for almost two years, from the fall of 1832 to June 1834. [2] During that period the Kembles played to delighted audiences in Philadelphia, Baltimore, Washington, and Boston, as well as a whole series of engagements in New York. In the United States, as in England, all doors were open to Fanny Kemble. In Washington she played before Dolly Madison and John Quincy Adams; she was presented to President Andrew Jackson. In New York she met America's foremost woman novelist, Catharine Maria Sedgwick, who conceived a deep affection for the English girl. [3] In Boston she was introduced to Dr. William Ellery Channing, the spiritual leader of New England liberalism. "Miss Kemble looked remarkably handsome," reported the daughter of the President of Harvard, "there is something exceedingly striking in her face, it is one of those that haunt you, after you have seen it, like some Sibyl or enchantress . . . ." [4]

[1] George C. D. Odell: *Annals of the New York Stage* (New York: 1928), III, 598. That inveterate theatergoer, Philip Hone, had the Kembles to dinner, and took Fanny out horseback riding with his wife Margaret and daughter Mary. "We have never seen her equal on the American stage," he wrote. *The Diary of Philip Hone 1828–51*, Allan Nevins, ed. (New York: 1927), I, 77–8.

[2] Fanny Kemble's own recollections of this period, from the departure from England in 1832 to marriage in 1834, are contained in her *Journal* (London and Philadelphia: 1835). This book has some beautiful writing in it though its youthful indiscretions gave much offense at the time.

[3] "We are just now," she wrote in 1833, "in the full flush of excitement about Fanny Kemble. She is a most captivating creature, steeped to the very lips in genius . . . . I have never seen any woman on the stage to be compared with her, nor ever an actor that delighted me so much." Letter to Mrs. Frank Channing, New York, February 12, 1833. *Life and Letters of Catharine Maria Sedgwick*, Mary E. Dewey, ed. (New York: 1871), 230.

[4] Anna Quincy, *Diary*, entry of April 23, 1833, quoted in M. A. De-Wolfe Howe: "Young Fanny Kemble as Seen in an Old Diary," *Atlantic Monthly*, CLXXIV (December, 1944), 101.

Outwardly the brilliant and beautiful young woman whose acting showed the deepest understanding of her chosen roles combined with the most passionate illustration of them, was at the gateway of a career that, in conventional terms, promised everything she could wish. Fame and fortune were at her feet. But on June 7, 1834, she married Pierce Mease Butler of Philadelphia, abandoned her theatrical career and her native land, and said farewell to her father, Charles, who returned to England alone. A discussion of this strange turn in Fanny Kemble's fortunes is important, for it takes us to the heart of her personal problem and helps explain and illuminate the circumstances from which the *Journal of a Residence on a Georgian Plantation* sprang.

Fanny Kemble was a woman of literary, rather than of dramatic, tastes and ambitions. She was part of the same Romantic movement that produced Shelley, Byron, and Keats. Even though Shakespeare's ideas and his poetry captivated her and swept her away, she still found the theatrical profession itself highly repugnant. "My going on the stage," she wrote, "was absolutely an act of duty and conformity to the will of my parents, strengthened by my own conviction that I was bound to help them by every means in my power. The theatrical profession, however, was utterly distasteful to me . . . nor did custom ever render the aversion less." [5] This attitude stemmed from the status of the acting profession, and from the nature of Shakespearian acting in particular, in Fanny Kemble's day. Traditionally the puritan English looked upon acting as sinful; actors they regarded with mingled awe and contempt. But the gypsy freedom of the strolling player and the bright play of stage passions and finery were mere illusions. An actor's life was an unending round of drudgery, a poor, proletarian occupation that claimed the lives and health of those Fanny loved best. [6]

[5] *Records of a Girlhood,* 191.
[6] See the bitter comments on Marie Thérèse De Camp's career as a child actress in *Records of a Girlhood,* 4–5: ". . . the calling of a player alone has the grotesque ele-

Perhaps if Shakespeare could have been played on bare boards in undiluted splendor, the true artist might have felt some compensation for the poverty and insecurity of the actor's lot. In actuality Shakespearian drama was obliged to compete for public patronage with all sorts of rival attractions and hence had to dress itself up in curious ways to maintain box-office appeal. Performing animals, circus acts, and double-features were used to provide sandwich meat for the Shakespearian loaf. The great tragedies were even rewritten in order to eliminate the gloom and to provide the desired happy ending. All of this to Fanny was a profanation not only of artistic integrity but of her most sacred feelings. In her estimation human nature, above all the human nature revealed by the genius of Shakespeare, was a profound and mystically beautiful thing, the scene of struggles that conducted both spectator and participant at once to the threshold of morality and religion.[7]

If, at the outset, the drudgery and emotional prostitution that Fanny associated with acting had social compensations in the excitement of universal acclaim, financial security, and a world of new experiences, tragedy very soon darkened the scene of her labors, rendering them intolerable and odious. Aunt Dall, Fanny's childhood mentor, teacher, and friend, had accompanied father and daughter on the transatlantic tour. During a vacation trip to Niagara and Canada in the summer of 1833, the party, which included Pierce Mease Butler and the explorer, Edward Trelawney,

---

ment of fiction, with all the fantastic accompaniments of sham splendor thrust into close companionship with the sordid details of poverty; for the actor alone, the livery of labor is a harlequin's jerkin lined with tatters, and the jester's cap and bells tied to the beggar's wallet."

[7] "Music and painting," wrote Kemble to Mrs. A. J. Scott from Rome on May 16, 1853, "and architecture and sculpture may none of them touch my sacred things directly, but though I perversely reject their ministration whenever it attempts to dedicate itself to my religion, I never hear or see the noblest and highest achievements of which they are capable without finding them stepping stones to that sanctuary from which they are invariably shut out—I do not much love religious art, *but art is to me religious.*" Kemble Mss., Box 60, Folger Shakespeare Library, Washington, D.C. Italics not in original.

was involved in a coach accident. Dall received a severe injury to her spine. She became seriously ill in Boston toward the close of the second American season, 1833–4. In the intervals of acting to audiences frantic with enthusiasm, cheering, shouting, crowning their heroine with roses, Fanny sat beside the sickbed, tormented with agonies of grief and remorse over a self-sacrificing love she had accepted so lightly and requited so little. "I am beginning to know," she wrote, "what care and sorrow really are . . . ." [8]

By this time Fanny had decided that she was in love with the wealthy young Philadelphian who had been pursuing her devotedly almost since her first arrival in America. Pierce Mease Butler was one of a crowd of admirers who had seen the star in Philadelphia in October 1832, had become infatuated with her, and had thenceforth dogged the theaters where she played. Aunt Dall died in Boston in April 1834, and was buried in Mount Auburn Cemetery. Early in June Fanny was married in Philadelphia. In that same month she made over to her father her share of the proceeds of the American tour, and bade him and the stage farewell.

TWO TRADITIONS MEET

Butler Mease, who changed his name to Pierce Butler in compliance with a proviso in his grandfather's will, was Fanny's junior by one year. At the time of his marriage he was, with his elder brother John, the heir to a Georgia plantation that boasted upwards of seven hundred slaves and was one of the most productive in that state. In 1836, two years after the marriage, the Georgia property fell under the direct control of the two brothers as a result of the death of their aunt, Frances Butler, who was the trustee of the estate and one of its two co-administrators.[9]

---

[8] *Records of a Girlhood*, 588.

[9] The history of the Butler family is of great interest in terms of its connection with both Pennsylvania and Georgia. Little has appeared in print, even less that is reliable. The principal sources are manuscript collections of the Pennsylvania Historical Society, where the materials are dispersed and may be found under

Butler and John Mease were the grandsons of Pierce Butler, who came to America in 1766 as a major in the British army. In 1771 Major Butler married a South Carolina heiress, Polly Middleton, and settled down in the colonies. In 1776 he cast his fortunes with the revolutionaries, participated in the Constitutional Convention, and was twice elected to the United States Senate. Polly died in 1790 leaving the Major four daughters to care for, Sarah, Harriet, Elizabeth, and Frances; and a son, Thomas. Shortly after his wife's death, Major Butler began to acquire large holdings of land in Georgia. Between 1793 and 1800 he purchased a number of tracts on the seacoast in the rich delta land of the Altamaha River, and proceeded to constitute these into two estates, Hampton, or Butler, Point on the northern extremity of St. Simons Island, and Butler Island, some nine miles westward (as the crow flies) in the estuary of the Altamaha River.

Major Butler was one among a number of planters who abandoned their impoverished Carolina or Virginia lands in the late eighteenth and early nineteenth centuries and moved to Georgia

---

the following categories: (1) *Butler Papers, 1771–1900.* A large collection of account books, invoices, bills, and correspondence which relate primarily to the administration of the Georgia estate, but contain information also on the Butlers' Philadelphia properties. (2) *H. E. Drayton Collection.* Two boxes of important papers, which deal with the affairs of Frances and Thomas Butler, and include Thomas's letter of May 24, 1825, to his sister, detailing the inner history of family relationships. (3) *Cadwalader Collection.* Butler papers and correspondence of F. A. Kemble are to be found in four separate divisions of this collection. The papers of Thomas Cadwalader include files on Major Pierce Butler's majestic speculations in Venango and Warren County real estate. The papers of General George Cadwalader have several folders on the Butler estate, 1822–70, and the correspondence of Fanny Kemble with Mrs. J. F. Fisher in the 1840's. See also the papers of Judge John Cadwalader, and the McCall Legal Section. (4) *Miscellaneous.* A number of Kemble letters are to be found in the Simon Gratz Collection and in the Pennsylvania Historical Society's own files.

Other unpublished materials are in the possession of Mrs. Margaret Davis Cate of St. Simons Island, Georgia. See also Burnette Vanstory: *Georgia's Land of the Golden Isles* (Athens, Ga.: 1956); and Robert Lee Meriwether: "Pierce Butler," in the *Dictionary of American Biography* (New York: 1943), III.

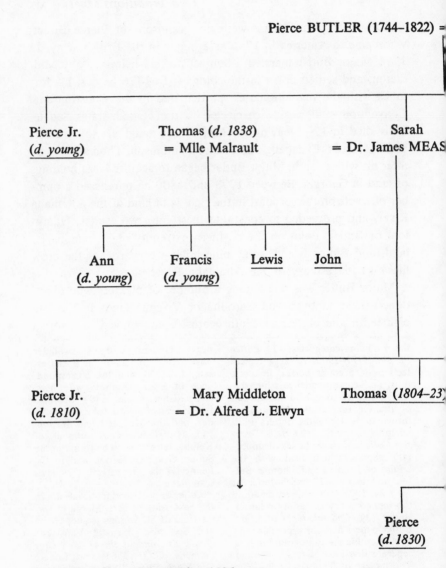

Pierce BUTLER (1744–1822) =

Pierce Jr.
(*d. young*)

Thomas (*d. 1838*)
= Mlle Malrault

Sarah
= Dr. James MEAS

Ann
(*d. young*)

Francis
(*d. young*)

Lewis

John

Pierce Jr.
(*d. 1810*)

Mary Middleton
= Dr. Alfred L. Elwyn

Thomas (*1804–23*)

Pierce
(*d. 1830*)

[1] changed name to John Butler, 1836
[2] changed name to Pierce Butler, c. 1826.

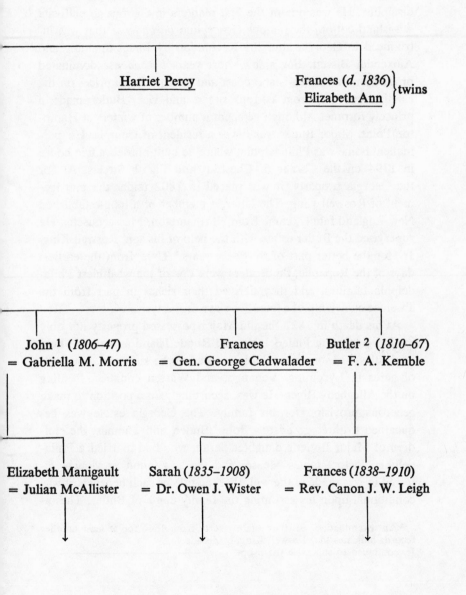

Mary Middleton (*d. 1790*)

Harriet Percy

Frances (*d. 1836*)
Elizabeth Ann } twins

John ¹ (*1806–47*)
= Gabriella M. Morris

Frances
= Gen. George Cadwalader

Butler ² (*1810–67*)
= F. A. Kemble

Elizabeth Manigault
= Julian McAllister

Sarah (*1835–1908*)
= Dr. Owen J. Wister

Frances (*1838–1910*)
= Rev. Canon J. W. Leigh

in search of new and fertile soil. The Major brought most of his slaves with him from South Carolina and ruled them with military discipline. He was one of the first planters in Georgia to cultivate sea-island cotton, the famous Gossypium *barbadense* that was introduced to Georgia after the Revolution by James Spalding and Alexander Bissett. For a few short years *barbadense* dominated production on the sea-island coast and brought fancy prices on the English market. From cotton, sugar, and rice, Butler made a princely fortune. Although he spent a number of winters at Hampton Point, Major Butler was never a resident of Georgia. His permanent home was Philadelphia, where he built himself a fine house in 1794 on the Corner of Chestnut and Eighth Streets. As for the Georgia property, it was placed in 1802 under the management of Roswell King. The latter, a member of a long-established New England family, came from Northampton, Massachusetts. He supervised the Butler estate with the help of his son, Roswell King, Jr., for the better part of thirty-six years.[1] Thus, from the earliest days of the Republic, the Butlers were one of the wealthiest Philadelphia families, and they derived their riches in part from the absentee ownership of a lucrative slave property.

At his death in 1822 the old Major possessed property not only in Georgia, but in Philadelphia and Rhode Island as well. He held land titles—of somewhat dubious value, to be sure—to thousands of acres in Lycoming, Venango, and Warren counties, fronting on the Allegheny River. He was, accordingly, in a position to make generous provision for his family. The Georgia estate was bequeathed to three grandsons, John, Butler, and Thomas, the children of Major Butler's daughter Sarah, who had married a Philadelphia doctor, James Mease; and the stipulation previously referred to was made in the will, that the title of each beneficiary was conditional upon his assuming the family name of Butler. The in-

---

[1] An examination of the estate records indicates that Roswell King, Jr. continued to supervise the property from 1844 for at least another decade.

come from the property was assigned during her lifetime to the Major's unmarried daughter Frances, who was also named trustee and, with Roswell King, co-administrator of the property on behalf of her nephews. "The death of an elderly lady," wrote Fanny on the demise of Aunt Frances in 1836, "puts us in possession of our property, which she had held in trust during her life . . . ." [2]

Up to this time the wider political and social issues of the new industrial age into which she was born had not been of major interest to Fanny. Now they moved into the center of her vision and came to dominate her thinking. For the wife of one of Georgia's largest slaveowners was herself a woman of antislavery sympathies with an unquestioning faith in the virtues and superiority of a free labor system.

The young actress had grown to maturity in a society in which rapid industrialization was creating a factory system based upon private enterprise and wage labor. Her early writings reveal a full awareness of this fact. In 1827 Fanny visited the Thames Tunnel, then under construction, and marveled at the spectacle of the workmen "all begrimed, with their brawny arms and legs bare, some standing in black water up to their knees, others laboriously shovelling the black earth in their cages (while they sturdily sung at their task), with the red, murky light of links and lanterns flashing and flickering about them . . . ." [3] The sight of this heroic labor, she said, made her *"humanity proud."* Again, when she had become a celebrity, Fanny was present at the opening of the Stockton-Darlington Railway on September 15, 1830, and was actually on the train when the accident occurred which resulted in the death of Charles Huskisson.[4] Her writings of this period breathe an

---

[2] *Records of Later Life* (London: 1882), I, 52. This work, in three volumes, continues Fanny's autobiography from 1834 to 1848. Only John and Pierce lived to enjoy the Georgia estate; their brother Thomas died young.

[3] *Records of a Girlhood,* 121.

[4] An excellent account of this tragedy will be found in *Records of a Girlhood,* 298–300.

awareness of great changes, of titanic labors, of factory smoke, of the clamor of steel and steam. George Stephenson, designer of the *Rocket,* became a personal friend, with whom, she confessed, she was "horribly in love." Stephenson took her with him behind the engine on a trial run on the railway in August 1830. The object of her worship was "a common coal digger," a man "of the most indefatigable industry and perseverance," a master of marvels.[5]

If Fanny brought with her to America an intense interest in the strange new world of industry that was transforming society on both sides of the Atlantic, she had also absorbed, so naturally as to be almost unaware of the fact, British antislavery traditions. *"I am going* [to Georgia]," she wrote in 1838, *"prejudiced against slavery, for I am an Englishwoman, in whom the absence of such a prejudice would be disgraceful."* [6] Antislavery feeling in England had grown along with the advance of the Industrial Revolution and the creation of a system of wage labor. Fanny was born and grew up precisely in the crucial years in which the British people under a reform leadership came to grips with the slavery question, abolished the slave trade, and finally outlawed slave institutions in British dependencies.

Prior to the nineteenth century, England had been one of the major slave-owning and slave-trading powers of the world. The focus of the slavery interest was the Caribbean, into which the British had moved, hard upon the heels of the Spanish, in the seventeenth century, when they secured control of a number of West Indian islands, of which the most important were Barbados and Jamaica. Although small freeholders and landless men emigrated

---

[5] Fanny Kemble's story of "a railroad and my ecstasies" will be found in *Records of a Girlhood,* 279–84. She described the great inventor as "a man of from fifty to fifty-five years of age; his face is fine, though careworn, and bears an expression of deep thoughtfulness."

[6] Frances Anne Kemble: *Journal of a Residence on a Georgian Plantation in 1838–1839,* 11. Italics not in the original. For the reader's convenience all page references to the *Journal* are to the present edition and not to the original edition of 1863.

from England, by the end of the seventeenth century the era of petty settlement was over. A fatal revolution got under way which harnessed the islands to the cultivation of sugar for the European market, drove off the small holders, and implanted a regime of slavery and large estates.[7]

Sugar production used up enormous quantities of labor. When the supply of white laborers gave out, their place was taken by African slaves. Production of sugar, linked with the supply of slaves, grew into a huge and hideous vested interest. A handful of planters constituted a tight oligarchy whose members usually lived in England and presided as absentee owners over the destinies of their swarms of black dependents. With the merchants who conducted the slave trade and the bankers who financed the business, they established the West India Interest that dominated British political, economic, and social life for much of the eighteenth century. The Interest bought seats in Parliament, controlled votes, boosted the manufacture of the iron and cotton goods requisite for purchasing slaves. They acquired country estates and titles, and married the daughters of the aristocracy.[8] England itself became a

---

[7] "There was an inexorable tenacity about sugar; once a mill and boiling-house had been established, land bought and planted to cane, slaves acquired and trained, there was no breaking the grip of sugar on the place. The preparation was too costly and too specialized to allow of change . . . . During the eighteenth century the scale of manufacture tended to increase, and with it the intensity and completeness of monoculture. The slow and primitive cattle mills gave place to windmills, which ground much faster; their ruined towers can be seen on every side in the Leeward Islands. Windmills in their turn were replaced, wherever the supply of water allowed, by more powerful and reliable water mills . . . . All this improvement in machinery demanded a quicker flow of cane to feed the iron maws of the mills. More land had to be taken in, more slaves bought and trained . . . ." J. H. Parry and P. M. Sherlock: *A Short History of the West Indies* (London: 1956), 144–5.

[8] Eric Williams, in his brilliant and suggestive study, *Capitalism and Slavery* (Chapel Hill, N.C.: 1947), goes so far as to say that "there are few, if any, noble houses in England without a West India strain," 94.

center for buying, selling, and transporting slaves. So complete was the acceptance of this by public opinion that the holding of men in slavery on English soil was not declared unlawful until the famous *Somerset* decision was handed down in 1772.

The Sugar Interest reached the climax of its power by 1763, and thereafter—for a variety of reasons that do not concern us here— fell into a more or less rapid decline.[9] At the same time, there developed in England itself a two-pronged attack upon the entrenched political and economic power of the Interest, and upon the theory and practice of slavery that lay at its base. As a result of these vehement assaults over a period of about half a century, from 1783 to 1833, the public influence of the oligarchy was broken, and it passed from the scene forever. This struggle for political, social, and moral reform gave rise in England to an anti-slavery tradition that is of immediate concern at this place.

Until the time of the American Revolution only a few voices were raised to cry out in the wilderness against the iniquity of slavery as a barbaric expression of human greed, exploitation, and cruelty. One of these was James Oglethorpe, founder of Georgia. Another was John Wesley, the great revivalist whose words reached the masses in the open fields of two continents, who was a close friend of Oglethorpe, and who conducted divine service at Frederica a century before Kemble came there. Wesley uttered a curse against slavery in 1774:

> It were better that all those islands should remain unculti-
> vated forever; yea, it were more desirable that they were alto-
> gether sunk in the depth of the sea, than that they should be
> cultivated at so high a price as the violation of justice, mercy,
> and truth; and it would be better that none should labor there,
> that the work should be left undone, than that myriads of

[9] For the details, see Parry and Sherlock: *West Indies,* chaps. ix–xi, and J. L. Ragatz: *The Fall of the* *Planter Class in the British Caribbean* (New York: 1928).

innocent men should be murdered, and myriads more dragged into the basest slavery.[1]

After the American Revolution the movement against slavery in England began to assume an organized form. Abolitionism began to take shape and to find for itself political spokesmen, literary champions, and mass propagandists. Granville Sharp, who had won fame by undertaking the legal battle for the freedom of Somerset in 1772, achieved in 1783 a brilliant indictment of the West India Interest by his handling of the *Zong* case.[2] James Ramsey, who had himself lived in the Caribbean and knew slavery from first-hand experience, in 1784 published his *Essay on the Treatment and Conversion of African Slaves in the British Sugar Colonies.*[3] Quakers, who had voiced antislavery sentiments as early as the late seventeenth century, sprang into action circulating antislavery pamphlets and deluging Parliament with antislavery petitions. Thomas Clarkson, a young antislavery minister, began a massive collection of facts about the slave trade that was to constitute one of the most remarkable social indictments ever made.[4]

Thus began a struggle which was to go on intermittently for half a century against the West Indian oligarchy, which won a first victory of limited significance with the abolition of the slave trade in 1807, and which came to a climax in the years 1823 to 1833. In that decade a campaign was mounted for the abolition of slavery itself; abolition, along with Catholic emancipation and parliamen-

---

[1] John Wesley: *Thoughts on Slavery* (London: 1774), 15.

[2] The captain of the *Zong* had thrown one hundred and thirty-two sick slaves to the sharks in order to place the loss on the underwriters rather than the owners. Sharp publicized the case and demanded that the entire crew be placed on trial for murder. Thomas Clarkson: *The History of the Rise, Progress, and Accomplishment of the Abolition of the African Slave Trade by the British Parliament* (London: 1808), I, 95–7.

[3] London: 1784.

[4] See Clarkson: *History . . . of the Abolition of the African Slave Trade;* also *An Essay on the Slavery and Commerce of the Human Species, Particularly the African* (London: 1788); and *The Cries of Africa to the Inhabitants of Europe; or, A Survey of that Bloody Commerce called the Slave Trade* (London: 1822).

tary reform, became one of three main and linked issues agitating the British public mind.[5] The details of this historic campaign are not of concern here. What is important is the fact that the agitation for half a century against slavery and the slave trade ended in a victory that established the dominance of antislavery *mores* in English society; and created an imperishable tradition of thought and action against a hated institution and all its works.

The union of Fanny Kemble and Pierce Butler, as may be seen, brought together representatives of sharply conflicting traditions and ways of life. Neither partner seems to have been aware of this fact and of its ominous implications at the time of their marriage. "When I married Mr. Butler," wrote Fanny in 1839, "I knew nothing of these dreadful possessions of his . . . ."[6] This was undoubtedly true, and in the circumstances, entirely natural; Pierce Butler had presented himself as a wealthy Philadelphian of private means. The source of his family's wealth and the nature of his own expectations would not have been matters which a man, in those days, would have felt himself obliged to talk about to his bride.[7] But very soon after marriage, when the couple settled down to a quiet existence in the village of Branchtown on the outskirts of Philadelphia, Fanny became aware of the truth; and at once the existence of slavery in America became a matter of intense personal concern to her, for she was now living in idleness off the fruits of this iniquity. She was now personally involved and directly answerable to God and man for her part in this sin:

> The family into which I have married [she wrote in 1835] are large slaveholders; our present and future fortune depend

[5] For further details of the ideological movement in England against slavery, see Frank J. Klingberg: *The Antislavery Movement in England: A Study in English Humanitarianism* (New Haven, Conn.: 1926).

[6] *Journal of a Residence on a Georgian Plantation*, 138.

[7] Margaret Armstrong is of the opinion that at the time of her marriage, Fanny was too naïve to realize that owning plantations implied ownership of slaves. *Fanny Kemble, a Passionate Victorian* (New York: 1938), 189–90.

greatly upon extensive plantations in Georgia. But the experience of every day, besides our faith in the great justice of God, forbids dependence on the duration of the mighty abuse by which one race of men is held in abject physical and mental slavery by another. As for me, though the toilsome earning of my bread were to be my lot again tomorrow, I should rejoice with unspeakable thankfulness that we had not to answer for what I consider so grievous a sin against humanity.[8]

Henceforth, for the next five years, till the disintegration of her marriage overwhelmed her, slavery was to be the central, most passionate concern in Fanny Kemble's life. We must examine the nature of this concern a little more closely, for Fanny's antislavery thinking led directly to her visit to Georgia and found a unique expression in the *Journal* that resulted from her Southern experience.

SLAVERY AND THE CHRISTIAN CONSCIENCE

How to discharge the responsibility laid upon her husband and herself for the welfare of hundreds of human beings;[9] how to care for these people, and, above all, how to prepare them for the emancipation that must surely come; such were the problems of slavery as they presented themselves to Fanny Kemble. "How can I bear to think," she cried, "the day will come, as come it surely must, when we shall say: we once had it in our power to lift this burden from four hundred heads and hearts, and stirred no finger

---

[8] Letter to Anna Jameson, Branchtown, June 1835. *Records of Later Life,* I, 67.

[9] "You do not know," wrote Fanny, "how profoundly this subject [slavery] interests me, and engrosses my thoughts; it is not alone the cause of humanity that so powerfully affects my mind; it is, above all, the deep responsibility in which we are involved, and which makes it a matter of such vital and paramount importance to me . . . . It seems to me that we are possessed of power and opportunity to do a great work; how can I not feel the keenest anxiety as to the use we make of this talent which God has entrusted us with?" Letter to Harriet St. Leger, Branchtown, October 5, 1836, I, 67.

to do it; but carelessly and indolently, or selfishly and cowardly, turned our back upon so great a duty and so great a privilege." [1]

In the long quiet days that began in 1835 on the Branchtown farm, Fanny devoted herself to reading, to writing, and to the elaboration of her thoughts on slavery and its abolition. Her endeavors filled her husband and his family with unspeakable dismay.[2] It was only four years, we must remember, since William Lloyd Garrison in 1831 had organized the New England Antislavery Society and its organ the *Liberator,* thus flinging down the gauntlet before the country's slavery interests. The emancipation of the West Indian slaves in 1833, furthermore, had a twofold impact upon the American scene. It stimulated the rising tide of apprehension over the advance of slavery in the United States, and it also heightened the alarm of slaveowners at the growing militancy of the antislavery movement. In 1835 this movement—that was to culminate in the Civil War and in emancipation—was, insofar as the United States was concerned, still in its infancy. But at the very time when Fanny Kemble abandoned the stage and turned with passionate concern to the slavery question, a new debate had begun that filled the slaveowners with fear and dread. Abolitionists, despite their oft-repeated denial of intent to bring about emancipation by violent means, were regarded as the wildest of radicals who deserved—and not infrequently received—lashing, lynching, or a coat of tar and feathers.

The thinking of Fanny Kemble on the slavery question underlines the fact that much of abolitionism in the 1830's flowed from a Christian belief in right action and a Christian desire to turn fellow citizens from the path of sin. Such thinking was eminently humane and rational in its objectives and its assumptions. It blended an ar-

---

[1] The number of slaves involved is understated. The Butlers owned more than six hundred.

[2] "I must have appeared to them," wrote Fanny in her old age, "nothing but a mischievous madwoman." *Records of Later Life,* I, 51.

dent desire for reform with an insistence that reform itself be based upon the main precepts of the Christian creed.

The first evidence that Fanny had put her mind to the slavery problem and its solution is her own statement that she had composed, in the first months of 1835, "a long and vehement treatise against Negro slavery." This she originally proposed to include in her *Journal,* which the Philadelphia publisher, Henry Carey, brought out that same year. Fanny had begun this *Journal*—which, of course, must not be confused with the later *Journal of a Residence on a Georgian Plantation*—before her marriage. In it she gave her impressions of America and the story of her travels from 1832 to 1834, from the time she left England to the termination of her American tour. Pierce Butler was opposed for a number of reasons to its publication and tried vainly to persuade the publisher to suppress it. He did succeed, however, in persuading his wife to eliminate from it her tirade against slavery.[3] The manuscript of this work has disappeared. Fanny's horrified husband saw to it, no doubt, that she consigned it to the flames.

Though the disappearance of this manuscript is a loss, we have a good indication of the nature of Fanny's antislavery thinking in this period from her relationship with William Ellery Channing. She was first introduced to the Unitarian divine in New York in May 1833 by Catharine Maria Sedgwick, who knew Channing intimately and was a member of his church.[4] Thereafter Channing became an important influence in Fanny's life. She spoke of him, in her letters, in terms of love and reverence. She missed no opportunity, when in his neighborhood, to enjoy "the honor of his intercourse, and the privilege of hearing him preach." She visited him

[3] Butler warned Fanny that the infuriated citizenry would "tear our house down, and make a bonfire of our furniture—a favorite mode of remonstrance in these parts with those who advocate the rights of the unhappy blacks." Letter to Harriet St. Leger, Branchtown, June 27, 1835, ibid., I, 35–6.

[4] Letter to Harriet St. Leger, New York, May 24, 1833, *Records of a Girlhood,* 577.

at his country cottage at Newport. These ties were encouraged by Mr. Butler, who was himself a Unitarian, and took Fanny with him to worship at the Unitarian Church.[5]

William Ellery Channing, minister of the Federal Street Church in Boston, was the acknowledged leader of New England liberalism in that day. He was the architect of the Unitarian Association which organized the departure of the protestant theology and ministry from the strict dogmatic path of the unreformed New England Calvinist creed. A speaker of great power and a writer of almost luminous beauty, Channing was the intellectual fountain-head from which flowed so much in the social, literary, and philosophic movement of transcendentalism. In 1835 as his contribution to the debate on the slavery question he published a little book entitled *Slavery,* which went through four editions within a year of its first issue. Fanny read this in the early months of 1836, and she gave it unqualified praise. "It is," she said, "like everything else of his, written in the pure spirit of Christianity, with judgment, temper, and moderation, yet with abundant warmth and energy." [6] It expressed to perfection the attitude of sincere but moderate anti-slavery people of that time, who wanted to think through the Christian answer to the problem. Fanny Kemble's own ideas on the subject, and her conduct when she went to Georgia, were in close accordance with the views expressed by Channing; his views, indeed, provide a key to understanding the *Journal of a Residence on a Georgian Plantation.*

Slavery, Channing tells his readers, must be faced boldly, and it must be discussed. But the purpose of discussion is not to instigate insurrection, which will avail nothing, but *to plead the cause of*

[5] "I attend a Unitarian Church . . . being taken thither by the people to whom I belong, who are of that mode of thinking . . . and where I hear admirable instruction and exhortation, and eloquent, excellent preaching, that does my soul good . . . ." Letter to Harriet St. Leger, Branchtown, October 31, 1835, *Records of Later Life,* I, 39.

[6] Letter to Harriet St. Leger, Branchtown (n.d.), 1836, *Records of Later Life,* I, 49.

the slave with his owner. The Christian must seek to win the soul of the slaveowner, to make him understand the nature of his sin, to win him to repentance.[7] Fanny Kemble was in complete agreement with this position. From the moment she learned the truth about the source of the wealth of the Butler family, she cast herself in the role of her husband's conscience and mentor. Her Georgia *Journal,* from one viewpoint, tells the story of how those passionate pleas reached their agonizing climax during the months of residence on the Butler estate.

A slave, Channing continues, is property. But a right to property in man cannot exist. To hold a person in this way is to incur the guilt of oppression. To practice slavery is an offense against God since it deprives man of the right to obey his own moral law and to be master of himself. Nor can slavery be defended on the plea that the public welfare depends upon it, for "no greater calamity can befall a people than to prosper by crime." [8] But, he goes on, because the slave is wronged it does *not* necessarily follow that the master is depraved, for men born and reared in the atmosphere of slavery have difficulty in recognizing moral truth and accepting it. The master may only be condemned if he persists in holding his slaves deliberately for base reasons, for the sake of personal enrichment. Such a man has sunk so low that his spiritual condition is far worse than that of the man whom he exploits.[9] With this position, too, Fanny was in complete agreement. It was to provide the basis for the Georgia *Journal*'s excoriation of a social system that sacrificed

[7] "Who can measure the power of Christian philanthropy, of enlightened goodness, pouring itself forth in prayers and persuasions, from the press and pulpit, from the lips and hearts of devoted men . . . ?" *Slavery,* 4th ed. (Boston: 1836), 6–7.

[8] Ibid., 44.

[9] "He, who has nothing to urge against emancipation, but that it will make him poorer, is bound to urge Immediate Emancipation. He has no excuse for wresting from his brethren their rights. The plea of benefit to the slave and to the state will avail him nothing. He extorts, by the lash, that labor to which he has no claim, through a base selfishness. Every morsel of food, thus forced from the injured, ought to be bitterer than gall. The sweat of the slave taints the luxuries from which it streams." Ibid., 63–4.

human happiness, including the supreme blessing of liberty itself, to mere greed of gain. "I used to pity the slaves," she wrote when in Georgia, "and I do pity them with all my soul; but oh dear! oh dear! their case is a bed of roses to that of their owners, and I would go to the slave block in Charleston tomorrow cheerfully to be purchased if my only option was to go thither as a purchaser." [1]

As for the evils generated by slavery, Channing does not shrink from the most explicit denunciation. His indictment is long, careful, dispassionate, but devastating. The evils of the system, he says, are readily apparent even from a distance. Slavery crushes the human spirit. It denies the dignity of labor. It extinguishes the light of reason in man. It dissolves the most sacred domestic ties. It breeds, on the part of masters, overseers, and drivers, cruelty and irresponsibility. It generates a caste system within a free society.

Fanny agreed with the central points of this indictment, and her Georgia *Journal* would, in time, document and illustrate them in harrowing detail. But how was this evil to be ended? Again, Channing's views were explicit, and Fanny would be the instrument to test their practical application. Emancipation, he says, is a *duty* that rests with the slaveowner. The history of the Caribbean, where the masters opposed emancipation, presents in the case of Haiti, a grim warning of the consequences if slaveowners neglect that duty. The slaves must be educated, introduced to the wage system, to stable domestic relations, and to a moral life. If, says he, the owner *wills* and *desires* emancipation, "a new light will break upon his path." Channing and Fanny, as moderates, distinguished themselves very carefully from more radical abolitionists. The latter, as Channing pointed out, carried on mass propaganda and organized abolition clubs, the effect of which—whether they realized it or not—was to create social antagonism and bring about a political cleavage between the people and the slaveholder. Both Channing and Fanny condemned this tactic and wished to avoid it.

---

[1] *Journal of a Residence on a Georgian Plantation*, 125.

They believed, as we have seen, in moral suasion. As far as re-education of slaves was concerned, personal example and personal ministration would prove more than enough. If, said Channing, the slave could be brought to understand the true spirit of Christianity, he would be fit for freedom.[2] "The personal character," wrote Fanny, "and influence of a few Christian men and women living daily among them [will] put an end to slavery, more speedily and effectually than any other means whatsoever." [3]

This conclusion of Channing's, *that immediate action was necessary for eventual emancipation,* Fanny took very seriously. It was this that led directly to the writing of the Georgia *Journal.* When Pierce Butler asked her one day, jokingly, if she would be willing to migrate to virgin lands of Alabama and make a fortune from cotton production, Fanny answered "in most solemn earnest, that I would go with delight, if we might take that opportunity of at once placing our slaves upon a more humane and Christian footing." [4] Fanny's manumission plans, as might be expected of a young woman with no experience of conditions in the South, were Utopian. But the missionary spirit was upon her. It was a Christian love for God's poor, downtrodden, and outcast. Nothing would satisfy her but that she should visit her husband's Georgia plantations. She began to importune him to that end.[5]

THE GEORGIA RESIDENCE AND COMPOSITION
OF THE *Journal*

For more than two years Pierce Butler firmly opposed his wife's wish, but in this time, his family's resistance to her making the trip lessened. Fanny's determination was as fixed as ever. In 1838

[2] Channing: *Slavery,* 126.

[3] *Records of Later Life,* 67.

[4] "Oh, Harriet!" she exclaimed, "I cannot tell you with what joy it would fill me, if we could only have the energy and courage, the humanity and justice, to do this . . . ." Letter to Harriet St. Leger, Branchtown, Spring, 1836, *Records of Later Life,* I, 48.

[5] Letter to Harriet St. Leger, Branchtown, July 31, 1836, ibid., I, 57.

the plantation overseers, the Roswell Kings, who had run the estate for so many years for the absentee owners, announced their resignation. John Butler, being indisposed, could not travel South to induct new managers, and things would be much easier for Pierce if his wife accompanied him. After a month spent at Lenox, Massachusetts, in the summer of 1838 with the Sedgwicks, the Butlers returned to Philadelphia and prepared for the long and arduous trip to the South. The family left the city on December 21, 1838. With the parents went their two daughters, Sally, who was three, Fan, who had been born in the spring of that very year, and the Irish nursemaid, Margery O'Brien. After nine days by railroad, stagecoach, and steamboat—the chronicle of which constitutes chapters II and III of this edition of the *Journal*—the party arrived at Darien, Georgia, on December 30, 1838, and was ferried over to Butler Island on the same day. "I purpose," wrote Fanny two or three days later, "while I reside here, keeping a sort of journal . . . ." [6]

When Fanny Kemble came to Georgia, English settlement there was barely a century old. But the coastal lands and sea islands were the center of an affluent and cultivated slaveowning aristocracy. On taking up residence on her husband's estate, Fanny was thrust into the heart of Georgian plantation society. It was this society that would be mirrored in her pages.

Georgia was planted in 1733 as a settlement for freeholders. James Oglethorpe, the colony's founding father and first governor, was himself a shareholder in the Africa Company, had coined money out of the infamous traffic in slaves, and knew only too well the dangers and evils attendant upon slavery. His colony stemmed from a shrewd combination of humanitarian zeal and mercantilist calculation. Georgia would help relieve England of her unwanted poor, stimulate the market for British manufactures, provide needed raw materials, and set up a buffer between South Carolina

[6] *Journal of a Residence on a Georgian Plantation*, 53.

on the north and the Spanish enemy on the south.[7] Freemen would provide a sturdier militia and a better defense than rebellious slaves.[8] The latter, indeed, must be banned altogether in view of the fatal tendency for the slave economy to swallow up the free.[9]

The dangers of slavery and the value to the Empire of the free farmer thus were stressed at the outset of Georgian history. The spiritual cradle of the colony lay at Frederica on St. Simons Island, only five miles from Pierce Mease Butler's Hampton Point estate. Frederica was the walled town which Oglethorpe built as the center of defense against the Spanish.[1] Near it he made his own home. St. Simons Island and the surrounding area was peopled with Inverness highlanders, McDonalds, McIntoshes, and McBains, who fled from proscription after the abortive Jacobite rebellion of 1715. It was they who uttered the most vehement protest against the proposed legalization of slavery in 1739.[2]

Oglethorpe left St. Simons Island in 1743 after ten years of service to the infant colony. Following a brief struggle, slavery became legal in 1749. Virginia and Carolina planters moved down to Georgia and began to exploit the virgin coastal lands. Here the

[7] *A Brief Account of the Establishment of the Colony of Georgia* (London: 1733). Reproduced in *Tracts and Other Papers Relating Principally to the Origin, Settlement, and Progress of the Colonies in North America,* Peter Force ed. (New York: 1947), I.

[8] Sir Robert Montgomery: *A Discourse Concerning the Design'd Establishment of a New Colony to the South of Carolina* (London: 1717). Reprinted ibid.

[9] *An Account Showing the Progress of the Colony in Georgia in America from its First Establishment* (London: 1741). Reprinted ibid. This is a document of extraordinary interest. In it the Crown defends itself from "the low-witted Sneer" of disgruntled settlers clamoring for slaves and explains in some detail the reasons for its ban on slavery in the colony.

[1] Fort Frederica is now a national monument administered by the National Park Service of the United States Department of the Interior. Recent excavations have laid bare the original layout of the town and yielded a rich harvest of colonial artifacts.

[2] See the text of the antislavery petition reproduced in *The Colonial Records of the State of Georgia,* Allen D. Candler, comp. (Atlanta, Ga.: 1905), III, 427–8.

fresh-water swamps were well suited to the cultivation of rice. They attracted planters who disposed of capital, owned slaves, and were in possession of the necessary experience for this form of enterprise.[3] The influx of such people was interrupted by the American Revolution, but continued thereafter into the nineteenth century. The development, in particular, of the enormously fertile and extensive ricelands of the Altamaha River region got under way in the 1790's, and the regime of large estates in the area dates from that time.[4] For awhile, to be sure, other crops competed with rice for dominion; first it was sea-island cotton, which from 1795 until 1830 was the boom crop that made fortunes for planters until poor prices, exhausted lands, and the competition of the short-staple cotton grown in the interior brought about a decline; and then it was sugar cane, which in the late 1820's and early 1830's enjoyed a brief boom. But when Fanny Kemble came to Georgia, rice had re-established itself, after the cotton and sugar crazes, as the dominant crop of the Altamaha River estuary.[5] Its cultivation was the type of enterprise well suited to the needs of a wealthy owner disposing of many slaves.[6]

On Pierce Mease Butler's estate the shift in production from cotton to rice also brought a shift in the relative importance of his

[3] W. W. Abbot: *The Royal Governors of Georgia, 1754–1775* (Chapel Hill, N.C.: 1959), 23–4.

[4] "The impetus for this change," writes House, "came largely from the Carolinas where the old rice kings were faced with declining profits due to rising costs, soil deterioration, exhaustion of protecting timber in the uplands, and the disastrous erosion which resulted from the introduction of clean culture crops such as cotton in the piedmont." *Plantation Management and Capitalism in Ante-Bellum Georgia: the Journal of Hugh Fraser Grant, Ricegrower*, Albert V. House, ed. (New York: 1954), 4.

[5] This fact is well illustrated in the careful records which James Hamilton Couper kept for his Hopeton estate near Butler Island on the southern shore of the Altamaha River. The cotton acreage on this estate dwindled from a high of 614 in 1822 to zero in 1838. Rice, on the other hand, rose from 60 acres in 1822 to a high of 684 in 1840. Sugar cane at Hopeton was an important crop from 1829–35. *Record Book of Hopeton Plantation*, Copy in the Division of Manuscripts of the Library of Congress.

[6] Ralph Flanders: *Plantation Slavery in Georgia* (Chapel Hill, N.C.: 1933), 107–8.

two plantations, Butler Island and Hampton Point. By 1838 Butler Island, a swampland given over almost entirely to the production of rice, was economically the center of the Butler property. Hampton Point on St. Simons Island lay on higher ground and had been in Major Pierce Butler's time the main source of the family fortunes. By 1838 it was of secondary importance. When Fanny Kemble came there in 1839, pine and oak had once more begun to claim abandoned and exhausted soil.[7]

In 1840 Georgia had 280,000 slaves who comprised more than fifty per cent of the total population of the state. This constituted one of the densest slave populations in the Union. Butler Island was in McIntosh County, and St. Simons Island in Glynn. In these two counties, slaves made up over eighty per cent of the population. Their owners and managers were a small group of wealthy and powerful families, Grants, Bryans, Brailsfords, Dents, Du-Bignons, Butlers, Kings, Troups, Spaldings, Coupers, and Hamiltons, to name only the most prominent, with the biggest estates of the Altamaha River estuary. They were a clan whose children intermarried and which was thus knit by a complex net of blood relationships.[8] Some of these families owned delta islands where they ruled as petty despots in their isolated riverine domains. This was

[7] ". . . the plantation here [at Hampton Point], which was once the chief source of its owners' wealth, is becoming a secondary one," *Journal of a Residence on a Georgian Plantation,* 227. Production figures for the plantation are not available for the early period. Later records indicate that by 1844 Butler Island was producing upwards of a million pounds of rice *per annum* on its 1800 acres. This would include an unspecified quantity of rice taken as toll for threshing other planters' rice at the Butler mill.

[8] This was not true of the Butlers. Living in the North and only visiting their estate occasionally, they were absentee owners in the fullest sense of the term. Pierce Butler looked for his bride in Philadelphia, and not among the plantation belles. This does not mean that absenteeism was not a widespread evil of plantation life in the Altamaha area. Ricegrowers, in particular, could not stay in their swamplands from May to December. During those months the hired manager took over. Further information about most of the families mentioned here is given in the Biographical Notes in Appendix (C).

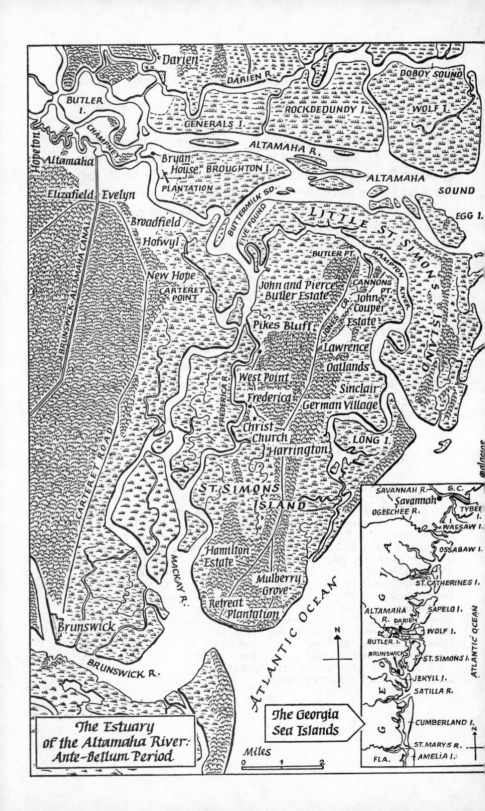

The Estuary of the Altamaha River: Ante-Bellum Period

The Georgia Sea Islands

Miles
0   1   2

N

true of Thomas Spalding of Sapelo Island, of Thomas Bryan of Broughton Island, of Dr. J. Champney Tunno of Champney's Island, and of Pierce Butler of Butler Island. Others, such as Hugh Fraser Grant of Elizafield, James Hamilton Couper of Hopeton, or William Brailsford of Broadfield, owned and operated huge tracts of rich swamplands fringing the Altamaha's southern shores. Still others settled on St. Simons Island, the largest of the delta islands, divided it up, and converted it into a center of cotton production. At the beginning of the nineteenth century there were four large estates on St. Simons, John Couper's at Cannon's Point, Major Pierce Butler's at Hampton Point, James Hamilton's at Gascoigne Bluff, and Major William Page's at Retreat. The rest of the island was divided up into a number of smaller properties owned by Hazzards, Demeres, Wyllys, Grants, Frasers, Caters, Gowens, Armstrongs, and Goulds.[9]

Fanny Kemble began to keep her *Journal* at the beginning of January 1839, though we have no means of knowing the precise day. She worked at it, with frequent interruptions, until the end of her stay in Georgia. The last entry was dated April 17, and the Butler family left for the North on April 18 or 19, 1839. The *Journal* thus covers a span of almost exactly fifteen weeks, or one week short of four lunar months. The family first stayed on Butler Island, then moved down the river to Hampton Point when the weather in the swamplands became too warm for comfort. Almost

[9] Still the best general introduction to the social history of the Altamaha River estuary is Charles Spalding Wylly: *The Seed that was Sown in the Colony of Georgia: the Harvest and Aftermath, 1740–1870* (New York: 1910). See, in addition, Margaret Davis Cate and Orrin S. Wightman: *Early Days of Coastal Georgia* (St. Simons Island, Ga.: 1955); Vanstory: *Georgia's Land of the Golden Isles,* op. cit.; and Caroline Couper Lovell: *The Golden Isles of Georgia* (Boston: 1932). Two special studies, House: *Planter Management,* op. cit., and E. Merton Coulter: *Thomas Spalding of Sapelo* (University, La.: 1941), are of great value, and also provide guidance to the study of the manuscript sources. Useful information is also contained in Georgia Bryan Conrad's charming *Reminiscences of a Southern Woman* (Hampton, Va., n.d.), and in Guion Griffes Johnson: *A Social History of the Sea Islands* (Chapel Hill, N.C.: 1930).

exactly one half of the *Journal* is devoted to the Butler Island period of residence, from December 30, 1838, to February 16, 1839; and one half to the St. Simons Island period of residence, from February 16 to April 17, 1839.

Little explanation is necessary as to why Fanny kept this *Journal*. Writing down her thoughts, keeping a record of her life, came naturally to her, and, indeed, seems to have been indispensable to her in the unfolding of her own inner life. A theoretical understanding, furthermore, of the evils of slavery was but poor preparation for the shock of contact with reality. She experienced agonies of grief. An outlet for her feelings was imperative, and she resorted to the supreme and ultimate consolation in her life, writing. But some comment is necessary about the form in which Fanny expressed her thoughts and the mechanics of writing them down, since this, in the actual reading, can be a fertile source of confusion. As originally published, the *Journal* consisted of thirty-one separate letters, each of them addressed to "Dear Elizabeth," and most of them undated. These letters were not written and mailed; we do not have to do, as would appear at first sight, with a collection of correspondence. Nor are these letters genuine journal entries; a close examination shows that some of them lack internal unity and are a collection of random items written down over the course of several days. Fanny Kemble wrote in haste, never knowing when she would be interrupted, nor when she would be able to resume.

But if these letters were not literally written *to* Elizabeth, they were written *for* her. Eventually she would read them. The Elizabeth to whom Fanny Kemble's passionate outpourings were addressed was Mrs. Elizabeth Dwight Sedgwick of Lenox, Massachusetts. In 1819 Elizabeth Dwight of Northampton had married Charles, the brother of Catharine Maria Sedgwick, and had thus become a member of her sister-in-law's circle. Catharine Maria was at the height of her fame in 1833 as one of New England's leading women of letters. She was an intimate of Dr. William Ellery Channing and a convert to that enlightened Christianity of which he was the champion. Her father was Theodore Sedgwick, an eminent Federalist divine. After his death in 1813, Catharine Maria, who never married, presided over his house and devoted herself to writing. She became the center of a group that included not only her brothers' and sisters' families, but some of New England's most important figures. Fanny was drawn into this circle in 1833; she soon met Elizabeth and her husband and became their close friend. Elizabeth had established an elementary school in her own home in 1828, and conducted it without interruption until her death in 1864. She enjoyed a considerable reputation as an educator; Jennie Jerome, mother of Winston Churchill, was among her pupils. She even permitted little girls to wear pants on their rambles in the woods—a very daring innovation for those days—and she was an authoress.[1]

The friendship thus begun between Fanny and the Sedgwicks was to continue for many years. After her divorce from Pierce Butler in 1849, Fanny bought a cottage at Lenox called "The Perch" and passed many summers there in the company of her friends. To the Charles Sedgwicks she confided the heartbreak arising from her marriage, and it was they who sustained and advised her in the difficulties that arose almost from the start.[2] To Elizabeth, finally, Fanny dedicated her Georgia *Journal*.

In the year following her return from Georgia, Fanny occupied herself with making a fair copy of the *Journal*.[3] This was necessary since the original was written amid constant interruptions and some of it was recorded virtually in note form.[4] This fair copy,

---

[1] See in particular her *A Talk with My Pupils* (New York: 1862).

[2] Fanny Kemble to Eliza Middleton Fisher, 1848. J. F. Fisher Section of the Gen. George Cadwalader Papers, Historical Society of Pennsylvania.

[3] Letter to Harriet St. Leger, Branchtown, October 26, 1840, *Records of Later Life,* II, 40.

[4] "The time that I passed in the South was so crowded with daily and hourly occupations that, though I kept a regular journal, it was hastily written, and received constant additional notes of things that occurred, and that I wished to remember, inserted in a very irregular fashion in it . . . ." Ibid., II, 39.

Fanny hoped, would provide a basis for further revision in the event that she were able to spend a second winter in Georgia, as she confidently expected to do. But this plan was not carried out; John Butler absolutely forbade it. The *Journal,* therefore, could not be filled out from additional first-hand observations. Though Fanny did make further revisions from time to time, these were in the nature of commentary upon what she had already written, and some rearrangement of her original material.

From this time, too, Fanny was considering publication. She wanted to tell the truth about slavery and felt it was her duty. "I have sometimes been haunted," she wrote to Harriet, "with the idea that it was an imperative duty, knowing what I know, and having seen what I have seen, to do all that lies in my power to show the dangers and the evils of this frightful institution." [5] Nonetheless Fanny, in spite of the urgings of her New England friends, kept her silence for nearly a quarter of a century. The manuscript was not prepared for publication, but circulated privately among the Sedgwicks and other friends in the Old World and the New.[6] It was not only that publishing it would involve an abuse of the privileged position Fanny had enjoyed; [7] by the end of 1840 she was facing a personal crisis that drove all thought of publication from her mind and that ended only with the disintegration of her marriage and her

[5] Ibid., 40.

[6] Ibid., I, 261, where Fanny refers to a reading of the manuscript "many years before [the Civil War]," at Lady Dacre's. See also a possible reference to the Georgia *Journal* in Fanny's letter to Charles B. Sedgwick from Lenox [? December 17, 1848], No. 8 in the Columbia University collection of F. A. Kemble's letters to Mr. and Mrs. Charles B. Sedgwick.

[7] "I think," wrote Fanny on October 26, 1840, to Harriet St. Leger, "such a publication would be a breach of confidence, an advantage taken on my part of the situation of trust, which I held on the estate. As my condemnation of the whole system is unequivocal, and all my illustrations of its evils must be drawn from our own plantation, I do not think I have the right to exhibit the interior management and economy of that property to the world at large, as a sample of Southern slavery, especially as I did not go thither with any such purpose." *Records of Later Life,* II, 39–40.

home. Throughout the decade of the forties Fanny cast every consideration to the winds save the central one of salvaging her marriage and of keeping her children. This crisis erupted when the Butlers sailed to England in the fall of 1840 to visit Fanny's father, who was seriously ill; and it continued without intermission for nearly ten years until the Court of Common Pleas of Pennsylvania decreed the couple's divorce on September 22, 1849, and awarded custody of the children to the father.

The sad personal history of these years and its sensational climax in the courts is not of relevance here.[8] But it should be pointed out that the initiative for the separation came from Pierce Butler and that Fanny strove, with a frenzy bordering on desperation, to defend her home and marriage. "For God's sake," she wrote when they were in England in 1843 and already living under separate roofs, "and for your children's sake, Pierce, my husband, oh still my most tenderly beloved, let us be wise before it is too late . . . I implore you by that love which you once had for me, by that unalterable love which I still bear you, forgive me, forgive me. . . ." Fanny's *Journal*, evidently, was not written by a woman soured against slavery by an unhappy marriage, but rather by one in whom love and moral conviction battled with equal and tempestuous force.

PUBLICATION OF THE *Journal*

Another decade lay between the divorce in 1849 and the coming of age of Fanny Kemble's younger daughter Fan. Waiting during the long years for the day when her children could be reunited with her, Fanny buried her anguish in work. She returned to her career as an actress, but now in a mature role of her own choos-

---

[8] For a report of the divorce proceedings and circumstances, see the *Philadelphia Ledger and Transcript,* November 28, 29, 30, and December 1, 2, and 4, 1848; Armstrong: *Fanny Kemble,* Chaps. xxi–xxiii.

ing, and delighted the public on both sides of the Atlantic with her Shakespearian readings.[9] Her art, her numerous friends, and the anticipation of reunion with her daughters filled all of Fanny's mind. What need was there to resurrect the past? During the fifties, nothing was further from the actress's thoughts than the publication of her Georgia *Journal*. Fanny had never become Americanized. She had, as she wrote later to her friend Harriet St. Leger, "grown more and more *English* in contradistinction to American as I have grown older." If slavery, from which she had quite literally been divorced, were an American problem, why should an Englishwoman concern herself with it? The more so as the turning up of old wounds, which publication of the *Journal* would involve, might endanger her relationship with her children and jeopardize her reunion with them.

Yet the course of events was pushing Fanny toward a decision. The divorce took away the restraining influence and the dictates of her husband. The very estate about which she had written ceased to exist in 1859, when four hundred of its slaves went under the hammer to pay the owner's debts.[1] And with the new decade came the Civil War.

The opening of the war found Fanny in the United States, sharing the complacency which many Northerners felt as to the outcome of the struggle, convinced that "after an unlimited amount of brag and bluster" the South would be obliged to knuckle under to the vastly superior resources and more enduring determination of

[9] For a remarkable tribute to Fanny Kemble's genius as a reader of Shakespeare, see Pauline Craven: *La Jeunesse de Fanny Kemble* (Paris, 1888). Philip Hone recorded that "delicate women, grave gentlemen, belles, beaux, and critics, flock to the doors of entrance and rush into such places as they can find, two or three hours before the time of the lady's appearance." March 13, 1849; *Diary*, II, 863.

[1] Pierce Butler fell deeply into debt as the result of the 1857 financial crash. His share of the Georgia estate was sold to pay his debts, and netted close to $250,000. See Mortimer Thomson's article in *The Tribune*, March 9, 1859, reprinted by the American Antislavery Society as a pamphlet (n.d.) entitled *Great Auction Sale of Slaves at Savannah, Georgia, March 2 and 3, 1859*.

the other side. All would be well, thought Fanny, provided that foreign countries, *and England in particular,* did not intervene.[2] But the course of events belied these expectations. Not only was it apparent, by the beginning of 1862, that the war was going to be a long one, but there was undisguised British sympathy with the rebels and an evident desire on the part of the British government, under Palmerston and his Foreign Secretary Earl Russell, to abandon neutrality and to recognize the Confederacy. The inevitable result of such a policy, in view of the Northern blockade of the Southern ports, would be war with the Union. The *Trent* case, which reached its climax in January 1862 and brought the two countries to the brink of war, underlined the perilousness of the situation. Fanny's mood became one of deep concern. War between England and the United States would have been to her the supreme catastrophe. It would set the cause of human progress back fifty to a hundred years. It was at all costs to be avoided.[3]

In June 1862 Mrs. Kemble returned to England for a visit. She arrived in London when Anglo-American relations were approaching their gravest wartime crisis. That summer Lee, fresh in command of the Confederate army, drove McClellan off from Richmond, marched north, routed an army under Pope at Manassas, and crossed the Potomac west of Washington. He was headed for Maryland and Pennsylvania in the South's first major invasion of the free states. Lincoln turned the command back to McClellan. The world watched as the North rallied its forces for the decisive battles that appeared to be at hand.

The English friends of the Confederacy were exuberant. They expected a Northern defeat and the end of the policy of neutrality

[2] *Further Records* (London: 1890), II, 230.

[3] Her change of heart was noted with satisfaction by her New England friends. "Mrs. Kemble," wrote Susan Sedgwick to her sister-in-law Jane, "is in exactly that state of mind which we would wish about England—weeping over her country's wickedness." Letter from Susan R. to Jane Sedgwick, February 1862, in the possession of the Stockbridge Library Association. See also the letter from Fanny to Charles B. Sedgwick, No. 26 of the Columbia University Kemble Mss.

that kept Southern cotton from English looms and English arms from the South. The government-inspired London *Times* prepared its readers for the speedy collapse of the Union:

> The North [the *Times* told its readers on the eve of Antietam] has tried the great experiment of coercion, and failed; the South has tried the great experiment of independence, and made good its position. The North is much further from its purpose now than when Mr. Lincoln first called for 75,000 men to carry it into effect. The South is much nearer to the accomplishment of its design than when, a year ago, its armies first besieged Washington from Manassas. In the interval, amid many shiftings and twistings of fortune, nothing has been so evident to all men as the ultimate hopelessness of the Northern project.[4]

On September 17, 1862, Lee's forces received a check at Antietam. On September 22, Lincoln issued his first, or preliminary, emancipation proclamation, which announced his intention to free, on January 1, 1863, all slaves in states which remained at that time in rebellion against the Union. This news reached England on the *Australasian,* which docked at Queenstown on October 4, and was printed in the *Times* on October 6. It was greeted with howls of execration from the *Times* and the rest of the London pro-slavery organs.[5] But the government hastened to make clear that its policy and its attitude toward the South was unchanged either by the unfavorable outcome of Antietam or by the threat of a "servile war." On the following day W. E. Gladstone, Chancellor of the Exchequer, made a major governmental pronouncement at Newcastle-on-Tyne. "We may anticipate," he said, "with certainty the success of the Southern states, so far as regards their separa-

---

[4] Dispatch from New York, September 16, 1862. Printed in the *Times,* September 30, 1862.

[5] "As an act of policy," fulminated the *Times,* "it is, if possible, more contemptible than it is wicked. . . . The most consummate folly ever perpetrated by a ruler." October 7 and 9, 1862.

tion from the North." He implied that recognition was only a question of time.[6]

Fanny was appalled at the hysteria of the London press, the hatred shown for the North, and the complete hostility to the emancipation proclamation of September 22, whose historic significance escaped the British press which derided it as an empty, hypocritical, and vengeful gesture.[7] Some time between the statement of the preliminary emancipation proclamation in September 1862, and its confirmation by the decree of January 1, 1863—we cannot say precisely when—Mrs. Kemble decided to publish her *Journal.* She felt she would thereby illuminate the nature of the Union's newly declared war aim, convince her English friends of its justness and necessity, and strike a blow at the proslavery apologetics of the government and of the London press. In addition she hoped to contribute to a true understanding in England of the American struggle, help rally English opinion to the side of the North, and hence minimize the danger of British intervention on behalf of the Confederacy.

Fanny's main concern was to produce an English edition of her *Journal,* and not an American one. But events in the United States, too, were moving toward a climax. By January 1863, the Union had committed itself to the eradication of slavery by fire and sword. Abolition was removed from the sphere of the Christian duty of the slaveowner to that of national policy. Fanny's position now came

[6] Speech of October 7, 1862. Reported in the *Times,* October 9. "The terrible rent," the *Times* had editorialized a few days earlier, "yawns as widely as ever, and appears beyond the carpenter's skill."

[7] "I am deeply grieved," she wrote, "at the tone of our press upon the subject of your national troubles and am frequently surprised and pained by the total absence of sympathy here with the Northern cause, but am always met by the assertion that though right-minded people here would rejoice in the suppression of the institution of slavery, they cannot sympathize with the Northerners upon whom that result is being merely forced as the natural consequence of the war itself, and who show no desire to deal with the question otherwise than as a matter of inevitable necessity." Letter to Joshua Francis Fisher, London, 1862. McCall Legal Section of the Cadwalader Collection, Historical Society of Pennsylvania.

close to the radical abolitionists who had maintained all along that control of slavery was a Federal concern, and who had been pressing since the beginning of the war for emancipation and military utilization of the slaves.[8] Her final objection to the publication of the *Journal* in America—that it would be used as an instrument of radical abolitionism—was removed. The American abolitionist movement scored a long waited-for victory when in May 1863, Fanny assigned the American copyright to Francis G. Shaw, a Massachusetts abolitionist friend, and authorized him to negotiate its sale.[9]

The London edition of the *Journal* was published by Longman and Company in May 1863; the New York edition, issued by Harper and Brothers, appeared in July. What, we must ask, was the impact of this event upon contemporary opinion?

In the absence of any careful investigation of this fascinating aspect of Anglo-American intellectual history, all sorts of wild statements have been made, and indeed a veritable mythology has arisen. Southerners have written, and some still believe, that Fanny Kemble singlehanded prevented England's recognition of the Confederacy, and hence turned the balance of advantage against the South.[1] What is more remarkable, they have even suc-

---

[8] *Journal*, 369–70.

[9] Letter from Frances Anne Kemble to Frances G. Shaw, London, May 1863. Original in the possession of Harper and Brothers, New York. On July 18, two days after the issue of the American edition of the *Journal*, the Shaw family's young immortal, Robert Gould, was killed at the assault of Fort Wagner on Morris Island, South Carolina. For Fanny's lament at this new sea-island sorrow, see her letter to Henry Lee, Bishop's Waltham, Hants, December 8, 1864. Kemble Mss., Harvard College Library Theater Collection, Cambridge, Mass.

[1] "The book," wrote Medora Field Perkerson, "created a sensation little short of that which followed the appearance of *Uncle Tom's Cabin*. English sympathy promptly swung away from the South and the hoped-for English support was lost." *White Columns in Georgia* (New York: 1952), 133–4. The Georgia Historical Commission has immortalized its conjecture in cast iron in the following words on a historical marker planted at the edge of U.S. Route 17 on Butler Island: "During a visit here with her husband in 1839–40 [sic], Pierce Butler's wife, the brilliant English actress, Fanny Kemble,

ceeded in convincing Mrs. Kemble's own biographers that she accomplished this feat.[2] On the other side, it has been argued that both in England and America the contemporary importance of the *Journal* was small, its sales minor, and its influence negligible.[3]

There is, in truth, at the present time no way of estimating the impact the *Journal* made at the time it was published. While the contemporary reviews still make interesting reading, they afford no indication of the book's reception by the wider public. Nor can we consult circulation statistics. Harper and Brothers have no sales records. Longman and Company's files, whatever they contained, were destroyed by enemy action in the second World War.

In this situation conjecture must advance along different lines. By May 1863, when Fanny's English edition appeared, the danger of English recognition of the Confederacy was past. The news of Gettysburg and Vicksburg, arriving in July, administered the *coup de grâce* to whatever hope remained. Fanny's *Journal* simply came on the scene too late to affect the outcome at all. But what is perhaps of more significance, the emancipation proclamation of January 1, 1863, had let loose a flood of pro-Union sentiment in Eng-

---

wrote her *Journal of a Residence on a Georgian Plantation,* which is said to have influenced England against the Confederacy."

[2] According to Margaret Armstrong, the *Journal* was "read and discussed, with anger and tears, from one end of England to the other." And, as though this flight of fancy were not enough for one page, she adds: "There is no reason to doubt that Fanny Kemble accomplished what she had hoped to accomplish; she helped to tip the wavering scales in favor of the North by weakening England's admiration for the Confederacy and thus preventing the loan that would have prolonged the war and perhaps destroyed the Union." *Fanny Kemble,* 342. The

Confederate Cotton Loan, to which this author is here referring, was launched on March 19, 1863; but—alas for Miss Armstrong's version!—within two weeks its price had fallen below par, and by the end of April, well before the publication of Fanny's *Journal,* the public had virtually abandoned it. See E. D. Adams: *Great Britain and the American Civil War* (New York: n.d.), II, 155–62.

[3] This thesis is developed by Mildred E. Lombard: "Contemporary Opinions of Mrs. Kemble's *Journal of a Residence on a Georgian Plantation,*" *Georgia Historical Quarterly,* XIV (December, 1930), 335–43.

land. Now that the moral issue had been clearly raised, the English working class, with its deep-rooted antislavery traditions, rallied round the North, and the spring of 1863 witnessed an avalanche of mass meetings supporting the proclamation. Lincoln was showered with addresses from British workers congratulating him upon the historic step. English supporters of the South were placed upon the defensive as the antislavery forces during these months circulated thousands of books and tracts demonstrating the horror of slavery in the United States, and, a fortiori, the justness of a war to eliminate it. We can be sure that Fanny Kemble's *Journal* was among the literature thus circulated. It would have a special significance for English workers because it not only showed the evils of slavery but—as the English reviewers were quick to point out—the evils of aristocracy.[4]

It was no secret in England that the upper and middle classes feared the advance of the movement toward universal suffrage, and looked with some misgivings on the "leveling" example of the American republican experiment. These people had naturally enough sympathized with the Confederacy. For was the latter not governed by an aristocracy, and would not its victory curb the impetuosity of the rash Northern democracy? But the English working class looked with admiration upon the American experiment in popular government and democratic rule. Thousands of its sons and daughters, indeed, had crossed the seas to build the new state, and had found home and happiness there. We may be reasonably certain that Fanny Kemble was carefully read by some of these English workers. The *Journal* was a dreadful indictment of a ruling class. It pointed a moral to voteless Englishmen who had grounds for dissatisfaction with their own rulers. And indeed, it is no coincidence that the second great nineteenth-century step in the broadening of suffrage came in England in 1867, hard upon the

---

[4] With rare discernment the *Athenæum* reviewer devoted more than one half of a lengthy six-column article to Fanny's treatment of the Southern white slave-owning class. June 6, 1863.

heels of the conclusion of the American Civil War and the vindication of government of, by, and for the people.

As for the impact of the *Journal* in the United States, we have two clues to its popularity. A second printing of the 1863 edition was issued in 1864. Surviving copies of this run are extremely rare, and there is no way of estimating its size. Another clue is to be found in the pamphlet entitled *The Views of Judge Woodward and Bishop Hopkins on Negro Slavery at the South,* published in Philadelphia in 1863. This pamphlet was, essentially, a reprint of portions of the *Journal;* evidently its reception had been sufficiently enthusiastic for an enterprising publisher to conclude that its chances of sale in pamphlet form were good.

FANNY KEMBLE'S PICTURE OF SLAVERY

Contemporary reviewers of the *Journal* gave a number of reasons for accepting the authenticity of Mrs. Kemble's facts about plantation life. The *London Review* argued that it would have required the imagination of a Dante to have conjured this picture out of thin air.[5] The *North American Review* pointed out that the *Journal* had been composed a quarter of a century before the Civil War; it could not have been written with a view to publication, and therefore was not a *pièce d'occasion* prompted by the war crisis itself.[6] One writer noted that Mrs. Kemble had good reason to look only for the best side of slavery, and to put the best face upon it; for was she not the master's wife, a young woman passionately in love, wishing above all things to protect her family and her marriage?[7] Several reviewers were struck by the unique nature of the *Journal* as an "inside story," and underlined the point that facts were observed by the author which no visitor, not even an Olmsted, could have had access to. Mrs. Kemble's, said the *Atlan-*

---

[5] *The London Review of Politics, Society, Literature, Art, and Science,* June 6, 1863.

[6] XCVII (October, 1863), 582.
[7] *Atlantic Monthly,* XII (August, 1863), 261.

tic Monthly, was "the decisive voice" that hitherto had been silent in the great debate; hers was "the first ample, lucid, faithful, detailed account, from the actual headquarters of a slave plantation in this country, of the workings of the system . . . ." [8] Reviewers on both sides of the Atlantic agreed that one of the most remarkable features of the *Journal* was the picture it gave of the lot of women under slavery.[9] Though the *Athenæum* thought that the slave women may have made many exaggerated statements to a mistress who had sympathy for their sufferings, the reviewers in general did not challenge the depth of the author's insight in this area. "Her sex," concluded the New York *Evening Post,* "brought her specially in contact with slave women. A man, unless he had been a physician, would have known nothing of most of the sorrows and sufferings which were confided to her without scruple."

In the years since the publication of the *Journal* scholarly evaluation, as might be expected, has divided along sectional lines. Southern historians have either ignored the *Journal* or have dismissed it as the product of bias.[1] Northern historians have accepted much of Fanny's evidence, in particular where it has been confirmed by similar evidence from other sources. Of these historians the most important are Rhodes,[2] Gray,[3] Franklin,[4] and Stampp.[5]

[8] Ibid., 260. See also *Harper's Magazine,* XXVII (August, 1863), 416.

[9] *Athenæum,* op. cit. *Atlantic Monthly,* op. cit., 261. *London Spectator,* May 30, 1863.

[1] Clement Eaton stated that "She [Kemble] has left a bitterly prejudiced account of slavery and the life of a rice planter," *A History of the Old South* (New York: 1949), 240. U. B. Phillips, who was an authority on slavery, cited Kemble only in order to prove the existence of anti-Negro bias in the North. His short notice of the *Journal* in *Life and Labor in the Old South* (Boston: 1929), 259–65, is so full of inaccuracies that one cannot believe that he gave the work careful examination. Fletcher Green went even further when he wrote that "She [Kemble] was so decidedly fixed in her opinions that it was impossible for her to see or understand the viewpoint of the American people, North or South," Book review, *Journal of Southern History,* I (May, 1935), 220. William B. Hesseltine: *The South in American History* (New York: 1943), made one allusion to Kemble, but clearly had no firsthand knowledge of the *Journal.*

[2] James Ford Rhodes: *A History of the United States from the Compromise of 1850* (New York: 1893),

A careful reading of the *Journal* reveals a number of minor factual inaccuracies. In the present edition these have been pointed out in the editor's footnotes. There is no reason to believe that Fanny would not have corrected the most important of these herself had she had the opportunity of a second visit to Georgia. But into one incident in the *Journal,* the Wylly-Hazzard duel, Mrs. Kemble deliberately introduced an element of fiction. In Chapters XXVII to XXXII she told the story of a quarrel between two neighboring planters on St. Simons Island which resulted in the death of one of the participants; and she gave the date of this encounter as the first week of April 1839, when in fact the quarrel occurred in 1838 and the fatal shooting on December 3 of that year. Mrs. Kemble was here recounting something that had not

---

devoted Chapter iv of Vol. I to a survey of slavery based largely on F. L. Olmsted, Frederick Douglass, Sir Charles Lyell, James S. Buckingham, and F. A. Kemble. "Her description," he wrote, "of the little Negroes begging her piteously for meat is as pathetic as the incident of the hungry demand of Oliver Twist," I, 305. With respect to slave women he said that ". . . her daily record of what she saw and heard is as pitiful as it is true," I, 311. Rhodes cited Kemble on slave diet, foulness of living quarters, brutalization, overwork, slave breeding, exploitation of women, flogging, education, poor whites, dueling, and owners' fears of insurrection, I, 303–83, *passim.*

[3] Lewis Cecil Gray: *A History of Agriculture in the Southern United States to 1860* (Washington, D.C.: 1933, reissued Gloucester, Mass.: 1941). This eminent economic historian observed that "Mrs. Kemble's oversympathetic, but apparently truthful, diary of her observations

on a Georgia rice plantation reflects graphically the burdens endured by female laborers," I, 562. Gray cited Kemble on the status of Southern poor whites, organization and management of slave labor, task labor, and on health and sanitation, I, 485, 548, 551, 562.

[4] John Hope Franklin: *The Militant South 1800–61* (Cambridge, Mass.: 1956). This leading Negro historian makes effective use of Fanny's *Journal* in his study of the influence of slavery on the *mores* of the Southern ruling class and of the white population in general. Her *Journal,* he says, "is especially important in understanding the influence of slavery on the character of the planters," 256.

[5] Kenneth M. Stampp: *The Peculiar Institution: Slavery in the Ante-Bellum South* (New York: 1956). This excellent and dispassionate survey cites Kemble on health and on social, family, and religious life on the plantation.

come under her immediate observation as if it had. How then, asks a recent writer, can one distinguish fact from fiction in the *Journal?* [6]

Fanny Kemble was a woman, evidently, who found it difficult to conceal her true thoughts and feelings. She felt obliged to take her stand on slavery before her husband even though this led to the collapse of her home, the disintegration of her marriage, and the vanishing of her hopes for happiness.[7] We must look for some unusual reason for her decision to postdate the Wylly-Hazzard duel and to introduce it into the *Journal* as personal experience rather than as recent St. Simons history. The fact is that shortly after returning from Georgia, Fanny had an intimate and harrowing experience. On Monday, April 15, 1844, Pierce Butler fought a duel at Bladensburg, Maryland, with a Philadelphia neighbor and friend, James Schott. Pistols were used, two rounds were fired by each man, and both escaped unharmed. It is noteworthy that the duel took place at the insistence of Pierce Butler, even after his opponent had tried to cancel it on the grounds that his heel was so painfully swollen he could not stand straight to deliver his shot accurately.[8] The encounter came about as a result of a charge by Schott that on a visit to New York he had found Butler at midnight of March 9, 1844, in a compromising relationship with his wife, Ellen Schott. Fanny was living in Philadelphia at that time, apart from her husband and children. The charge of Butler's infidelity was a matter of public gossip, and the duel was the sensation of the hour. Fanny read the whole affair in the public press.

While she was in Georgia, Fanny had had ample opportunity to

[6] Margaret Davis Cate: "Mistakes in Fanny Kemble's Journal," *Georgia Historical Quarterly*, XLIV (March, 1960), 17.

[7] Polite society judged Mrs. Kemble harshly for such unpardonable quixotry. Far better, it thought, that she should have put aside conscience and concentrated upon making her husband happy. See Charles Greville: *Memoirs,* Lytton Strachey and Roger Fulford eds. (London: 1938), V, 62–3.

[8] For the full story, see the Butler-Schott Duel folder in Box Miscellaneous B of the George Cadwalader Papers, Historical Society of Pennsylvania.

realize the role played by the duel in Southern life. The shadow of a famous murder hung over the Butler estate itself; it was there, at Hampton Point, that Aaron Burr took refuge from New Jersey justice after slaying Alexander Hamilton in 1804. The mistress of Hampton, we know, read the local newspaper, the Brunswick *Advocate,* while she was in Georgia.[9] The March 30, 1839 issue had a lead article, evidently designed for the improvement of its readers, entitled "The Horrors of Duelling." The same issue reported an encounter which resulted in the murder of George Cumberland, a commission merchant from Mobile, Alabama, by E. B. Church, also a merchant, at the latter's home; in addition it told of a duel near Moscow, Tennessee, between Alex Donelson, adopted son of the Seventh President of the United States, and Henry Robeson, in which both men were slightly wounded. Other issues of the *Advocate* reported duels in which the opponents placed their pistols in each other's mouths; [1] and one in which a judge fought an army captain with rifles and finished his antagonist off with a bowie knife.[2] While Fanny was on St. Simons Island the conversation must have turned constantly to the recent duel between Wylly and Hazzard. Whatever local indignation had been aroused, it was not sufficient to prevent Hazzard's acquittal upon a charge of manslaughter, and this occurred shortly after Mrs. Kemble left Georgia.

We must conclude that dueling was a fact of Fanny's Georgia experience. It was in her husband's family tradition, in his own personal conduct, and in the mental agony which she suffered as a consequence. Postdating the Wylly-Hazzard affair was a device which enabled Fanny to introduce into the *Journal* the agonies of her own encounter with the duello without revealing the secrets of her personal life.

The picture that Mrs. Kemble paints of slavery on her husband's plantation is a dark one lightened by exquisite word pictures of the

[9] *Journal,* 104, where Fanny mentions reading the Couper-Nightingale advertisement for labor for the Brunswick Canal.
[1] April 13, 1839.
[2] March 2, 1839.

landscape, of birds, waterways, trees, skies, and flowers. Incidents, too, of a deep tenderness lighten the gloom, but also accentuate the sadness of the world of toil and misery into which the reader is plunged. If the slaves are the heroes of the scene, they are not romanticized, but presented in their dirt-incrusted, animal existence. If the planter society seems vapid and ignorant, idle and cruel, some of its members are likeable people. John Couper is shown as a kindly, thrifty old soul with a passion for flowers, and his son James Hamilton Couper, the hero of the *Pulaski*, is described in complimentary terms. Dr. James Holmes appears as courteous and friendly; Captain John Fraser and his wife, Ann, are depicted as thoughtful hosts and neighbors.

Mrs. Kemble's picture of slavery has a many-sided complexity. Its almost inexhaustible detail points up the powers of observation of a woman who reflected the varied life about her with a brilliant intensity. But to what extent was the Butler estate typical or representative of conditions under slavery? Fanny's experience was of a large plantation which utilized slaves in gangs, represented a considerable capital investment, and produced an enormous monetary profit. Her *Journal* tells us nothing of conditions on farms employing only a few slaves where more patriarchal relationships prevailed. But in many parts of the South, notably in much of Kentucky and Tennessee, small slaveholdings were the rule.[3] Even insofar as large plantations are concerned, there is no norm by which the Butler estate can be measured as typical or representative. Undoubtedly there were many plantations more humanely run than this, and many, particularly in the deep South, far more cruel in their mode of operation. The most we can say is that Fanny gives a picture of conditions on an estate where absenteeism was the rule, where the owners had for many years been indif-

[3] In Tennessee, according to the census of 1860, over 5,000 landowners, or more than 85 per cent of the total, owned nearly 38,000 slaves, or more than 50 per cent of the total, an average of seven to eight slaves per landowner.

ferent to all save the monetary income yielded by their property, and where care of slaves was given over to hired managers and overseers. The evils of absentee ownership are clearly depicted in the *Journal,* and absenteeism, as we know, was widespread among the owners of large estates. For the rest, it is enough to say that the *Journal* captured many of the inevitable features of slave labor on big plantations, and that much of its detail has been corroborated by the evidence of other observers.

The *Journal* brings to life for us both a slave community and a segment of Southern society, and because it does this, its literary and historical value is evident. Mrs. Kemble was a white woman who cast aside the apologetics which rationalized and defended the oppression of the Negro people, and who won a true perception of their strength, dignity, and beauty. This achievement was nonetheless impressive for being—as the pages of the *Journal* bear eloquent witness—the result of a constant struggle to penetrate to the heart of things through the repulsive outer circumstance of dirt, ugliness, and disease. Fanny Kemble fought, in a difficult time, her own battle on behalf of the brotherhood of man. The *Journal* is a contribution to the antislavery literature which constitutes an important part of the cultural and moral heritage of the American people.

* * * * * * * * * * * * * * * * * * *

The present edition follows closely the original edition of 1863, but certain changes have been made in the interests of clarity, including slight modifications of punctuation and spelling. In the original edition most of the people to whom Fanny Kemble referred were not mentioned by name. Her pages were strewn with blanks that made a full understanding of the text often difficult and sometimes impossible. In the present edition practically all such references have been identified, and the blanks filled in. The persons so identified have been listed in Appendix (C), and biographical information about them has been provided. This Appendix will enable the reader to become acquainted with the people whom Fanny knew or to whom she makes reference.

In the original edition of the *Journal* the entries followed each other without number or title. Now both number and title have been given to the entries, which are, accordingly, presented in chapter form. Chapters II and III of the present edition did not appear in the original. However, this material was written from Butler Island in January 1839 to Harriet St. Leger, and constitutes such a vital link in the story that the editor considered it essential to include it here in the appropriate place.

Each entry has been dated as precisely as possible from an examination of the entry itself and its position in relation to succeeding and preceding entries. Where possible exact dates have been assigned; dates mentioned by the author have been checked and errors rectified. The editor's dating is placed at the head of each chapter in brackets. In the earlier part of the *Journal,* it is possible only to identify the month in which the letter was written; further along greater exactness is possible. The headings then refer to the day, or the span of days, during which that particular chapter was actually written. Thus the reader will have a chronology of the diary entries that is clear enough for practical purposes. In addition to Fanny Kemble's own Appendices, (A) and (B), one further Appendix, (D), has been provided. This consists of a guide to the main sources consulted in the preparation of this edition of the *Journal.*

In the editorial work I have received help from a great many people. My thanks go especially to the staffs of the Columbia University and Amherst College Libraries, of the Library of Congress, the Folger Shakespeare Library, and of the Stockbridge and Lenox Library Associations, for their assistance. The Massachusetts and New York Historical Societies, and the Historical Society of Pennsylvania placed their resources at my disposal. The Harvard College Library gave me the use of its Theater Collection. Mrs.

Lilla Hawes of the Georgia Historical Society helped in a number of ways. Harper and Brothers, publishers of the original American edition of the *Journal,* generously provided me with copies of documents in their possession. Professor Stanley J. Stein of Princeton University read the Introduction and offered useful suggestions. Mrs. Margaret Davis Cate, eminent St. Simons Island historian, gave me freely of her time, allowed me to use her unique historical collection, and read and criticized portions of the manuscript. Mrs. John D. McLanahan of New York City gave valuable help in the elaboration of the Butler family genealogy. Mr. Alvin Cannon, Project Leader of the Altamaha Waterfowl Management Area of the Georgia State Game and Fish Commission, discussed the history of Butler Island with me, and provided a copy of an invaluable old map. Miss Ophelia Dent permitted me to use a portion of her grandmother's memoirs and offered information about the history of the Dent and Troup families. Mrs. Walter Stokes of St. Davids, Pennsylvania, gave me her kind permission to quote from Mrs. Kemble's unpublished writings. Miss Elizabeth Hall, Librarian of the New York Botanical Gardens, provided technical information on rice and cotton. Mr. Arthur Kinoy helped in a search for manuscripts in England. Dr. Julius Parker gave help with the identification of clinical symptoms. Mrs. Eve Lederman gave invaluable secretarial help; and my wife, Maria Scott, assisted with the proof.

JOHN ANTHONY SCOTT

JOURNAL

OF

A RESIDENCE ON A

GEORGIAN PLANTATION

IN 1838–1839.

BY FRANCES ANNE KEMBLE.

SLAVERY THE CHIEF CORNER STONE.

'This stone (Slavery), which was rejected by the first builders, is become the chief stone of the corner in our new edifice.'—*Speech of* ALEXANDER H. STEPHENS, *Vice-President of the Confederate States: delivered March* 21, 1861.

NEW YORK:

HARPER & BROTHERS, PUBLISHERS,

FRANKLIN SQUARE.

1863.

TO

ELIZABETH DWIGHT SEDGWICK,

This Journal,

Originally Kept for Her,

is

Most Affectionately

Dedicated.

PREFACE

THE FOLLOWING DIARY was kept in the winter and spring of 1838–9, on an estate consisting of rice and cotton plantations, in the islands at the entrance of the Altamaha, on the coast of Georgia.

The slaves in whom I then had an unfortunate interest were sold some years ago. The islands themselves are at present in the power of the Northern troops. The record contained in the following pages is a picture of conditions of human existence which I hope and believe have passed away.

LONDON, *January 16, 1863.*

CONTENTS

FROM PHILADELPHIA

TO GEORGIA.

December 1838

[The author's notes are indicated throughout with an asterisk (*), the editor's by arabic numbers 1 through 9.]

I

Thoughts on Slavery

[Philadelphia. December, 1838]

My dear E[lizabeth],

I return you Mr. ——'s letter.[1] I do not think it answers any of the questions debated in our last conversation at all satisfactorily: the *right* one man has to enslave another, he has not the hardihood to assert; but in the reasons he adduces to defend that act of injustice, the contradictory statements he makes appear to me to refute each other. He says, that to the Continental European protesting against the abstract iniquity of slavery, his answer would be, "the slaves are infinitely better off than half the Continental peasantry"; to the Englishman, "they are happy compared with the miserable Irish." But supposing that this answered the question of original injustice, which it does not, it is not a true reply. Though the Negroes are fed, clothed, and housed, and though the Irish peasant is starved, naked, and roofless, the bare name of freemen—the lordship over his own person, the power to choose and will—are blessings beyond food, raiment, or shelter; possessing which, the want of every comfort of life is yet more tolerable than their fullest enjoyment without them. Ask the thousands of ragged destitutes who yearly land upon these shores

[1] The original of this letter remains untraced and its authorship uncertain.

to seek the means of existence—ask the friendless, penniless foreign emigrant if he will give up his present misery, his future uncertainty, his doubtful and difficult struggle for life at once, for the secure, and, as it is called, fortunate dependence of the slave: the indignation with which he would spurn the offer will prove that he possesses one good beyond all others, and that his birthright as a man is more precious to him yet than the mess of pottage for which he is told to exchange it because he is starving.

Of course the reverse alternative cannot be offered to the slaves, for at the very word the riches of those who own them would make themselves wings and flee away. But I do not admit the comparison between your slaves and even the lowest class of European free laborers, for the former are *allowed* the exercise of no faculties but those which they enjoy in common with the brutes that perish. The just comparison is between the slaves and the useful animals to whose level your laws reduce them; and I will acknowledge that the slaves of a kind owner may be as well cared for, and as happy, as the dogs and horses of a merciful master; but the latter condition—i.e., that of happiness—must again depend upon the complete perfection of their moral and mental degradation.

Mr. ——, in his letter, maintains that they *are* an inferior race, and, compared with the whites, *"animals,* incapable of mental culture and moral improvement"': to this I can only reply, that if they are incapable of profiting by instruction, I do not see the necessity for laws inflicting heavy penalties on those who offer it to them. If they really are brutish, witless, dull, and devoid of capacity for progress, where lies the *danger* which is constantly insisted upon of offering them that of which they are incapable? We have no laws forbidding us to teach our dogs and horses as much as they can comprehend; nobody is fined or imprisoned for reasoning upon knowledge and liberty to the beasts of the field, for they are incapable of such truths. But these themes are forbidden to slaves, not because they cannot, but because they can and would seize on them with avidity—receive them gladly, comprehend them quickly; and the masters' power over them would be annihilated at once and forever.

But I have more frequently heard not that they were incapable of receiving instruction, but something much nearer the truth—that knowledge only makes them miserable: the moment they are in any degree enlightened, they become unhappy. In the letter I return to you Mr. —— says that the very slightest amount of education, merely teaching them to read, "impairs their value as slaves, for it instantly destroys their contentedness, and, since you do not contemplate changing their condition, it is surely doing them an ill service to destroy their acquiescence in it"; but this is a very different ground of argument from the other. The discontent they evince upon the mere dawn of an advance in intelligence proves not only that they can acquire, but combine ideas, a process to which it is very difficult to assign a limit; and there indeed the whole question lies, and there and nowhere else the shoe really pinches. A slave is ignorant; he eats, drinks, sleeps, labors, and is happy. He learns to read; he feels, thinks, reflects, and becomes miserable. He discovers himself to be one of a debased and degraded race, deprived of the elementary rights which God has granted to all men alike; every action is controlled, every word noted; he may not stir beyond his appointed bounds, to the right hand or to the left, at his own will, but at the will of another he may be sent miles and miles of weary journeying—tethered, yoked, collared, and fettered—away from whatever he may know as home, severed from all those ties of blood and affection which he alone of all human, of all living creatures on the face of the earth, may neither enjoy in peace nor defend when they are outraged. If he is well treated, if his master be tolerably humane or even understand his own interest tolerably, this is probably *all* he may have to endure: it is only to the consciousness of these evils that knowledge and reflection awaken him. But how is it if his master be severe, harsh, cruel—or even only careless—

leaving his creatures to the delegated dominion of some overseer or agent, whose love of power, or other evil dispositions, are checked by no considerations of personal interest? Imagination shrinks from the possible result of such a state of things; nor must you, or Mr. ——, tell me that the horrors thus suggested exist only in imagination. The Southern newspapers, with their advertisements of Negro sales and personal descriptions of fugitive slaves, supply details of misery that it would be difficult for imagination to exceed. Scorn, derision, insult, menace—the handcuff, the lash— the tearing away of children from parents, of husbands from wives—the weary trudging in droves along the common highways, the labor of body, the despair of mind, the sickness of heart— these are the realities which belong to the system, and form the rule, rather than the exception, in the slave's experience. And this system exists here in this country of yours, which boasts itself the asylum of the oppressed, the home of freedom, the one place in all the world where all men may find enfranchisement from all thraldoms of mind, soul, or body—the land elect of liberty.

Mr. —— lays great stress, as a proof of the natural inferiority of the blacks, on the little comparative progress they have made in those states where they enjoy their freedom, and the fact that, whatever quickness of parts they may exhibit while very young, on attaining maturity they invariably sink again into inferiority, or at least mediocrity, and indolence. But surely there are other causes to account for this besides natural deficiency, which must, I think, be obvious to any unprejudiced person observing the condition of the free blacks in your Northern communities. If, in the early portion of their life, they escape the contempt and derision of their white associates—if the blessed unconsciousness and ignorance of childhood keeps them for a few years unaware of the conventional proscription under which their whole race is placed (and it is difficult to walk your streets, and mark the tone of insolent superiority assumed by even the gutter urchins over their dusky contemporaries, and imagine this possible)—as soon as they acquire the first rudiments of knowledge, as soon as they begin to grow up and pass from infancy to youth, as soon as they cast the first observing glance upon the world by which they are surrounded, and the society of which they are members, they must become conscious that they are marked as the Hebrew lepers of old, and are condemned to sit, like those unfortunates, without the gates of every human and social sympathy. From their own sable color, a pall falls over the whole of God's universe to them, and they find themselves stamped with a badge of infamy of Nature's own devising, at sight of which all natural kindliness of man to man seems to recoil from them. They are not slaves indeed, but they are pariahs; debarred from all fellowship save with their own despised race—scorned by the lowest white ruffian in your streets, not tolerated as companions even by the foreign menials in your kitchen. They are free certainly, but they are also degraded, rejected, the offscum and the offscouring of the very dregs of your society; they are free from the chain, the whip, the enforced task and unpaid toil of slavery; but they are not the less under a ban. Their kinship with slaves forever bars them from a full share of the freeman's inheritance of equal rights, and equal consideration and respect. All hands are extended to thrust them out, all fingers point at their dusky skin, all tongues—the most vulgar, as well as the self-styled most refined—have learned to turn the very name of their race into an insult and a reproach. How, in the name of all that is natural, probable, possible, should the spirit and energy of any human creature support itself under such an accumulation of injustice and obloquy? Where shall any mass of men be found with power of character and mind sufficient to bear up against such a weight of prejudice? Why, if one individual rarely gifted by heaven were to raise himself out of such a slough of despond, he would be a miracle; and what would be his reward? Would he be admitted to an equal share in your political rights? Would he ever be allowed to cross the threshold of your doors? Would any of you give your daughter to his son, or your son to his daughter? Would you, in any one particular, admit him to the footing of equality which any man with a white skin would claim, whose ability and worth had so raised him from the lower degrees of the social scale? You would turn from such propositions with abhorrence, and the servants in your kitchen and stable—the ignorant and boorish refuse of foreign populations, in whose countries no such prejudice exists, imbibing it with the very air they breathe here—would shrink from eating at the same table with such a man, or holding out the hand of common fellowship to him. Under the species of social proscription in which the blacks in your Northern cities exist, if they preserved energy of mind, enterprise of spirit, or any of the best attributes and powers of free men, they would prove themselves, instead of the lowest and least of human races, the highest and first, not only of all that do exist, but of all that ever have existed; for they alone would seek and cultivate knowledge, goodness, truth, science, art, refinement, and all improvement, purely for the sake of their own excellence, and without one of those incentives of honor, power, and fortune, which are found to be the chief, too often the only, inducements which lead white men to the pursuit of the same objects.

You know very well, dear E[lizabeth], that in speaking of the free blacks of the North I here state nothing but what is true, and of daily experience. Only last week I heard in this very town of Philadelphia of a family of strict probity and honor, highly principled, intelligent, well-educated, and accomplished, and (to speak in the world's language) respectable in every way—i.e., *rich*. Upon an English lady's stating it to be her intention to visit these persons when she came to Philadelphia, she was told that if she did nobody else would visit *her;* and she probably would excite a malevolent feeling, which might find vent in some violent demonstration against this family. All that I have now said of course bears only upon the condition of the free colored population of the North, with which I am familiar enough to speak confidently of it. As for the slaves, and their capacity for progress, I can say nothing, for I have never been among them to judge what faculties their unhappy social position leaves to them unimpaired. But it seems to me that no experiment on a sufficiently large scale can have been tried for a sufficient length of time to determine the question of their incurable inferiority. Physiologists say that three successive generations appear to be necessary to produce an effectual change of constitution (bodily and mental), be it for health or disease. There are positive physical defects which produce positive mental ones; the diseases of the muscular and nervous systems descend from father to son. Upon the agency of one corporal power how much that is not corporal depends; from generation to generation internal disease and external deformity, vices, virtues, talents, and deficiencies are transmitted, and by the action of the same law it must be long indeed before the offspring of slaves—creatures begotten of a race debased and degraded to the lowest degree, themselves born in slavery, and whose progenitors have eaten the bread and drawn the breath of slavery for years—can be measured, with any show of justice, by even the least favored descendants of European nations, whose qualities have been for centuries developing themselves under the beneficent influences of freedom, and the progress it inspires.

I am rather surprised at the outbreak of violent disgust which Mr. ——— indulges in on the subject of amalgamation, as that formed no part of our discussion, and seems to me a curious subject for abstract argument. I should think the intermarrying between blacks and whites a matter to be as little insisted upon if repugnant, as prevented if agreeable to the majority of the two races. At the same time, I cannot help being astonished at the furious and ungoverned execration which all reference to the possibility of a fusion of the races draws down upon those who suggest it, because nobody pretends to deny that, throughout the South, a large proportion of the population is the offspring of white men and colored women. In New Orleans, a class of unhappy females exists whose mingled blood does not prevent their being remarkable for their beauty, and with whom no man, no *gentleman,* in that city shrinks from associating; and while the slaveowners of the Southern states insist vehemently upon the mental and physical inferiority of the blacks, they are benevolently doing their best, in one way at least, to raise and improve the degraded race, and the bastard population which forms so ominous an element in the social safety of their cities certainly exhibit in their forms and features the benefit they derive from their white progenitors. It is hard to conceive that some mental improvement does not accompany this physical change. Already the finer forms of the European races are cast in these dusky molds: the outward configuration can hardly thus improve without corresponding progress in the inward capacities. The white man's blood and bones have begotten this bronze race, and bequeathed to it, in some degree, qualities, tendencies, capabilities, such as are the inheritance of the highest order of human animals.

Mr. ———, and many others, speak as if there were a natural repugnance in all whites to any alliance with the black race; and yet it is notorious, that almost every Southern planter has a family more or less numerous of illegitimate colored children. Most certainly, few people would like to assert that such connections are formed because it is the *interest* of these planters to increase the number of their human property, and that they add to their revenue by the closest intimacy with creatures that they loathe, in order to reckon among their wealth the children of their body. Surely that is a monstrous and unnatural supposition, and utterly unworthy of belief. That such connections exist commonly is a sufficient proof that they are not abhorrent to nature; but it seems, indeed, as if marriage (and not concubinage) was the horrible enormity which cannot be tolerated, and against which, moreover, it has been deemed expedient to enact laws. Now it appears very evident that there is no law in the white man's nature which prevents him from making a colored woman the mother of his children, but there *is* a law on his statute books forbidding

him to make her his wife; and if we are to admit the theory that
the mixing of the races is a monstrosity, it seems almost as curious
that laws should be enacted to prevent men marrying women
toward whom they have an invincible natural repugnance, as that
education should by law be prohibited to creatures incapable of
receiving it.

As for the exhortation with which Mr. —— closes his letter,
that I will not "go down to my husband's plantation prejudiced
against what I am to find there," I know not well how to answer
it. Assuredly I *am* going prejudiced against slavery, for I am an
Englishwoman, in whom the absence of such a prejudice would
be disgraceful. Nevertheless, I go prepared to find many mitiga-
tions in the practice to the general injustice and cruelty of the
system—much kindness on the part of the masters, much content
on that of the slaves; and I feel very sure that you may rely upon
the carefulness of my observation, and the accuracy of my report,
of every detail of the working of the thing that comes under my
notice; and certainly, on the plantation to which I am going, it
will be more likely that I should some things extenuate, than set
down aught in malice.

II
Maryland, Virginia, and North Carolina

Dearest Harriet,[1]

On Friday morning [December 21, 1838] we started from Philadelphia, by railroad, for Baltimore. It is a curious fact enough, that half the routes that are traveled in America are either temporary or unfinished—one reason, among several, for the multitudinous accidents which befall wayfarers. At the very outset of our journey, and within scarce a mile of Philadelphia, we crossed the Schuylkill, over a bridge, one of the principal piers of which

[1] The content of this chapter and the following one was written by Mrs. Kemble while on Butler Island, and formed part of her correspondence with a lifelong friend, Harriet St. Leger. But it was not included in the original edition of the *Journal*. It has been thought well to incorporate these letters here since they give a vivid picture of the journey from Philadelphia to Georgia in late December 1838; and because they effectively fill the gap that would otherwise exist between the first chapter of the *Journal* and the succeeding ones. These letters were originally published in Frances Kemble: *Records of Later Life* (London: 1882), I, 170–218. A series of dots in the text indicates material deleted by Mrs. Kemble herself in preparing the manuscript for publication. The beginning of each new day throughout the voyage has been indicated by the addition of the appropriate date in brackets.

is yet incomplete, and the whole building (a covered wooden one, of handsome dimensions) filled with workmen, yet occupied about its construction. But the Americans are impetuous in the way of improvement, and have all the impatience of children about the trying of a new thing, often greatly retarding their own progress by hurrying unduly the completion of their works, or using them in a perilous state of incompleteness. Our road lay for a considerable length of time through flat low meadows that skirt the Delaware, which at this season of the year, covered with snow and bare of vegetation, presented a most dreary aspect. We passed through Wilmington (Delaware), and crossed a small stream called the Brandywine, the scenery along the banks of which is very beautiful. For its historical associations I refer you to the life of Washington. I cannot say that the aspect of the town of Wilmington, as viewed from the railroad cars, presented any very exquisite points of beauty; I shall therefore indulge in a few observations upon these same railroad cars just here.

And first, I cannot but think that it would be infinitely more consonant with comfort, convenience, and common sense, if persons obliged to travel during the intense cold of an American winter (in the Northern states), were to clothe themselves according to the exigency of the weather, and so do away with the present deleterious custom of warming close and crowded carriages with sheet iron stoves, heated with anthracite coal. No words can describe the foulness of the atmosphere, thus robbed of all vitality by the vicious properties of that dreadful combustible, and tainted besides with the poison emitted at every respiration from so many pairs of human lungs. These are facts which the merest tyro in physiological science knows, and the utter disregard of which on the part of the Americans renders them the amazement of every traveler from countries where the preservation of health is considered worth the care of a rational creature. I once traveled to Harrisburg in a railroad car, fitted up to carry sixty-four persons, in the midst of which glowed a large stove. The trip was certainly a delectable one. Nor is there any remedy for this: an attempt to open a window is met by a universal scowl and shudder; and indeed it is but incurring the risk of one's death of cold, instead of one's death of heat. The windows, in fact, form the walls on each side of the carriage, which looks like a long greenhouse upon wheels; the seats, which each contain two persons (a pretty tight fit too), are placed down the whole length of the vehicle, one behind the other, leaving a species of aisle in the middle for the uneasy (a large portion of the traveling community here) to fidget up and down, for the tobacco chewers to spit in, and for a whole tribe of little itinerant fruit and cake sellers to rush through, distributing their wares at every place where the train stops. Of course nobody can well sit immediately in the opening of a window when the thermometer is twelve degrees below zero; yet this, or suffocation in foul air, is the only alternative. I generally prefer being half frozen to death to the latter mode of martyrdom.

Attached to the Baltimore cars was a separate apartment for women. It was of comfortable dimensions, and without a stove; and here I betook myself with my children, escaping from the pestilential atmosphere of the other compartment, and performing our journey with ease enough. My only trial here was one which I have to encounter in whatever direction I travel in America, and which, though apparently a trivial matter in itself, has caused me infinite trouble, and no little compassion for the rising generation of the United States—I allude to the ignorant and fatal practice of the women of stuffing their children from morning till night with every species of trash which comes to hand . . . . I once took the liberty of asking a young woman who was traveling in the same carriage with me, and stuffing her child incessantly with heavy cakes, which she also attempted to make mine eat, her reason for this system,—she replied, it was to "keep her baby good." I looked at her own sallow cheeks and rickety teeth, and could not forbear suggesting to her how much she was injuring her poor child's health. She stared in astonishment, and pursued the process, no doubt wondering what I meant, and how I could be so cruel as not to allow poundcake to my child. Indeed, as may easily be supposed, it becomes a matter of no little difficulty to enforce my own rigid discipline in the midst of the various offers of dainties which tempt my poor little girl at every turn; but I persevere, nevertheless, and am not seldom rewarded by the admiration which her appearance of health and strength excites wherever she goes.

I remember being excessively amused at the woeful condition of an unfortunate gentleman on board one of the Philadelphia boats, whose sickly looking wife, exhausted with her vain attempts to quiet three sickly looking children, had in despair given them into his charge. The miserable man furnished each of them with a lump of cake, and during the temporary lull caused by this diversion, took occasion to make acquaintance with my child, to whom he tendered the same indulgence. Upon my refusing it for her, he exclaimed in astonishment—"Why, madam, don't you allow the little girl cake?"

"No, sir."

"What does she eat, pray?" (as if people lived upon cake generally).

"Bread and milk, and bread and meat."

"What! no butter? no tea or coffee?"

"None whatever."

"Ah!" sighed the poor man, as the chorus of woe arose again from his own progeny, the cake having disappeared down their throats, "I suppose that's why she looks so healthy."

I supposed so, too, but did not inquire whether the gentleman extended his inference.

We pursued our way from Wilmington to Havre de Grace on the railroad, and crossed one or two inlets from the Chesapeake, of considerable width, upon bridges of a most perilous construction, and which, indeed, have given way once or twice in various parts already. They consist merely of wooden piles driven into the river, across which the iron rails are laid, only just raising the train above the level of the water. To traverse with an immense train, at full steam-speed, one of these creeks, nearly a mile in width, is far from agreeable, let one be never so little nervous; and it was with infinite cordiality each time that I greeted the first bush that hung over the water, indicating our approach to terra firma. At Havre de Grace we crossed the Susquehanna in a steamboat, which cut its way through the ice an inch in thickness with marvelous ease and swiftness, and landed us on the other side, where we again entered the railroad carriages to pursue our road.

We arrived in Baltimore at about half past two, and went immediately on board the Alabama steamboat, which was to convey us to Portsmouth, and which started about three quarters of an hour after, carrying us down the Chesapeake Bay to the shores of Virginia. We obtained an unutterably hard beefsteak for our dinner, having had nothing on the road, but found ourselves but little fortified by the sight of what we really could not swallow. Between six and seven, however, occurred that most comprehensive repast, a steamboat tea; after which, and the ceremony of choosing our berths, I betook myself to the reading of *Oliver Twist* till half past eleven at night. I wonder if Mr. Dickens had any sensible perception of the benedictions which flew to him from the bosom of the broad Chesapeake as I closed his book; I am afraid not. Helen says: "It is pity well-wishing has no body," so it is that gratitude, admiration, and moral approbation have none, for the sake of such a writer, and yet he might, peradventure, be smothered.

I had a comical squabble with the stewardess—a dirty, funny, good-humored old Negress,[2] who was driven almost wild by my exorbitant demands for towels, of which she assured me one was a quite ample allowance. Mine, alas! were deep down in my trunk, beyond all possibility of getting at, even if I could have got at the trunk, which I very much doubt. Now I counted no less than

[2] Since Mrs. Kemble's day the term "Negress" has acquired insulting overtones and conveys a meaning she could not have intended.

seven handsome looking glasses on board of this steamboat, where one towel was considered all that was requisite, not even for each individual, but for each washing room. This addiction to ornament, and neglect of comfort and convenience, is a strong characteristic of Americans at present, luxuries often abounding where decencies cannot be procured. It is the necessary result of a young civilization, and reminds me a little of Rosamond's purple jar, or Sir Joshua Reynolds's charming picture of the naked child, with a court cap full of flowers and feathers stuck on her head.

After a very wretched night on board the boat, we landed at about nine o'clock [Saturday, December 22, 1838] at Portsmouth, Virginia. I must not omit to mention that my morning ablutions were as much excepted to by the old Negress as those of the preceding evening. Indeed, she seemed perfectly indignant at the forbearance of one lady, who withdrew from the dressing room, on finding me there, exclaiming: "Go in, go in, I tell you; they always washes two at a time in them rooms."

At Portsmouth there is a fine dry dock, and navy yard, as I was informed . . . . The appearance of the place in general was mean and unpicturesque. Here I encountered the first slaves I ever saw, and the sight of them in no way tended to alter my previous opinions upon this subject. They were poorly clothed; looked horribly dirty, and had a lazy recklessness in their air and manner as they sauntered along, which naturally belongs to creatures without one of the responsibilities which are the honorable burthen of rational humanity.

Our next stopping place was a small town called Suffolk. Here the Negroes gathered in admiring crowds round the railroad carriages. They seem full of idle merriment and unmeaning glee, and regard with an intensity of curiosity, perfectly ludicrous, the appearance and proceedings of such whites as they easily perceive are strangers in their part of the country. As my child leaned from the carriage window, her brilliant complexion drew forth sundry exclamations of delight from the sooty circle below, and one woman, grinning from ear to ear, and displaying a most dazzling set of grinders, drew forward a little mahogany-colored imp, her grandchild, and offered her to the little "Missis" for her waiting maid. I told her the little missis waited upon herself; whereupon she set up a most incredulous giggle, and reiterated her proffers, in the midst of which our kettle started off, and we left her.

To describe to you the tract of country through which we now passed would be impossible, so forlorn a region it never entered my imagination to conceive. Dismal by nature, indeed, as well as by name, is that vast swamp, of which we now skirted the northern edge, looking into its endless pools of black water, where the melancholy cypress and juniper trees alone overshadowed the thick-looking surface, their roots all globular, like huge bulbous plants, and their dark branches woven together with a hideous matting of giant creepers, which clung round their stems, and hung about the dreary forest like a drapery of withered snakes.

It looked like some blasted region lying under an enchanter's ban, such as one reads of in old stories. Nothing lived or moved throughout the loathsome solitude, and the sunbeams themselves seemed to sicken and grow pale as they glided like ghosts through these watery woods. Into this wilderness it seems impossible that the hand of human industry, or the foot of human wayfaring should ever penetrate; no wholesome growth can take root in its slimy depths; a wild jungle chokes up parts of it with a reedy, rattling covert for venomous reptiles; the rest is a succession of black ponds, sweltering under black cypress boughs—a place forbid.

The wood which is cut upon its borders is obliged to be felled in winter, for the summer, which clothes other regions with flowers, makes this pestilential waste alive with rattlesnakes, so that none dare venture within its bounds, and I should even apprehend that, traveling as rapidly as one does on the railroad, and only skirting this district of dismay, one might not escape the fetid breathings it sends forth when the warm season has quickened its stagnant waters and poisonous vegetation.

After passing this place, we entered upon a country little more cheerful in its aspect, though the absence of the dark swamp water was something in its favor—apparently endless tracks of pine forest, well called by the natives, Pine Barrens. The soil is pure sand; and, though the holly, with its coral berries, and the wild myrtle, grow in considerable abundance, mingled with the pines, these preponderate, and the whole land presents one wearisome extent of arid soil and gloomy vegetation. Not a single decent dwelling did we pass: here and there, at rare intervals, a few miserable Negro huts squatting round a mean framed building, with brick chimneys built on the outside, the residence of the owner of the land, and his squalid serfs, were the only evidences of human existence in this forlorn country.

Toward four o'clock, as we approached the Roanoke, the appearance of the land improved; there was a good deal of fine soil well farmed, and the river, where we crossed it, although in all the naked unadornment of wintry banks, looked very picturesque and refreshing as it gushed along, broken by rocks and small islands into rapid reaches and currents. Immediately after crossing it, we stopped at a small knot of houses, which, although christened Weldon, and therefore pretending to be a place, was rather the place where a place was intended to be. Two or three rough pine warerooms, or station houses, belonging to the railroad; a few miserable dwellings, which might be either not half built up, or not quite fallen down, on the banks of a large millpond; one exceedingly dirty-looking old wooden house, whither we directed our steps as to the inn; but we did not take our ease in it, though we tried as much as we could.

However, one thing I will say for North Carolina—it has the best material for fire, and the noblest liberality in the use of it, of any place in the world. Such a spectacle as one of those rousing

pine-wood chimneyfuls, is not to be described, nor the revivifica-
tion it engenders even in the absence of every other comfort or
necessary of life. They are enough to make one turn Gheber [3]—
such noble piles of fire and flame, such hearty brilliant life—full
altars of light and warmth. These greeted us upon our entrance
into this miserable inn, and seemed to rest and feed, as well as
warm us. We (the women) were shown up a filthy flight of wooden
stairs, into a dilapidated room, the plastered walls of which were
all smeared and discolored, the windows begrimed, and darkened
with dirt. Upon the three beds, which nearly filled up this wretched
apartment, lay tattered articles of male and female apparel; and
here we drew round the pine-wood fire, which blazed up the
chimney, sending a ruddy glow of comfort and cheerfulness even
through this disgusting den. We were to wait here for the arrival
of the cars from a branch railroad, to continue our route; and in
the meantime a so-called dinner was provided for us, to which we
were presently summoned. Of the horrible dirt of everything at
this meal, from the eatables themselves to the tablecloth, and the
clothes of the Negroes who waited upon us, it would be impossible
to give any idea. The poultry, which formed here, as it does all
through the South, the chief animal part of the repast (except the
consumers always understood), were so tough that I should think
they must have been alive when we came into the house, and
certainly died very hard. They were swimming in black grease,
and stuffed with some black ingredient that was doubt and dismay
to us uninitiated; but, however, knowledge would probably have
been more terrible in this case than ignorance. We had no bread,
but lumps of hot dough, which reminded me forcibly of certain
juvenile creations of my brothers, yclept dumps. I should think
they would have eaten very much alike.

I was amused to observe that while our tea was poured out, and
handed to us by a black girl of most disgustingly dirty appearance,
no sooner did the engine drivers, and persons connected with the

[3] Fire worshiper.

railroads and coaches, sit down to their meal, than the landlady herself, a portly dame, with a most dignified carriage, took the head of the table, and did the honors with all the grace of a most accomplished hostess. Our male fellow travelers no sooner had dispatched their dinner, than they withdrew in a body to the other end of the apartment, and large rattling folding doors being drawn across the room, the separation of men and women so rigidly observed by all traveling Americans, took place. This is a most peculiar and amusing custom, though sometimes I have been not a little inclined to quarrel with it, inasmuch as it effectually deprives one of the assistance of the men under whose protection one is traveling, as well as all the advantages or pleasure of their society. Twice during this southward trip of ours my companion has been most peremptorily ordered to withdraw from the apartment where he was conversing with me, by colored cabin girls, who told him it was against the rules for any gentleman to come into the ladies' room. This making rules by which ladies and gentlemen are to observe the principles of decorum and good breeding, may be very necessary, for aught I can tell, but it seems rather sarcastical, I think, to have them enforced by servant girls.

The gentlemen, on their side, are intrenched in a similar manner; and if a woman has occasion to speak to the person with whom she is traveling, her entrance into the male den, if she has the courage to venture there, is the signal for a universal stare and whisper. But, for the most part, the convenient result of this arrangement is, that such men as have female companions with them pass their time in prowling about the precincts of the "ladies' apartment"; while their respective ladies pop their heads first out of one door and then out of another, watching in decorous discomfort the time when "their man" shall come to pass. Our sole resource on the present occasion was to retire again to the horrible hole above stairs, where we had at first taken refuge, and here we remained until summoned down again by the arrival of the expected train. My poor little children, overcome with fatigue and sleep, were carried, and we walked from the *hotel* at Weldon to the railroad, and by good fortune obtained a compartment to ourselves.

It was now between eight and nine o'clock, and perfectly dark. The carriages were furnished with lamps, however, and, by the rapid glance they cast upon the objects which we passed, I endeavored in vain to guess at the nature of the country through which we were traveling; but, except the tall shafts of the everlasting pine trees which still pursued us, I could descry nothing, and resigned myself to the amusing contemplation of the attitudes of my companions, who were all fast asleep.

Between twelve and one o'clock [in the early morning of Sunday, December 23, 1838], the engine stopped, and it was announced to us that we had traveled as far upon the railroad as it was yet completed, and that we must transfer ourselves to stagecoaches; so in the dead middle of the night we crept out of the train, and taking our children in our arms, walked a few yards into an open space in the woods, where three four-horse coaches stood waiting to receive us. A crowd of men, principally Negroes, were collected here round a huge fire of pinewood, which, together with the pine torches, whose resinous glare streamed brilliantly into the darkness of the woods, created a ruddy blaze, by the light of which we reached our vehicles in safety, and, while they were adjusting the luggage, had leisure to admire our jetty torchbearers, who lounged round in a state of tattered undress, highly picturesque—the staring whites of their eyes, and glittering ranges of dazzling teeth, exhibited to perfection by the expression of grinning amusement in their countenances, shining in the darkness almost as brightly as the lights which they reflected.

We had especially requested that we might have a coach to ourselves, and had been assured that there would be one for the use of our party. It appeared, however, that the outside seat of this had been appropriated by someone, for our coachman, who was traveling with us, was obliged to take a seat inside with us; and though it then contained five grown persons and two children, it seems that the coach was by no means considered full. The horrors of that night's journey I shall not easily forget. The road lay almost the whole way through swamps, and was frequently itself under water. It was made of logs of wood (a corduroy road), and so dreadfully rough and unequal, that the drawing a coach over it at all seemed perfectly miraculous. I expected every moment that we must be overturned into the marsh, through which we splashed, with hardly any intermission, the whole night long. Their drivers in this part of the country deserve infinite praise both for skill and care; but the roadmakers, I think, are beyond all praise for their noble confidence in what skill and care can accomplish.

You will readily imagine how thankfully I saw the first whitening of daylight in the sky. I do not know that any morning was ever more welcome to me than that which found us still surrounded by the pine swamps of North Carolina, which, brightened by the morning sun, and breathed through by the morning air, lost something of their dreary desolateness to my senses. . . .

Not long after daybreak we arrived at a place called Stantonsborough. I do not know whether that is the name of the district, or what; for I saw no village—nothing but the one lonely house in the wood at which we stopped. I should have mentioned, that the unfortunate individual who took our coachman's place outside, toward daybreak became so perished with cold, that an exchange was effected between them, and thus the privacy (if such it could be called) of our carriage was invaded, in spite of the promise which we had received to the contrary. As I am nursing my own baby, and have been compelled to travel all day and all night, of course this was a circumstance of no small annoyance; but as our company was again increased some time after, and subsequently I had to travel in a railroad carriage that held upwards of twenty people, I had to resign myself to this, among the other miseries of this most miserable journey.

As we alighted from our coach, we encountered the comical spectacle of the two coachloads of gentlemen who had traveled the same route as ourselves, with wristbands and coat cuffs turned back, performing their morning ablutions all together at a long wooden dresser in the open air, though the morning was piercing cold. Their toilet accommodations were quite of the most primitive order imaginable, as indeed were ours. We (the women) were all shown into one small room, the whole furniture of which consisted of a chair and wooden bench: upon the latter stood one basin, one ewer, and a relic of soap, apparently of great antiquity. Before, however, we could avail ourselves of these ample means of cleanliness, we were summoned down to breakfast; but as we had traveled all night, and all the previous day, and were to travel all the ensuing day and night, I preferred washing to eating, and determined, if I could not do both, at least to accomplish the first. There was neither towel, nor glass for one's teeth, nor hostess or chambermaid to appeal to. I ran through all the rooms on the floor, of which the doors were open; but though in one I found a magnificent veneered chest of drawers, and large looking glass, neither of the above articles [was] discoverable. Again the savage passion for ornament occurred to me as I looked at this piece of furniture, which might have adorned the most luxurious bedroom of the wealthiest citizen in New York—here in this wilderness, in a house which seemed but just cut out of the trees, where a tin pan was brought to me for a basin, and where the only kitchen, of which the window of our room, to our sorrow, commanded an uninterrupted prospect, was an open shed, not fit to stable a well-kept horse in.

As I found nothing that I could take possession of in the shape of towel or tumbler, I was obliged to wait on the stairs, and catch one of the dirty black girls who were running to and fro serving the breakfast room. Upon asking one of these nymphs for a towel, she held up to me a horrible cloth, which, but for the evidence to the contrary which its filthy surface presented, I should have supposed had been used to clean the floors. Upon my objecting to this, she flounced away, disgusted, I presume, with my fastidiousness, and appeared no more. As I leaned over the banisters in a state of considerable despondency, I espied a man who appeared to be the host himself, and to him I ventured to prefer my humble petition for a clean towel. He immediately snatched from the dresser where the gentlemen had been washing themselves a wet and dirty towel, which lay by one of the basins, and offered it to me. Upon my suggesting that that was not a *clean* towel, he looked at me from head to foot with ineffable amazement, but at length desired one of the Negroes to fetch me the unusual luxury.

Of the breakfast at this place no words can give any idea. There were plates full of unutterable-looking things, which made one feel as if one should never swallow food again. There were some eggs, all begrimed with smoke, and powdered with cinders; some unbaked dough, cut into little lumps, by way of bread; and a white hard substance, calling itself butter, which had an infinitely nearer resemblance to tallow. The mixture presented to us by way of tea was absolutely undrinkable; and when I begged for a glass of milk, they brought a tumbler covered with dust and dirt, full of such sour stuff that I was obliged to put it aside, after endeavoring to taste it. Thus *refreshed,* we set forth again through the eternal pinelands, on and on, the tall stems rising all round us for miles and miles in dreary monotony, like a spell-land of dismal enchantment, to which there seemed no end . . . .

North Carolina is, I believe, the poorest state in the Union: the part of it through which we traveled should seem to indicate as much. From Suffolk to Wilmington we did not pass a single town —scarcely anything deserving the name of a village. The few detached houses on the road were mean and beggarly in their appearance; and the people whom we saw when the coach stopped had a squalid, and at the same time fierce air, which at once bore witness to the unfortunate influences of their existence. Not the least of these is the circumstance that their subsistence is derived in great measure from the spontaneous produce of the land, which yielding without cultivation the timber and turpentine, by the sale of which they are mainly supported, denies to them all the blessings which flow from labor.

How is it that the fable ever originated of God's having cursed man with the doom of toil? How is it that men have ever been blind to the exceeding profitableness of labor, even for its own sake, whose moral harvest alone—industry, economy, patience, foresight, knowledge—is in itself an exceeding great reward, to which add the physical blessings which wait on this universal law —health, strength, activity, cheerfulness, the content that springs from honest exertions, and the lawful pride that grows from conquered difficulty. How invariably have the inhabitants of southern countries, whose teeming soil produced, unurged, the means of life, been cursed with indolence, with recklessness, with the sleepy slothfulness which, while basking in the sunshine, and gathering the earth's spontaneous fruits, satisfied itself with this animal existence, forgetting all the nobler purposes of life in the mere ease of living? Therefore, too, southern lands have always been the prey of northern conquerors; and the bleak regions of Upper Europe and Asia have poured forth from time to time the hungry hordes, whose iron sinews swept the nerveless children of the gardens of the earth from the face of their idle paradises: and, but for this stream of keener life and nobler energy, it would be difficult to imagine a more complete race of lotus-eaters than would now cumber the fairest regions of the earth.

Doubtless it is to counteract the enervating effects of soil and climate that this northern tide of vigorous life flows forever toward the countries of the sun, that the races may be renewed, the earth reclaimed, and the world, and all its various tribes, rescued from disease and decay by the influence of the stern northern vitality, searching and strong, and purifying as the keen piercing winds that blow from that quarter of the heavens. To descend to rather a familiar illustration of this, it is really quite curious to

observe how many New England adventurers come to the Southern states, and bringing their enterprising active character to bear
upon the means of wealth, which in the North they lack, but
which abound in these more favored regions, return home after a
short season of exertion, laden with the spoils of the indolent
Southerners. The Southern people are growing poorer every day,
in the midst of their slaves and their vast landed estates: whilst
every day sees the arrival amongst them of some penniless Yankee,
who presently turns the very ground he stands upon into wealth,
and departs a lord of riches at the end of a few years, leaving
the sleepy population among whom he has amassed them floated
still farther down the tide of dwindling prosperity . . . .

At a small place called Waynesborough . . . I asked for a glass
of milk, and they told me they had no such thing. Upon entering
our new vehicle, we found another stranger added to our party, to
my unspeakable annoyance. Complaint or remonstrance I knew,
however, would be of no avail, and I therefore submitted in
silence to what I could not help. At a short distance beyond
Waynesborough we were desired to alight, in order to walk over a
bridge, which was in so rotten a condition as to render it very
probable that it would give way under our weight. This same
bridge, whose appearance was indeed most perilous, is built at a
considerable height over a broad and rapid stream, called the
Neuse, the color of whose water we had an excellent opportunity
of admiring through the numerous holes in the plankage, over
which we walked as lightly and rapidly as we could, stopping af-
terwards to see our coach come at a foot's pace after us. This may
be called safe and pleasant traveling.

The ten miles which followed were over heavy sandy roads, and
it was near sunset when we reached the place where we were to
take the railroad. The train, however, had not arrived, and we sat
still in the coaches, there being neither town, village, nor even
roadside inn at hand, where we might take shelter from the bitter
blast which swept through the pinewoods by which we were sur-

rounded; and so we waited patiently, the day gradually drooping, the evening air becoming colder, and the howling wilderness around us more dismal every moment.

In the meantime the coaches were surrounded by a troop of gazing boors, who had come from far and near to see the hot-water carriages come up for only the third time into the midst of their savage solitude. A more forlorn, fierce, poor, and wild-looking set of people, short of absolute savages, I never saw. They wandered round and round us, with a stupid kind of dismayed wonder. The men clothed in the coarsest manner, and the women also, of whom there were not a few, with the grotesque addition of pink and blue silk bonnets, with artificial flowers, and imitation-blonde veils. Here the gentlemen of our party informed us that they observed, for the first time, a custom prevalent in North Carolina, of which I had myself frequently heard before—the women chewing tobacco, and that, too, in a most disgusting and disagreeable way, if one way can be more disgusting than another. They carry habitually a small stick, like the implement for cleaning the teeth, usually known in England by the name of a root—this they thrust away in their glove, or their garter string, and, whenever occasion offers, plunge it into a snuffbox, and begin chewing it. The practice is so common, that the proffer of the snuffbox, and its passing from hand to hand, is the usual civility of a morning visit among the country people; and I was not a little amused at hearing the gentlemen who were with us describe the process as they witnessed it in their visit to a miserable farm house across the fields, whither they went to try to obtain something to eat.

It was now becoming dark, and the male members of our caravan held council round a pine fire as to what course had better be adopted for sheltering themselves and us during the night, which we seemed destined to pass in the woods. After some debate, it was recollected that one Colonel ——, a man of some standing in that neighborhood, had a farm about a mile distant, immediately upon the line of the railroad; and thither it was determined we should all repair, and ask quarters for the night. Fortunately, an empty truck stood at hand upon the iron road, and to this the luggage, and the women and children of the party, were transferred. A number of Negroes, who were loitering about, were pressed into the service, and pushed it along; and the gentlemen, walking, brought up the rear. I don't know that I ever in my life felt so completely desolate as during that half hour's slow progress. We sat cowering among the trunks, my faithful Margery and I, each with a baby in our arms, sheltering ourselves and our poor little burthens from the bleak northern wind that whistled over us.

The last embers of daylight were dying out in dusky red streaks along the horizon, and the dreary waste around us looked like the very shaggy edge of all creation. The men who pushed us along encouraged each other with wild shouts and yells, and every now and then their labor was one of no little danger, as well as difficulty—for the road crossed one or two deep ravines and morasses at a considerable height, and, as it was not completed, and nothing but the iron rails were laid across piles driven into these places, it became a service of considerable risk to run along these narrow ledges, at the same time urging our car along. No accident happened, however, fortunately, and we presently beheld, with no small satisfaction, a cluster of houses in the fields at some little distance from the road. To the principal one I made my way, followed by the rest of the poor womankind, and, entering the house without further ceremony, ushered them into a large species of wooden room, where blazed a huge pine-wood fire. By this welcome light we descried, sitting in the corner of the vast chimney, an old ruddy-faced man, with silver hair, and a good-humored countenance, who, welcoming us with ready hospitality, announced himself as Colonel ——, and invited us to draw near the fire.

The worthy Colonel seemed in no way dismayed at this sudden inbreak of distressed women, which was very soon followed by the arrival of the gentlemen, to whom he repeated the same courteous reception he had given us, replying to their rather hesitating demands for something to eat, by ordering to the right and left a tribe of staring Negroes, who bustled about preparing supper, under the active superintendence of the hospitable colonel. His residence (considering his rank) was quite the most primitive imaginable—a rough brick-and-plank chamber, of considerable dimensions, not even whitewashed, with the great beams and rafters by which it was supported displaying the skeleton of the building, to the complete satisfaction of any one who might be curious in architecture. The windows could close neither at the top, bottom, sides, nor middle, and were, besides, broken so as to admit several delightful currents of air, which might be received as purely accidental. In one corner of this primitive apartment stood a clean-looking bed, with coarse furniture; while in the opposite one, an old case clock was ticking away its time and its master's, with cheerful monotony. The rush-bottomed chairs were of as many different shapes and sizes as those in a modern fine lady's drawing room, and the walls were hung all round with a curious miscellany, consisting principally of physic phials, turkey-feather fans, bunches of dried herbs, and the Colonel's arsenal, in the shape of one or two old guns, etc.

According to the worthy man's hearty invitation, I proceeded to make myself and my companions at home, pinning, skewering, and otherwise suspending our cloaks and shawls across the various intentional and unintentional air gaps, thereby increasing both the comfort and the grotesqueness of the apartment in no small degree. The babies had bowls of milk furnished them, and the elder portion of the caravan was regaled with a taste of the Colonel's homemade wine, pending the supper, to which he continued to entreat our stay. Meantime he entered into conversation with the gentlemen; and my veneration waxed deep, when the old man, unfolding his history, proclaimed himself one of the heroes of the revolution—a fellow fighter with Washington. I, who, comforted to a degree of high spirits by our sudden transition from the cold and darkness of the railroad to the light and shelter of this rude mansion, had been flippantly bandying jokes, and [had] proceeded some way in a lively flirtation with this illustrious American, grew thrice respectful, and hardly ventured to raise either my eyes or my voice as I inquired if he lived alone in this remote place. Yes, alone now; his wife had been dead near upon two years.

Suddenly we were broken in upon the arrival of the expected train. It was past eight o'clock. If we delayed we should have to travel all night; but, then, the Colonel pressed us to stay and sup (the bereaved Colonel, the last touching revelation of whose lonely existence had turned all my mirth into sympathizing sadness). The gentlemen were famished, and well inclined to stay; the ladies were famished too, for we had eaten nothing all day. The bustle of preparation, urged by the warmhearted Colonel, began afresh; the Negro girls shambled in and out more vigorously than ever, and finally we were called to eat and refresh ourselves with—dirty water—I cannot call it tea, old cheese, bad butter, and old dry biscuits. The gentlemen bethought them of the good supper they might have secured a few miles further, and groaned; but the hospitable Colonel merely asked them half a dollar apiece (there were about ten of them); paying which, we departed, with our enthusiasm a little damped for the warrior of the revolution; and a tinge of rather deeper misgiving as to some of his virtues stole over our minds, on learning that three of the sable damsels who trudged about at our supper service were the Colonel's own progeny. I believe only three—though the young Negro girl, whose loquacity made us aware of the fact, added, with a burst of commendable pride and gratitude: "Indeed, he is a father to us all!" Whether she spoke figuratively, or literally, we could not determine. So much for a three-hours' shelter in North Carolina . . . .

III

Charleston
and the Sea-Island Coast

Dearest Harriet,

I had been very much struck with the appearance of the horses we passed occasionally in enclosures, or gathered round some lonely roadside pine-wood shop, or post office, fastened to trees in the surrounding forest, and waiting for their riders. I had been always led to expect a great improvement in the breed of horses as we went southward, and the appearance of those I saw on the road was certainly in favor of the claim. They were generally small, but in good condition, and remarkable well made. They seemed to be tolerably well cared for, too; and those which we saw caparisoned were ornamented with gay saddlecloths, and rather a superfluity of trappings for *civil* animals.

At our dismal halt in the woods, while waiting for the railroad train, among our other spectators was a woman on horseback. Her steed was uncommonly pretty and well-limbed; but her costume was quite the most eccentric that can be imagined, accustomed as I am to the not over-rigid equipments of the Northern villages. But the North Carolinian damsel beat all Yankee girls I ever saw hollow, in the glorious contempt she exhibited for the external fitness of things in her exceeding short skirts and huge sunbonnet.

After our departure from Colonel ——'s, we traveled all night on the railroad. One of my children slept in my lap, the other on the narrow seat opposite to me, from which she was jolted off every quarter of an hour by the uneasy motion of the carriage, and the checks and stops of the engine, which was out of order. The carriage, though full of people, was heated with a stove, and every time this was replenished with coals we were almost suffocated with the clouds of bituminous smoke which filled it. Five hours, they said, was the usual time consumed in this part of the journey; but we were the whole mortal night upon that uneasy railroad, and it was five o'clock in the morning [Monday, December 24, 1838] before we reached Wilmington, North Carolina. When the train stopped it was yet quite dark, and most bitterly cold; nevertheless, the distance from the railroad to the only inn where we could be accommodated was nothing less than a mile; and, weary and worn out, we trudged along, the poor little sleeping children carried by their still more unfortunate, sleepless nurses—and so by the cheerless winter starlight we walked along the brink of the Cape Fear River, to seek where we might lay our heads.

We were shown into a room without window curtains or shutters, the windows, as usual, not half-shut, and wholly incapable of shutting. Here, when I asked if we could have some tea (having fasted the whole previous day, with the exception of Colonel ——'s bountiful supper), the host pleasantly informed us, that the "public breakfast would not be ready for some hours yet." I really could not help once again protesting against this abominable tyranny of the traveling many over the traveling few in this free country. It is supposed impossible that any individual can hunger, thirst, or desire sleep at any other than the "public hours"—the consequence is, that let one arrive starved at an inn, one can obtain nothing till such hours when those who are not starving desire to eat; and if one is foredone with travel, weary, and wanting rest, the pitiless alarum bell, calling those who may have had twelve hours' sleep from their beds, must startle those who have only just closed their eyes for the first time, perhaps, for three nights,—as if the whole traveling community were again at boarding school, and as if a private summons by the boots [1] or chambermaid to each apartment would not answer the same purpose.

We were, however, so utterly exhausted, that waiting for the public appetite was out of the question; and, by dint of much supplication, we at length obtained some breakfast. When, however, we stated that we had not been in bed for two successive nights, and asked to be shown to our rooms, the same gentleman, our host, an exceedingly pleasant person, informed us that *our* chamber was prepared, adding, with the most facetious familiarity, when I exclaimed: "Our chamber!" (we were three, and two children),

"Oh! madam, I presume you will have no objection to sleeping with *your infant*" (he lumped the two into one); "and these two ladies (Miss [Butler] [2] and Margery) will sleep together. I dare say they have done it a hundred times."

This unheard-of proposition, and the man's cool impudence in making it, so astonished me, that I could hardly speak. At last, however, I found words to inform him that none of our party were in the habit of sleeping with each other, and that the arrangement was such as we were not at all inclined to submit to. The gentleman, apparently very much surprised at our singular habits, said: "Oh! he didn't know that the ladies were not acquainted" (as if, forsooth, one went to bed with all one's acquaintance!) "but that he had but that one room in the ladies' part of the house."

Miss [Butler] immediately professed her readiness to take one in the gentlemen's "part of the house," when it appeared that there

---

[1] In the Queen's English *boots* denotes servant, as at a large hotel, whose duties include the shining of boots and shoes.

[2] The lady here referred to was an aunt of Pierce Butler's who accompanied the family as far as Charleston, where she intended to visit friends.

was none vacant there which had a fireplace in it. As the morning was intensely cold, this could not be thought of. I could not take shelter in [Mr. Butler]'s room; for he, according to this decent and comfortable mode of lodging travelers, had another man to share it with him. To our common dormitory we therefore repaired, as it was impossible that we could any of us go any longer without rest. I established Margery and the two babies in the largest bed; poor Miss [Butler] betook herself to a sort of curtainless cot that stood in one corner; and I laid myself down on a mattress on the floor; and we soon all forgot the [in]conveniences of a Wilmington hotel in the supreme convenience of sleep.

It was bright morning, and drawing toward one o'clock, when we rose, and were presently summoned to the "public dinner." The dirt and discomfort of everything was so intolerable, that I could not eat; and having obtained some tea, we set forth to walk to the steamboat *Governor Dudley,* which was to convey us to Charleston. The midday sun took from Wilmington some of the desolateness which the wintry darkness of the morning gave it; yet it looked to me like a place I could sooner die than live in— ruinous, yet not old—poor, dirty, and mean, and unvenerable in its poverty and decay. The river that runs by it is called Cape Fear River; above, on the opposite shore, lies Mount Misery— and heaven-forsaken enough seemed place and people to me. How good one should be to live in such places! How heavenly would one's thoughts and imaginations of hard necessity become, if one existed in Wilmington, North Carolina! The afternoon was beautiful, golden, mild, and bright—the boat we were in extremely comfortable and clean, and the captain especially courteous. The whole furniture of this vessel was remarkably tasteful, as well as convenient—not forgetting the fawn-colored and blue curtains to the berths.

But what a deplorable mistake it is—be-draperying up these narrow nests, so as to impede the poor meagre mouthfuls of air which their dimensions alone necessarily limit one to. These crimson and yellow, or even fawn-colored and blue silk suffocators, are a poor compensation for free ventilation; and I always look at these elaborate adornments of sea beds as ingenious and elegant incentives to seasickness, graceful emetics in themselves, all provocation from the water set aside. The captain's wife and ourselves were the only passengers; and, after a most delightful walk on deck in the afternoon, and comfortable tea, we retired for the night, and did not wake till we bumped on the Charleston bar on the morning of Christmas Day [Tuesday, December 25, 1838].

The *William Seabrook,* the boat which is to convey us from hence to Savannah, only goes once a week. . . . This unfrequent communication between the principal cities of the great Southern states is rather a curious contrast to the almost unintermitting intercourse which goes on between the Northern towns. The boat itself, too, is a species of small monopoly being built and chiefly used for the convenience of certain wealthy planters residing on Edisto Island, a small insulated tract between Charleston and Savannah, where the finest cotton that is raised in this country grows. This city is the oldest I have yet seen in America—I should think it must be the oldest in it. I cannot say that the first impression produced by the wharf at which we landed, or the streets we drove through in reaching our hotel, was particularly lively. Rickety, dark, dirty, tumble-down streets and warehouses, with every now and then a mansion of loftier pretensions, but equally neglected and ruinous in its appearance, would probably not have been objects of special admiration to many people on this side the water; but I belong to that infirm, decrepit, bedridden old country, England, and must acknowledge, with a blush for the stupidity of the prejudice, that it is so very long since I have seen anything old, that the lower streets of Charleston, in all their dinginess and decay, were a refreshment and a rest to my spirit.

I have had a perfect red-brick and white-board fever ever since I came to this country; and once more to see a house which looks as if it had stood long enough to get warmed through, is a balm to my senses, oppressed with newness. Boston had two or three fine old dwelling houses, with antique gardens and old-fashioned courtyards; but they have come down to the dust before the improving spirit of the age. One would think, that after ten years a house gets weak in the knees. Perhaps these houses do; but I have lodged under rooftrees that have stood hundreds of years, and may stand hundreds more—marry, they have good foundations.

In walking about Charleston, I was forcibly reminded of some of the older country towns in England—of Southampton a little. The appearance of the city is highly picturesque, a word which can apply to none other of the American towns; and although the place is certainly pervaded with an air of decay, it is a genteel infirmity, as might be that of a distressed elderly gentlewoman. It has none of the smug mercantile primness of the Northern cities, but a look of state, as of quondam wealth and importance, a little gone down in the world, yet remembering still its former dignity. The Northern towns, compared with it, are as the spruce citizen rattling by the faded splendors of an old family coach in his newfangled chariot—they certainly have got on before it. Charleston has an air of eccentricity, too, and peculiarity, which formerly were not deemed unbecoming the wellborn and well-bred gentlewoman, which her gentility itself sanctioned and warranted—none of the vulgar dread of vulgar opinion, forcing those who are possessed by it to conform to a general standard of manners, unable to conceive one peculiar to itself—this "what-'ll-Mrs.-Grundy-say" devotion to conformity in small things and great, which pervades the American body-social from the matter of churchgoing to the trimming of women's petticoats—this dread of singularity, which has eaten up all individuality amongst them, and makes their population like so many moral and mental lithographs, and their houses like so many thousand hideous brick twins.

I believe I am getting excited; but the fact is, that being politically the most free people on earth, the Americans are socially the least so; and it seems as though, ever since that little affair of establishing their independence among nations, which they managed so successfully, every American mother's son of them has been doing his best to divest himself of his own private share of that great public blessing, liberty.

But to return to Charleston. It is in this respect a far more aristocratic (should I not say democratic?) city than any I have yet seen in America, inasmuch as every house seems built to the owner's particular taste; and in one street you seem to be in an old English town, and in another in some continental city of France or Italy. This variety is extremely pleasing to the eye; not less so is the intermixture of trees with the buildings, almost every house being adorned, and gracefully screened, by the beautiful foliage of evergreen shrubs. These, like ministering angels, cloak with nature's kindly ornaments the ruins and decays of the mansions they surround; and the latter, time-mellowed (I will not say stained, and a painter knows the difference), harmonize in their forms and coloring with the trees, in a manner most delightful to an eye that knows how to appreciate this species of beauty.

There are several public buildings of considerable architectural pretensions in Charleston, all of them apparently of some antiquity (for the New World), except a very large and handsome edifice which is not yet completed, and which, upon inquiry, we found was intended for a guardhouse. Its very extensive dimensions excited our surprise; but a man who was at work about it, and who answered our questions with a good deal of intelligence, informed us that it was by no means larger than the necessities of the city required; for that they not unfrequently had between fifty and sixty persons (colored and white) brought in by the patrol in one night.

"But," objected we, "the colored people are not allowed to go out without passes after nine o'clock."

"Yes," replied our informant, "but they will do it, nevertheless; and every night numbers are brought in who have been caught endeavoring to evade the patrol."

This explained to me the meaning of a most ominous tolling of bells and beating of drums, which, on the first evening of my arrival in Charleston, made me almost fancy myself in one of the old fortified frontier towns of the Continent, where the tocsin is sounded, and the evening drum beaten, and the guard set as regularly every night as if an invasion were expected. In Charleston, however, it is not the dread of foreign invasion, but of domestic insurrection, which occasions these nightly precautions; and, for the first time since my residence in this free country, the curfew (now obsolete in mine, except in some remote districts, where the ringing of an old church bell at sunset is all that remains of the tyrannous custom) recalled the associations of early feudal times, and the oppressive insecurity of our Norman conquerors. But truly it seemed rather anomalous hereabouts, and nowadays; though, of course, it is very necessary where a large class of persons exists in the very bosom of a community whose interests are known to be at variance and incompatible with those of its other members. And no doubt these daily and nightly precautions are but trifling drawbacks upon the manifold blessings of slavery (for which, if you are stupid, and cannot conceive them, see the late Governor McDuffie's speeches [3]); still I should prefer going to sleep without the apprehension of my servants' cutting my throat in my bed, even to having a guard provided to prevent their doing so. However, this peculiar prejudice of mine may spring from the fact of my having known many instances in which servants were the trusted and most trustworthy friends of their employers, and entertaining, besides, some odd notions of the reciprocal duties of *all* the members of families one towards the other.

The extreme emptiness which I observed in the streets, and absence of anything like bustle or business, is chiefly owing to the season, which the inhabitants of Charleston, with something akin

[3] George McDuffie was governor of South Carolina for two terms, 1834–8. His annual message to the legislature in 1835 attracted nation- wide attention for its bold defense of slavery as "the cornerstone of our republican edifice."

to old English feeling, generally spend in hospitable festivity upon their estates; a goodly custom, at least in my mind. It is so rare for any of the wealthier people to remain in town at Christmas, that poor Miss [Butler], who had come on with us to pay a visit to some friends, was not a little relieved to find that they were (contrary to their custom) still in the city. I went to take my usual walk this morning, and found that the good citizens of Charleston were providing themselves with a most delightful promenade upon the river, a fine, broad, well-paved esplanade, of considerable length, open to the water on one side, and on the other overlooked by some very large and picturesque old houses, whose piazzas, arches, and sheltering evergreens reminded me of buildings in the vicinity of Naples. This delightful walk is not yet finished, and I fear, when it is, it will be little frequented; for the Southern women, by their own account, are miserable pedestrians, of which fact, indeed, I had one curious illustration today; for I received a visit from a young lady residing in the same street where we lodged, who came in her carriage a distance of less than a quarter of a mile, to call upon me.

It is impossible to conceive anything funnier, and at the same time more provokingly stupid, dirty, and inefficient, than the tribe of black-faced heathen divinities and classicalities who make believe to wait upon us here—the Dianas, Phyllises, Floras, Caesars, etc., who stand grinning in wonderment and delight round our table, and whom I find it impossible, by exhortation or entreaty, to banish from the room, so great is their amusement and curiosity at my outlandish modes of proceeding. This morning, upon my entreating them not to persist in waiting upon us at breakfast, they burst into an ungovernable titter, and withdrawing from our immediate vicinity, kept poking their woolly heads and white grinders in at the door every five minutes, keeping it conveniently open for that purpose.

A fine large new hotel was among the buildings which the late fire at Charleston destroyed [Summer, 1838], and the house

where we now are is the best at present in the city. It is kept by a
very obliging and civil colored woman, who seems extremely desirous of accommodating us to our minds; but her servants (they
are her slaves, in spite of her and their common complexion)
would defy the orderly genius of the superintendent of the Astor
House. Their laziness, their filthiness, their inconceivable stupidity, and unconquerable good humor, are enough to drive one
stark-staring mad.

The sitting room we occupy is spacious, and not ill-furnished,
and especially airy, having four windows and a door, none of
which can or will shut. We are fortunately rid of that familiar
fiend of the North, the anthracite coal, but do not enjoy the luxury
of burning wood. Bituminous coal, such as is generally used in
England, is the combustible preferred here; and all my national
predilections cannot reconcile me to it, in preference to the brilliant, cheerful, wholesome, poetical warmth of a wood fire. Our
bedrooms are dismal dens, open to "a' the airts the wind can blaw,"
half furnished, and not by any means half clean. The furniture
itself is old, and very infirm—the tables all peach [4] with one or
other leg—the chairs are most of them minus one or two bars—
the tongs cross their feet when you attempt to use them—and one
poker travels from room to room, that being our whole allowance for two fires.

We have had occasion to make only two trifling purchases
since we have been here; but the prices (if these articles are any
criterion) must be infinitely higher than those of the Northern
shopkeepers; but this we must expect as we go further south, for,
of course, they have to pay double profits upon all the commonest
necessaries of life, importing them, as they do, from distant districts. I must record a curious observation of Margery's, on her
return from church, Tuesday morning. She asked me if the people
of this place were not very proud? I was struck with the question,

---

[4] Colloquially, to have one leg shorter than the others, hence to tip
or tilt on one side.

as coinciding with a remark sometimes made upon the South, and supposed by some farfetching cause-hunters to have its origin in some of their "domestic institutions." I told her that I knew no more of them than she did; and that I had had no opportunity of observing whether they were or not.

"Well," she replied, "I think they are, for I was in church early, and I observed the countenances and manner of the people as they came in, and they struck me as the haughtiest, proudest-looking people I ever saw!"

This very curious piece of observation of hers I note down without comment. I asked her if she had ever heard, or read, the remark as applied to the Southern people? She said, "Never," and I was much amused at this result of her physiognomical church speculations.

Last Thursday evening [December 27, 1838] we left our hotel in Charleston for the steamboat which was to carry us to Savannah: it was not to start until two in the morning, but, of course, we preferred going on board rather earlier, and getting to bed. The ladies' cabin, however, was so crowded with women and children, and so inconveniently small, that sleeping was out of the question in such an atmosphere. I derived much amusement from the very empresslike airs of an uncommonly handsome mulatto woman, who officiated as stewardess, but whose discharge of her duties appeared to consist in telling the ladies what they ought, and what they ought not to do, and lounging about with an indolent dignity, which was irresistibly droll, and peculiarly Southern.

The boat in which we were, not being considered seaworthy, as she is rather old, took the inner passage, by which we were two nights and a day accomplishing this most tedious navigation, creeping through cuts and small muddy rivers, where we stuck sometimes to the bottom, and sometimes to the banks, which presented a most dismal succession of dingy, low, yellow swamps, and reedy marshes, beyond expression wearisome to the eye. About the middle of the day on Friday [December 28, 1838], we touched at the island of Edisto, where some of the gentlemen passengers had business, that being the seat of their plantations, and where the several families reside—after the eldest member of which, Mr. Seabrook, the boat we were in was named.

Edisto, as I have mentioned before, is famous for producing the finest cotton in America—therefore, I suppose in the world. As we were to wait here some time, we went on shore to walk. The appearance of the cotton fields at this season of the year was barren enough; but, as a compensation, I here, for the first time, saw the evergreen oak trees (the ilex, I presume), of the South. They were not very fine specimens of their kind, and disappointed me a good deal. The advantage they have of being evergreen is counterbalanced by the dark and almost dingy color of the foliage, and the leaf being minute in size, and not particularly graceful in form. These trees appeared to me far from comparable, either in size or beauty, to the European oak, when it has attained its full growth. We were walking on the estate of one of the Mr. Seabrooks, which lay unenclosed on each side of what appeared to be the public road through the island.

At a short distance from the landing we came to what is termed a ginning house—a building appropriated to the process of freeing the cotton from the seed. It appeared to be open to inspection; and we walked through it. Here were about eight or ten stalls on either side, in each of which a man was employed at a machine, worked like a turner's or knife grinder's wheel, by the foot, which, as fast as he fed it with cotton, parted the snowy flakes from the little black first cause, and gave them forth soft, silky, clean, and fit to be woven into the finest lace or muslin. This same process of ginning is performed in many places, and upon our own cotton estate, by machinery; the objection to which, however, is, that the staple of the cotton—in the length of which consists its chief excellence—is supposed by some planters to be injured, and the threads broken, by the substitution of an engine for the task performed by the human fingers in separating the cotton and presenting it to the gin.

After walking through this building, we pursued our way past a large, rambling, white wood house, and down a road, bordered on each side with evergreen oaks. While we were walking, a young man on horseback passed us, whose light hair, in a very picturesque contempt of modern fashion, absolutely flowed upon the collar of his coat, and was blown back as he rode, like the disheveled tresses of a woman. On Edisto Island such a noble exhibition of individuality would probably find few censors.

As we returned toward the boat we stopped to examine an irregular scrambling hedge of the wild orange, another of the exquisite shrubs of this paradise of evergreens. The form and foliage of this plant are beautiful, and the leaf, being bruised, extremely fragrant; but, as its perfume indicates, it is a rank poison, containing a great portion of prussic acid. It grows from cuttings rapidly and freely, and might be formed into the most perfect hedge, being well adapted, by its close bushy growth, to that purpose.

After leaving Edisto we pursued the same tedious meandering course, over turbid waters, and between low-lying swamps, till the evening closed in. The afternoon had been foggy, and rainy, and wretched. The cabin was darkened by the various outer protections against the weather, so that we could neither read nor work. Our party, on leaving the island, had received an addition of some young ladies, who were to go on shore again in the middle of the night, at a stopping place called Hilton Head. As they did not intend to sleep, they seemed to have no idea of allowing any one else to do so; and the giggling and chattering with which they enlivened the dreary watches of the night, certainly rendered anything like repose impossible; so I lay, devoutly wishing for Hilton Head, where the boat stopped between one and two in the morning. I had just time to see our boarding-school angels leave us, and a monstrous awkward-looking woman, who at first struck me as a man in disguise, enter the cabin, before my eyes sealed themselves in sleep, which had been hovering over them, kept aloof only by the incessant conversational racket of my young fellow travelers.

I was extremely amused at two little incidents which occurred the next morning [Saturday, December 29, 1838] before we were called to breakfast. The extraordinary-looking woman who came into the boat during the night, and who was the most masculine-looking lady I ever saw, came and stood by me, and, seeing me nursing my baby, abruptly addressed me, with: "Got a baby with you?" I replied in the affirmative, which trouble her eyes might have spared me. After a few minutes' silence, she pursued her unceremonious catechism with: "Married woman?" This question was so exceedingly strange, though put in the most matter-of-course sort of way, that I suppose my surprise exhibited itself in my countenance, for the lady presently left me—not, however, appearing to imagine that she had said or done anything at all unusual. The other circumstance which amused me was to hear another lady observe to her neighbor, on seeing Margery bathe my children (a ceremony never omitted night and morning, where water can be procured): "How excessively ridiculous!" Which same worthy lady, on leaving the boat at Savannah, exclaimed, as she huddled on her cloak, that she never had felt so *"mean* in her life!" Considering that she had gone to bed two nights with the greater part of her day clothes on her, and had abstained from any "ridiculous" ablutions, her *mean* sensations did not, I confess, much surprise me.

When the boat stopped at Savannah, it poured with rain; and in a perfect deluge we drove up to the Pulaski House, thankful to escape from the tedious confinement of a *slow* steamboat—an intolerable nuisance and anomaly in the nature of things. The hotel was, comparatively speaking, very comfortable; infinitely superior to the one where we had lodged at Charleston, as far as bed accommodations went. Here, too, we obtained the inestimable luxury of a warm bath; and the only disagreeable thing we had to encounter was that all but universal pest in this crowd-loving country, a public table. This is always a trial of the first water to me; and that day particularly I was fatigued, and out of spirits, and the din and confusion of a long table d'hôte was perfectly intolerable, in spite of the assiduous attentions of a tiresome worthy old gentleman, who sat by me, and persisted in endeavoring to make me talk. Finding me impracticable, however, he turned, at length, in despair, to the hostess, who sat at the head of her table, and inquired in a most audible voice if it were true, as he had understood, that Mr. and Mrs. Butler were in the hotel? This, of course, occasioned some little amusement; and the good old gentleman being informed that I was sitting at his elbow, went off into perfect convulsions of apologies, and renewed his exertions to make me discourse, with more zeal than ever, asking me, among other things, when he had ascertained that I had never before been to the South: "How I liked the appearance of 'our blackies' (the Negroes)?—no want of cheerfulness, no despondency, or misery in their appearance, eh, madam?" As I thought this was rather begging the question, I did not trouble the gentleman with my impressions. He was a Scotchman, and his adoption of "our blackies" was, by his own account, rather recent, to be so perfectly satisfactory; at least, so it seems to me, who have some small prejudices in favor of freedom and justice yet to overcome before I can enter into all the merits of this beneficent system, so productive of cheerfulness and contentment in those whom it condemns to perpetual degradation.

Our night wanderings were not yet ended, for the steamer in which we were to proceed to Darien was to start at ten o'clock that evening, so that we had but a short interval of repose at this same Pulaski House, and I felt sorry to leave it, in proportion to the uncertainty of our meeting with better accommodation for a long time. The *Ocmulgee* (the Indian name of a river in Georgia, and the cognomen of our steamboat) was a tiny, tidy little vessel, the exceeding small ladies' cabin of which we, fortunately, had entirely to ourselves.

On Sunday morning [December 30, 1838] the day broke most brilliantly over those Southern waters, and as the sun rose, the atmosphere became clear and warm, as in the early Northern summer. We crossed two or three sounds of the sea. The land in sight was a mere forest of reeds, and the fresh, sparkling, crisping waters had a thousand times more variety and beauty. At the mouth of the Altamaha is a small cluster of houses, scarce deserving the name of a village, called Doboy. At the wharf lay two trading vessels; the one with the harp of Ireland waving on her flag; the other with the union jack flying at her mast. I felt vehemently stirred to hail the beloved symbol; but, upon reflection, forbore outward demonstrations of the affectionate yearnings of my heart toward the flag of England; and so we boiled by them into this vast volume of turbid waters, whose noble width, and rapid rolling current, seem appropriately called by that most euphonious and sonorous of Indian names, the Alatamaha, which, in the common mode of speaking it, gains by the loss of the second syllable, and becomes more agreeable to the ear, as it is usually pronounced the Altamaha.

On either side lay the low reedy swamps, yellow, withered Lilliputian forests, rattling their brittle canes in the morning breeze . . . . Through these dreary banks we wound a most sinuous course for a long time; at length the irregular buildings of the little town of Darien appeared, and as we grazed the side of the wharf it seemed to me as if we had touched the outer bound of civilized creation. As soon as we showed ourselves on the deck we were hailed by a shout from the men in two pretty boats, which had pulled alongside of us; and the vociferations of "Oh, massa! how you do, massa? Oh, missis! oh! lily missis! me too glad to see you!" accompanied with certain interjectional shrieks, whoops, whistles and grunts, that could only be written down in Negro language, made me aware of our vicinity to our journey's end. The strangeness of the whole scene, its wildness (for now beyond the broad river and the low swamp lands the savage-looking woods arose to meet the horizon), the rapid retrospect which my mind hurried through of the few past years of my life; the singular contrasts which they presented to my memory; the affectionate shouts of welcome of the poor people, who seemed to hail us as descending divinities, affected me so much that I burst into tears, and could hardly answer their demonstrations of delight. We were presently transferred into the larger boat, and the smaller one being freighted with our luggage, we pulled off from Darien, not, however, without a sage remark from Margery, that, though we seemed to have traveled to the very end of the world, here yet were people and houses, ships, and even steamboats; in which evidences that we were not to be plunged into the deepest abysses of savageness she seemed to take no small comfort.

We crossed the river, and entered a small arm of it, which presently became still narrower and more straight, assuming the appearance of an artificial cut or canal, which indeed it is, having been dug by General Oglethorpe's men (tradition says, in one night), and [which] afforded him the only means of escape from the Spaniards and Indians, who had surrounded him on all sides, and [who] felt secure against all possibility of his eluding them. The cut is neither very deep nor very long, and yet both sufficiently to render the general's exploit rather marvelous. General Oglethorpe was the first British governor of Georgia; Wesley's friend and disciple.

The banks of this little canal were mere dikes, guarding rice swamps, and presented no species of beauty; but in the little creek, or inlet, from which we entered it, I was charmed with the beauty and variety of the evergreens growing in thick and luxuriant underwood, beneath giant straggling cypress trees, whose branches were almost covered with the pendant wreaths of gray moss peculiar to these Southern woods. Of all parasitical plants (if, indeed, it properly belong to that class) it assuredly is the most melancholy and dismal. All creepers, from the polished, dark-leaved ivy, to the delicate clematis, destroy some portion of the strength of the trees around which they cling, and from which they gradually suck the vital juices; but they, at least, adorn the forest shafts round which they twine, and hide, with a false smiling beauty, the gradual ruin and decay they make. Not so this dismal moss: it does not appear to grow, or to have root, or even clinging fiber of any sort, by which it attaches itself to the bark or stem. It hangs in dark, gray, drooping masses from the boughs, swinging in every breeze like matted grizzled hair. I have seen a naked cypress with its straggling arms all hung with this banner of death, looking like a gigantic tree of monstrous cobwebs—the most funereal spectacle in all the vegetable kingdom.

After emerging from the cut, we crossed another arm of the Altamaha (it has as many as Briareus)—I should rather, perhaps, call them mouths, for this is near its confluence with the sea, and these various branches are formed by a numerous sisterhood of small islands, which divide this noble river into three or four streams, each of them wider than England's widest, the Thames. We now approached the low, reedy banks of Butler Island, and passed the rice mill and buildings surrounding it, all of which, it being Sunday, were closed. As we neared the bank, the steersman took up a huge conch, and in the barbaric fashion of early times in the Highlands, sounded out our approach. A pretty schooner,[5] which carries the produce of the estate to Charleston and Savannah, lay alongside the wharf, which began to be crowded with Negroes, jumping, dancing, shouting, laughing, and clapping their hands (a usual expression of delight with savages and children), and using the most extravagant and ludicrous gesticulations to express their ecstasy at our arrival.

[5] This refers to the *Roswell King,* a boat named after the plantation overseer who had resigned his position in 1838 after thirty-four years of service on the Butler estate.

On our landing from the boat, the crowd thronged about us like a swarm of bees; we were seized, pulled, pushed, carried, dragged, and all but lifted in the air by the clamorous multitude. I was afraid my children would be smothered. Fortunately Mr. O＿＿＿,* the overseer, and the captain of the little craft above-mentioned, came to our assistance, and by their good offices the babies and nurse were protected through the crowd. They seized our clothes, kissed them—then our hands, and almost wrung them off. One tall, gaunt Negress flew to us, parting the throng on either side, and embraced us in her arms. I believe I was almost frightened; and it was not until we were safely housed, and the door shut upon our riotous escort, that we indulged in a fit of laughing, quite as full, on my part, of nervousness as of amusement.

Later in the day I attempted to take some exercise, and thought I had escaped observation; but, before I had proceeded a quarter of a mile, I was again enveloped in a cloud of these dingy dependents, who gathered round me, clamoring welcome, staring at me, stroking my velvet pelisse, and exhibiting at once the wildest delight and the most savage curiosity. I was obliged to relinquish my proposed walk, and return home. Nor was the door of the room where I sat, and which was purposely left open, one moment free from crowds of eager faces, watching every movement of myself and the children, until evening caused our audience to disperse. This zeal in behalf of an utter stranger, merely because she stood to them in the relation of a mistress, caused me not a little speculation. These poor people, however, have a very distinct notion of the duties which ownership should entail upon their proprietors, however these latter may regard their obligation towards their dependents; and as to their vehement professions of regard and affection for me, they reminded me of the saying of the satirist, that "gratitude is a lively sense of benefits to come."

* EDITOR'S NOTE: Since the publication of the earlier edition, the overseer has been identified as Mr. Thomas Oden.

BUTLER ISLAND.

December 30, 1838–

February 16, 1839

IV

Exploring Butler Island

[Butler Island. January, 1839]

Dear E[lizabeth],

Minuteness of detail, and fidelity in the account of my daily doings, will hardly, I fear, render my letters very interesting to you now; but, cut off as I am here from all the usual resources and amusements of civilized existence, I shall find but little to communicate to you that is not furnished by my observations on the novel appearance of external nature, and the moral and physical condition of Mr. [Butler]'s people. The latter subject is, I know, one sufficiently interesting in itself to you, and I shall not scruple to impart all the reflections which may occur to me relative to their state during my stay here, where inquiry into their mode of existence will form my chief occupation, and, necessarily also, the staple commodity of my letters. I purpose, while I reside here, keeping a sort of journal, such as Monk Lewis [1] wrote during his visit to his West India plantations. I wish I had any prospect of rendering my diary as interesting and amusing to you as his was to me.

In taking my first walk on the island, I directed my steps toward

[1] Matthew Gregory Lewis was known as Monk Lewis, after the title of one of his novels. His *Journal of a* *West Indian Proprietor* was first published in London in 1834.

the rice mill, a large building on the banks of the river, within a few yards of the house we occupy. Is it not rather curious that Miss Martineau [2] should have mentioned the erection of a steam mill for threshing rice somewhere in the vicinity of Charleston as a singular novelty, likely to form an era in Southern agriculture, and to produce the most desirable changes in the system of labor by which it is carried on? Now on this estate alone there are three threshing mills—one worked by steam, one by the tide, and one by horses; there are two private steam mills on plantations adjacent to ours, and a public one at Savannah, where the planters who have none on their own estates are in the habit of sending their rice to be threshed at a certain percentage; these have all been in operation for some years, and I therefore am at a loss to understand what made her hail the erection of the one at Charleston as likely to produce such immediate and happy results. By-the-by—of the misstatements, or rather mistakes, for they are such, in her books, with regard to certain facts—her only disadvantage in acquiring information was not by any means that natural infirmity on which the periodical press, both here and in England, has commented with so much brutality. She had the misfortune to possess, too, that unsuspecting reliance upon the truth of others which they are apt to feel who themselves hold truth most sacred; and this was a sore disadvantage to her in a country where I have heard it myself repeatedly asserted—and, what is more, much gloried in —that she was purposely misled by the persons to whom she addressed her inquiries, who did not scruple to disgrace themselves by imposing in the grossest manner upon her credulity and anxiety to obtain information. It is a knowledge of this very shameful proceeding which has made me most especially anxious to avoid *fact hunting*. I might fill my letters to you with accounts received from others, but, as I am aware of the risk which I run in so doing,

[2] Harriet Martineau visited the South in the winter of 1834—5. Despite the handicap of severe deafness she conversed with a great many people and published her impressions of the United States, *Society in America*, in 1837.

I shall furnish you with no details but those which come under my own immediate observation.

To return to the rice mill: it is worked by a steam engine of thirty horsepower, and, besides threshing [a] great part of our own rice, is kept constantly employed by the neighboring planters, who send their grain to it in preference to the more distant mill at Savannah, paying, of course, the same percentage, which makes it a very profitable addition to the estate. Immediately opposite to this building is a small shed, which they call the cook's shop, and where the daily allowance of rice and corn grits of the people is boiled and distributed to them by an old woman, whose special business this is. There are four settlements or villages (or, as the Negroes call them, camps) on the island, consisting of from ten to twenty houses, and to each settlement is annexed a cook's shop with capacious caldrons, and the oldest wife of the settlement for officiating priestess. Pursuing my walk along the river's bank, upon an artificial dike, sufficiently high and broad to protect the fields from inundation by the ordinary rising of the tide—for the whole island is below high-water mark—I passed the blacksmith's and cooper's shops. At the first all the common iron implements of husbandry or household use for the estate are made, and at the latter all the rice barrels necessary for the crop, besides tubs and buckets, large and small, for the use of the people, and cedar tubs, of noble dimensions and exceedingly nea. vorkmanship, for our own household purposes. The fragrance ot these when they are first made, as well as their ample size, renders them preferable as dressing-room furniture, in my opinion, to all the china foot tubs that ever came out of Staffordshire. After this I got out of the vicinity of the settlement, and pursued my way along a narrow dike—the river on the one hand, and, on the other, a slimy, poisonous-looking swamp, all rattling with sedges of enormous height, in which one might lose one's way as effectually as in a forest of oaks. Beyond this, the low rice fields, all clothed in their rugged stubble, divided by dikes into monotonous squares, a species of prospect by no means beautiful to the mere lover of the picturesque. The only thing that I met with to attract my attention was a most beautiful species of ivy, the leaf longer and more graceful than that of the common English creeper, glittering with the highest varnish, delicately veined, and of a rich brown-green, growing in profuse garlands from branch to branch of some stunted evergreen bushes which border the dike, and which the people call salt-water bush. My walks are rather circumscribed, inasmuch as the dikes are the only promenades. On all sides of these lie either the marshy rice fields, the brimming river, or the swampy patches of yet unreclaimed forest, where the huge cypress trees and exquisite evergreen undergrowth spring up from a stagnant sweltering pool, that effectually forbids the foot of the explorer.

As I skirted one of these thickets today, I stood still to admire the beauty of the shrubbery. Every shade of green, every variety of form, every degree of varnish, and all in full leaf and beauty in the very depth of winter. The stunted dark-colored oak; the Magnolia bay (like our own culinary and fragrant bay), which grows to a very great size; the wild myrtle, a beautiful and profuse shrub, rising to a height of six, eight, and ten feet, and branching on all sides in luxuriant tufted fullness; most beautiful of all, that pride of the South, the Magnolia *grandiflora,* whose lustrous dark green perfect foliage would alone render it an object of admiration, without the queenly blossom whose color, size, and perfume are unrivaled in the whole vegetable kingdom. This last magnificent creature grows to the size of a forest tree in these swamps, but seldom adorns a high or dry soil, or suffers itself to be successfully transplanted. Under all these the spiked palmetto forms an impenetrable covert, and from glittering graceful branch to branch hang garlands of evergreen creepers, on which the mockingbirds are swinging and singing even now; while I, bethinking me of the pinching cold that is at this hour tyrannizing over your region, look round on this strange scene—on these green woods, this unfettered

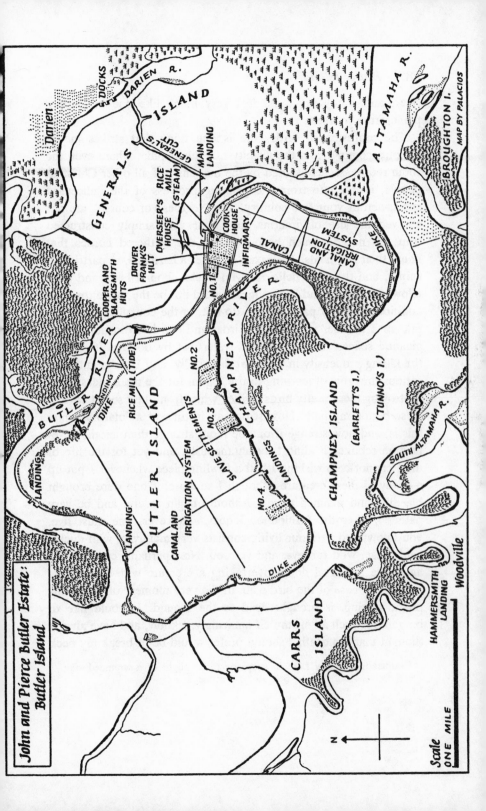

John and Pierce Butler Estate: Butler Island

DARIEN R.
Darien
DOCKS
GENERALS ISLAND
GENERAL'S CUT
MAIN LANDING
OVERSEER'S RICE MILL (STEAM)
COOK HOUSE
INFIRMARY
CANAL AND IRRIGATION SYSTEM
DIKE SYSTEM
CANAL
NO. 1
DRIVER FRANK'S HUT
COOPER AND BLACKSMITH HUTS
BUTLER RIVER
LANDING
DIKE
RICE MILL (TIDE)
NO. 2
CHAMPNEY RIVER
BUTLER ISLAND
SLAVE SETTLEMENTS
NO. 3
CANAL AND IRRIGATION SYSTEM
NO. 4
LANDINGS
DIKE
CHAMPNEY ISLAND (BARRETT'S I.)
(TUNNO'S I.)
ALTAMAHA R.
BROUGHTON I.
MAP BY PALACIOS
SOUTH ALTAMAHA R.
CARRS ISLAND
HAMMERSMITH LANDING
Woodville

Scale
ONE MILE

N

river, and sunny sky—and feel very much like one in another planet from yourself.

The profusion of birds here is one thing that strikes me as curious, coming from the vicinity of Philadelphia, where even the robin redbreast, held sacred by the humanity of all other Christian people, is not safe from the *gunning* prowess of the unlicensed sportsmen of your free country. The Negroes (of course) are not allowed the use of firearms, and their very simply constructed traps do not do much havoc among the feathered hordes that haunt their rice fields. Their case is rather a hard one, as partridges, snipes, and the most delicious wild ducks abound here, and their allowance of rice and Indian meal would not be the worse for such additions. No day passes that I do not, in the course of my walk, put up a number of the land birds, and startle from among the gigantic sedges the long-necked waterfowl by dozens. It arouses the killing propensity in me most dreadfully, and I really entertain serious thoughts of learning to use a gun, for the mere pleasure of destroying these pretty birds as they whirr from their secret coverts close beside my path. How strong an instinct of animal *humanity* this is, and how strange if one be more strange than another. Reflection rebukes it almost instantaneously, and yet for the life of me I cannot help wishing I had a fowling piece whenever I put up a covey of these creatures; though I suppose, if one were brought bleeding and maimed to me, I should begin to cry, and be very pathetic, after the fashion of Jaques.[3] However, one must live, you know; and here our living consists very mainly of wild ducks, wild geese, wild turkeys, and venison. Nor, perhaps, can one imagine the universal doom overtaking a creature with less misery than in the case of the bird who, in the very moment of his triumphant soaring, is brought dead to the ground. I should like to bargain for such a finis myself amazingly, I know, and have always thought that the death I should prefer would be to break my neck

[3] Jaques in *As You Like It* weeps over the plight of a wounded stag. See Act II, scene 1.

off the back of my horse at a full gallop on a fine day. Of course a bad shot should be hung—a man who shatters his birds' wings and legs; if I undertook the trade, I would learn of some Southern duelist, and always shoot my bird through the head or heart—as an expert murderer knows how.

Besides these birds of which we make our prey, there are others that prey upon their own fraternity. Hawks of every sort and size wheel their steady rounds above the rice fields; and the great turkey buzzards—those most unsightly carrion birds—spread their broad black wings, and soar over the river like so many mock eagles. I do not know that I ever saw any winged creature of so forbidding an aspect as these same turkey buzzards; their heavy flight, their awkward gait, their bald-looking head and neck, and their devotion to every species of foul and detestable food, render them almost abhorrent to me. They abound in the South, and in Charleston are held in especial veneration for their scavenger-like propensities, killing one of them being, I believe, a finable offense by the city police regulations. Among the Brobdignagian sedges that in some parts of the island fringe the Altamaha, the night-shade (apparently the same as the European creeper) weaves a perfect matting of its poisonous garlands, and my remembrance of its prevalence in the woods and hedges of England did not reconcile me to its appearance here. How much of this is mere association I cannot tell; but, whether the wild duck makes its nest under its green arches, or the alligators and snakes of the Altamaha have their secret bowers there, it is an evil-looking weed, and I shall have every leaf of it cleared away.

I must inform you of a curious conversation which took place between my little girl and the woman who performs for us the offices of chambermaid here—of course one of Mr. [Butler]'s slaves. What suggested it to the child, or whence indeed she gathered her information, I know not; but children are made of eyes and ears, and nothing, however minute, escapes their microscopic observation. She suddenly began addressing this woman.

"Mary, some persons are free and some are not (the woman made no reply). I am a free person (of a little more than three years old). I say, I am a free person, Mary—do you know that?"

"Yes, missis."

"Some persons are free and some are not—do you know that, Mary?"

"Yes, missis, *here,*" was the reply; "I know it is so here, in this world."

Here my child's white nurse, my dear Margery, who had hitherto been silent, interfered, saying: "Oh, then you think it will not always be so?"

"Me hope not, missis."

I am afraid, E[lizabeth], this woman actually imagines that there will be no slaves in heaven; isn't that preposterous, now, when, by the account of most of the Southerners, slavery itself must be heaven, or something uncommonly like it? Oh, if you could imagine how this title "Missis," addressed to me and to my children, shocks all my feelings! Several times I have exclaimed: "For God's sake do not call me that!" and only been awakened, by the stupid amazement of the poor creatures I was addressing, to the perfect uselessness of my thus expostulating with them; once or twice, indeed, I have done more—I have explained to them, and they appeared to comprehend me well, that I had no ownership over them, for that I held such ownership sinful, and that, though I was the wife of the man who pretends to own them, I was, in truth, no more their mistress than they were mine. Some of them, I know, understood me, more of them did not.

Our servants—those who have been selected to wait upon us in the house—consist of a man, who is quite a tolerable cook (I believe this is a natural gift with them, as with Frenchmen); a dairy-woman, who churns for us; a laundrywoman; her daughter, our housemaid, the aforesaid Mary; and two young lads of from fifteen to twenty, who wait upon us in the capacity of footmen. As, however, the latter are perfectly filthy in their persons and clothes

—their faces, hands, and naked feet being literally incrusted with dirt—their attendance at our meals is not, as you may suppose, particularly agreeable to me, and I dispense with it as often as possible. Mary, too, is so intolerably offensive in her person that it is impossible to endure her proximity, and the consequence is that, among Mr. [Butler]'s slaves, I wait upon myself more than I have ever done in my life before. About this same personal offensiveness, the Southerners, you know, insist that it is inherent with the race, and it is one of their most cogent reasons for keeping them as slaves. But, as this very disagreeable peculiarity does not prevent Southern women from hanging their infants at the breasts of Negresses, nor almost every planter's wife and daughter from having one or more little pet blacks sleeping like puppy dogs in their very bedchamber, nor almost every planter from admitting one or several of his female slaves to the still closer intimacy of his bed, it seems to me that this objection to doing them right is not very valid. I cannot imagine that they would smell much worse if they were free, or come in much closer contact with the delicate organs of their white fellow countrymen; indeed, inasmuch as good deeds are spoken of as having a sweet savor before God, it might be supposed that the freeing of the blacks might prove rather an odoriferous process than the contrary. However this may be, I must tell you that this potent reason for enslaving a whole race of people is no more potent with me than most of the others adduced to support the system, inasmuch as, from observation and some experience, I am strongly inclined to believe that peculiar ignorance of the laws of health and the habits of decent cleanliness are the real and only causes of this disagreeable characteristic of the race, thorough ablutions and change of linen, when tried, having been perfectly successful in removing all such objections; and if ever you have come into anything like neighborly proximity with a low Irishman or woman, I think you will allow that the same causes produce very nearly the same effects. The stench in an Irish, Scotch, Italian, or French hovel is quite as intolerable as any I ever found in our Negro houses, and the filth and vermin which abound about the clothes and persons of the lower peasantry of any of those countries as abominable as the same conditions in the black population of the United States. A total absence of self-respect begets these hateful physical results, and in proportion as moral influences are remote, physical evils will abound. Well-being, freedom, and industry induce self-respect, self-respect induces cleanliness and personal attention, so that slavery is answerable for all the evils that exhibit themselves where it exists—from lying, thieving, and adultery, to dirty houses, ragged clothes, and foul smells.

But to return to our Ganymedes.[4] One of them—the eldest son of our laundrywoman, and Mary's brother, a boy of the name of Aleck (Alexander)—is uncommonly bright and intelligent; he performs all the offices of a well-instructed waiter with great efficiency, and anywhere out of slaveland would be able to earn fourteen or fifteen dollars a month for himself; he is remarkably good tempered and well disposed. The other poor boy is so stupid that he appears sullen from absolute darkness of intellect; instead of being a little lower than the angels, he is scarcely a little higher than the brutes, and to this condition are reduced the majority of his kind by the institutions under which they live. I should tell you that Aleck's parents and kindred have always been about the house of the overseer, and in daily habits of intercourse with him and his wife; and wherever this is the case the effect of involuntary education is evident in the improved intelligence of the degraded race. In a conversation which Mr. [Butler] had this evening with Mr. O——, the overseer, the latter mentioned that two of our carpenters had in their leisure time made a boat, which they had disposed of to some neighboring planter for sixty dollars.

Now, E[lizabeth], I have no intention of telling you a onesided

[4] Ganymede in Greek mythology was a Trojan youth whom the gods had made immortal and taken up into heaven as their cupbearer. The use of the term in the present context is a shaft of sarcasm.

story, or concealing from you what are cited as the advantages which these poor people possess; you, who know that no indulgence is worth simple justice, either to him who gives or him who receives, will not thence conclude that their situation thus mitigated is, therefore, what it should be. On this matter of the sixty dollars earned by Mr. [Butler]'s two men much stress was laid by him and his overseer. I look at it thus: if these men were industrious enough, out of their scanty leisure, to earn sixty dollars, how much more of remuneration, of comfort, of improvement might they not have achieved were the price of their daily labor duly paid them, instead of being unjustly withheld to support an idle young man and his idle family, i.e., myself and my children.

And here it may be well to inform you that the slaves on this plantation are divided into field hands and mechanics or artisans. The former, the great majority, are the more stupid and brutish of the tribe; the others, who are regularly taught their trades, are not only exceedingly expert at them, but exhibit a greater general activity of intellect, which must necessarily result from even a partial degree of cultivation. There are here a gang (for that is the honorable term) of coopers, of blacksmiths, of bricklayers, of carpenters, all well acquainted with their peculiar trades. The latter constructed the washhand stands, clothespresses, sofas, tables, etc., with which our house is furnished, and they are very neat pieces of workmanship—neither veneered or polished indeed, nor of very costly materials, but of the white pinewood planed as smooth as marble—a species of furniture not very luxurious perhaps, but all the better adapted therefore to the house itself, which is certainly rather more devoid of the conveniences and adornments of modern existence than anything I ever took up my abode in before. It consists of three small rooms, and three still smaller, which would be more appropriately designated as closets, a wooden recess by way of pantry, and a kitchen detached from the dwelling —a mere wooden outhouse, with no floor but the bare earth, and for furniture a congregation of filthy Negroes, who lounge in and out of it like hungry hounds at all hours of the day and night, picking up such scraps of food as they can find about, which they discuss squatting down upon their hams, in which interesting position and occupation I generally find a number of them whenever I have sufficient hardihood to venture within those precincts, the sight of which and its tenants is enough to slacken the appetite of the hungriest hunter that ever lost all nice regards in the mere animal desire for food. Of our three apartments, one is our sitting, eating, and *living* room, and is sixteen feet by fifteen. The walls are plastered indeed, but neither painted nor papered; it is divided from our bedroom (a similarly elegant and comfortable chamber) by a dingy wooden partition covered all over with hooks, pegs, and nails, to which hats, caps, keys, etc., etc., are suspended in graceful irregularity. The doors open by wooden latches, raised by means of small bits of packthread—I imagine, the same primitive order of fastening celebrated in the touching chronicle of Red Riding Hood; how they shut I will not attempt to describe, as the shutting of a door is a process of extremely rare occurrence throughout the whole Southern country. The third room, a chamber with sloping ceiling, immediately over our sitting room and under the roof, is appropriated to the nurse and my two babies. Of the closets, one is Mr. O——, the overseer's, bedroom, the other his office or place of business; and the third, adjoining our bedroom, and opening immediately out of doors, is Mr. [Butler]'s dressing room and *cabinet d'affaires,* where he gives audiences to the Negroes, redresses grievances, distributes red woolen caps (a singular gratification to a slave), shaves himself, and performs the other offices of his toilet. Such being our abode, I think you will allow there is little danger of my being dazzled by the luxurious splendors of a Southern slave residence. Our sole mode of summoning our attendants is by a packthread bell-rope suspended in the sitting room. From the bedrooms we have to raise the windows and our voices, and bring them by power of lungs, or help ourselves—which, I thank God, was never yet a hardship to me.

I mentioned to you just now that two of the carpenters had made a boat in their leisure time. I must explain this to you, and this will involve the mention of another of Miss Martineau's mistakes with regard to slave labor, at least in many parts of the Southern states. She mentions that on one estate of which she knew, the proprietor had made the experiment, and very successfully, of appointing to each of his slaves a certain task to be performed in the day, which once accomplished, no matter how early, the rest of the four-and-twenty hours were allowed to the laborer to employ as he pleased. She mentions this as a single experiment, and rejoices over it as a decided amelioration in the condition of the slave, and one deserving of general adoption. But in the part of Georgia where this estate is situated, the custom of task labor is universal, and it prevails, I believe, throughout Georgia, South Carolina, and parts of North Carolina; in other parts of the latter state, however—as I was informed by our overseer, who is a native of that state—the estates are small, rather deserving the name of farms, and the laborers are much upon the same footing as the laboring men at the North, working from sunrise to sunset in the fields with the farmer and his sons, and coming in with them to their meals, which they take immediately after the rest of the family. In Louisiana and the new Southwestern slave states, I believe, task labor does not prevail; but it is in those that the condition of the poor human cattle is most deplorable. As you know it was there that the humane calculation was not only made, but openly and unhesitatingly avowed, that the planters found it, upon the whole, their most profitable plan to work off (kill with labor) their whole number of slaves about once in seven years, and renew the whole stock. By-the-by, the Jewish institution of slavery is much insisted upon by the Southern upholders of the system; perhaps this is their notion of the Jewish jubilee, when the slaves were by Moses' strict enactment to be all set free.

Well, this task system is pursued on this estate; and thus it is that the two carpenters were enabled to make the boat they sold for sixty dollars. These tasks, of course, profess to be graduated according to the sex, age, and strength of the laborer; but in many instances this is not the case, as I think you will agree when I tell you that on Mr. [Butler]'s first visit to his estates he found that the men and the women who labored in the fields had the same task to perform. This was a noble admission of female equality, was it not?—and thus it had been on the estate for many years past. Mr. [Butler], of course, altered the distribution of the work, diminishing the quantity done by the women.

I had a most ludicrous visit this morning from the midwife of the estate—rather an important personage both to master and slave, as to her unassisted skill and science the ushering of all the young Negroes into their existence of bondage is entrusted. I heard a great deal of conversation in the dressing room adjoining mine while performing my own toilet, and presently Mr. [Butler] opened my room door, ushering in a dirty, fat, good-humored looking old Negress, saying: "The midwife, Rose, wants to make your acquaintance."

"Oh massa!" shrieked out the old creature, in a paroxysm of admiration, "where you get this lilly alabaster baby!"

For a moment I looked round to see if she was speaking of my baby; but no, my dear, this superlative apostrophe was elicited by the fairness of *my skin:* so much for degrees of comparison. Now I suppose that if I chose to walk arm in arm with the dingiest mulatto through the streets of Philadelphia, nobody could possibly tell by my complexion that I was not his sister, so that the mere quality of mistress must have had a most miraculous effect upon my skin in the eyes of poor Rose. But this species of outrageous flattery is as usual with these people as with the low Irish, and arises from the ignorant desire, common to both the races, of propitiating at all costs the fellow creature who is to them as a Providence—or rather, I should say, a fate—for 'tis a heathen and no Christian relationship.

Soon after this visit, I was summoned into the wooden porch or piazza of the house, to see a poor woman who desired to speak to me. This was none other than the tall, emaciated-looking Negress who, on the day of our arrival, had embraced me and my nurse with such irresistible zeal. She appeared very ill today, and presently unfolded to me a most distressing history of bodily afflictions. She was the mother of a very large family, and complained to me that, what with childbearing and hard field labor, her back was almost broken in two. With an almost savage vehemence of gesticulation, she suddenly tore up her scanty clothing, and exhibited a spectacle with which I was inconceivably shocked and sickened. The facts, without any of her corroborating statements, bore tolerable witness to the hardships of her existence. I promised to attend to her ailments and give her proper remedies; but these are natural results, inevitable and irremediable ones, of improper treatment of the female frame; and, though there may be alleviation, there cannot be any cure when once the beautiful and wonderful structure has been thus made the victim of ignorance, folly, and wickedness.

After the departure of this poor woman, I walked down the settlement toward the infirmary or hospital, calling in at one or two of the houses along the row. These cabins consist of one room, about twelve feet by fifteen, with a couple of closets smaller and closer than the staterooms of a ship, divided off from the main room and each other by rough wooden partitions, in which the inhabitants sleep. They have almost all of them a rude bedstead, with the gray moss of the forests for mattress, and filthy, pestilential-looking blankets for covering. Two families (sometimes eight and ten in number) reside in one of these huts, which are mere wooden frames pinned, as it were, to the earth by a brick chimney outside, whose enormous aperture within pours down a flood of air, but little counteracted by the miserable spark of fire, which hardly sends an attenuated thread of lingering smoke up its huge throat. A wide ditch runs immediately at the back of these dwellings, which is filled and emptied daily by the tide. Attached to each hovel is a small scrap of ground for a garden, which, however, is for the most part untended and uncultivated.

Such of these dwellings as I visited today were filthy and wretched in the extreme, and exhibited that most deplorable consequence of ignorance and an abject condition, the inability of the inhabitants to secure and improve even such pitiful comfort as might yet be achieved by them. Instead of the order, neatness, and ingenuity which might convert even these miserable hovels into tolerable residences, there was the careless, reckless, filthy indolence which even the brutes do not exhibit in their lairs and nests, and which seemed incapable of applying to the uses of existence the few miserable means of comfort yet within their reach. Firewood and shavings lay littered about the floors, while the half-naked children were cowering round two or three smouldering cinders. The moss with which the chinks and crannies of their ill-protecting dwellings might have been stuffed was trailing in dirt and dust about the ground, while the back door of the huts, opening upon a most unsightly ditch, was left wide open for the fowls and ducks, which they are allowed to raise, to travel in and out, increasing the filth of the cabin by what they brought and left in every direction.

In the midst of the floor, or squatting round the cold hearth, would be four or five little children from four to ten years old, the latter all with babies in their arms, the care of the infants being taken from the mothers (who are driven afield as soon as they recover from child labor), and devolved upon these poor little nurses, as they are called, whose business it is to watch the infant, and carry it to its mother whenever it may require nourishment. To these hardly human little beings I addressed my remonstrances about the filth, cold, and unnecessary wretchedness of their room, bidding the older boys and girls kindle up the fire, sweep the floor, and expel the poultry. For a long time my very words seemed unintelligible to them, till, when I began to sweep and make up the fire, etc., they first fell to laughing, and then imitating me. The incrustations of dirt on their hands, feet, and faces were my next object of attack, and the stupid Negro practice (by-the-by, but a short time since nearly universal in enlightened Europe) of keeping the babies with their feet bare, and their heads, already well capped by nature with their woolly hair, wrapped in half a dozen hot, filthy coverings.

Thus I traveled down the "street," in every dwelling endeavoring to awaken a new perception, that of cleanliness, sighing, as I went, over the futility of my own exertions, for how can slaves be improved? Nathless, thought I, let what can be done; for it may be that, the two being incompatible, improvement may yet expel slavery; and so it might, and surely would, if, instead of beginning at the end, I could but begin at the beginning of my task. If the mind and soul were awakened, instead of mere physical good attempted, the physical good would result, and the great curse vanish away; but my hands are tied fast, and this corner of the work is all that I may do. Yet it cannot be but, from my words and actions, some revelations should reach these poor people; and going in and out among them perpetually, I shall teach, and they learn involuntarily a thousand things of deepest import. They must learn, and who can tell the fruit of that knowledge alone, that there are beings in the world, even with skins of a different color from their own, who have sympathy for their misfortunes, love for their virtues, and respect for their common nature—but oh! my heart is full almost to bursting as I walk among these most poor creatures.

The infirmary is a large two-story building, terminating the broad orange-planted space between the two rows of houses which form the first settlement; it is built of whitewashed wood, and contains four large-sized rooms. But how shall I describe to you the spectacle which was presented to me on entering the first of these? But half the casements, of which there were six, were glazed, and these were obscured with dirt, almost as much as the other window-less ones were darkened by the dingy shutters, which the shivering inmates had fastened to in order to protect themselves from the cold. In the enormous chimney glimmered the powerless embers of a few sticks of wood, round which, however, as many of the sick women as could approach were cowering, some on wooden settles, most of them on the ground, excluding those who were too ill to rise; and these last poor wretches lay prostrate on the floor, without bed, mattress, or pillow, buried in tattered and fithy blankets, which, huddled round them as they lay strewed about, left hardly space to move upon the floor. And here, in their hour of sickness and suffering, lay those whose health and strength are spent in unrequited labor for us—those who, perhaps even yesterday, were being urged on to their unpaid task—those whose husbands, fathers, brothers, and sons were even at that hour sweating over the earth, whose produce was to buy for us all the luxuries which health can revel in, all the comforts which can alleviate sickness. I stood in the midst of them, perfectly unable to speak, the tears pouring from my eyes at this sad spectacle of their misery, myself and my emotion alike strange and incomprehensible to them. Here lay women expecting every hour the terrors and agonies of childbirth, others who had just brought their doomed offspring into the world, others who were groaning over the anguish and bitter disappointment of miscarriages—here lay some burning with fever, others chilled with cold and aching with rheumatism, upon the hard cold ground, the draughts and dampness of the atmosphere increasing their sufferings, and dirt, noise, and stench, and every aggravation of which sickness is capable, combined in their condition—here they lay like brute beasts, absorbed in physical suffering; unvisited by any of those Divine influences which may ennoble the dispensations of pain and illness, forsaken, as it seemed to me, of all good; and yet, O God, Thou surely hadst not forsaken them! Now pray take notice that this is the hospital of an estate where the owners are supposed to be humane, the overseer efficient and kind, and the Negroes remarkably well cared for and comfortable.

As soon as I recovered from my dismay, I addressed old Rose the midwife, who had charge of this room, bidding her open the shutters of such windows as were glazed, and let in the light. I next proceeded to make up the fire; but, upon my lifting a log for that purpose, there was one universal outcry of horror, and old Rose, attempting to snatch it from me, exclaimed: "Let alone, missis— let be; what for you lift wood? you have nigger enough, missis, to do it!" I hereupon had to explain to them my view of the purposes for which hands and arms were appended to our bodies, and forth- with began making Rose tidy up the miserable apartment, remov- ing all the filth and rubbish from the floor that could be removed, folding up in piles the blankets of the patients who were not using them, and placing, in rather more sheltered and comfortable posi- tions, those who were unable to rise. It was all that I could do, and having enforced upon them all my earnest desire that they should keep their room swept, and as tidy as possible, I passed on to the other room on the ground floor, and to the two above, one of which is appropriated to the use of the men who are ill. They were all in the same deplorable condition, the upper rooms being rather the more miserable, inasmuch as none of the windows were glazed at all, and they had, therefore, only the alternative of utter dark- ness, or killing draughts of air from the unsheltered casements. In all, filth, disorder, and misery abounded; the floor was the only bed, and scanty begrimed rags of blankets the only covering. I left this refuge for Mr. [Butler]'s sick dependents with my clothes covered with dust, and full of vermin, and with a heart heavy enough, as you will well believe. My morning's work had fatigued me not a little, and I was glad to return to the house, where I gave vent to my indignation and regret at the scene I had just witnessed to Mr. [Butler] and his overseer, who, here, is a member of our family. The latter told me that the condition of the hospital had appeared to him, from his first entering upon his situation (only within the last year), to require a reform, and that he had proposed it to the former manager, Mr. K[ing], and Mr. [Butler]'s brother, who is part proprietor of the estate, but, receiving no encouragement from them, had supposed that it was a matter of indifference to the owners, and had left it in the condition in which he had found it, in which condition it has been for the last nineteen years and upward.

This new overseer of ours has lived fourteen years with an old Scotch gentleman, who owns an estate adjoining Mr. [Butler]'s, on the island of St. Simons, upon which estate, from everything I can gather, and from what I know of the proprietor's character, the slaves are probably treated with as much humanity as is consistent with slavery at all, and where the management and comfort of the hospital in particular had been most carefully and judiciously attended to. With regard to the indifference of our former manager upon the subject of the accommodation for the sick, he was an excellent overseer, *videlicet* the estate returned a full income under his management, and such men have nothing to do with sick slaves: they are tools, to be mended only if they can be made available again; if not, to be flung by as useless, without further expense of money, time, or trouble.

I am learning to row here, for circumscribed, as my walks necessarily are, impossible as it is to resort to my favorite exercise on horseback upon these narrow dikes, I must do something to prevent my blood from stagnating; and this broad brimming river, and the beautiful light canoes which lie moored at the steps, are very inviting persuaders to this species of exercise. My first attempt was confined to pulling an oar across the stream, for which I rejoiced in sundry aches and pains altogether novel, letting alone a delightful row of blisters on each of my hands.

I forgot to tell you that in the hospital were several sick babies, whose mothers were permitted to suspend their field labor in order to nurse them. Upon addressing some remonstrances to one of these, who, besides having a sick child, was ill herself, about the horribly dirty condition of her baby, she assured me that it was impossible for them to keep their children clean; that they went out to work at daybreak, and did not get their tasks done till evening, and that then they were too tired and worn out to do anything but throw themselves down and sleep. This statement of hers I mentioned on my return from the hospital, and the overseer appeared extremely annoyed by it, and assured me repeatedly that it was not true.

In the evening Mr. [Butler], who had been over to Darien, mentioned that one of the storekeepers there had told him that, in the course of a few years, he had paid the Negroes of this estate several thousand dollars for moss, which is a very profitable article of traffic with them: they collect it from the trees, dry and pick it, and then sell it to the people in Darien for mattresses, sofas, and all sorts of stuffing purposes, which, in my opinion, it answers better than any other material whatever that I am acquainted with, being as light as horsehair, as springy and elastic, and a great deal less harsh and rigid. It is now bedtime, dear E[lizabeth], and I doubt not it has been sleepy time with you over this letter long ere you came thus far. There is a preliminary to my repose, however, in this agreeable residence, which I rather dread, namely, the hunting for, or discovering without hunting, in fine relief upon the white-washed walls of my bedroom, a most hideous and detestable species of *reptile* called centipedes, which come out of the cracks and crevices of the walls, and fill my very heart with dismay. They are from an inch to two inches long, and appear to have not a hundred, but a thousand legs. I cannot ascertain very certainly from the Negroes whether they sting or not, but they look exceedingly as if they might, and I visit my babies every night in fear and trembling, lest I should find one or more of these hateful creatures mounting guard over them. Good night; you are well to be free from centipedes—better to be free from slaves.

V

Further Explorations

[January, 1839]

Dear E[lizabeth],

This morning I paid my second visit to the infirmary, and found there had been some faint attempt at sweeping and cleaning, in compliance with my entreaties. The poor woman Harriet, however, whose statement with regard to the impossibility of their attending properly to their children had been so vehemently denied by the overseer, was crying bitterly. I asked her what ailed her, when, more by signs and dumb show than words, she and old Rose informed me that Mr. O—— had flogged her that morning for having told me that the women had not time to keep their children clean. It is part of the regular duty of every overseer to visit the infirmary at least once a day, which he generally does in the morning, and Mr. O——'s visit had preceded mine but a short time only, or I might have been edified by seeing a man horsewhip a woman. I again and again made her repeat her story, and she again and again affirmed that she had been flogged for what she told me, none of the whole company in the room denying it or contradicting her. I left the room because I was so disgusted and indignant that I could hardly restrain my feelings, and to express them could have produced no single good result.

In the next ward, stretched upon the ground, apparently either asleep or so overcome with sickness as to be incapable of moving, lay an immense woman; her stature, as she cumbered the earth, must have been, I should think, five feet seven or eight, and her bulk enormous. She was wrapped in filthy rags, and lay with her face on the floor. As I approached, and stooped to see what ailed her, she suddenly threw out her arms, and, seized with violent convulsions, rolled over and over upon the floor, beating her head violently upon the ground, and throwing her enormous limbs about in a horrible manner. Immediately upon the occurrence of this fit, four or five women threw themselves literally upon her, and held her down by main force; they even proceeded to bind her legs and arms together, to prevent her dashing herself about; but this violent coercion and tight bandaging seemed to me, in my profound ignorance, more likely to increase her illness by impeding her breathing and the circulation of her blood, and I bade them desist, and unfasten all the strings and ligatures not only that they had put round her limbs, but which, by tightening her clothes round her body, caused any obstruction. How much I wished that, instead of music, and dancing, and such stuff, I had learned something of sickness and health, of the conditions and liabilities of the human body, that I might have known how to assist this poor creature, and to direct her ignorant and helpless nurses! The fit presently subsided, and was succeeded by the most deplorable prostration and weakness of nerves, the tears streaming down the poor woman's cheeks in showers, without, however, her uttering a single word, though she moaned incessantly. After bathing her forehead, hands, and chest with vinegar, we raised her up, and I sent to the house for a chair with a back (there was no such thing in the hospital), and we contrived to place her in it. I have seldom seen finer women than this poor creature and her younger sister, an immense strapping lass called Chloe—tall, straight, and extremely well made—who was assisting her sister, and whom I had remarked, for the extreme delight and merriment which my cleansing propensities seemed to give her, on my last visit to the hospital. She was here taking care of a sick baby, and helping to nurse her sister Molly, who, it seems, is subject to those fits, about which I spoke to our physician here—an intelligent man residing in Darien, who visits the estate whenever medical assistance is required. He seemed to attribute them to nervous disorder, brought on by frequent childbearing. This woman is young, I suppose at the outside not thirty, and her sister informed me that she had had ten children —ten children, E[lizabeth]! Fits and hard labor in the fields, unpaid labor, labor exacted with stripes—how do you fancy that? I wonder if my mere narration can make your blood boil as the facts did mine?

Among the patients in this room was a young girl, apparently from fourteen to fifteen, whose hands and feet were literally rotting away piecemeal, from the effect of a horrible disease, to which the Negroes are subject here, and I believe in the West Indies, and when it attacks the joints of the toes and fingers, the pieces absolutely decay and come off, leaving the limb a maimed and horrible stump! I believe no cure is known for this disgusting malady, which seems confined to these poor creatures. Another disease, of which they complained much, and which, of course, I was utterly incapable of accounting for, was a species of lockjaw, to which their babies very frequently fall victims in the first or second week after their birth, refusing the breast, and the mouth gradually losing the power of opening itself. The horrible diseased state of the head, common among their babies, is a mere result of filth and confinement, and therefore, though I never anywhere saw such distressing and disgusting objects as some of these poor little woolly skulls presented, the cause was sufficiently obvious. Pleurisy, or a tendency to it, seems very common among them; also peripneumonia, or inflammation of the lungs, which is terribly prevalent, and generally fatal. Rheumatism is almost universal; and as it proceeds from exposure, and want of knowledge and care, attacks indiscriminately the young and old. A great number of the women are victims to falling of the womb and weakness in the spine; but these are necessary results of their laborious existence, and do not belong either to climate or constitution.

I have ingeniously contrived to introduce bribery, corruption, and pauperism, all in a breath, upon this island, which, until my advent, was as innocent of these pollutions, I suppose, as Prospero's isle of refuge. Wishing, however, to appeal to some perception, perhaps a little less dim in their minds than the abstract loveliness of cleanliness, I have proclaimed to all the little baby nurses that I will give a cent to every little boy or girl whose baby's face shall be clean, and one to every individual with clean face and hands of their own. My appeal was fully comprehended by the majority, it seems, for this morning I was surrounded, as soon as I came out, by a swarm of children carrying their little charges on their backs and in their arms, the shining, and, in many instances, wet faces and hands of the latter bearing ample testimony to the ablutions which had been inflicted upon them. How they will curse me and the copper cause of all their woes in their baby bosoms! Do you know that, little as grown Negroes are admirable for their personal beauty (in my opinion, at least), the black babies of a year or two old are very pretty; they have, for the most part, beautiful eyes and eyelashes, the pearly perfect teeth, which they retain after their other juvenile graces have left them; their skins are all (I mean of blacks generally) infinitely finer and softer than the skins of white people. Perhaps you are not aware that among the white race the *finest grained* skins generally belong to persons of dark complexion. This, as a characteristic of the black race, I think might be accepted as some compensation for the coarse woolly hair. The nose and mouth, which are so peculiarly displeasing in their conformation in the face of a Negro man or woman, being the features least developed in a baby's countenance, do not at first present the ugliness which they assume as they become more marked; and when the very unusual operation of washing has been performed, the blood shines through the fine texture of the skin, giving life and richness to the dingy color, and displaying a species of beauty which I think scarcely anybody who observed it would fail to acknowledge. I have seen many babies on this plantation who were quite as pretty as white children, and this very day stooped to kiss a little sleeping creature that lay on its mother's knees in the infirmary—as beautiful a specimen of a sleeping infant as I ever saw. The caress excited the irrepressible delight of all the women present—poor creatures! who seemed to forget that I was a woman, and had children myself, and bore a woman's and a mother's heart toward them and theirs; but, indeed, the Honorable Mr. Slumkey [1] could not have achieved more popularity by his performances in that line than I by this exhibition of feeling; and, had the question been my election, I am very sure nobody else would have had a chance of a vote through the island. But wisely is it said that use is second nature, and the contempt and neglect to which these poor people are used make the commonest expression of human sympathy appear a boon and gracious condescension.

While I am speaking of the Negro countenance, there is another beauty which is not at all infrequent among those I see here—a finely-shaped oval face—and those who know (as all painters and sculptors, all who understand beauty do) how much expression there is in the outline of the head, and how very rare it is to see a well-formed face, will be apt to consider this a higher matter than any coloring, of which, indeed, the red and white one so often admired is by no means the most rich, picturesque, or expressive. At first the dark color confounded all features to my eye, and I could hardly tell one face from another. Becoming, however, accustomed to the complexion, I now perceive all the variety among these black countenances that there is among our own race, and as much difference in features and in expression as among the same number of whites. There is another peculiarity which I have remarked

---

[1] The Dickensian prototype, from *The Pickwick Papers,* of the baby-kissing political campaigner.

among the women here—very considerable beauty in the make of the hands; their feet are very generally ill-made, which must be a natural, and not an acquired defect, as they seldom injure their feet by wearing shoes. The figures of some of the women are handsome, and their carriage, from the absence of any confining or tightening clothing, and the habit they have of balancing great weights on their heads, erect and good.

At the upper end of the row of houses, and nearest to our over-seer's residence, is the hut of the head driver. Let me explain, by the way, his office. The Negroes, as I before told you, are divided into troops or gangs, as they are called; at the head of each gang is a driver, who stands over them, whip in hand, while they perform their daily task, who renders an account of each individual slave and his work every evening to the overseer, and receives from him directions for their next day's tasks. Each driver is allowed to inflict a dozen lashes upon any refractory slave in the field, and at the time of the offense; they may not, however, extend the chastisement, and if it is found ineffectual, their remedy lies in reporting the unmanageable individual either to the head driver or the overseer, the former of whom has power to inflict three dozen lashes at his own discretion, and the latter as many as he himself sees fit, within the number of fifty; which limit, however, I must tell you, is an arbitrary one on this plantation, appointed by the founder of the estate, Major [Butler], Mr. [Butler]'s grandfather, many of whose regulations, indeed I believe most of them, are still observed in the government of the plantation. Limits of this sort, however, to the power of either driver, head driver, or overseer, may or may not exist elsewhere; they are, to a certain degree, a check upon the power of these individuals; but in the absence of the master, the overseer may confine himself within the limit or not, as he chooses; and as for the master himself, where is his limit? He may, if he likes, flog a slave to death, for the laws which pretend that he may not are a mere pretense, inasmuch as the testimony of a black is never taken against a white; and upon this plantation of ours, and a thousand more, the overseer is the *only* white man, so whence should come the testimony to any crime of his? With regard to the oft-repeated statement that it is not the owner's interest to destroy his human property, it answers nothing; the instances in which men, to gratify the immediate impulse of passion, sacrifice not only their eternal, but their evident, palpable, positive worldly interest, are infinite. Nothing is commoner than for a man under the transient influence of anger to disregard his worldly advantage; and the black slave, whose preservation is indeed supposed to be his owner's interest, may be, will be, and is occasionally sacrificed to the blind impulse of passion.

To return to our head driver, or, as he is familiarly called, headman, Frank—he is second in authority only to the overseer, and exercises rule alike over the drivers and the gangs in the absence of the sovereign white man from the estate, which happens whenever Mr. O—— visits the other two plantations at Woodville and St. Simons. He is sole master and governor of the island, appoints the work, pronounces punishments, gives permission to the men to leave the island (without it they never may do so), and exercises all functions of undisputed mastery over his fellow slaves, for you will observe that all this [occurs] while he is just as much a slave as any of the rest. Trustworthy, upright, intelligent, he may be flogged tomorrow if Mr. O—— or Mr. [Butler] so please it, and sold the next day, like a cart horse, at the will of the latter. Besides his various other responsibilities, he has the key of all the stores, and gives out the people's rations weekly; nor is it only the people's provisions that are put under his charge—meat, which is only given out to them occasionally, and provisions for the use of the family, are also entrusted to his care. Thus you see, among these *inferior* creatures, their own masters yet look to find, surviving all their best efforts to destroy them, good sense, honesty, self-denial, and all the qualities, mental and moral, that make one man worthy to be trusted by another. From the imperceptible but inevitable effect of the sympathies and influences of human creatures toward and over each other, Frank's intelligence has become uncommonly developed by intimate communion in the discharge of his duty with the former overseer [Roswell King, Jr.], a very intelligent man, who has only just left the estate, after managing it for nineteen years; the effect of this intercourse, and of the trust and responsibility laid upon the man, are that he is clearheaded, well judging, active, intelligent, extremely well-mannered, and, being respected, he respects himself. He is as ignorant as the rest of the slaves; but he is always clean and tidy in his person, with a courteousness of demeanor far removed from servility, and exhibits a strong instance of the intolerable and wicked injustice of the system under which he lives, having advanced thus far toward improvement, in spite of all the bars it puts to progress; and here being arrested, not by want of energy, want of sense, or any want of his own, but by being held as another man's property, who can only thus hold him by forbidding him further improvement. When I see that man, who keeps himself a good deal aloof from the rest, in his leisure hours looking, with a countenance of deep thought, as I did today, over the broad river, which is to him as a prison wall, to the fields and forest beyond, not one inch or branch of which his utmost industry can conquer as his own, or acquire and leave an independent heritage to his children, I marvel what the thoughts of such a man may be. I was in his house today, and the same superiority in cleanliness, comfort, and propriety exhibited itself in his dwelling as in his own personal appearance and that of his wife—a most active, trustworthy, excellent woman, daughter of the oldest, and probably most highly respected of all Mr. [Butler]'s slaves. To the excellent conduct of this woman, and, indeed, every member of her family, both the present and the last overseer bear unqualified testimony.

As I was returning toward the house after my long morning's lounge, a man rushed out of the blacksmith's shop, and, catching me by the skirt of my gown, poured forth a torrent of self-gratulations on having at length found the "right missis." They have no idea, of course, of a white person performing any of the offices of a servant, and as throughout the whole Southern country the owner's children are nursed and tended, and sometimes *suckled* by their slaves (I wonder how this inferior milk agrees with the lordly *white* babies?), the appearance of M[argery] with my two children had immediately suggested the idea that she must be the missis. Many of the poor Negroes flocked to her, paying their profound homage under this impression; and when she explained to them that she was not their owner's wife, the confusion in their minds seemed very great—Heaven only knows whether they did not conclude that they had two mistresses, and Mr. [Butler] two wives; for the privileged race must seem, in their eyes, to have such absolute masterdom on earth, that perhaps they thought polygamy might be one of the sovereign white men's numerous indulgences. The ecstasy of the blacksmith on discovering the "right missis" at last was very funny, and was expressed with such extraordinary grimaces, contortions, and gesticulations, that I thought I should have died of laughing at this rapturous identification of my most melancholy relation to the poor fellow.

Having at length extricated myself from the group which forms round me whenever I stop but for a few minutes, I pursued my voyage of discovery by peeping into the kitchen garden. I dared do no more; the aspect of the place would have rejoiced the very soul of Solomon's sluggard of old—a few cabbages and weeds innumerable filled the neglected-looking enclosure, and I ventured no farther than the entrance into its most uninviting precincts. You are to understand that upon this swamp island of ours we have quite a large stock of cattle, cows, sheep, pigs, and poultry in the most enormous and inconvenient abundance. The cows are pretty miserably off for pasture, the banks and pathways of the dikes being their only grazing ground, which the sheep perambulate also, in earnest search of a nibble of fresh herbage; both the cows and sheep are fed with rice flour in great abundance, and are pretty often carried down for change of air and more sufficient grazing to Hampton, Mr. [Butler]'s estate, on the island of St. Simons, fifteen miles from this place, farther down the river—or rather, indeed, I should say in the sea, for it is salt water all round, and one end of the island has a noble beach open to the vast Atlantic. The pigs thrive admirably here, and attain very great perfection of size and flavor, the rice flour upon which they are chiefly fed tending to make them very delicate. As for the poultry, it being one of the few privileges of the poor blacks to raise as many as they can, their abundance is literally a nuisance—ducks, fowls, pigeons, turkeys (the two latter species, by-the-by, are exclusively the master's property), cluck, scream, gabble, gobble, crow, cackle, fight, fly, and flutter in all directions, and to their immense concourse, and the perfect freedom with which they intrude themselves even into the piazza of the house, the pantry, and kitchen, I partly attribute the swarms of fleas, and other still less agreeable vermin, with which we are most horribly pestered.

My walk lay today along the bank of a canal, which has been dug through nearly the whole length of the island, to render more direct and easy the transportation of the rice from one end of the estate to another, or from the various distant fields to the principal mill at Settlement Number One. It is of considerable width and depth, and opens by various locks into the river. It has, unfortunately, no trees on its banks, but a good footpath renders it, in spite of that deficiency, about the best walk on the island. I passed again today one of those beautiful evergreen thickets, which I described to you in my last letter; it is called a reserve, and is kept uncleared and uncultivated in its natural swampy condition, to allow of the people's procuring their firewood from it. I cannot get accustomed, so as to be indifferent to this exquisite natural ornamental growth, and think, as I contemplate the various and beautiful foliage of these watery woods, how many of our finest English parks and gardens owe their chiefest adornments to plantations of these shrubs, procured at immense cost, reared with infinite pains and care, which are here basking in the winter's sunshine, waiting to be cut down for firewood! These little groves are peopled with wild pigeons and birds, which they designate here as blackbirds. These sometimes rise from the rice fields with a whirr of multitudinous wings that is almost startling, and positively overshadow the ground beneath like a cloud.

I had a conversation that interested me a good deal, during my walk today, with my peculiar slave, Jack. This lad, whom Mr. [Butler] has appointed to attend me in my roamings about the island, and rowing expeditions on the river, is the son of the last head driver, a man of very extraordinary intelligence and faithfulness—such, at least, is the account given of him by his employers (in the burial ground of the Negroes is a stone dedicated to his memory, a mark of distinction accorded by his masters, which his son never failed to point out to me when we passed that way). Jack appears to inherit his quickness of apprehension; his questions, like those of an intelligent child, are absolutely inexhaustible; his curiosity about all things beyond this island, the prison house of his existence, is perfectly intense; his countenance is very pleasing, mild, and not otherwise than thoughtful; he is, in common with the rest of them, a stupendous flatterer, and, like the rest of them, also seems devoid of physical and moral courage. Today, in the midst of his torrent of inquiries about places and things, I suddenly asked him if he would like to be free. A gleam of light absolutely shot over his whole countenance, like the vivid and instantaneous lightning; he stammered, hesitated, became excessively confused, and at length replied: "Free, missis! what for me wish to be free? Oh no, missis, me no wish to be free, if massa only let we keep pig!" The fear of offending by uttering that forbidden wish—the dread of admitting, by its expression, the slightest discontent with his present situation—the desire to conciliate my favor, even at the expense of strangling the intense natural longing that absolutely glowed in his every feature—it was a sad spectacle, and I repented my question. As for the pitiful request, which he reiterated several times, adding: "No, missis, me no want to be free; me work till me die for missis and massa," with increased emphasis; it amounted only to this, that Negroes once were, but no longer are, permitted to keep pigs. The increase of filth and foul smells consequent upon their being raised is, of course, very great; and, moreover, Mr. [Butler] told me, when I preferred poor Jack's request to him, that their allowance was no more than would suffice their own necessity, and that they had not the means of feeding the animals. With a little good management they might very easily obtain them, however; their little "kail-yard" [2] alone would suffice to it, and the pork and bacon would prove a most welcome addition to their farinaceous diet. You perceive at once (or, if you could have seen the boy's face, you would have perceived at once) that his situation was no mystery to him; that his value to Mr. [Butler], and, as he supposed, to me, was perfectly well known to him, and that he comprehended immediately that his expressing even the desire to be free might be construed by me into an offense, and sought, by eager protestations of his delighted acquiescence in slavery, to conceal his soul's natural yearning, lest I should resent it. It was a sad passage between us, and sent me home full of the most painful thoughts.

I told Mr. [Butler], with much indignation, of poor Harriet's flogging, and represented that if the people were to be chastised for anything they said to me, I must leave the place, as I could not but hear their complaints, and endeavor, by all my miserable limited means, to better their condition while I was here. He said he would ask Mr. O—— about it, assuring me, at the same time, that it was impossible to believe a single word any of these people said. At dinner, accordingly, the inquiry was made as to the cause of her punishment, and Mr. O—— then said it was not at all for what she had told me that he had flogged her, but for having answered him impertinently; that he had ordered her into the field, whereupon she had said she was ill and could not work; that he retorted he knew better, and bade her get up and go to work; she

[2] This is a Scottish term for a cabbage patch.

replied: "Very well, I'll go, but I shall just come back again!" meaning that when in the field she would be unable to work, and obliged to return to the hospital.

"For this reply," Mr. O—— said, "I gave her a good lashing; it was her business to have gone into the field without answering me, and then we should have soon seen whether she could work or not; I gave it to Chloe too for some such impudence."

I give you the words of the conversation, which was prolonged to a great length, the overseer complaining of the sham sicknesses of the slaves, and detailing the most disgusting struggle which is going on the whole time, on the one hand to inflict, and on the other to evade oppression and injustice. With this sauce I ate my dinner, and truly it tasted bitter.

Toward sunset I went on the river to take my rowing lesson. A darling little canoe, which carries two oars and a steersman, and rejoices in the appropriate title of the *Dolphin,* is my especial vessel; and with Jack's help and instructions, I contrived this evening to row upward of half a mile, coasting the reed-crowned edge of the island to another very large rice mill, the enormous wheel of which is turned by the tide. A small bank of mud and sand, covered with reedy coarse grass, divides the river into two arms on this side of the island; the deep channel is on the outside of this bank, and as we rowed home this evening, the tide having fallen, we scraped sand almost the whole way. Mr. [Butler]'s domain, it seems to me, will presently fill up this shallow stream, and join itself to the above-mentioned mud bank. The whole course of this most noble river is full of shoals, banks, mud and sand bars, and the navigation, which is difficult to those who know it well, is utterly baffling to the inexperienced. The fact is, that the two elements are so fused hereabouts that there are hardly such things as earth or water proper; that which styles itself the former is a fat, muddy, slimy sponge, that, floating half under the turbid river, looks yet saturated with the thick waves which every now and then reclaim their late dominion, and cover it almost entirely; the water, again, cloudy and yellow, like pea soup, seems but a solution of such islands, rolling turbid and thick with alluvium, which it both gathers and deposits as it sweeps along with a swollen, smooth rapidity, that almost deceives the eye. Amphibious creatures, alligators, serpents, and wild fowl haunt these yet but half-formed regions, where land and water are of the consistency of hasty pudding—the one seeming too unstable to walk on, the other almost too thick to float in. But then the sky—if no human chisel ever yet cut breath, neither did any human pen ever write light; if it did, mine should spread out before you the unspeakable glories of these Southern heavens, the saffron brightness of morning, the blue intense brilliancy of noon, the golden splendor and the rosy softness of sunset. Italy and Claude Lorrain may go hang themselves together! Heaven itself does not seem brighter or more beautiful to the imagination than these surpassing pageants of fiery rays, and piled-up beds of orange, golden clouds, with edges too bright to look on, scattered wreaths of faintest rosy bloom, amber streaks and pale green lakes between, and amid sky all mingled blue and rose tints, a spectacle to make one fall over the side of the boat, with one's head broken off with looking adoringly upward, but which, on paper, means nothing.

At six o'clock our little canoe grazed the steps at the landing. These were covered with young women, and boys and girls, drawing water for their various household purposes. A very small cedar pail—a piggin as they termed it—serves to scoop up the river water; and having, by this means, filled a large bucket, they transfer this to their heads, and, thus laden, march home with the purifying element—what to do with it I cannot imagine, for evidence of its ever having been introduced into their dwellings I saw none. As I ascended the stairs, they surrounded me with shrieks and yells of joy, uttering exclamations of delight and amazement at my rowing. Considering that they dig, delve, carry burdens, and perform many more athletic exercises than pulling a light oar, I was rather amused at this; but it was the singular fact of seeing a white woman stretch her sinews in any toilsome exercise which astounded them, accustomed as they are to see both men and women of the privileged skin eschew the slightest shadow of labor as a thing not only painful, but degrading. They will learn another lesson from me, however, whose idea of heaven was pronounced by a friend of mine, to whom I once communicated it, to be "devilish hard work!" It was only just six o'clock, and these women had all done their tasks. I exhorted them to go home and wash their children, and clean their houses and themselves, which they professed themselves ready to do, but said they had no soap. Then began a chorus of mingled requests for soap, for summer clothing, and a variety of things, which, if "Missis only give we, we be so clean forever!"

This request for summer clothing, by-the-by, I think a very reasonable one. The allowance of clothes made yearly to each slave by the present regulations of the estate is a certain number of yards of flannel, and as much more of what they call plains—an extremely stout, thick, heavy woolen cloth, of a dark gray or blue color, which resembles the species of carpet we call drugget. This, and two pair of shoes, is the regular ration of clothing; but these plains would be intolerable to any but Negroes, even in winter, in this climate, and are intolerable to them in the summer. A far better arrangement, in my opinion, would be to increase their allowance of flannel and underclothing, and to give them dark chintzes instead of these thick carpets, which are very often the only covering they wear at all. I did not impart all this to my petitioners, but, disengaging myself from them, for they held my hands and clothes, I conjured them to offer us some encouragement to better their condition by bettering it as much as they could themselves—enforced the virtue of washing themselves and all belonging to them, and at length made good my retreat. As there is no particular reason why such a letter as this should ever come to an end, I had better spare you for the present. You shall have a faithful journal, I promise you, hence forward, as hitherto, from yours ever.

VI

Observations
upon Mr. Butler's Slaves

[January, 1839]

Dear E[lizabeth],

We had a species of fish this morning for our breakfast which
deserves more glory than I can bestow upon it. Had I been the ingenious man who wrote a poem upon fish, the white mullet of the
Altamaha should have been at least my heroine's cousin. It is the
heavenliest creature that goes upon fins. I took a long walk this
morning to Settlement Number Three, the third village on the island. My way lay along the side of the canal, beyond which, and
only divided from it by a raised narrow causeway, rolled the
brimming river, with its girdle of glittering evergreens, while on my
other hand a deep trench marked the line of the rice fields. It really
seemed as if the increase of merely a shower of rain might join all
these waters together, and lay the island under its original covering
again. I visited the people and houses here. I found nothing in any
respect different from what I have described to you at Settlement
Number One. During the course of my walk, I startled from its repose in one of the rice fields a huge blue heron. You must have
seen, as I often have, these creatures stuffed in museums; but it is
another matter, and far more curious, to see them stalking on their

stilts of legs over a rice field, and then, on your near approach, see them spread their wide heavy wings, and throw themselves upon the air, with their long shanks flying after them in a most grotesque and laughable manner. They fly as if they did not know how to do it very well; but standing still, their height (between four and five feet) and peculiar color, a dusky, grayish blue, with black about the head, render their appearance very beautiful and striking.

In the afternoon I and Jack rowed ourselves over to Darien. It is Saturday—the day of the week on which the slaves from the island are permitted to come over to the town to purchase such things as they may require and can afford, and to dispose, to the best advantage, of their poultry, moss, and eggs. I met many of them paddling themselves singly in their slight canoes, scooped out of the trunk of a tree, and parties of three and four rowing boats of their own building, laden with their purchases, singing, laughing, talking, and apparently enjoying their holiday to the utmost. They all hailed me with shouts of delight as I pulled past them, and many were the injunctions bawled after Jack to "mind and take good care of missis!" We returned home through the glory of a sunset all amber-colored and rosy, and found that one of the slaves, a young lad for whom Mr. [Butler] has a particular regard, was dangerously ill. Dr. H[olmes] was sent for; and there is every probability that he, Mr. [Butler], and Mr. O—— will be up all night with the poor fellow. I shall write more tomorrow.

Today being Sunday, dear E[lizabeth], a large boat full of Mr. [Butler]'s people from Hampton came up, to go to church at Darien, and to pay their respects to their master, and see their new "missis." The same scene was acted over again that occurred on our first arrival. A crowd clustered round the house door, to whom I and my babies were produced, and with every individual of whom we had to shake hands some half a dozen times. They brought us up presents of eggs (their only wealth), beseeching us to take them; and one young lad, the son of headman Frank, had a beautiful pair of chickens, which he offered most earnestly to S[ally]. We took one of them, not to mortify the poor fellow, and a green ribbon being tied round its leg, it became a sacred fowl, "little missis's chicken." By-the-by, this young man had so light a complexion, and such regular straight features, that, had I seen him anywhere else, I should have taken him for a southern European, or, perhaps, in favor of his tatters, a gipsy; but certainly it never would have occurred to me that he was the son of Negro parents. I observed this to Mr. [Butler], who merely replied: "He is the son of headman Frank and his wife Betty, and they are both black enough, as you see." The expressions of devotion and delight of these poor people are the most fervent you can imagine. One of them, speaking to me of Mr. [Butler], and saying that they had heard that he had not been well, added: "Oh! we hear so, missis, and we not know what to do. Oh! missis, massa sick, all him people *broken!*"

Dr. H[olmes] came again today to see the poor sick boy, who is doing much better, and bidding fair to recover. He entertained me with an account of the Darien society, its aristocracies and democracies, its little grandeurs and smaller pettinesses, its circles higher and lower, its social jealousies, fine invisible lines of demarkation, imperceptible shades of different respectability, and delicate divisions of genteel, genteeler, genteelest. "For me," added the worthy doctor, "I cannot well enter into the spirit of these nice distinctions; it suits neither my taste nor my interest, and my house is, perhaps, the only one in Darien where you would find all these opposite and contending elements combined." The doctor is connected with the aristocracy of the place, and, like a wise man, remembers, notwithstanding, that those who are not [so connected] are quite as liable to be ill, and call in medical assistance, as those who are. He is a shrewd, intelligent man, with an excellent knowledge of his profession, much kindness of heart, and apparent cheerful good temper. I have already severely tried the latter by the unequivocal expression of my opinions on the subject of slavery, and, though I perceived that it required all his self-command to listen with anything like patience to my highly incendiary and inflammatory doctrines, he yet did so, and though he was, I have no doubt, perfectly horror-stricken at the discovery, lost nothing of his courtesy or good humor. By-the-by, I must tell you that, at an early period of the conversation, upon my saying: "I put all other considerations out of the question, and first propose to you the injustice of the system alone," "Oh," replied my friend the doctor, "if you put it upon that ground, you *stump* the question at once; I have nothing to say to that whatever, but," and then followed the usual train of pleadings—happiness, tenderness, care, indulgence, etc., etc., etc.—all the substitutes that may or may not be put in the place of *justice,* and which these slaveholders attempt to persuade others, and perhaps themselves, effectually supply its want.

After church hours the people came back from Darien. They are only permitted to go to Darien to church once a month. On the intermediate Sundays they assemble in the house of London, Mr. [Butler]'s head cooper, an excellent and pious man, who, Heaven alone knows how, has obtained some little knowledge of reading, and who reads prayers and the Bible to his fellow slaves, and addresses them with extemporaneous exhortations. I have the greatest desire to attend one of these religious meetings, but fear to put the people under any, the slightest restraint. However, I shall see by-and-by how they feel about it themselves.

You have heard, of course, many and contradictory statements as to the degree of religious instruction afforded to the Negroes of the South, and their opportunities of worship, etc. Until the late abolition movement, the spiritual interests of the slaves were about as little regarded as their physical necessities. The outcry which has been raised with threefold force within the last few years against the whole system has induced its upholders and defenders to adopt, as measures of personal extenuation, some appearance of religious instruction (such as it is), and some pretense at physical indulgences (such as they are), bestowed apparently voluntarily upon their dependents. At Darien a church is appropriated to the especial use of the slaves, who are almost all of them Baptists here; and a gentleman officiates in it (of course, white), who, I understand, is very zealous in the cause of their spiritual well-being. He, like most Southern men, clergy or others, jump the present life in their charities to the slaves, and go on to furnish them with all requisite conveniences for the next. There were a short time ago two free black preachers in this neighborhood, but they have lately been ejected from the place. I could not clearly learn, but one may possibly imagine, upon what grounds.

I do not think that a residence on a slave plantation is likely to be peculiarly advantageous to a child like my oldest. I was observing her today among her swarthy worshipers, for they follow her as such, and saw, with dismay, the universal eagerness with which they sprang to obey her little gestures of command. She said something about a swing, and in less than five minutes headman Frank had erected it for her, and a dozen young slaves were ready to swing little "missis." [Elizabeth], think of learning to rule despotically your fellow creatures before the first lesson of self-government has been well spelled over! It makes me tremble; but I shall find a remedy, or remove myself and the child from this misery and ruin.

You cannot conceive anything more grotesque than the Sunday trim of the poor people, their ideality, as Mr. Combe would say, being, I should think, twice as big as any rational bump in their head. Their Sabbath toilet really presents the most ludicrous combination of incongruities that you can conceive—frills, flounces, ribbons; combs stuck in their woolly heads, as if they held up any portion of the stiff and ungovernable hair; filthy finery, every color in the rainbow, and the deepest possible shades blended in fierce companionship round one dusky visage; head handkerchiefs, that put one's very eyes out from a mile off; chintzes with sprawling patterns, that might be seen if the clouds were printed with them; beads, bugles, flaring sashes, and, above all, little fanciful aprons, which finish these incongruous toilets with a sort of airy grace, which I assure you is perfectly indescribable. One young man, the oldest son and heir of our washerwoman Hannah, came to pay his respects to me in a magnificent black satin waistcoat, shirt gills which absolutely engulfed his black visage, and neither shoes nor stockings on his feet.

Among our visitors from St. Simons today was Hannah's mother (it seems to me that there is not a girl of sixteen on the plantations but has children, nor a woman of thirty but has grandchildren). Old House Molly, as she is called, from the circumstance of her having been one of the slaves employed in domestic offices during Major [Butler]'s residence on the island, is one of the oldest and most respected slaves on the estate, and was introduced to me by Mr. [Butler] with especial marks of attention and regard; she absolutely embraced him, and seemed unable sufficiently to express her ecstasy at seeing him again. Her dress, like that of her daughter, and all the servants who have at any time been employed about the family, bore witness to a far more improved taste than the half-savage adornment of the other poor blacks, and upon my observing to her how agreeable her neat and cleanly appearance was to me, she replied that her old master (Major [Butler]) was extremely particular in this respect, and that in his time all the house servants were obliged to be very nice and careful about their persons.

She named to me all her children, an immense tribe; and, by-the-by, E[lizabeth], it has occurred to me that whereas the increase of this ill-fated race is frequently adduced as a proof of their good treatment and well-being, it really and truly is no such thing, and springs from quite other causes than the peace and plenty which a rapidly increasing population are supposed to indicate. If you will reflect for a moment upon the overgrown families of the half-starved Irish peasantry and English manufacturers, you will agree with me that these prolific shoots by no means necessarily spring from a rich or healthy soil. Peace and plenty are certainly causes of human increase, and so is recklessness; and this, I take it, is the impulse in the instance of the English manufacturer, the Irish peasant, and the Negro slave. Indeed here it is more than reckless-ness, for there are certain indirect premiums held out to obey the early commandment of replenishing the earth which do not fail to have their full effect. In the first place, none of the cares, those noble cares, that holy thoughtfulness which lifts the human above the brute parent, are ever incurred here by either father or mother. The relation indeed resembles, as far as circumstances can possibly make it do so, the short-lived connection between the animal and its young. The father, having neither authority, power, responsi-bility, or charge in his children, is of course, as among brutes, the least attached to his offspring; the mother, by the natural law which renders the infant dependent on her for its first year's nourishment, is more so; but as neither of them is bound to educate or to support their children, all the unspeakable tenderness and so-lemnity, all the rational, and all the spiritual grace and glory of the connection, is lost, and it becomes mere breeding, bearing, suckling, and there an end. But it is not only the absence of the conditions which God has affixed to the relation which tends to encourage the reckless increase of the race; they enjoy, by means of numerous children, certain positive advantages. In the first place, every woman who is pregnant, as soon as she chooses to make the fact known to the overseer, is relieved of a certain portion of her work in the field, which lightening of labor continues, of course, as long as she is so burdened. On the birth of a child certain additions of clothing and an additional weekly ration are bestowed on the fam-ily; and these matters, small as they may seem, act as powerful in-ducements to creatures who have none of the restraining influences actuating them which belong to the parental relation among all other people, whether civilized or savage. Moreover, they have all of them a most distinct and perfect knowledge of their value to their owners as property; and a woman thinks, and not much amiss, that the more frequently she adds to the number of her mas-ter's livestock by bringing new slaves into the world, the more claims she will have upon his consideration and good will. This was perfectly evident to me from the meritorious air with which the women always made haste to inform me of the number of children they had borne, and the frequent occasions on which the older slaves would direct my attention to their children, exclaiming: "Look, missis! little niggers for you and massa; plenty little niggers for you and little missis!" A very agreeable apostrophe to me indeed, as you will believe.

I have let this letter lie for a day or two, dear E[lizabeth], from press of more immediate avocations. I have nothing very particular to add to it. On Monday evening I rowed over to Darien with Mr. [Butler] to fetch over the doctor, who was coming to visit some of our people. As I sat waiting in the boat for the return of the gentlemen, the sun went down, or rather seemed to dissolve bodily into the glowing clouds, which appeared but a fusion of the great orb of light; the stars twinkled out in the rose-colored sky, and the evening air, as it fanned the earth to sleep, was as soft as a summer's evening breeze in the North. A sort of dreamy stillness seemed creeping over the world and into my spirit as the canoe just tilted against the steps that led to the wharf, raised by the scarce perceptible heaving of the water. A melancholy, monotonous boat horn sounded from a distance up the stream, and presently, floating slowly down with the current, huge, shapeless, black, relieved against the sky, came one of those rough barges piled with cotton, called, hereabouts, Ocone[e] boxes. The vessel itself is really nothing but a monstrous square box, made of rough planks, put together in the roughest manner possible to attain the necessary object of keeping the cotton dry. Upon this great tray are piled the swollen, apoplectic-looking cotton bags, to the height of ten, twelve, and fourteen feet. This huge water wagon floats lazily down the river, from the upper country to Darien. They are flat-bottomed, and, of course, draw little water. The stream from whence they are named is an up-country river, which, by its junction with the Ocmulgee, forms the Altamaha. Here at least, you perceive, the Indian names remain, and long may they do so, for they seem to me to become the very character of the streams and mountains they indicate, and are indeed significant to the learned in savage tongues, which is more than can be said of such titles as Jones's Creek, Onion Creek, etc. These Ocone[e] boxes are broken up at Darien, where the cotton is shipped either for the Savannah, Charleston, or Liverpool markets, and the timber of which they are constructed sold.

We rowed the doctor over to see some of his patients on the island, and before his departure a most animated discussion took place upon the subject of the President of the United States, his talents, qualifications, opinions—above all, his views with regard to the slave system. Mr. [Butler], who you know is no abolitionist, and is a very devoted Van Buren man, maintained with great warmth the President's straightforwardness, and his evident and expressed intention of protecting the rights of the South. The doctor, on the other hand, quoted a certain speech of the President's upon the question of abolishing slavery in the District of Columbia, which his fears interpreted into a mere evasion of the matter, and an indication that at some future period he (Mr. Van Buren) might take a different view of the subject. I confess, for my own part, that if the doctor quoted the speech right, and if the President is not an honest man, and if I were a Southern slaveholder, I should not feel altogether secure of Mr. Van Buren's present opinions or future conduct upon this subject. These three *ifs,* however, are material points of consideration. Our friend the doctor inclined vehemently to Mr. Clay as one on whom the slaveholders could depend. Georgia, however, as a state, is perhaps the most democratic in the Union; though here, as well as in other places that you and I know of, a certain class, calling themselves the first, and honestly believing themselves the best, set their faces against the modern-fashioned republicanism, professing, and, I have no doubt, with great sincerity, that their ideas of democracy are altogether of a different kind.

I went again today to the infirmary, and was happy to perceive that there really was an evident desire to conform to my instructions, and keep the place in a better condition than formerly. Among the sick I found a poor woman suffering dreadfully from the earache. She had done nothing to alleviate her pain but apply some leaves, of what tree or plant I could not ascertain, and tie up her head in a variety of dirty cloths, till it was as large as her whole body. I removed all these, and found one side of her face and neck very much swollen, but so begrimed with filth that it was really no very agreeable task to examine it. The first process, of course, was washing, which, however, appeared to her so very unusual an operation, that I had to perform it for her myself. Sweet oil and laudanum, and raw cotton, being then applied to her ear and neck, she professed herself much relieved, but I believe in my heart that the warm-water sponging had done her more good than anything else. I was sorry not to ascertain what leaves she had applied to her ear. These simple remedies resorted to by savages, and people as ignorant, are generally approved by experience, and sometimes condescendingly adopted by science. I remember once, when Mr. [Butler] was suffering from a severe attack of inflammatory rheumatism, Dr. C[hapman] [1] desired him to bind round his knee the leaves of the tulip tree—poplar I believe you call it —saying that he had learned that remedy from the Negroes in Virginia, and found it a most effectual one.

My next agreeable office in the infirmary this morning was superintending the washing of two little babies, whose mothers were nursing them with quite as much ignorance as zeal. Having ordered a large tub of water, I desired Rose to undress the little creatures and give them a warm bath; the mothers looked on in unutterable dismay; and one of them, just as her child was going to be put into the tub, threw into it all the clothes she had just taken off it, as she said, to break the unusual shock of the warm water. I immediately rescued them; not but what they were quite as much in want of

---

[1] Dr. Nathaniel Chapman was an eminent Philadelphia physician and a native of Virginia. His daughter Emily was a leading beauty whom Fanny supplanted in the affections of Pierce Butler.

washing as the baby, but it appeared, upon inquiry, that the woman had none others to dress the child in when it should have taken its bath; they were immediately wrung and hung by the fire to dry; and the poor little patients, having undergone this novel operation, were taken out and given to their mothers. Anything, however, much more helpless and inefficient than these poor ignorant creatures you cannot conceive; they actually seemed incapable of drying or dressing their own babies, and I had to finish their toilet myself. As it is only a very few years since the most absurd and disgusting customs have become exploded among ourselves, you will not, of course, wonder that these poor people pin up the lower part of their infants, bodies, legs, and all, in red flannel as soon as they are born, and keep them in the selfsame envelope till it literally falls off.

In the next room I found a woman lying on the floor in a fit of epilepsy, barking most violently. She seemed to excite no particular attention or compassion; the women said she was subject to these fits, and took little or no notice of her, as she lay barking like some enraged animal on the ground. Again I stood in profound ignorance, sickening with the sight of suffering which I knew not how to alleviate, and which seemed to excite no commiseration merely from the sad fact of its frequent occurrence. Returning to the house, I passed up the "street." It was between eleven o'clock and noon, and the people were taking their first meal in the day. By-the-by E[lizabeth], how do you think Berkshire county farmers would relish laboring hard all day upon *two meals* of Indian corn or hominy? Such is the regulation on this plantation, however, and I beg you to bear in mind that the Negroes on Mr. [Butler]'s estate are generally considered well off. They go to the fields at daybreak, carrying with them their allowance of food for the day, which toward noon, *and not till then,* they eat, cooking it over a fire, which they kindle as best they can, where they are working. Their second meal in the day is at night, after their labor is over, having worked, at the *very least,* six hours without intermission of rest or refreshment since their noonday meal (properly so called, for it is meal, and nothing else). Those that I passed to-day, sitting on their doorsteps, or on the ground round them eating, were the people employed at the mill and threshing floor. As these are near to the settlement, they had time to get their food from the cookshop. Chairs, tables, plates, knives, forks, they had none; they sat, as I before said, on the earth or doorsteps, and ate either out of their little cedar tubs or an iron pot, some few with broken iron spoons, more with pieces of wood, and all the children with their fingers. A more complete sample of savage feeding I never beheld.

At one of the doors I saw three young girls standing, who might be between sixteen and seventeen years old; they had evidently done eating, and were rudely playing and romping with each other, laughing and shouting like wild things. I went into the house, and such another spectacle of filthy disorder I never beheld. I then ad-dressed the girls most solemnly, showing them that they were wast-ing in idle riot the time in which they might be rendering their abode decent, and told them that it was a shame for any woman to live in so dirty a place and so beastly a condition. They said they had seen buckree (white) women's houses just as dirty, and they could not be expected to be cleaner than white women. I then told them that the only difference between themselves and buckree women was, that the latter were generally better informed, and, for that reason alone, it was more disgraceful to them to be dis-orderly and dirty. They seemed to listen to me attentively, and one of them exclaimed, with great satisfaction, that they saw I made no difference between them and white girls, and that they never had been so treated before. I do not know anything which strikes me as a more melancholy illustration of the degradation of these people than the animal nature of their recreations in their short seasons of respite from labor. You see them, boys and girls, from the youngest age to seventeen and eighteen, rolling, tumbling, kick-ing, and wallowing in the dust, regardless alike of decency, and incapable of any more rational amusement; or lolling, with half-closed eyes, like so many cats and dogs, against a wall, or upon a bank in the sun, dozing away their short leisure hour, until called to resume their labors in the field or the mill.

After this description of the meals of our laborers, you will, perhaps, be curious to know how it fares with our house servants in this respect. Precisely in the same manner, as far as regards allowance, with the exception of what is left from our table, but, if possible, with even less comfort, in one respect, inasmuch as no time whatever is set apart for their meals, which they snatch at any hour, and in any way that they can—generally, however, standing, or squatting on their hams round the kitchen fire. They have no sleeping rooms in the house, but when their work is over, retire, like the rest, to their hovels, the discomfort of which has to them all the addition of comparison with our mode of living. Now, in all establishments whatever, of course some disparity exists between the comforts of the drawing room and best bedrooms, and the servants' hall and attics, but here it is no longer a matter of degree. The young woman who performs the office of lady's maid, and the lads who wait upon us at table, have neither table to feed at nor chair to sit down upon themselves. The boys sleep at night on the hearth by the kitchen fire, and the women upon a rough board bedstead, strewed with a little tree moss. All this shows how very torpid the sense of justice is apt to lie in the breasts of those who have it not awakened by the peremptory demands of others. In the North we could not hope to keep the worst and poorest servant for a single day in the wretched discomfort in which our Negro servants are forced habitually to live.

I received a visit this morning from some of the Darien people. Among them was a most interesting young person, from whose acquaintance, if I have any opportunity of cultivating it, I promise myself much pleasure. The ladies that I have seen since I crossed the Southern line have all seemed to me extremely sickly in their appearance—delicate in the refined term, but unfortunately sickly in the truer one. They are languid in their deportment and speech, and seem to give themselves up, without an effort to counteract it, to the enervating effect of their warm climate. It is undoubtedly a most relaxing and unhealthy one, and therefore requires the more imperatively to be met by energetic and invigorating habits both of body and mind. Of these, however, the Southern ladies appear to have, at present, no very positive idea. Doctor [Holmes] told us today of a comical application which his Negro man had made to him for the coat he was then wearing. I forget whether the fellow wanted the loan, or the absolute gift of it, but his argument was (it might have been an Irishman's) that he knew his master intended to give it to him by-and-by, and that he thought he might as well let him have it at once as keep him waiting any longer for it. This story the doctor related with great glee, and it furnishes a very good sample of what the Southerners are fond of exhibiting, the degree of license to which they capriciously permit their favorite slaves occasionally to carry their familiarity. They seem to consider it as an undeniable proof of the general kindness with which their dependents are treated. It is as good a proof of it as the maudlin tenderness of a fine lady to her lapdog is of her humane treatment of animals in general. Servants whose claims to respect are properly understood by themselves and their employers, are not made pets, playthings, jesters, or companions of, and it is only the degradation of the many that admits of this favoritism to the few—a system of favoritism which, as it is perfectly consistent with the profoundest contempt and injustice, degrades the object of it quite as much, though it oppresses him less, than the cruelty practiced upon his fellows. I had several of these favorite slaves presented to me, and one or two little Negro children, who their owners assured me were quite pets. The only real service which this arbitrary good will did to the objects of it was quite involuntary and unconscious on the part of their kind masters—I mean the inevitable improvement in intelligence which resulted to them from being more constantly admitted to the intercourse of the favored white race.

I must not forget to tell you of a magnificent bald-headed eagle which Mr. [Butler] called me to look at early this morning. I had never before seen alive one of these national types of yours, and stood entranced as the noble creature swept, like a black cloud, over the river, his bald white head bent forward and shining in the sun, and his fierce eyes and beak directed toward one of the beautiful wild ducks on the water, which he had evidently marked for his prey. The poor little duck, who was not ambitious of such a glorification, dived, and the eagle hovered above the spot. After a short interval, its victim rose to the surface several yards nearer shore. The great king of birds stooped nearer, and again the watery shield was interposed. This went on until the poor waterfowl, driven by excess of fear into unwonted boldness, rose, after repeatedly diving, within a short distance of where we stood. The eagle, who, I presume, had read how we were to have dominion over the fowls of the air (bald-headed eagles included), hovered sulkily awhile over the river, and then, sailing slowly toward the woods on the opposite shore, alighted and furled his great wings on a huge cypress limb, that stretched itself out against the blue sky, like the arm of a giant, for the giant bird to perch upon.

I am amusing myself by attempting to beautify, in some sort, this residence of ours. Immediately at the back of it runs a ditch, about three feet wide, which empties and fills twice a day with the tide. This lies like a moat on two sides of the house. The opposite bank is a steep dike, with a footpath along the top. One or two willows droop over this very interesting ditch, and I thought I would add to their company some Magnolias and myrtles, so as to make a little evergreen plantation round the house. I went to the swamp reserves I have before mentioned to you, and chose some beautiful bushes—among others, a very fine young pine, at which our overseer and all the Negroes expressed much contemptuous surprise; for, though the tree is beautiful, it is also common, and with them, as with wiser folk, it is "nothing pleases but rare accidents." In spite of their disparaging remarks, however, I persisted in having my pine tree planted, and I assure you it formed a very pleasing variety among the broad, smooth-leaved evergreens about it. While forming my plantation, I had a brand thrown into a bed of tall yellow sedges which screen the brimming waters of the noble river from our parlor window, and which I therefore wished removed. The small sample of a Southern conflagration which ensued was very picturesque, the flames devouring the light growth, absolutely licking it off the ground, while the curling smoke drew off in misty wreaths across the river. The heat was intense, and I thought how exceedingly and unpleasantly warm one must feel in the midst of such a forest burning as Cooper describes. Having worked my appointed task in the garden, I rowed over to Darien and back, the rosy sunset changing meantime to starry evening, as beautiful as the first the sky ever was arrayed in.

I saw an advertisement this morning in the paper which occasioned me much thought. Mr. J[ames Hamilton] C[ouper] and a Mr. N[ightingale], two planters of this neighborhood, have contracted to dig a canal, called the Brunswick Canal [2] and, not having hands enough for the work, advertise at the same time for Negroes on hire and for Irish laborers. Now the Irishmen are to have twenty dollars a month wages, and to be "found" (to use the technical phrase), which finding means abundant food, and the best accommodations which can be procured for them. The Negroes are hired from their masters, who will be paid, of course, as high a price as they can obtain for them—probably a very high one, as the demand for them is urgent—they, in the meantime, receiving no wages, and nothing more than the miserable Negro

[2] In 1834 a group of sea-island planters secured from the State of Georgia an Act incorporating the Brunswick Canal and Railroad Company, to build a canal and/or railroad connecting Brunswick with the Altamaha River. The enterprise strove to interest Boston capital, and commenced cutting the canal in 1837. Fanny read the canal contractors' advertisements in the Brunswick *Advocate*, the local weekly newspaper. For further details see Loammi Baldwin, *Report on the Brunswick Canal and Railroad Company* (Boston, 1836).

fare of rice and corn grits. Of course the Irishmen and these slaves are not allowed to work together, but are kept at separate stations on the canal. This is every way politic, for the low Irish seem to have the same sort of hatred of Negroes which sects, differing but little in their tenets, have for each other. The fact is, that a condition in their own country nearly similar has made the poor Irish almost as degraded a class of beings as the Negroes are here, and their insolence toward them, and hatred of them, are precisely in proportion to the resemblance between them. This hiring out of Negroes is a horrid aggravation of the miseries of their condition; for if, on the plantations, and under the masters to whom they belong, their labor is severe and their food inadequate, think what it must be when they are hired out for a stipulated sum to a temporary employer, who has not even the interest which it is pretended an owner may feel in the welfare of his slaves, but whose chief aim it must necessarily be to get as much out of them, and expend as little on them, as possible. Ponder this new form of iniquity, and believe me ever your most sincerely attached.

VII

Roswell King, Jr.

Dearest E[lizabeth],

After finishing my last letter to you, I went out into the clear starlight to breathe the delicious mildness of the air, and was surprised to hear, rising from one of the houses of the settlement, a hymn sung apparently by a number of voices. The next morning I inquired the meaning of this, and was informed that those Negroes on the plantation who were members of the Church were holding a prayer meeting. There is an immensely strong devotional feeling among these poor people. The worst of it is, that it is zeal without understanding, and profits them but little; yet light is light, even that poor portion that may stream through a keyhole, and I welcome this most ignorant profession of religion in Mr. [Butler]'s dependents as the herald of better and brighter things for them. Some of the planters are entirely inimical to any such proceedings, and neither allow their Negroes to attend worship, or to congregate together for religious purposes, and truly I think they are wise in their own generation. On other plantations, again, the same rigid discipline is not observed; and some planters and overseers go even farther than toleration, and encourage these devotional exercises and professions of religion, having actually discovered that a man may become more faithful and trustworthy, even as a slave, who acknowledges the higher influences of Christianity, no matter in how small a degree. Slaveholding clergymen, and certain piously inclined planters, undertake, accordingly, to enlighten these poor creatures upon these matters, with a safe understanding, however, of what truth is to be given to them, and what is not; how much they may learn to become better slaves, and how much they may not learn, lest they cease to be slaves at all. The process is a very ticklish one, and but for the Northern public opinion, which is now pressing the slaveholders close, I dare say would not be attempted at all. As it is, they are putting their own throats and their own souls in jeopardy by this very endeavor to serve God and Mammon. The light that they are letting in between their fingers will presently strike them blind, and the mighty flood of truth which they are straining through a sieve to the thirsty lips of their slaves, sweep them away like straws from their cautious moorings, and overwhelm them in its great deeps, to the waters of which man may in nowise say, thus far shall ye come and no farther.

The community I now speak of, the white population of Darien, should be a religious one, to judge by the number of churches it maintains. However, we know the old proverb, and, at that rate, it may not be so godly after all. Mr. [Butler] and his brother have been called upon at various times to subscribe to them all; and I saw this morning a most fervent appeal, extremely ill-spelled, from a gentleman living in the neighborhood of the town, and whose slaves are notoriously ill-treated, reminding Mr. [Butler] of the precious souls of his human cattle, and requesting a farther donation for the Baptist Church, of which most of the people here are members. Now this man is known to be a hard master; his Negro houses are sheds not fit to stable beasts in; his slaves are ragged, half-naked, and miserable; yet he is urgent for their religious comforts, and writes to Mr. [Butler] about "their souls—their precious souls." He was over here a few days ago, and pressed me very much to attend his church. I told him I would not go to a church where the people who worked for us were parted off from us as if they had the pest, and we should catch it of them. I asked him, for I was curious to know, how they managed to administer the sacrament to a mixed congregation? He replied, oh, very easily; that the white portion of the assembly received it first, and the blacks afterward. *A new commandment I give unto you, that ye love one another, even as I have loved you.* Oh, what a shocking mockery! However, they show their faith, at all events, in the declaration that God is no respecter of persons, since they do not pretend to exclude from His table those whom they most certainly would not admit to their own.

I have, as usual, allowed this letter to lie by, dear E[lizabeth], not in the hope of the occurrence of any event—for that is hopeless—but until my daily avocations allowed me leisure to resume it, and afforded me, at the same time, matter wherewith to do so. I really never was so busy in all my life as I am here. I sit at the receipt of custom (involuntarily enough) from morning till night. No time, no place, affords me a respite from my innumerable petitioners; and whether I be asleep or awake, reading, eating, or walking—in the kitchen, my bedroom, or the parlor—they flock in with urgent entreaties and pitiful stories, and my conscience forbids my ever postponing their business for any other matter; for, with shame and grief of heart I say it, by their unpaid labor I live —their nakedness clothes me, and their heavy toil maintains me in luxurious idleness. Surely the least I can do is to hear these, my most injured benefactors; and, indeed, so intense in me is the sense of the injury they receive from me and mine, that I should scarce dare refuse them the very clothes from my back, or food from my plate, if they asked me for it.

In taking my daily walk round the banks yesterday, I found that I was walking over violet roots. The season is too little advanced for them to be in bloom, and I could not find out whether they were the fragrant violet or not.

Mr. [Butler] has been much gratified today by the arrival of Mr. K[ing],[1] who, with his father, for nineteen years was the sole manager of these estates, and discharged his laborious task with great ability and fidelity toward his employers. How far he understood his duties to the slaves, or whether, indeed, an overseer can, in the nature of things, acknowledge any duty to them, is another question. He is a remarkable man, and is much respected for his integrity and honorable dealing by everybody here. His activity and energy are wonderful; and the mere fact of his having charge of for nineteen years, and personally governing, without any assistance whatever, seven hundred people scattered over three large tracts of land, at a considerable distance from each other, certainly bespeaks efficiency and energy of a very uncommon order. The character I had heard of him from Mr. [Butler] had excited a great deal of interest in me, and I was very glad of this opportunity of seeing a man who for so many years had been sovereign over the poor people here. I met him walking on the banks with Mr. [Butler] as I returned from my own ramble, during which nothing occurred or appeared to interest me, except, by-the-by, my unexpectedly coming quite close to one of those magnificent scarlet birds which abound here, and which dart across your path like a winged flame. Nothing can surpass the beauty of their plumage, and their voice is excellently melodious—they are lovely.

My companions, when I do not request the attendance of my friend Jack, are a couple of little terriers, who are endowed to perfection with the ugliness and the intelligence of their race; they are of infinite service on the plantation, as, owing to the immense quantity of grain, and chaff, and such matters, rats and mice abound in the mills and storehouses. I crossed the threshing floor today—a very large square, perfectly level, raised by artificial means about half a foot from the ground, and covered equally all

[1] Roswell was the given name of both father and son. The references in this and the following chapter are to Roswell King, Jr.

over, so as to lie quite smooth, with some preparation of tar. It lies immediately between the house and the steam mill, and on it much of the Negroes' work is done—the first threshing is given to the rice, and other labors are carried on. As I walked across it to-day, passing through the busy groups, chiefly of women, that covered it, I came opposite to one of the drivers, who held in his hand his whip, the odious insignia of his office. I took it from him; it was a short stick of moderate size, with a thick square leather thong attached to it. As I held it in my hand, I did not utter a word; but I conclude, as is often the case, my face spoke what my tongue did not, for the driver said: "Oh, missis, me use it for measure; me seldom strike nigger with it." For one moment I thought I must carry the hateful implement into the house with me. An instant's reflection, however, served to show me how useless such a proceeding would be. The people are not mine, nor their drivers, nor their whips. I should but have impeded, for a few hours, the man's customary office, and a new scourge would have been easily provided, and I should have done nothing, perhaps worse than nothing.

After dinner I had a most interesting conversation with Mr. K[ing]. Among other subjects, he gave me a lively and curious description of the yeomanry of Georgia, more properly termed pinelanders. Have you visions now of well-to-do farmers with comfortable homesteads, decent habits, industrious, intelligent, cheerful, and thrifty? Such, however, is not the yeomanry of Georgia. Labor being here the especial portion of slaves, it is thenceforth degraded, and considered unworthy of all but slaves. No white man, therefore, of any class puts hand to work of any kind soever. This is an exceedingly dignified way of proving their gentility for the lazy planters who prefer an idle life of semistarvation and barbarism to the degradation of doing anything themselves; but the effect on the poorer whites of the country is terrible. I speak now of the scattered white population, who, too poor to possess land or slaves, and having no means of living in the towns, squat (most appropriately is it so termed) either on other men's land or government districts—always here swamp or pine barren—and claim masterdom over the place they invade till ejected by the rightful proprietors. These wretched creatures will not, for they are whites (and labor belongs to blacks and slaves alone here), labor for their own subsistence. They are hardly protected from the weather by the rude shelters they frame for themselves in the midst of these dreary woods. Their food is chiefly supplied by shooting the wildfowl and venison, and stealing from the cultivated patches of the plantations nearest at hand. Their clothes hang about them in filthy tatters, and the combined squalor and fierceness of their appearance is really frightful.

This population is the direct growth of slavery. The planters are loud in their execrations of these miserable vagabonds; yet they do not see that so long as labor is considered the disgraceful portion of slaves, these free men will hold it nobler to starve or steal than till the earth, with none but the despised blacks for fellow laborers. The blacks themselves—such is the infinite power of custom—acquiesce in this notion, and, as I have told you, consider it the lowest degradation in a white to use any exertion. I wonder, considering the burdens they have seen me lift, the digging, the planting, the rowing, and the walking I do, that they do not utterly contemn me, and, indeed, they seem lost in amazement at it.

Talking of these pinelanders—gypsies, without any of the romantic associations that belong to the latter people—led us to the origin of such a population, slavery; and you may be sure I listened with infinite interest to the opinions of a man of uncommon shrewdness and sagacity, who was born in the very bosom of it, and has passed his whole life among slaves. If anyone is competent to judge of its effects, such a man is the one; and this was his verdict: "I hate slavery with all my heart; I consider it an absolute curse wherever it exists. It will keep those states where it does exist fifty years behind the others in improvement and prosperity."

Farther on in the conversation he made this most remarkable

observation: "As for its being an irremediable evil—a thing not to be helped or got rid of—that's all nonsense; for, as soon as people become convinced that it is their interest to get rid of it, they will soon find the means to do so, depend upon it."

And undoubtedly this is true. This is not an age, nor yours a country, where a large mass of people will long endure what they perceive to be injurious to their fortunes and advancement. Blind as people often are to their highest and truest interests, your countryfolk have generally shown remarkable acuteness in finding out where their worldly progress suffered let or hindrance, and have removed it with laudable alacrity. Now the fact is not at all as we at the North are sometimes told, that the Southern slaveholders deprecate the evils of slavery quite as much as we do; that they see all its miseries; that, moreover, they are most anxious to get rid of the whole thing, but want the means to do so, and submit most unwillingly to a necessity from which they cannot extricate themselves. All this I thought might be true before I went to the South, and often has the charitable supposition checked the condemnation which was indignantly rising to my lips against these murderers of their brethren's peace. A little reflection, however, even without personal observation, might have convinced me that this could not be the case. If the majority of Southerners were satisfied that slavery was contrary to their worldly fortunes, slavery would be at an end from that very moment; but the fact is—and I have it not only from observation of my own, but from the distinct statement of some of the most intelligent Southern men that I have conversed with—the only obstacle to immediate abolition throughout the South is the immense value of the human property, and, to use the words of a very distinguished Carolinian, who thus ended a long discussion we had on the subject: "I'll tell you why abolition is impossible: because every healthy Negro can fetch a thousand dollars in the Charleston market at this moment." And this opinion, you see, tallies perfectly with the testimony of Mr. K[ing].

He went on to speak of several of the slaves on this estate as persons quite remarkable for their fidelity and intelligence, instancing old Molly, Ned the engineer, who has the superintendence of the steam engine in the rice mill, and headman Frank, of whom, indeed, he wound up the eulogium by saying he had quite the principles of a white man, which I thought most equivocal praise, but he did not intend it as such. As I was complaining to Mr. [Butler] of the terribly neglected condition of the dikes, which are in some parts so overgrown with gigantic briers that it is really impossible to walk over them, and the trench on one hand, and river on the other, afford one extremely disagreeable alternatives, Mr. K[ing] cautioned me to be particularly on my guard not to step on the thorns of the orange tree. These, indeed, are formidable spikes, and, he assured me, were peculiarly poisonous to the flesh. Some of the most painful and tedious wounds he had ever seen, he said, were incurred by the Negroes running these large green thorns into their feet.

This led him to speak of the glory and beauty of the orange trees on the island before a certain uncommonly severe winter, a few years ago, destroyed them all. For five miles round the banks grew a double row of noble orange trees, as large as our orchard apple trees, covered with golden fruit and silver flowers. It must have been a most magnificent spectacle, and Captain F[raser], too, told me, in speaking of it, that he had brought Basil Hall [2] here in the season of the trees blossoming, and he had said it was as well worth crossing the Atlantic to see that as to see the Niagara. Of all these noble trees nothing now remains but the roots, which

---

[2] Basil Hall visited the Sea Islands in the winter of 1827–8 with his wife, Margaret, and his daughter, Eliza. Hall's account of this visit (*Travels in North America*, 3rd ed. [Edinburgh: 1830], III, 215 ff.) does not refer to Butler Island, but it is mentioned in a letter from Margaret Hall to her sister Jane. "In coming from Hopeton to Darien," she wrote, "we stopped at Butler's Island, the most valuable plantation on this river. . . . We walked across the island, on which there is the greatest number of oranges, sour oranges, that I have ever seen." *Letters 1827–28*, No. 21: Library of Congress Mss.

bear witness to their size, and some young sprouts shooting up, affording some hope that, in the course of years, the island may wear its bridal garland again. One huge stump close to the door is all that remains of an enormous tree that overtopped the house, from the upper windows of which oranges have been gathered from off its branches, and which, one year, bore the incredible number of 8,542 oranges. Mr. K[ing] assured me of this as a positive fact, of which he had at the time made the entry in his journal, considering such a crop from a single tree well worthy of record.

Mr. [Butler] was called out this evening to listen to a complaint of overwork from a gang of pregnant women. I did not stay to listen to the details of their petition, for I am unable to command myself on such occasions, and Mr. [Butler] seemed positively degraded in my eyes as he stood enforcing upon these women the necessity of their fulfilling their appointed tasks. How honorable he would have appeared to me begrimed with the sweat and soil of the coarsest manual labor, to what he then seemed, setting forth to these wretched, ignorant women, as a duty, their unpaid exacted labor! I turned away in bitter disgust. I hope this sojourn among Mr. [Butler]'s slaves may not lessen my respect for him, but I fear it; for the details of slaveholding are so unmanly, letting alone every other consideration, that I know not how anyone with the spirit of a man can condescend to them.

I have been out again on the river, rowing. I find nothing new. Swamps crowned with perfect evergreens are the only land (that's Irish!) about here, and, of course, turn which way I will, the natural features of river and shore are the same. I do not weary of these most exquisite watery woods, but you will of my mention of them, I fear. Adieu.

VIII

Sinda

Dearest E[lizabeth],

Since I last wrote to you I have been actually engaged in receiving and returning visits; for even to this *ultima Thule* of all civilization do these polite usages extend. I have been called upon by several families residing in and about Darien, and rowed over in due form to acknowledge the honor. How shall I describe Darien to you? The abomination of desolation is but a poor type of its forlorn appearance, as, half-buried in sand, its straggling, tumble-down wooden houses peer over the muddy bank of the thick slimy river. The whole town lies in a bed of sand: sidewalks, or mid-walks, there be none distinct from each other; at every step I took my feet were ankle deep in the soil, and I had cause to rejoice that I was booted for the occasion. Our worthy doctor, whose lady I was going to visit, did nothing but regret that I had not allowed him to provide me a carriage, though the distance between his house and the landing is not a quarter of a mile. The magnitude of the exertion seemed to fill him with amazement, and he over and over again repeated how impossible it would be to prevail on any of the ladies there to take such a walk. The houses seemed scattered about here and there, apparently without any design, and looked, for the most part, either unfinished or ruinous. One feature of the scene alone recalled the villages of New England—the magnificent oaks, which seemed to add to the meanness and insignificance of the human dwellings they overshadowed by their enormous size and grotesque forms. They reminded me of the elms of New Haven and Stockbridge. They are quite as large, and more picturesque, from their somber foliage and the infinite variety of their forms—a beauty wanting in the New England elm, which invariably rises and spreads in a way which, though the most graceful in the world, at length palls on the capricious human eye, which seeks, above all other beauties, variety. Our doctor's wife is a New England woman; how can she live here? She had the fair eyes and hair, and fresh complexion of your part of the country, and its dearly beloved snuffle, which seemed actually dearly beloved when I heard it down here. She gave me some violets and narcissus, already blossoming profusely—in January—and expressed, like her husband, a thousand regrets at my having walked so far.

A transaction of the most amusing nature occurred today with regard to the resources of the Darien Bank, and the mode of carrying on business in that liberal and enlightened institution, the funds of which I should think quite incalculable—impalpable, certainly, they appeared by our experience this morning.

The river, as we came home, was covered with Ocone[e] boxes. It is well for them they are so shallow-bottomed, for we rasped sand all the way home through the cut and in the shallows of the river.

I have been over the rice mill, under the guidance of the overseer and headman Frank, and have been made acquainted with the whole process of threshing the rice, which is extremely curious; and here I may again mention another statement of Miss Martineau's, which I am told is, and I should suppose, from what I see here, must be a mistake. She states that the chaff of the husks of the rice is used as a manure for the fields, whereas the people have today assured me that it is of so hard, stony, and untractable a nature as to be literally good for nothing. Here I know it is thrown away by cartloads into the river, where its only use appears to be to act like ground bait, and attract a vast quantity of small fish to its vicinity. The number of hands employed in this threshing mill is very considerable, and the whole establishment, comprising the fires, and boilers, and machinery of a powerful steam engine, are all under Negro superintendence and direction. After this survey I occupied myself with my infant plantation of evergreens round the dike, in the midst of which interesting pursuit I was interrupted by a visit from Mr. B[arrett], a neighboring planter,[1] who came to transact some business with Mr. [Butler] about rice which he had sent to our mill to have threshed, and the price to be paid for such threshing. The Negroes have presented a petition today that they may be allowed to have a ball in honor of our arrival, which demand has been acceded to, and furious preparations are being set on foot.

On visiting the infirmary today, I was extremely pleased with the increased cleanliness and order observable in all the rooms. Two little filthy children, however, seemed to be still under the *ancien régime* of nonablution; but upon my saying to the old nurse Molly, in whose ward they were: "Why, Molly, I don't believe you have bathed those children today," she answered, with infinite dignity: "Missis no b'lieve me wash um pickaninny! and yet she 'tress me wid all um niggar when 'em sick." The injured innocence and lofty conscious integrity of this speech silenced and abashed me; and yet I can't help it, but I don't believe to this present hour

---

[1] This is a tentative identification. Jacob Barrett was the owner of a plantation on an island directly adjacent to Butler Island and known by the various names of Champney's, Tunno's, and Barrett's Island after the planters who at one time or another owned or cultivated it. Mr. B—— might also have been Thomas Bryan, owner of Broughton Island. This seems less likely. We know that Bryan, unlike the local planters who used the Butler mill, was in the habit of threshing his own rice. But Fanny tells us explicitly that on this occasion the discussion had to do with rice "which he had sent to our mill to have threshed."

that those children had had any experience of water, at least not washing water, since they first came into the world.

I rowed over to Darien again, to make some purchases, yesterday, and, inquiring the price of various articles, could not but wonder to find them at least three times as dear as in your Northern villages. The profits of these Southern shopkeepers (who for the most part are thoroughbred Yankees, with the true Yankee propensity to trade, no matter on how dirty a counter, or in what manner of wares) are enormous. The prices they ask for everything, from colored calicoes for Negro dresses to pianofortes (one of which, for curiosity sake, I inquired the value of), are fabulous, and such as none but the laziest and most reckless people in the world would consent to afford. On our return we found the water in the cut so extremely low that we were obliged to push the boat through it, and did not accomplish it without difficulty. The banks of this canal, when they are thus laid bare, present a singular appearance enough—two walls of solid mud, through which matted, twisted, twined, and tangled, like the natural veins of wood, runs an everlasting net of indestructible roots, the thousand toes of huge cypress feet. The trees have been cut down long ago from the soil, but these fangs remain in the earth without decaying for an incredible space of time. This long endurance of immersion is one of the valuable properties of these cypress roots; but, though excellent binding stuff for the sides of a canal, they must be pernicious growth in any land used for cultivation that requires deep tillage. On entering the Altamaha, we found the tide so low that we were much obstructed by the sandbanks, which, but for their constant shifting, would presently take entire possession of this noble stream, and render it utterly impassable from shore to shore, as it already is in several parts of the channel at certain seasons of the tide.

On landing, I was seized hold of by a hideous old Negress, named Sinda, who had come to pay me a visit, and of whom Mr. [Butler] told me a strange anecdote. She passed at one time for a prophetess among her fellow slaves on the plantation, and had acquired such an ascendency over them that, having given out, after the fashion of Mr. Miller,[2] that the world was to come to an end at a certain time, and that not a very remote one, the belief in her assertion took such possession of the people on the estate that they refused to work, and the rice and cotton fields were threatened with an indefinite fallow in consequence of this strike on the part of the cultivators. Mr. K[ing], who was then overseer of the property, perceived the impossibility of arguing, remonstrating, or even flogging this solemn panic out of the minds of the slaves. The great final emancipation which they believed at hand had stripped even the lash of its prevailing authority, and the terrors of an overseer for once were as nothing, in the terrible expectation of the advent of the universal Judge of men. They were utterly impracticable; so, like a very shrewd man as he was, he acquiesced in their determination not to work; but he expressed to them his belief that Sinda was mistaken, and he warned her that if, at the appointed time, it proved so, she would be severely punished. I do not know whether he confided to the slaves what he thought likely to be the result if she was in the right; but poor Sinda was in the wrong. Her day of judgment came indeed, and a severe one it proved, for Mr. K[ing] had her tremendously flogged, and her end of things ended much like Mr. Miller's; but whereas he escaped unhanged in spite of his atrocious practices upon the fanaticism and credulity of his countrypeople, the spirit of false prophecy was mercilessly scourged out of her, and the faith of her people of course reverted from her to the omnipotent lash again. Think what a dream that must have been while it lasted for those infinitely oppressed people—freedom without entering it by the grim gate of death, brought down to them at once by the second coming of Christ, whose first advent has left them yet so far from it! Farewell; it makes me giddy to think of having been a slave while that delusion lasted and after it vanished.

[2] William Miller's millenialist movement reached its climax in the years 1842–4, i.e., three to four years after Fanny had left Georgia.

IX

Slave Settlements

[January, 1839]

Dearest E[lizabeth],

I received early this morning a visit from a young Negro called Morris, who came to request permission to be baptized. The master's leave is necessary for this ceremony of acceptance into the bosom of the Christian Church; so all that can be said is, that it is to be hoped the rite itself may *not* be indispensable for salvation, as, if Mr. [Butler] had thought proper to refuse Morris's petition, he must infallibly have been lost, in spite of his own best wishes to the contrary. I could not, in discoursing with him, perceive that he had any very distinct ideas of the advantages he expected to derive from the ceremony; but perhaps they appeared all the greater for being a little vague. I have seldom seen a more pleasing appearance than that of this young man; his figure was tall and straight, and his face, which was of a perfect oval, rejoiced in the grace, very unusual among his people, of a fine high forehead, and the much more frequent one of a remarkably gentle and sweet expression. He was, however, jet-black, and certainly did not owe these personal advantages to any mixture in his blood. There is a certain African tribe from which the West Indian slave market is chiefly recruited, who have these same characteristic features, and do not at all present the ignoble and ugly Negro type, so much more commonly seen here. They are a tall, powerful people, with remarkably fine figures, regular features, and a singularly warlike and fierce disposition, in which respect they also differ from the race of Negroes existing on the American plantations. I do not think Morris, however, could have belonged to this tribe, though perhaps Othello did, which would at once settle the difficulties of those commentators who, abiding by Iago's very disagreeable suggestions as to his purely African appearance, are painfully compelled to forego the mitigation of supposing him a Moor and not a Negro. Did I ever tell you of my dining in Boston, at the H———'s,[1] on my first visit to that city, and sitting by Mr. John Quincy Adams, who, talking to me about Desdemona, assured me, with a most serious expression of sincere disgust, that he considered all her misfortunes as a very just judgment upon her for having married a "nigger?" I think, if some ingenious American actor of the present day, bent upon realizing Shakespeare's finest conceptions, with all the advantages of modern enlightenment, could contrive to slip in that opprobrious title, with a true South Carolinian antiabolitionist expression, it might really be made quite a point for Iago, as, for instance, in his first soliloquy—"I hate the nigger," given in proper Charleston or Savannah fashion, I am sure would tell far better than "I hate the Moor." Only think, E[lizabeth], what a very new order of interest the whole tragedy might receive, acted throughout from this standpoint, as the Germans call it in this country, and called *Amalgamation, or the Black Bridal.*

On their return from their walk this afternoon the children brought home some pieces of sugar cane, of which a small quantity

[1] The house at which Charles and Fanny Kemble dined with John Quincy Adams in Boston was Dr. George Parkman's, according to Adams. The meeting took place on May 11, 1833, and in his recollection the conversation turned mainly upon horsemanship. *Memoirs of John Quincy Adams,* Charles F. Adams, ed. (Philadelphia: 1874–7), VIII, 544.

grows on the island. When I am most inclined to deplore the condition of the poor slaves on these cotton and rice plantations, the far more intolerable existence and harder labor of those employed on the sugar estates occurs to me, sometimes producing the effect of a lower circle in Dante's "Hell of Horrors," opening beneath the one where he seems to have reached the climax of infernal punishment. You may have seen this vegetable, and must at any rate, I should think, be familiar with it by description. It is a long green reed, like the stalk of the maize, or Indian corn, only it shoots up to a much more considerable height, and has a consistent pith, which, together with the rind itself, is extremely sweet. The principal peculiarity of this growth, as perhaps you know, is that they are laid horizontally in the earth when they are planted for propagation, and from each of the notches or joints of the recumbent cane a young shoot is produced at the germinating season.

A very curious and interesting circumstance to me just now in the neighborhood is the projection of a canal, to be called the Brunswick Canal, which, by cutting through the lower part of the mainland, toward the southern extremity of Great St. Simons Island, is contemplated as a probable and powerful means of improving the prosperity of the town of Brunswick, by bringing it into immediate communication with the Atlantic. The scheme, which I think I have mentioned to you before, is, I believe, chiefly patronized by your state's folk—Yankee enterprise and funds being very essential elements, it appears to me, in all Southern projects and achievements. This speculation, however, from all I hear of the difficulties of the undertaking, from the nature of the soil, and the impossibility almost of obtaining efficient labor, is not very likely to arrive at any very satisfactory result; and, indeed, I find it hard to conceive how this part of Georgia can possibly produce a town which can be worth the digging of a canal, even to Yankee speculators. There is one feature of the undertaking, however, which more than all the others excites my admiration, namely, that Irish laborers have been advertised for to work upon the canal, and the terms offered them are twenty dollars a month per man and their board. Now these men will have for fellow laborers Negroes who not only will receive nothing at all for their work, but who will be hired by the contractors and directors of the works from their masters, to whom they will hand over the price of their slaves' labor; while it will be the interest of the person hiring them not only to get as much work as possible out of them, but also to provide them as economically with food, combining the two praiseworthy endeavors exactly in such judicious proportions as not to let them neutralize each other. You will observe that this case of a master hiring out his slaves to another employer, from whom he receives their rightful wages, is a form of slavery which, though extremely common, is very seldom adverted to in those arguments for the system which are chiefly founded upon the master's presumed regard for his human property. People who have ever let a favorite house to the temporary occupation of strangers can form a tolerable idea of the difference between one's own regard and care of one's goods and chattels and that of the most conscientious tenant; and whereas I have not yet observed that ownership is a very effectual protection to the slaves against ill-usage and neglect, I am quite prepared to admit that it is a vastly better one than the temporary interest which a lessee can feel in the livestock he hires, out of whom it is his manifest interest to get as much, and into whom to put as little, as possible. Yet thousands of slaves throughout the Southern states are thus handed over by the masters who own them to masters who do not; and it does not require much demonstration to prove that their estate is not always the more gracious.

Now you must not suppose that these same Irish free laborers and Negro slaves will be permitted to work together at this Brunswick Canal. They say that this would be utterly impossible; for why? there would be tumults, and risings, and broken heads, and bloody bones, and all the natural results of Irish intercommunion with their fellow creatures, no doubt—perhaps even a little more riot and violence than merely comports with their usual habits of Milesian [2] good fellowship; for, say the masters, the Irish hate the Negroes more even than the Americans do, and there would be no bound to their murderous animosity if they were brought in contact with them on the same portion of the works of the Brunswick Canal. Doubtless there is some truth in this; the Irish laborers who might come hither would be apt enough, according to a universal moral law, to visit upon others the injuries they had received from others. They have been oppressed enough themselves to be oppressive whenever they have a chance; and the despised and degraded condition of the blacks, presenting to them a very ugly resemblance of their own home, circumstances naturally excite in them the exercise of the disgust and contempt of which they themselves are very habitually the objects; and that such circular distribution of wrongs may not only be pleasant, but have something like the air of retributive right to very ignorant folks, is not much to be wondered at. Certain is the fact, however, that the worst of all tyrants is the one who has been a slave; and, for that matter (and I wonder if the Southern slaveholders hear it with the same ear that I do, and ponder it with the same mind?), the command of one slave to another is altogether the most uncompromising utterance of insolent truculent despotism that it ever fell to my lot to witness or listen to. "You nigger—I say, you black nigger—you no hear me call you—what for you no run quick?"

All this, dear E[lizabeth], is certainly reasonably in favor of division of labor on the Brunswick Canal; but the Irish are not only quarrelers, and rioters, and fighters, and drinkers, and despisers of niggers—they are a passionate, impulsive, warmhearted, generous people, much given to powerful indignations, which break out suddenly when not compelled to smoulder sullenly—pestilent sympathizers too, and with a sufficient dose of American atmos-

[2] The Milesian tales were a collection of witty and bawdy stories brought together by Aristides of Miletus. Though they have not sur- vived, they have given their name to the genre and to the kind of company in which such tales are told.

pheric air in their lungs, properly mixed with a right proportion of ardent spirits, there is no saying but what they might actually take to sympathy with the slaves, and I leave you to judge of the possible consequences. You perceive, I am sure, that they can by no means be allowed to work together on the Brunswick Canal.

I have been taking my daily walk round the island, and visited the sugar mill and the threshing mill again.

Mr. [Butler] has received another letter from Parson S[mith] upon the subject of more church building in Darien. It seems that there has been a very general panic in this part of the slave states lately, occasioned by some injudicious missionary preaching, which was pronounced to be of a decidedly abolitionist tendency. The offensive preachers, after sowing God only knows what seed in this tremendous soil, where one grain of knowledge may spring up a gigantic upas tree to the prosperity of its most unfortunate possessors, were summarily and ignominiously expelled; and now some shortsighted, uncomfortable Christians in these parts, among others this said Parson S[mith], are possessed with the notion that something had better be done to supply the want created by the cessation of these dangerous exhortations, to which the Negroes have listened, it seems, with complacency. Parson S[mith] seems to think that, having driven out two preachers, it might be well to build one church, where, at any rate, the Negroes might be exhorted in a safe and salutary manner, *"qui ne leur donnerait point d'idées,"* [3] as the French would say. Upon my word, E[lizabeth], I used to pity the slaves, and I do pity them with all my soul; but, oh dear! oh dear! their case is a bed of roses to that of their owners, and I would go to the slave block in Charleston tomorrow cheerfully to be purchased if my only option was to go thither as a purchaser. I was looking over this morning, with a most indescribable mixture of feelings, a pamphlet published in the South upon the subject of the religious instruction of the slaves, and the difficulty of the task undertaken by these reconcilers of God and

[3] Which would not put any dangerous ideas into their heads.

Mammon really seems to me nothing short of piteous. "We must give our involuntary servants" (they seldom call them slaves, for it is an ugly word in an American mouth, you know) "Christian enlightenment," say they; and where shall they begin? "Whatsoever ye would that men should do unto you, do ye also unto them"? No; but "Servants, obey your masters"; and there, I think, they naturally come to a full stop. This pamphlet forcibly suggested to me the necessity for a slave Church Catechism, and also, indeed, if it were possible, a slave Bible. If these heaven-blinded Negro enlighteners persist in their pernicious plan of making Christians of their cattle, something of the sort must be done, or they will infallibly cut their own throats with this two-edged sword of truth, to which they should in no wise have laid their hand, and would not, doubtless, but that it is now thrust at them so threateningly that they have no choice. Again and again, how much I do pity them!

I have been walking to another cluster of Negro huts, known as Number Two, and here we took a boat and rowed across the broad brimming Altamaha to a place called Woodville, on a part of the estate named Hammersmith, though why that very thriving suburb of the great city of London should have been selected as the name of the lonely plank house in the midst of the pinewoods which here enjoys that title I can not conceive, unless it was suggested by the contrast. This settlement is on the mainland, and consists apparently merely of this house (to which the overseer retires when the poisonous malaria of the rice plantations compels him to withdraw from it), and a few deplorably miserable hovels, which appeared to me to be chiefly occupied by the most decrepit and infirm samples of humanity it was ever my melancholy lot to behold.

The air of this pine barren is salubrious compared with that of the rice islands, and here some of the oldest slaves who will not die yet, and cannot work any more, are sent, to go, as it were, out of the way. Remote recollections of former dealings with civilized human beings in the shape of masters and overseers seemed to me to be the only idea not purely idiotic in the minds of the poor old tottering creatures that gathered to stare with dim and blear eyes at me and my children.

There were two very aged women, who had seen different, and, to their faded recollections, better times, who spoke to me of Mr. [Butler]'s grandfather, and of the early days of the plantation, when they were young and strong, and worked as their children and grandchildren were now working, neither for love nor yet for money. One of these old crones, a hideous, withered, wrinkled piece of womanhood, said that she had worked as long as her strength had lasted, and that then she had still been worth her keep, for, said she: "Missus, tho' we no able to work, we make little niggers for massa." Her joy at seeing her present owner was unbounded, and she kept clapping her horny hands together and exclaiming: "While there is life there is hope; we seen massa before we die." These demonstrations of regard were followed up by piteous complaints of hunger and rheumatism, and their usual requests for pittances of food and clothing, to which we responded by promises of additions in both kinds; and I was extricating myself as well as I could from my petitioners, with the assurance that I would come by-and-by and visit them again, when I felt my dress suddenly feebly jerked, and a shrill cracked voice on the other side of me exclaimed: "Missus, no go yet—no go away yet; you no see me, missus, when you come by-and-by; but," added the voice, in a sort of wail, which seemed to me as if the thought was full of misery, "you see many, many of my offspring." These melancholy words, particularly the rather unusual one at the end of the address, struck me very much. They were uttered by a creature which *was* a woman, but looked like a crooked, ill-built figure set up in a field to scare crows, with a face infinitely more like a mere animal's than any human countenance I ever beheld, and with that peculiar, wild, restless look of indefinite and, at the same time, intense sadness that is so remarkable in the countenance of some monkeys. It was almost with an effort that I commanded myself so as not to withdraw my dress from the yellow, crumpled, filthy claws that gripped it, and it was not at last without the authoritative voice of the overseer that the poor creature released her hold of me.

We returned home certainly in the very strangest vehicle that ever civilized gentlewoman traveled in—a huge sort of cart, made only of some loose boards, on which I lay, supporting myself against one of the four posts which indicated the sides of my carriage; six horned creatures, cows or bulls, drew this singular equipage, and a yelping, howling, screaming, leaping company of half-naked Negroes ran all round them, goading them with sharp sticks, frantically seizing hold of their tails, and inciting them by every conceivable and inconceivable encouragement to quick motion: thus, like one of the ancient Merovingian monarchs, I was dragged through the deep sand from the settlement back to the river, where we re-embarked for the island.

As we crossed the broad flood, whose turbid waters always look swollen as if by a series of freshets, a flight of birds sprang from the low swamp we were approaching, and literally, as it rose in the air, cast a shadow like that of a cloud, which might be said, with but little exaggeration, to darken the sun for a few seconds. How well I remember my poor Aunt Whitlock [4] describing such phenomena as of frequent occurrence in America, and the scornful incredulity with which we heard, without accepting, these legends of her Western experience! How little I then thought that I should have to cry peccavi to her memory from the bottom of such ruts, and under the shadow of such flights of winged creatures as she

[4] Elizabeth Whitlock, a sister of Charles Kemble and a well-known actress in her day, had toured the United States some forty-five years before Fanny's *Journal* was written. On returning home Mrs. Whitlock regaled the family with horrendous tales of her American experience which, as Fanny recalled, were "always received with extreme incredulity." *Records of a Girlhood*, 41.

used to describe from the muddy ways of Pennsylvania and the muddy waters of Georgia.

The vegetation is already in an active state of demonstration, sprouting into lovely pale green and vivid red-brown buds and leaflets, though it is yet early in January.

After our return home we had a visit from Mr. C[ouper],[5] one of our neighbors, an intelligent and humane man, to whose account of the qualities and characteristics of the slaves, as he had observed and experienced them, I listened with great interest. The Brunswick Canal was again the subject of conversation, and again the impossibility of allowing the Negroes and Irish to work in proximity was stated, and admitted as an indisputable fact. It strikes me with amazement to hear the hopeless doom of incapacity for progress pronounced upon these wretched slaves, when in my own country the very same order of language is perpetually applied to these very Irish, here spoken of as a sort of race of demigods by Negro comparison. And it is most true that in Ireland nothing can be more savage, brutish, filthy, idle, and incorrigibly and hopelessly helpless and incapable than the Irish appear; and yet, transplanted to your Northern states, freed from the evil influences which surround them at home, they and their children become industrious, thrifty, willing to learn, able to improve, and forming, in the course of two generations, a most valuable accession to your laboring population. How is it that it never occurs to these emphatical denouncers of the whole Negro race that the Irish at home are esteemed much as they esteem their slaves, and that the sentence pronounced against their whole country by one of the greatest men of our age, an Irishman, was precisely that

[5] This is almost certainly a reference to James Hamilton Couper, manager and part owner of Hopeton, and not to his father, John Couper, who lived at Cannon's Point on St. Simons Island. Both men were neighbors of the Butlers, but the son was one of the contractors engaged in building the Brunswick Canal, and the conversation would have turned naturally to that subject.

nothing could save, redeem, or regenerate Ireland unless, as a preparatory measure, the island were submerged, and all its inhabitants drowned off?

I have had several women at the house today asking for advice and help for their sick children: they all came from Number Two, as they call it, that is, the settlement or cluster of Negro huts nearest to the main one, where we may be said to reside. In the afternoon I went thither, and found a great many of the little children ailing: there had been an unusual mortality among them at this particular settlement this winter. In one miserable hut I heard that the baby was just dead; it was one of thirteen, many of whom had been, like itself, mercifully removed from the life of degradation and misery to which their birth appointed them; and whether it was the frequent repetition of similar losses, or an instinctive consciousness that death was indeed better than life for such children as theirs, I know not, but the father and mother, and old Rose, the nurse, who was their little baby's grandmother, all seemed apathetic, and apparently indifferent to the event. The mother merely repeated over and over again: "I've lost a many; they all goes so"; and the father, without word or comment, went out to his enforced labor.

As I left the cabin, rejoicing for them at the deliverance out of slavery of their poor child, I found myself suddenly surrounded by a swarm of young ragamuffins in every stage of partial nudity, clamoring from out of their filthy remnants of rags for donations of scarlet ribbon for the ball, which was to take place that evening. The melancholy scene I had just witnessed, and the still sadder reflection it had given rise to, had quite driven all thoughts of the approaching festivity from my mind; but the sudden demand for these graceful luxuries by Mr. [Butler]'s half-naked dependents reminded me of the grotesque mask which life wears on one of its mysterious faces; and with as much sympathy for rejoicing as my late sympathy for sorrow had left me capable of, I procured the desired ornaments. I have considerable fellow feeling for the passion for all shades of red which prevails among these dusky fellow creatures of mine, a savage propensity for that same color in all its modifications being a tendency of my own.

At our own settlement (Number One) I found everything in a high fever of preparation for the ball. A huge boat had just arrived from the cotton plantation at St. Simons, laden with the youth and beauty of that portion of the estate who had been invited to join the party; and the greetings among the arrivers and welcomers, and the heaven-defying combinations of color in the gala attire of both, surpass all my powers of description. The ball, to which of course we went, took place in one of the rooms of the infirmary. As the room had, fortunately, but few occupants, they were removed to another apartment, and, without any very tender consideration for their not very remote, though invisible sufferings, the dancing commenced, and was continued. Oh, my dear E[lizabeth], I have seen Jim Crow—the veritable James: all the contortions, and springs, and flings, and kicks, and capers you have been beguiled into accepting as indicative of him are spurious, faint, feeble, impotent—in a word, pale Northern reproductions of that ineffable black conception. It is impossible for words to describe the things these people did with their bodies, and, above all, with their faces, the whites of their eyes, and the whites of their teeth, and certain outlines which either naturally and by the grace of heaven, or by the practice of some peculiar artistic dexterity, they bring into prominent and most ludicrous display. The languishing elegance of some—the painstaking laboriousness of others—above all, the feats of a certain enthusiastic banjo player, who seemed to me to thump his instrument with every part of his body at once, at last so utterly overcame any attempt at decorous gravity on my part that I was obliged to secede; and, considering what the atmosphere was that we inhaled during the exhibition, it is only wonderful to me that we were not made ill by the double effort not to laugh, and, if possible, not to breathe.

X

Psyche

[January 21, 1839]

My dearest E[lizabeth],

A rather longer interval than usual has elapsed since I last wrote to you, but I must beg you to excuse it. I have had more than a usual amount of small daily occupations to fill my time; and, as a mere enumeration of these would not be very interesting to you, I will tell you a story which has just formed an admirable illustration for my observation of all the miseries of which this accursed system of slavery is the cause, even under the best and most humane administration of its laws and usages. Pray note it, my dear friend, for you will find, in the absence of all voluntary or even conscious cruelty on the part of the master, the best possible comment on a state of things which, without the slightest desire to injure and oppress, produces such intolerable results of injury and oppression.

We have, as a sort of under nursemaid and assistant of my dear M[argery], whose white complexion, as I wrote you, occasioned such indignation to my Southern fellow travelers, and such extreme perplexity to the poor slaves on our arrival here, a much more orthodox servant for these parts, a young woman named Psyche, but commonly called Sack, not a very graceful abbreviation of the divine heathen appellation. She cannot be much over twenty, has a very pretty figure, a graceful, gentle deportment, and a face which, but for its color (she is a dingy mulatto), would be pretty, and is extremely pleasing, from the perfect sweetness of its expression; she is always serious, not to say sad and silent, and has always an air of melancholy and timidity, that has frequently struck me very much, and would have made me think some special anxiety or sorrow must occasion it, but that God knows the whole condition of these wretched people naturally produces such a deportment, and there is no necessity to seek for special or peculiar causes to account for it. Just in proportion as I have found the slaves on this plantation intelligent and advanced beyond the general brutish level of the majority, I have observed this pathetic expression of countenance in them, a mixture of sadness and fear, the involuntary exhibition of the two feelings, which I suppose must be the predominant experience of their whole lives, regret and apprehension, not the less heavy, either of them, for being, in some degree, vague and indefinite—a sense of incalculable past loss and injury, and a dread of incalculable future loss and injury.

I have never questioned Psyche as to her sadness, because, in the first place, as I tell you, it appears to me most natural, and is observable in all the slaves whose superior natural or acquired intelligence allows of their filling situations of trust or service about the house and family; and, though I cannot and will not refuse to hear any and every tale of suffering which these unfortunates bring to me, I am anxious to spare both myself and them the pain of vain appeals to me for redress and help, which, alas! it is too often utterly out of my power to give them. It is useless, and, indeed, worse than useless, that they should see my impotent indignation and unavailing pity, and hear expressions of compassion for them, and horror at their condition, which might only prove incentives to a hopeless resistance on their part to a system, under the hideous weight of whose oppression any individual or partial revolt must be annihilated and ground into the dust. Therefore, as I tell you, I asked Psyche no questions; but, to my great astonishment, the other day M[argery] asked me if I knew to whom Psyche belonged, as the poor woman had inquired of her with much hesitation and anguish if she could tell her who owned her and her children. She has two nice little children under six years old, whom she keeps as clean and tidy, and who are sad and as silent as herself. My astonishment at this question was, as you will readily believe, not small, and I forthwith sought out Psyche for an explanation. She was thrown into extreme perturbation at finding that her question had been referred to me, and it was some time before I could sufficiently reassure her to be able to comprehend, in the midst of her reiterated entreaties for pardon, and hopes that she had not offended me, that she did not know herself who owned her. She was, at one time, the property of Mr. K[ing], the former overseer, of whom I have already spoken to you, and who has just been paying Mr. [Butler] a visit. He, like several of his predecessors in the management, has contrived to make a fortune upon it (though it yearly decreases in value to the owners, but this is the inevitable course of things in the Southern states), and has purchased a plantation of his own in Alabama, I believe, or one of the Southwestern states. Whether she still belonged to Mr. K[ing] or not she did not know, and entreated me, if she did, to endeavor to persuade Mr. [Butler] to buy her. Now you must know that this poor woman is the wife of one of Mr. [Butler]'s slaves, a fine, intelligent, active, excellent young man, whose whole family are among some of the very best specimens of character and capacity on the estate. I was so astonished at the (to me) extraordinary state of things revealed by poor Sack's petition, that I could only tell her that I had supposed all the Negroes on the plantation were Mr. [Butler]'s property, but that I would certainly inquire, and find out for her, if I could, to whom she belonged, and if I could, endeavor to get Mr. [Butler] to purchase her, if she really was not his.

Now, E[lizabeth], just conceive for one moment the state of mind of this woman, believing herself to belong to a man who in a few days was going down to one of those abhorred and dreaded Southwestern states, and who would then compel her, with her poor little children, to leave her husband and the only home she had ever known, and all the ties of affection, relationship, and association of her former life, to follow him thither, in all human probability never again to behold any living creature that she had seen before; and this was so completely a matter of course that it was not even thought necessary to apprise her positively of the fact, and the only thing that interposed between her and this most miserable fate was the faint hope that Mr. [Butler] *might have* purchased her and her children. But if he had, if this great deliverance had been vouchsafed to her, the knowledge of it was not thought necessary; and with this deadly dread at her heart she was living day after day, waiting upon me and seeing me, with my husband beside me, and my children in my arms in blessed security, safe from all separation but the one reserved in God's great providence for all His creatures. Do you think I wondered any more at the woebegone expression of her countenance, or do you think it was easy for me to restrain within prudent and proper limits the expression of my feelings at such a state of things? And she had gone on from day to day enduring this agony, till I suppose its own intolerable pressure and M[argery]'s sweet countenance and gentle sympathizing voice and manner had constrained her to lay down this great burden of sorrow at our feet.

I did not see Mr. [Butler] until the evening; but, in the meantime, meeting Mr. O——, the overseer, with whom, as I believe I have already told you, we are living here, I asked him about Psyche, and who was her proprietor, when, to my infinite surprise, he told me that *he* had bought her and her children from Mr. K[ing], who had offered them to him, saying that they would be rather troublesome to him than otherwise down where he was going. "And so," said Mr. O——, "as I had no objection to investing a little money that way, I bought them." With a heart much lightened, I flew to tell poor Psyche the news, so that, at any rate, she might be relieved from the dread of any immediate separation from her husband. You can imagine better than I can tell you what her sensations were; but she still renewed her prayer that I would, if possible, induce Mr. [Butler] to purchase her, and I promised to do so.

Early the next morning, while I was still dressing, I was suddenly startled by hearing voices in loud tones in Mr. [Butler]'s dressing room, which adjoins my bedroom, and the noise increasing until there was an absolute cry of despair uttered by some man. I could restrain myself no longer, but opened the door of communication and saw Joe, the young man, poor Psyche's husband, raving almost in a state of frenzy, and in a voice broken with sobs and almost inarticulate with passion, reiterating his determination never to leave this plantation, never to go to Alabama, never to leave his old father and mother, his poor wife and children, and dashing his hat, which he was wringing like a cloth in his hands, upon the ground, he declared he would kill himself if he was compelled to follow Mr. K[ing]. I glanced from the poor wretch to Mr. [Butler], who was standing, leaning against a table with his arms folded, occasionally uttering a few words of counsel to his slave to be quiet and not fret, and not make a fuss about what there was no help for. I retreated immediately from the horrid scene, breathless with surprise and dismay, and stood for some time in my own room, with my heart and temples throbbing to such a degree that I could hardly support myself. As soon as I recovered myself I again sought Mr. O——, and inquired of him if he knew the cause of poor Joe's distress. He then told me that Mr. [Butler], who is highly pleased with Mr. K[ing]'s past administration of his property, wished, on his departure for his newly acquired slave plantation, to give him some token of his satisfaction, and *had made him a present* of the man Joe, who had just received the intelligence that he was to go down to Alabama with his new owner the next day, leaving father, mother, wife, and children behind. You will not wonder that the man required a little judicious soothing under such circumstances, and you will also, I hope, admire the humanity of the sale of his wife and children by the owner who was going to take him to Alabama, because *they* would be encumbrances rather than otherwise down there. If Mr. K[ing] did not do this after he knew that the man was his, then Mr. [Butler] gave him to be carried down to the South after his wife and children were sold to remain in Georgia. I do not know which was the real transaction, for I have not had the heart to ask; but you will easily imagine which of the two cases I prefer believing.

When I saw Mr. [Butler] after this most wretched story became known to me in all its details, I appealed to him, for his own soul's sake, not to commit so great a cruelty. Poor Joe's agony while remonstrating with his master was hardly greater than mine while arguing with him upon this bitter piece of inhumanity —how I cried, and how I adjured, and how all my sense of justice, and of mercy, and of pity for the poor wretch, and of wretchedness at finding myself implicated in such a state of things, broke in torrents of words from my lips and tears from my eyes! God knows such a sorrow at seeing anyone I belonged to commit such an act was indeed a new and terrible experience to me, and it seemed to me that I was imploring Mr. [Butler] to save himself more than to spare these wretches. He gave me no answer whatever, and I have since thought that the intemperate vehemence of my entreaties and expostulations perhaps deserved that he should leave me as he did without one single word of reply; and miserable enough I remained.

Toward evening, as I was sitting alone, my children having gone to bed, Mr. O—— came into the room. I had but one subject in my mind; I had not been able to eat for it. I could hardly sit still for the nervous distress which every thought of these poor people filled me with. As he sat down looking over some accounts, I

said to him: "Have you seen Joe this afternoon, Mr. O——?"
(I give you our conversation as it took place.)

"Yes, ma'am; he is a great deal happier than he was this morning."

"Why, how is that?" asked I, eagerly.

"Oh, he is not going to Alabama. Mr. K[ing] heard that he had
kicked up a fuss about it" (being in despair at being torn from one's
wife and children is called *kicking up a fuss;* this is a sample of
overseer appreciation of human feelings), "and said that if the
fellow wasn't willing to go with him, he did not wish to be bothered
with any niggers down there who were to be troublesome, so he
might stay behind."

"And does Psyche know this?"

"Yes, ma'am, I suppose so."

I drew a long breath; and whereas my needle had stumbled
through the stuff I was sewing for an hour before, as if my
fingers could not guide it, the regularity and rapidity of its evolu-
tions were now quite edifying. The man was for the present safe,
and I remained silently pondering his deliverance and the whole
proceeding, and the conduct of everyone engaged in it, and, above
all, Mr. [Butler]'s share in the transaction, and I think, for the
first time, almost a sense of horrible personal responsibility and
implication took hold of my mind, and I felt the weight of an
unimagined guilt upon my conscience; and yet, God knows, this
feeling of self-condemnation is very gratuitous on my part, since
when I married Mr. [Butler] I knew nothing of these dreadful
possessions of his, and even if I had I should have been much
puzzled to have formed any idea of the state of things in which I
now find myself plunged, together with those whose well-doing is
as vital to me almost as my own.

With these agreeable reflections I went to bed. Mr. [Butler]
said not a word to me upon the subject of these poor people all
the next day, and in the meantime I became very impatient of
this reserve on his part, because I was dying to prefer my request

that he would purchase Psyche and her children, and so prevent any future separation between her and her husband, as I supposed he would not again attempt to make a present of Joe, at least to anyone who did not wish to be *bothered* with his wife and children. In the evening I was again with Mr. O—— alone in the strange, bare, wooden-walled sort of shanty which is our sitting room, and revolving in my mind the means of rescuing Psyche from her miserable suspense, a long chain of all my possessions, in the shape of bracelets, necklaces, brooches, earrings, etc., wound in glittering procession through my brain, with many hypothetical calculations of the value of each separate ornament, and the very doubtful probability of the amount of the whole being equal to the price of this poor creature and her children; and then the great power and privilege I had foregone of earning money by my own labor occurred to me, and I think, for the first time in my life, my past profession assumed an aspect that arrested my thoughts most seriously. For the last four years of my life that preceded my marriage I literally coined money, and never until this moment, I think, did I reflect on the great means of good, to myself and others, that I so gladly agreed to give up forever for a maintenance by the unpaid labor of slaves—people toiling not only unpaid, but under the bitter conditions the bare contemplation of which was then wringing my heart. You will not wonder that when, in the midst of such cogitations, I suddenly accosted Mr. O——, it was to this effect: "Mr. O——, I have a particular favor to beg of you. Promise me that you will never sell Psyche and her children without first letting me know of your intention to do so, and giving me the option of buying them."

Mr. O—— is a remarkably deliberate man, and squints, so that, when he has taken a little time in directing his eyes to you, you are still unpleasantly unaware of any result in which you are concerned; he laid down a book he was reading, and directed his head and one of his eyes toward me and answered: "Dear me, ma'am, I am very sorry—I have sold them."

My work fell down on the ground, and my mouth opened wide, but I could utter no sound, I was so dismayed and surprised; and he deliberately proceeded: "I didn't know, ma'am, you see, at all, that you entertained any idea of making an investment of that nature; for I'm sure, if I had, I would willingly have sold the woman to you; but I sold her and her children this morning to Mr. [Butler].

My dear E[lizabeth], though [Mr. Butler] had resented my unmeasured upbraidings, you see they had not been without some good effect, and though he had, perhaps justly, punished my violent outbreak of indignation about the miserable scene I witnessed by not telling me of his humane purpose, he had bought these poor creatures, and so, I trust, secured them from any such misery in future. I jumped up and left Mr. O—— still speaking, and ran to find Mr. [Butler], to thank him for what he had done, and with that will now bid you good-by. Think, E[lizabeth], how it fares with slaves on plantations where there is no crazy English-woman to weep, and entreat, and implore, and upbraid for them, and no master willing to listen to such appeals.

XI

Shadrach's Death and Funeral

[January, 1839]

Dear E[lizabeth],

There is one privilege which I enjoy here which I think few Cockneyesses have ever had experience of, that of hearing my own extemporaneous praises chanted bard-fashion by our Negroes in rhymes as rude and to measures as simple as ever any illustrious female of the days of King Brian Boroihme [1] listened to. Rowing yesterday evening through a beautiful sunset into a more beautiful moonrise, my two sable boatmen entertained themselves and me with alternate strophe and antistrophe of poetical description of my personal attractions, in which my "wire waist" recurred repeatedly, to my intense amusement. This is a charm for the possession of which M[argery] (my white nursemaid) is also invariably celebrated; and I suppose that the fine round natural proportions of the uncompressed waists of the sable beauties of these regions appear less symmetrical to eyes accustomed to them than our stay-cased figures, since "nothing pleaseth but rare accidents." Occasionally I am celebrated in these rowing chants as "Massa's darling," and S[ally] comes in for endless glorification on account of the brilliant beauty of her complexion; the other

[1] An Irish king and legendary hero.

day, however, our poets made a diversion from the personal to the moral qualities of their small mistress, and after the usual tribute to her roses and lilies came the following rather significant couplet:

> Little Missis Sally,
> That's a ruling lady.

At which all the white teeth simultaneously lightened from the black visages, while the subject of this equivocal commendation sat with infantine solemnity (the profoundest, I think, that the human countenance is capable of), surveying her sable dependents with imperturbable gravity.

Yesterday morning I amused myself with an exercise of a talent I once possessed, but have so neglected that my performance might almost be called an experiment. I cut out a dress for one of the women. My education in France—where, in some important respects, I think girls are better trained than with us—had sent me home to England, at sixteen, an adept in the female mystery of needle work. Not only owing to the Saturday's discipline of clothes mending by all the classes—while Abbé Millot's history (of blessed boring memory) was being read aloud, to prevent "vain babblings," and insure wholesome mental occupation the while—was I an expert patcher and mender, darner and piecer (darning and marking were my specialties), but the white cotton embroidery of which every Frenchwoman has always a piece under her hand *pour les moments perdus,* which are thus anything but *perdus,* was as familiar to us as to the Irish cottagers of the present day, and cutting out and making my dresses was among the more advanced branches of *the* female accomplishment to which I attained.* The luxury of a lady's maid of my own, indulged in ever

---

* Some of our great English ladies are, I know, exquisite needle-women; but I do not think, in spite of these exceptional examples, that young English ladies of the higher classes are much skilled in this respect at the present day; and as for the democratic daughters of America, who for many reasons might be supposed likely to be well up in

since the days of my "coming out," has naturally enough caused my right hand to forget its cunning, and regret and shame at having lost any useful lore in my life made me accede, for my own sake, to the request of one of our multitudinous Dianas and innumerable Chloes to cut out dresses for each of them, especially as they (wonderful to relate) declared themselves able to stitch them if I would do the cutting. Since I have been on the plantation I have already spent considerable time in what the French call "confectioning" baby bundles, i.e., the rough and very simple tiny habiliments of coarse cotton and scarlet flannel which form a baby's layette here, and of which I have run up some scores; but my present task was far more difficult. Chloe was an ordinary mortal Negress, but Diana might have been the Huntress of the Woods herself, done into the African type. Tall, large, straight, well-made, profoundly serious, she stood like a bronze statue, while I, mounted on a stool (the only way in which I could attain to the noble shoulders and bust of my lay figure), pinned and measured, and cut and shaped, under the superintendence of M[argery], and had the satisfaction of seeing the fine proportions of my black goddess quite becomingly clothed in a high, tight-fitting body of the gayest chintz, which she really contrived to put together quite creditably.

I was so elated with my own part of this performance that I then and there determined to put into execution a plan I had long formed of endowing the little boat in which I take what the French

---

such housewifely lore, they are, for the most part, so ignorant of it that I have heard the most eloquent preacher of the city of New York advert to their incapacity in this respect as an impediment to their assistance of the poor, and ascribe to the fact that the daughters of his own parishioners did not know how to sew, the impossibility of their giving the most valuable species of help to the women of the needier classes, whose condition could hardly be more effectually improved than by acquiring such useful knowledge. I have known young American schoolgirls duly instructed in the nature of the parallaxes of the stars, but, as a rule, they do not know how to darn their stockings. Les Dames du Sacré Cœur do better for their highborn and well-bred pupils than this.

call my "walks on the water" with cushions for the back and seat of the benches usually occupied by myself and Mr. [Butler]; so, putting on my large straw hat, and plucking up a paper of pins, scissors, and my brown holland, I walked to the steps, and, jumping into the little canoe, began piecing, and measuring, and cutting the cushions, which were to be stuffed with the tree moss by some of the people who understand making a rough kind of mattress. My inanimate subject, however, proved far more troublesome to fit than my living lay figure, for the little cockleshell ducked, and dived, and rocked, and tipped, and courtesied, and tilted, as I knelt first on one side and then on the other, fitting her, till I was almost in despair; however, I got a sort of pattern at last, and by dint of some pertinacious efforts—which, in their incompleteness, did not escape some sarcastic remarks from Mr. [Butler] on the capabilities of "women of genius" applied to commonplace objects—the matter was accomplished, and the little *Dolphin* rejoiced in very tidy back and seat cushions, covered with brown holland, and bound with green serge. My ambition then began to contemplate an awning; but the boat being of the nature of a canoe—though not a real one, inasmuch as it is not made of a single log—does not admit of supports for such an edifice.

I had rather a fright the other day in that same small craft, into which I had taken S[ally], with the intention of paddling myself a little way down the river and back. I used to row tolerably well, and was very fond of it, and frequently here take an oar, when the men are rowing me in the longboat, as some sort of equivalent for my riding, of which, of course, I am entirely deprived on this little dikeland of ours; but paddling is a perfectly different process, and one that I was very anxious to achieve. My first strokes answered the purpose of sending the boat off from shore, and for a few minutes I got on pretty well; but presently I got tired of shifting the paddle from side to side, a maneuver which I accomplished very clumsily and slowly, and yet, with all my precautions, not without making the boat tip perilously. The immense breadth and volume of the river suddenly seized my eyes and imagination as it were, and I began to fancy that if I got into the middle of the stream I should not be able to paddle myself back against it— which, indeed, might very well have proved the case. Then I became nervous, and paddled all on one side, by which means, of course, I only turned the boat round. S[ally] began to fidget about, getting up from where I had placed her, and terrifying me with her unsteady motions and the rocking of the canoe. I was now very much frightened, and saw that I *must* get back to shore before I became more helpless than I was beginning to feel; so, laying S[ally] down in the bottom of the boat as a preliminary precaution, I said to her with infinite emphasis: "Now lie still there, and don't stir, or you'll be drowned"; to which, with her clear gray eyes fixed on me, and no sign whatever of emotion, she replied deliberately: "I shall lie still here, and won't stir, for I should not like to be drowned," which, for an atom not four years old, was rather philosophical. Then I looked about me, and of course having drifted, set steadily to work and paddled home, with my heart in my mouth almost till we grazed the steps, and I got my precious freight safe on shore again, since which I have taken no more paddling lessons without my slave and master, Jack.

We have had a death among the people since I last wrote to you. A very valuable slave called Shadrach was seized with a disease which is frequent, and very apt to be fatal here—peripneumonia; and, in spite of all that could be done to save him, sank rapidly, and died after an acute illness of only three days. The doctor came repeatedly from Darien, and the last night of the poor fellow's life [Mr. Butler] himself watched with him. I suppose the general low diet of the Negroes must produce some want of stamina in them; certainly, either from natural constitution or the effect of their habits of existence, or both, it is astonishing how much less power of resistance to disease they seem to possess than we do. If they are ill, the vital energy seems to sink immediately. This rice cultivation, too, although it does not affect them as it would whites—to whom, indeed, residence on the rice plantation after a certain season is impossible—is still, to a certain degree, deleterious even to the Negroes. The proportion of sick is always greater here than on the cotton plantation, and the invalids of this place are not unfrequently sent down to St. Simons to recover their strength, under the more favorable influences of the sea air and dry sandy soil of Hampton Point.

Yesterday afternoon the tepid warmth of the air and glassy stillness of the river seemed to me highly suggestive of fishing, and I determined, not having yet discovered what I could catch with what in these unknown waters, to try a little innocent paste bait—a mystery his initiation into which caused Jack much wonderment. The only hooks I had with me, however, had been bought in Darien—made, I should think, at the North expressly for this market; and so villainously bad were they, that, after trying them and my patience a reasonable time, I gave up the attempt and took a lesson in paddling instead. Among other items Jack told me of his own fishing experience was that he had more than once caught those most excellent creatures, Altamaha shad, by the fish themselves leaping out of the water and *landing,* as Jack expressed it, to escape from the porpoises, which come in large schools up the river to a considerable distance, occasioning, evidently, much emotion in the bosoms of the legitimate inhabitants of these muddy waters. Coasting the island on our return home, we found a trap, which the last time we examined it was tenanted by a creature called a mink, now occupied by an otter. The poor beast did not seem pleased with his predicament; but the trap had been set by one of the drivers, and, of course, Jack would not have meddled with it except upon my express order, which, in spite of some pangs of pity for the otter, I did not like to give him, as, in the extremely few resources of either profit or pleasure possessed by the slaves, I could not tell at all what might be the value of an otter to his captor.

Yesterday evening the burial of the poor man Shadrach took

place. I had been applied to for a sufficient quantity of cotton cloth to make a winding sheet for him, and just as the twilight was thickening into darkness I went with Mr. [Butler] to the cottage of one of the slaves whom I may have mentioned to you before—a cooper of the name of London, the head of the religious party of the inhabitants of the island, a Methodist preacher of no small intelligence and influence among the people—who was to perform the burial service. The coffin was laid on trestles in front of the cooper's cottage, and a large assemblage of the people had gathered round, many of the men carrying pine-wood torches, the fitful glare of which glanced over the strange assembly, where every pair of large white-rimmed eyes turned upon [Mr. Butler] and myself; we two poor creatures, on this more solemn occasion, as well as on every other when these people encounter us, being the objects of admiration and wonderment, on which their gaze is immovably riveted. Presently the whole congregation uplifted their voices in a hymn, the first high wailing notes of which—sung all in unison, in the midst of these unwonted surroundings—sent a thrill through all my nerves. When the chant ceased, cooper London began a prayer, and all the people knelt down in the sand, as I did also. Mr. [Butler] alone remained standing in the presence of the dead man and of the living God to whom his slaves were now appealing. I cannot tell you how profoundly the whole ceremony, if such it could be called, affected me; and there was nothing in the simple and pathetic supplication of the poor black artisan to check or interfere with the solemn influences of the whole scene. It was a sort of conventional Methodist prayer, and probably quite as conventional as all the rest was the closing invocation of God's blessing upon their master, their mistress, and our children; but this fairly overcame my composure, and I began to cry very bitterly; for these same individuals, whose implication in the state of things in the midst of which we are living, seemed to me as legitimate a cause for tears as for prayers.

When the prayer was concluded we all rose, and, the coffin

being taken up, proceeded to the people's burial ground,[2] when London read aloud portions of the funeral service from the Prayer Book—I presume the American Episcopal version of our Church service, for what he read appeared to be merely a selection from what was perfectly familiar to me; but whether he himself extracted what he uttered I did not inquire. Indeed, I was too much absorbed in the whole scene, and the many mingled emotions it excited of awe and pity, and an indescribable sensation of wonder at finding myself on this slave soil, surrounded by *my* slaves, among whom again I knelt while the words proclaiming to the living and the dead the everlasting covenant of freedom, "I am the resurrection and the life," sounded over the prostrate throng, and mingled with the heavy flowing of the vast river sweeping, not far from where we stood, through the darkness by which we were now encompassed (beyond the immediate circle of our torchbearers). There was something painful to me in [Mr. Butler]'s standing while we all knelt on the earth; for, though in any church in Philadelphia he would have stood during the praying of any minister, here I wished he would have knelt, to have given his slaves some token of his belief that—at least in the sight of that Master to whom we were addressing our worship—all men are equal.

The service ended with a short address from London upon the subject of Lazarus, and the confirmation which the story of his resurrection afforded our hopes. The words were simple and rustic, and of course uttered in the peculiar sort of jargon which is the habitual Negro speech; but there was nothing in the slightest degree incongruous or grotesque in the matter or manner, and the exhortations not to steal, or lie, or neglect to work well for massa, with which the glorious hope of immortality was blended in the poor slave preacher's closing address, was a moral adaptation, as wholesome as it was touching, of the great Christian theory to the ca-

[2] Nothing is known for certain about the location of the people's burial ground, and no indications are given on the old maps.

pacities and consciences of his hearers. When the coffin was lowered the grave was found to be partially filled with water— naturally enough, for the whole island is a mere swamp, off which the Altamaha is only kept from sweeping by the high dikes all round it. This seemed to shock and distress the people, and for the first time during the whole ceremony there were sounds of crying and exclamations of grief heard among them. Their chief expression of sorrow, however, when Mr. [Butler] and myself bade them good night at the conclusion of the service, was on account of my crying, which appeared to affect them very much, many of them mingling with their "Farewell, good night, massa and missis," affectionate exclamations of "God bless you, missis; don't cry!" "Lor, missis, don't you cry so!"

Mr. [Butler] declined the assistance of any of the torchbearers home, and bade them all go quietly to their quarters; and as soon as they had dispersed, and we had got beyond the fitful and un-equal glaring of the torches, we found the shining of the stars in the deep blue lovely night sky quite sufficient to light our way along the dikes. I could not speak to [Mr. Butler], but continued to cry as we walked silently home; and, whatever his cogitations were, they did not take the usual form with him of wordy demon-stration, and so we returned from one of the most striking religious ceremonies at which I ever assisted.

Arrived at the door of the house, we perceived that we had been followed the whole way by the naked, noiseless feet of a poor half-witted creature, a female idiot, whose mental incapacity, of course, in no respect unfits her for the life of toil, little more in-tellectual than that of any beast of burden, which is her allotted portion here. Some small gratification was given to her, and she departed gibbering and muttering in high glee. Think, E[lizabeth], of that man London, who, in spite of all the bitter barriers in his way, has learned to read, has read his Bible, teaches it to his un-fortunate fellows, and is used by his owner and his owner's agents, for all these causes, as an effectual influence for good over the slaves of whom he is himself the despised and injured companion. Like them, subject to the driver's lash; like them, the helpless creature of his master's despotic will, without a right or a hope in this dreary world. But, though the light he has attained must show him the terrible aspects of his fate hidden by blessed ignorance from his companions, it reveals to him also other rights and other hopes—another world, another life—toward which he leads, according to the grace vouchsafed to him, his poor fellow slaves. How can we keep this man in such a condition? How is such a cruel sin of injustice to be answered? Mr. [Butler], of course, sees and feels none of this as I do, and, I should think, must regret that he ever brought me here, to have my abhorrence of the theory of slavery deepened, and strengthened every hour of my life, by what I see of its practice.

This morning I went over to Darien upon the very female errands of returning visits and shopping. In one respect (assuredly in none other) our life here resembles existence in Venice: we can never leave home for any purpose or in any direction but by boat—not, indeed, by gondola, but the sharp-cut, well-made light craft in which we take our walks on the water is a very agreeable species of conveyance. One of my visits this morning was to a certain Miss [Troup],[3] whose rather grandiloquent name and very striking style of beauty exceedingly well became the daughter of an ex-governor of Georgia. As for the residence of this princess, it was like all the planters' residences that I have seen, and such as a well-to-do English farmer would certainly not inhabit. Occasional marks of former elegance or splendor survive sometimes in the size of the rooms, sometimes in a little carved woodwork about the mantelpieces or wainscotings of these mansions; but all things

[3] Orallie Troup was one of the two daughters of George Michael Troup, ex-governor of Georgia. She and her sister, Florida, lived for years with their cousins at the house of their uncle, Dr. James McGillivray Troup, in Darien. Orallie, her cousin Ophelia recalled, "was like a queen in her beauty, and her manners were graceful and elegant."

have a Castle Rackrent [4] air of neglect, and dreary, careless un-
tidiness, with which the dirty, barefooted Negro servants are in
excellent keeping. Occasionally a huge pair of dazzling shirt gills,
out of which a black visage grins as out of some vast white paper
cornet, adorns the sable footman of the establishment, but unfortunately without at all necessarily indicating any downward
prolongation of the garment; and the perfect tulip bed of a head
handkerchief with which the female attendants of these "great
families" love to bedizen themselves frequently stands them instead of every other most indispensable article of female attire.

As for my shopping, the goods, or rather "bads," at which I used
to grumble, in your village emporium at Lenox, are what may be
termed "first rate," both in excellence and elegance, compared
with the vile products of every sort which we wretched Southerners
are expected to accept as the conveniences of life in exchange for
current coin of the realm. I regret to say, moreover, that all these
infamous articles are Yankee made, expressly for this market,
where every species of *thing* (to use the most general term I can
think of), from list shoes to pianofortes, is procured from the
North, almost always New England, utterly worthless of its kind,
and dearer than the most perfect specimens of the same articles
would be anywhere else. The incredible variety and ludicrous combinations of goods to be met with in one of these Southern shops
beats the stock of your village omnium-gatherum hollow: to be
sure, one class of articles, and that probably the most in demand
here, is not sold over any counter in Massachusetts—cowhides and
mantraps, of which a large assortment enters necessarily into the
furniture of every Southern shop.

In passing today along the deep sand road calling itself the
street of Darien, my notice was attracted by an extremely hand-

[4] Maria Edgeworth's brief master-
piece of this title was written in
1800. It depicts an impoverished
Irish squire, Sir Condy Rackrent, on
his dilapidated and debt-ridden estate, Castle Rackrent.

some and intelligent-looking poodle, standing by a little wizen-looking knife grinder, whose features were evidently European, though he was nearly as black as a Negro, who, strange to say, was discoursing with him in very tolerable French. The impulse of curiosity led me to accost the man at the grindstone, when his companion immediately made off. The itinerant artisan was from Aix, in Provence: think of wandering thence to Darien in Georgia! I asked him about the Negro who was talking to him; he said he knew nothing of him but that he was a slave belonging to somebody in the town. And upon my expressing surprise at his having left his own beautiful and pleasant country for this dreary distant region, he answered, with a shrug and a smile: *"Oui, madame, c'est vrai; c'est un joli pays, mais dans ce pays-là, quand un homme n'a rien, c'est rien pour toujours."* [5] A property which many, no doubt, have come hither, like the little French knife grinder, to increase, without succeeding in the struggle much better than he appeared to have done.

[5] "Yes madam, it is true that my native land is beautiful, but over there a poor man is poor for good."

XII

Hospital Rounds and a Visit to Tunno's Island

[End of January or beginning of February, 1839]
Dear E[lizabeth],

Having made a fresh, and, as I thought, more promising purchase of fishing tackle, Jack and I betook ourselves to the river, and succeeded in securing some immense catfish, of which, to tell you the truth, I am most horribly afraid when I have caught them. The dexterity necessary for taking them off the hook so as to avoid the spikes on their backs, and the spikes on each side of their gills, the former having to be pressed down, and the two others pressed up, before you can get any purchase on the slimy beast (for it is smooth skinned and without scales, to add to the difficulty)— these conditions, I say, make the catching of catfish questionable sport. Then, too, they hiss, and spit, and swear at one, and are altogether devilish in their aspect and demeanor; nor are they good for food, except, as Jack with much humility said this morning, for colored folks: "Good for colored folks, missis; me 'spect not good enough for white people." That 'spect, meaning *expect*, has sometimes a possible meaning of *suspect*, which would give the sentence in which it occurs a very humorous turn, and I always take the benefit of that interpretation. After exhausting the charms of our occupation, finding that catfish were likely to be our principal haul, I left the river and went my rounds to the hospitals. On my way I encountered two batches of small black fry, Hannah's children and poor Psyche's children, looking really as neat and tidy as children of the bettermost class of artisans among ourselves. These people are so quick and so imitative that it would be the easiest thing in the world to improve their physical condition by appealing to their emulative propensities. Their passion for what is *genteel* might be used most advantageously in the same direction; and, indeed, I think it would be difficult to find people who offered such a fair purchase by so many of their characteristics to the hand of the reformer.

Returning from the hospital, I was accosted by poor old Teresa, the wretched Negress who had complained to me so grievously of her back being broken by hard work and childbearing. She was in a dreadful state of excitement, which she partly presently communicated to me, because she said Mr. O—— had ordered her to be flogged for having complained to me as she did. It seems to me that I have come down here to be tortured, for this punishing these wretched creatures for crying out to me for help is really converting me into a source of increased misery to them. It is almost more than I can endure to hear these horrid stories of lashings inflicted because I have been invoked; and though I dare say Mr. [Butler], thanks to my passionate appeals to him, gives me little credit for prudence or self-command, I have some, and I exercise it, too, when I listen to such tales as these with my teeth set fast and my lips closed. Whatever I may do to the master, I hold my tongue to the slaves, and I wonder how I do it.

In the afternoon I rowed with Mr. [Butler] to another island in the broad waters of the Altamaha, called Tunno's Island, to return the visit of a certain Dr. T[unno], the proprietor of the island, named after him, as our rice swamp is after Major [Butler]. I here saw growing in the open air the most beautiful Gardenias I ever beheld; the branches were as high and as thick as the largest clumps of kalmia that grow in your woods; but whereas the tough, stringy, fibrous branches of these gives them a straggling appearance, these magnificent masses of dark, shiny, glossy green leaves were quite compact, and I cannot conceive anything lovelier or more delightful than they would be starred all over with their thick-leaved, cream-white odoriferous blossoms.

In the course of our visit a discussion arose as to the credibility of any Negro assertion, though, indeed, that could hardly be called a discussion that was simply a chorus of assenting opinions. No Negro was to be believed on any occasion or any subject. No doubt they are habitual liars, for they are slaves; but there are some thrice honorable exceptions, who, being slaves, are yet not liars; and certainly the vice results much more from the circumstances in which they are placed than from any natural tendency to untruth in their case. The truth is that they are always considered as false and deceitful, and it is very seldom that any special investigation of the facts of any particular case is resorted to in their behalf. They are always prejudged on their supposed general characteristics, and never judged after the fact on the merit of any special instance.

A question which was discussed in the real sense of the term was that of plowing the land instead of having it turned with the spade or hoe. I listened to this with great interest, for Jack and I had had some talk upon this subject, which began in his ardently expressed wish that massa would allow his land to be plowed, and his despairing conclusion that he never would, " 'cause horses more costly to keep than colored folks," and plowing, therefore, dearer than hoeing or digging. I had ventured to suggest to Mr. [Butler] the possibility of plowing some of the fields on the island, and his reply was that the whole land was too moist, and too much interrupted with the huge masses of the cypress yam roots, which would turn the share of any plow; yet there is land belonging to our neighbor Mr. G[rant],[1] on the other side of the river, where the conditions of the soil must be precisely the same, and yet which is being plowed before our faces. On Mr. [Butler]'s adjacent plantation the plow is also used extensively and successfully.

On my return to our own island I visited another of the hospitals, and the settlements to which it belonged. The condition of these places and of their inhabitants is, of course, the same all over the plantation, and if I were to describe them I should but weary you with a repetition of identical phenomena: filthy, wretched, almost naked, always barelegged and barefooted children; negligent, ignorant, wretched mothers, whose apparent indifference to the plight of their offspring, and utter incapacity to alter it, are the inevitable result of their slavery. It is hopeless to attempt to reform their habits or improve their condition while the women are condemned to field labor; nor is it possible to overestimate the bad moral effect of the system as regards the women, entailing this enforced separation from their children, and neglect of all the cares and duties of mother, nurse, and even housewife, which are all merged in the mere physical toil of a human hoeing machine. It seems to me too—but upon this point I cannot, of course, judge as well as the persons accustomed to and acquainted with the physical capacities of their slaves—that the labor is not judiciously distributed in many cases, at least not as far as the women are concerned. It is true that every able-bodied woman is made the most of in being driven afield as long as, under all and any circumstances, she is able to wield a hoe; but, on the other hand, stout, hale, hearty girls and boys, of from eight to twelve and older, are allowed to lounge about, filthy and idle, with no pretense of an occupation but what they call "tend baby," i.e., see to the life and limbs of the little slave infants, to whose mothers, working in distant fields, they carry them during the day to be suckled, and for the rest of the time leave them to crawl and kick in the filthy

[1] Hugh Fraser Grant owned and operated the rice plantation of Eliza- field at the edge of the Altamaha River directly south of Butler Island.

cabins or on the broiling sand which surrounds them, in which industry, excellent enough for the poor babies, these big lazy youths and lasses emulate them. Again, I find many women who have borne from five to ten children rated as workers, precisely as young women in the prime of their strength who have had none; this seems a cruel carelessness. To be sure, while the women are pregnant their task is diminished, and this is one of the many indirect inducements held out to reckless propagation, which has a sort of premium offered to it in the consideration of less work and more food, counterbalanced by none of the sacred responsibilities which hallow and ennoble the relation of parent and child; in short, as their lives are for the most part those of mere animals, their increase is literally mere animal breeding, to which every encouragement is given, for it adds to the master's livestock and the value of his estate.

XIII

Three Days of Plantation Life

[February, 1839]

Dear E[lizabeth],

Today I have the pleasure of announcing to you a variety of improvements about to be made in the infirmary of the island. There is to be a third story—a mere loft, indeed—added to the building; but, by affording more room for the least distressing cases of sickness to be drafted off into, it will leave the ground floor and room above it comparatively free for the most miserable of these unfortunates. To my unspeakable satisfaction, these destitute apartments are to be furnished with bedsteads, mattresses, pillows, and blankets; and I feel a little comforted for the many heartaches my life here inflicts upon me—at least some of my twinges will have wrought this poor alleviation of their wretchedness for the slaves when prostrated by disease or pain.

I had hardly time to return home from the hospital this morning before one of the most tremendous storms I ever saw burst over the island. Your Northern hills, with their solemn pinewoods, and fresh streams and lakes, telling of a cold rather than a warm climate, always seem to me as if undergoing some strange and unnatural visitation when one of your heavy summer thunderstorms bursts over them. Snow and frost, hail and, above all, wind, trailing rain clouds and brilliant northern lights, are your appropriate sky phenomena; here, thunder and lightning seem as if they might have been invented. Even in winter (remember, we are now in February) they appear neither astonishing nor unseasonable, and I should think in summer (but Heaven defend me from ever making good my supposition) lightning must be as familiar to these sweltering lands and slimy waters as sunlight itself.

The afternoon cleared off most beautifully, and Jack and I went out on the river to catch what might be caught. Jack's joyful excitement was extreme at my announcing to him the fact that Mr. [Butler] had consented to try plowing on some of the driest portions of the island instead of the slow and laborious process of hoeing the fields; this is a disinterested exultation on his part, for, at any rate, as long as I am here, he will certainly be nothing but "my boy Jack," and I should think, after my departure, will never be degraded to the rank of a field hand or common laborer. Indeed, the delicacy of his health, to which his slight, slender figure and languid face bear witness, and which was one reason of his appointment to the eminence of being "my slave," would, I should think, prevent the poor fellow's ever being a very robust or useful working animal.

On my return from the river I had a long and painful conversation with Mr. [Butler] upon the subject of the flogging which had been inflicted on the wretched Teresa. These discussions are terrible: they throw me into perfect agonies of distress for the slaves, whose position is utterly hopeless; for myself, whose intervention in their behalf sometimes seems to me worse than useless; for Mr. [Butler], whose share in this horrible system fills me by turns with indignation and pity. But, after all, what can he do? how can he help it all? Moreover, born and bred in America, how should he care or wish to help it? and, of course, he does not; and I am in despair that he does not: *et voilà,* it is a happy and hopeful plight for us both. He maintained that there had been neither hardship nor injustice in the case of Teresa's flogging; and that, moreover, she had not been flogged at all for complaining to me, but simply because her allotted task was not done at the appointed time. Of course this was the result of her having come to appeal to me instead of going to her labor; and as she knew perfectly well the penalty she was incurring, he maintained that there was neither hardship nor injustice in the case; the whole thing was a regularly established law, with which all the slaves were perfectly well acquainted; and this case was no exception whatever. The circumstance of my being on the island could not, of course, be allowed to overthrow the whole system of discipline established to secure the labor and obedience of the slaves; and if they chose to try experiments as to that fact, they and I must take the consequences. At the end of the day, the driver of the gang to which Teresa belongs reported her work not done, and Mr. O—— ordered him to give her the usual number of stripes, which order the driver of course obeyed, without knowing how Teresa had employed her time instead of hoeing. But Mr. O—— knew well enough, for the wretched woman told me that she had herself told him she should appeal to me about her weakness, and suffering, and inability to do the work exacted from her.

He did not, however, think proper to exceed in her punishment the usual number of stripes allotted to the nonperformance of the appointed daily task, and Mr. [Butler] pronounced the whole transaction perfectly satisfactory and *en règle*. The common drivers are limited in their powers of chastisement, not being allowed to administer more than a certain number of lashes to their fellow slaves. Headman Frank, as he is called, has alone the privilege of exceeding this limit; and the overseer's latitude of infliction is only curtailed by the necessity of avoiding injury to life or limb. The master's irresponsible power has no such bound. When I was thus silenced on the particular case under discussion, I resorted, in my distress and indignation, to the abstract question, as I never can refrain from doing; and to Mr. [Butler]'s assertion of the justice of poor Teresa's punishment, I retorted the manifest injustice of unpaid and enforced labor; the brutal inhumanity of allowing a man to strip and lash a woman, the mother of ten children; to exact from her, toil, which was to maintain in luxury two idle young men, the owners of the plantation. I said I thought female labor of the sort exacted from these slaves, and corporal chastisement such as they endure, must be abhorrent to any manly or humane man. Mr. [Butler] said he thought it was *disagreeable,* and left me to my reflections with that concession.

My letter has been interrupted for the last three days—by nothing special, however. My occupations and interests here, of course, know no change; but Mr. [Butler] has been anxious for a little while past that we should go down to St. Simons, the cotton plantation. We shall suffer less from the heat, which I am beginning to find oppressive on this swamp island; and he himself wished to visit that part of his property, whither he had not yet been since our arrival in Georgia; so the day before yesterday he departed to make the necessary arrangements for our removal thither; and my time in the meanwhile has been taken up in fitting him out for his departure.

In the morning Jack and I took our usual paddle, and, having the tackle on board, tried fishing. I was absorbed in many sad and serious considerations, and, wonderful to relate (for you know, E[lizabeth], how keen an angler I am), had lost all consciousness of my occupation until, after I know not how long a time elapsing without the shadow of a nibble, I was recalled to a most ludicrous perception of my ill success by Jack's sudden observation: "Missis, fishing berry good fun when um fish bite." This settled the fishing for that morning, and I let Jack paddle me down the broad turbid stream, endeavoring to answer in the most comprehensible manner to his keen but utterly undeveloped intellects the innumerable questions with which he plied me about Philadelphia, about England, about the Atlantic, etc. He dilated much upon the charms of St. Simons, to which he appeared very glad that we were going; and, among other items of description, mentioned what I was very glad to hear, that it was a beautiful place for riding, and that I should be able to indulge to my heart's content in my favorite exercise, from which I have, of course, been utterly debarred in this small dikeland of ours. He insinuated more than once his hope and desire that he might be allowed to accompany me, but as I knew nothing at all about his capacity for equestrian exercises, or any of the arrangements that might or might not interfere with such a plan, I was discreetly silent, and took no notice of his most comically turned hints on the subject. In our row we started a quantity of wild duck, and he told me there was a great deal of game at St. Simons, but that the people did not contrive to catch much, though they laid traps constantly for it. Of course their possessing firearms is quite out of the question; but this abundance of what must be to them such especially desirable prey makes the fact a great hardship. I almost wonder they don't learn to shoot like savages with bows and arrows; but these would be weapons, and equally forbidden them.

In the afternoon I saw Mr. [Butler] off for St. Simons; it is fifteen miles lower down the river, and a large island at the very mouth of the Altamaha.

The boat he went in was a large, broad, rather heavy, though well-built craft, by no means as swift or elegant as the narrow eight-oared longboat in which he generally takes his walks on the water, but well-adapted for the traffic between the two plantations, where it serves the purpose of a sort of omnibus or stagecoach for the transfer of the people from one to the other, and of a baggage wagon or cart for the conveyance of all sorts of household goods, chattels, and necessaries. Mr. [Butler] sat in the middle of a perfect chaos of such freight; and as the boat pushed off, and the steersman took her into the stream, the men at the oars set up a chorus, which they continued to chant in unison with each other, and in time with their stroke, till the voices and oars were heard no more from the distance. I believe I have mentioned to you before the peculiar characteristics of this veritable Negro minstrelsy—how they all sing in unison, having never, it appears, attempted or heard anything like part singing. Their voices seem oftener tenor than any other quality, and the tune and time they keep, something quite wonderful; such truth of intonation and accent would make almost any music agreeable. That which I have heard these people say is often plaintive and pretty, but almost always has some resemblance to tunes with which they must have become acquainted through the instrumentality of white men; their overseers or masters whistling Scotch or Irish airs, of which they have produced by ear these *rifacciamenti*.[1] The note for note reproduction of "*Ah! vous dirai-je, maman?*" in one of the most popular of the so-called Negro melodies with which all America and England are familiar, is an example of this very transparent plagiarism; and the tune with which Mr. [Butler]'s rowers started him down the Altamaha, as I stood at the steps to see him off, was a very distinct descendant of "Coming Through the Rye." The words, however, were astonishingly primitive, especially the first line, which, when it burst from their eight throats in high unison, sent me into fits of laughter.

> Jenny shake her toe at me,
> Jenny gone away;
> Jenny shake her toe at me,
> Jenny gone away.
> Hurrah! Miss Susy, oh!
> Jenny gone away;
> Hurrah! Miss Susy, oh!
> Jenny gone away.

What the obnoxious Jenny meant by shaking her toe, whether defiance or mere departure, I never could ascertain, but her going away was an unmistakable subject of satisfaction; and the pause made on the last "oh!" before the final announcement of her departure, had really a good deal of dramatic and musical effect.

[1] This should read *rifacimenti*, which means musical versions or adaptations.

Except the extemporaneous chants in our honor, of which I have written to you before, I have never heard the Negroes on Mr. [Butler]'s plantation sing any words that could be said to have any sense. To one, an extremely pretty, plaintive, and original air, there was but one line, which was repeated with a sort of wailing chorus—

Oh! my massa told me, there's no grass in Georgia.

Upon inquiring the meaning of which, I was told it was supposed to be the lamentation of a slave from one of the more northerly states, Virginia or Carolina, where the labor of hoeing the weeds, or grass as they call it, is not nearly so severe as here, in the rice and cotton lands of Georgia. Another very pretty and pathetic tune began with words that seemed to promise something sentimental—

Fare you well, and good-by, oh, oh!
I'm goin' away to leave you, oh, oh!

but immediately went off into nonsense verses about gentlemen in the parlor drinking wine and cordial, and ladies in the drawing room drinking tea and coffee, etc. I have heard that many of the masters and overseers on these plantations prohibit melancholy tunes or words, and encourage nothing but cheerful music and senseless words, deprecating the effect of sadder strains upon the slaves, whose peculiar musical sensibility might be expected to make them especially excitable by any songs of a plaintive character, and having any reference to their particular hardships. If it is true, I think it a judicious precaution enough—these poor slaves are just the sort of people over whom a popular musical appeal to their feelings and passions would have an immense power.

In the evening, Mr. [Butler]'s departure left me to the pleasures of an uninterrupted *tête-à-tête* with his cross-eyed overseer, and I endeavored, as I generally do, to atone by my conversibleness and civility for the additional trouble which, no doubt, all my outlandish ways and notions are causing the worthy man. So suggestive (to use the new-fangled jargon about books) a woman as myself is, I suspect, an intolerable nuisance in these parts; and poor Mr. O—— cannot very well desire Mr. [Butler] to send me away, however much he may wish that he would; so that figuratively, as well as literally, I fear the worthy master *me voit d'un mauvais œil,* as the French say. I asked him several questions about some of the slaves who had managed to learn to read, and by what means they had been able to do so. As teaching them is strictly prohibited by the laws, they who instructed them, and such of them as acquired the knowledge, must have been not a little determined and persevering. This was my view of the case, of course, and of course it was not the overseer's. I asked him if many of Mr. [Butler]'s slaves could read.

He said: "No; very few, he was happy to say, but those few were just so many too many."

"Why, had he observed any insubordination in those who did?" And I reminded him of cooper London, the Methodist preacher, whose performance of the burial service had struck me so much some time ago, to whose exemplary conduct and character there is but one concurrent testimony all over the plantation. No; he had no special complaint to bring against the lettered members of his subject community, but he spoke by anticipation. Every step they take toward intelligence and enlightenment lessens the probability of their acquiescing in their condition. Their condition is not to be changed—ergo, they had better not learn to read; a very succinct and satisfactory argument as far as it goes, no doubt, and one to which I had not a word to reply, at any rate, to Mr. O——, as I did not feel called upon to discuss the abstract justice or equity of the matter with him; indeed he, to a certain degree, gave up that part of the position, starting with "I don't say whether it's right or wrong"; and in all conversations that I have had with the Southerners upon these subjects, whether out of civility to what may be supposed to be an Englishwoman's prejudices, or a forlorn respect to their own convictions, the question of the fundamental wrong of slavery is generally admitted, or, at any rate, certainly never denied. That part of the subject is summarily dismissed, and all its other aspects vindicated, excused, and even lauded, with untiring eloquence. Of course, of the abstract question I could judge before I came here, but I confess I had not the remotest idea how absolutely my observation of every detail of the system, as a practical iniquity, would go to confirm my opinion of its abomination.

Mr. O—— went on to condemn and utterly denounce all the preaching, and teaching, and moral instruction upon religious subjects which people in the South, pressed upon by Northern opinion, are endeavoring to give their slaves. The kinder and the more cowardly masters are anxious to evade the charge of keeping their Negroes in brutish ignorance, and so they crumble what they suppose and hope may prove a little harmless religious enlightenment, which, mixed up with much religious authority on the subject of submission and fidelity to masters, they trust their slaves may swallow without its doing them any harm—i.e., that they may be better Christians and better slaves—and so, indeed, no doubt they are; but it is a very dangerous experiment, and from Mr. O——'s point of view I quite agree with him. The letting out of water, or the letting in of light, in infinitesimal quantities, is not always easy. The half-wicked of the earth are the leaks through which wickedness is eventually swamped; compromises forerun absolute surrender in most matters, and fools and cowards are, in such cases, the instruments of Providence for their own defeat. Mr. O—— stated unequivocally his opinion that free labor would be more profitable on the plantations than the work of slaves, which, being compulsory, was of the worst possible quality and the smallest possible quantity; then the charge of them before and after they are able to work is onerous, the cost of feeding and clothing them very considerable, and, upon the whole, he, a Southern overseer, pronounced himself decidedly in favor of free labor, upon grounds of expediency. Having at the beginning of our conversation declined discussing the moral aspect of slavery, evidently not thinking that position tenable, I thought I had every right to consider Mr. [Butler]'s slave driver a decided abolitionist.

I had been anxious to enlist his sympathies on behalf of my extreme desire to have some sort of garden, but did not succeed in inspiring him with my enthusiasm on the subject; he said there was but one garden that he knew of in the whole neighborhood of Darien, and that was our neighbor, old Mr. C[ouper]'s,[2] a Scotchman on St. Simons. I remembered the splendid Gardenias on Tunno's Island, and referred to them as a proof of the material for ornamental gardening. He laughed, and said rice and cotton crops were the ornamental gardening principally admired by the planters, and that, to the best of his belief, there was not another decent kitchen or flower garden in the state but the one he had mentioned.

The next day after this conversation, I walked with my horticultural zeal much damped, and wandered along the dike by the broad river, looking at some pretty peach trees in blossom, and thinking what a curse of utter stagnation this slavery produces, and how intolerable to me a life passed within its stifling influence would be. Think of peach trees in blossom in the middle of February! It does seem cruel, with such a sun and soil, to be told that a garden is worth nobody's while here; however, Mr. O—— said that he believed the wife of the former overseer had made a "sort of a garden" at St. Simons. We shall see "what sort" it turns out to be. While I was standing on the dike, ruminating above the river, I saw a beautiful white bird of the crane species alight not far from me. I do not think a little knowledge of natural history would diminish the surprise and admiration with which I regard the, to me, unwonted specimens of animal existence that I en-

[2] John Couper owned the Cannon's Point plantation adjacent to Pierce Butler's Hampton Point property on St. Simons Island. He was a renowned horticulturist, and his estate has been called one of the country's first agricultural experiment stations.

counter every day, and of which I do not even know the names. Ignorance is an odious thing. The birds here are especially beautiful, I think. I saw one the other day, of what species of course I do not know, of a warm and rich brown, with a scarlet hood and crest—a lovely creature, about the size of your Northern robin, but more elegantly shaped.

This morning, instead of my usual visit to the infirmary, I went to look at the work and workers in the threshing mill: all was going on actively and orderly under the superintendence of headman Frank, with whom, and a very sagacious clever fellow who manages the steam power of the mill, and is honorably distinguished as Engineer Ned, I had a small chat. There is one among various drawbacks to the comfort and pleasure of our intercourse with these colored "men and brethren," at least in their slave condition, which certainly exercises my fortitude not a little. The swarms of fleas that cohabit with these sable dependents of ours are—well—incredible; moreover, they are by no means the only or most objectionable companions one borrows from them; and I never go to the infirmary, where I not infrequently am requested to look at very dirty limbs and bodies in very dirty draperies, without coming away with a strong inclination to throw myself into the water, and my clothes into the fire, which last would be expensive. I do not suppose that these hateful consequences of dirt and disorder are worse here than among the poor and neglected human creatures who swarm in the lower parts of European cities; but my call to visit them has never been such as that which constrains me to go daily among these poor people, and although on one or two occasions I have penetrated into fearfully foul and filthy abodes of misery in London, I have never rendered the same personal services to their inhabitants that I do to Mr. [Butler]'s slaves, and so have not incurred the same amount of entomological inconvenience.

After leaving the mill I prolonged my walk, and came, for the first time, upon one of the "gangs," as they are called, in full field work. Upon my appearance and approach there was a momentary suspension of labor, and the usual chorus of screams and ejaculations of welcome, affection, and infinite desires for infinite small indulgences. I was afraid to stop their work, not feeling at all sure that urging a conversation with me would be accepted as any excuse for an uncompleted task, or avert the fatal infliction of the usual award of stripes; so I hurried off and left them to their hoeing.

On my way home I was encountered by London, our Methodist preacher, who accosted me with a request for a Prayer Book and Bible, and expressed his regret at hearing that we were so soon going to St. Simons. I promised him his holy books, and asked him how he had learned to read, but found it impossible to get him to tell me. I wonder if he thought he should be putting his teacher, whoever he was, in danger of the penalty of the law against instructing the slaves, if he told me who he was; it was impossible to make him do so, so that, besides his other good qualities, he appears to have that most unusual one of all in an uneducated person—discretion. He certainly is a most remarkable man.

After parting with him, I was assailed by a small gang of children, clamoring for the indulgence of some meat, which they besought me to give them. Animal food is only allowed to certain of the harder working men, hedgers and ditchers, and to them only occasionally, and in very moderate rations. My small cannibals clamored round me for flesh, as if I had had a butcher's cart in my pocket, till I began to laugh, and then to run, and away they came, like a pack of little black wolves, at my heels, shrieking: "Missis, you gib me piece meat—missis, you gib me meat," till I got home. At the door I found another petitioner, a young woman named Maria, who brought a fine child in her arms, and demanded a present of a piece of flannel. Upon my asking her who her husband was, she replied, without much hesitation, that she did not possess any such appendage. I gave another look at her bonny baby, and went into the house to get the flannel for her. I afterward heard from Mr. [Butler] that she and two other girls of her age, about seventeen, were the only instances on the island of women with illegitimate children.

After I had been in the house a little while, I was summoned out again to receive the petition of certain poor women in the family way to have their work lightened. I was, of course, obliged to tell them that I could not interfere in the matter; that their master was away, and that, when he came back, they must present their request to him: they said they had already begged "massa," and he had refused, and they thought, perhaps, if "missis" begged "massa" for them, he would lighten their task. Poor "missis," poor "massa," poor woman, that I am to have such prayers addressed to me! I had to tell them that, if they had already spoken to their master, I was afraid my doing so would be of no use, but that when he came back I would try; so, choking with crying, I turned away from them, and re-entered the house, to the chorus of "Oh, thank you, missis! God bless you, missis!" E[lizabeth], I think an improvement might be made upon that caricature published a short time ago, called the "Chivalry of the South." I think an elegant young Carolinian or Georgian gentleman, whip in hand, driving a gang of "lusty women," as they are called here, would be a pretty version of the "Chivalry of the South"—a little coarse, I am afraid you will say. Oh! quite horribly coarse, but then so true—a great matter in works of art, which nowadays appear to be thought excellent only in proportion to their lack of ideal elevation. That would be a subject, and a treatment of it, which could not be accused of imaginative exaggeration, at any rate.

In the evening I mentioned the petitions of these poor women to Mr. O——, thinking that perhaps he had the power to lessen their tasks. He seemed evidently annoyed at their having appealed to me; said that their work was not a bit too much for them, and that constantly they were *shamming* themselves in the family way in order to obtain a diminution of their labor. Poor creatures! I suppose some of them do; but, again, it must be a hard matter for those who do not, not to obtain the mitigation of their toil which their condition requires; for their assertion and their evidence are never received: they can't be believed, even if they were upon oath, say their white taskmasters; why? because they have never been taught the obligations of an oath, to whom made, or wherefore binding; and they are punished both directly and indirectly for their moral ignorance, as if it were a natural and incorrigible element of their character, instead of the inevitable result of their miserable position. The oath of any and every scoundrelly fellow with a white skin is received, but not that of such a man as Frank, Ned, old Jacob, or cooper London.

XIV

Visitors

[February 13, 1839]

Dearest E[lizabeth],

I think it right to begin this letter with an account of a most prosperous fishing expedition Jack and I achieved the other morning. It is true we still occasionally drew up huge catfish, with their detestable beards and spikes, but we also captured some magnificent perch, and the Altamaha perch are worth one's while both to catch and to eat. On a visit I had to make on the mainland the same day, I saw a tiny strip of garden ground, rescued from the sandy road called the street, perfectly filled with hyacinths, double jonquils, and snowdrops, a charming nosegay for February 11. After leaving the boat on my return home, I encountered a curious creature walking all sideways, a small cross between a lobster and a crab. One of the Negroes to whom I applied for its denomination informed me that it was a land crab, with which general description of this very peculiar multipede you must be satisfied, for I can tell you no more. I went a little farther, as the nursery rhyme says, and met with a snake; and, not being able to determine, at ignorant first sight, whether it was a malignant serpent or not, I ingloriously took to my heels, and came home on the full run. It is the first of these exceedingly displeasing animals I have encountered here;

but Jack, for my consolation, tells me that they abound on St. Simons, whither we are going—"rattlesnakes, and all kinds," says he, with an affluence of promise in his tone that is quite agreeable. Rattlesnakes will be quite enough of a treat, without the vague horrors that may be comprised in the additional "all kinds." Jack's account of the game on St. Simons is really quite tantalizing to me, who cannot carry a gun any more than if I were a slave. He says that partridges, woodcocks, snipe, and wild duck abound, so that, at any rate, our table ought to be well supplied. His account of the bears that are still to be found in the woods of the mainland is not so pleasant, though he says they do no harm to the people if they are not meddled with, but that they steal the corn from the fields when it is ripe, and actually swim the river to commit their depredations on the islands. It seems difficult to believe this, looking at this wide and heavy stream, though, to be sure, I did once see a young horse swim across the St. Lawrence, between Montreal and Quebec, a feat of natation which much enlarged my belief in what quadrupeds may accomplish when they have no choice between swimming and sinking.

You cannot imagine how great a triumph the virtue next to godliness is making under my auspices and a judicious system of small bribery. I can hardly stir now without being assailed with cries of "Missis, missis, me mind chile, me bery clean," or the additional gratifying fact, "and chile too, him bery clean." This virtue, however, if painful to the practicers, as no doubt it is, is expensive, too, to me, and I shall have to try some moral influence equivalent in value to a cent current coin of the realm. What a poor chance, indeed, the poor abstract idea runs! However, it is really a comfort to see the poor little woolly heads now, in most instances, stripped of their additional filthy artificial envelopes.

In my afternoon's row today I passed a huge dead alligator, lying half in and half out of the muddy slime of the river bank; a most hideous object it was, and I was glad to turn my eyes to the beautiful surface of the midstream, all burnished with sunset glories, and broken with the vivacious gambols of a school of porpoises. It is curious, I think, that these creatures should come fifteen miles from the sea to enliven the waters round our little rice swamp.

While rowing this evening, I was led by my conversation with Jack to some of those reflections with which my mind is naturally incessantly filled here, but which I am obliged to be very careful not to give any utterance to. The testimony of no Negro is received in a Southern court of law, and the reason commonly adduced for this is, that the state of ignorance in which the Negroes are necessarily kept renders them incapable of comprehending the obligations of an oath, and yet, with an inconsistency which might be said to border on effrontery, these same people are admitted to the most holy sacrament of the Church, and are certainly thereby supposed to be capable of assuming the highest Christian obligations, and the entire fulfillment of God's commandments, including, of course, the duty of speaking the truth at all times.

As we were proceeding down the river, we met the flat, as it is called, a huge sort of clumsy boat, more like a raft than any other species of craft, coming up from St. Simons with its usual swarthy freight of Mr. [Butler]'s dependents from that place. I made Jack turn our canoe, because the universal outcries and exclamations very distinctly intimated that I should be expected to be at home to receive the homage of this cargo of "massa's people." No sooner, indeed, had I disembarked and reached the house, than a dark cloud of black life filled the piazza and swarmed up the steps, and I had to shake hands, like a popular president, till my arm ached at the shoulder joint.

When this tribe had dispersed itself, a very old woman, with a remarkably intelligent, nice-looking young girl, came forward and claimed my attention. The old woman, who must, I think, by her appearance, have been near seventy, had been one of the house servants on St. Simons Island in Major [Butler]'s time, and retained a certain dignified courtesy and respectfulness of manner which is by no means an uncommon attribute of the better class of slaves, whose intercourse with their masters, while tending to expand their intelligence, cultivates, at the same time, the natural turn for good manners which is, I think, a distinctive peculiarity of Negroes, if not in the kingdom of Dahomey, certainly in the United States of America. If it can be for a moment attributed to the beneficent influence of slavery on their natures (and I think slaveowners are quite likely to imagine so), it is curious enough that there is hardly any alloy whatever of cringing servility, or even humility, in the good manners of the blacks, but a rather courtly and affable condescension which, combined with their affection for, and misapplication of, long words, produces an exceedingly comical effect. Old House Molly, after congratulating herself, with many thanks to heaven, for having spared her to see "massa's" wife and children, drew forward her young companion, and informed me she was one of her numerous grandchildren. The damsel, ycleped Louisa, made rather a shamefaced obeisance, and her old grandmother went on to inform me that she had only lately been forgiven by the overseer for an attempt to run away from the plantation. I inquired the cause of her desire to do so—a "thrashing" she had got for an unfinished task—"but lor, missis," explained the old woman, "taint no use—what use nigger run away?—de swamp all round; dey get in dar, an' dey starve to def, or de snakes eat 'em up—massa's nigger, dey don't neber run away"; and if the good lady's account of their prospects in doing so is correct (which, substituting biting for eating on the part of the snakes, it undoubtedly is), one does not see exactly what particular merit the institution of slavery as practiced on Mr. [Butler]'s plantation derives from the fact that his "nigger don't neber run away."

After dismissing Molly and her granddaughter, I was about to re-enter the house, when I was stopped by Betty, headman Frank's wife, who came with a petition that she might be baptized. As usual with all requests involving anything more than an immediate physical indulgence, I promised to refer the matter to Mr. [Butler], but expressed some surprise that Betty, now by no means a young woman, should have postponed a ceremony which the religious among the slaves are apt to attach much importance to. She told me she had more than once applied for this permission to Massa K[ing] (the former overseer), but had never been able to obtain it, but that now she thought she would ask "de missis." *

Yesterday afternoon I received a visit from the wife of our neighbor, Dr. T[roup]. As usual, she exclaimed at my good fortune in having a white woman with my children when she saw M[argery], and, as usual, went on to expatiate on the utter impossibility of finding a trustworthy nurse anywhere in the South, to whom your children could be safely confided for a day or even

* Of this woman's life on the plantation I subsequently learned the following circumstances: she was the wife of headman Frank, the most intelligent and trustworthy of Mr. [Butler]'s slaves; [Frank was] the head driver—second in command to the overseer, and, indeed, second to none during the pestilential season, when the rice swamps cannot with impunity be inhabited by any white man, and when, therefore, the whole force employed in its cultivation on the island remains entirely under his authority and control. His wife—a tidy, trim, intelligent woman, with a pretty figure, but a decidedly Negro face—was taken from him by the overseer left in charge of the plantation by the Messrs. [Butler], the all-efficient and all-satisfactory Mr. K[ing], and she had a son by him, whose straight features and diluted color, no less than his troublesome, discontented, and insubmissive disposition, bear witness to his Yankee descent. I do not know how long Mr. K[ing]'s occupation of Frank's wife continued, or how the latter [i.e., Frank] endured the wrong done to him. When I visited the island Betty was again living with her husband—a grave, sad, thoughtful-looking man, whose admirable moral and mental qualities were extolled to me by no worse a judge of such matters than Mr. K[ing] himself, during the few days he spent with Mr. [Butler], while we were on the plantation. This outrage upon this man's rights was perfectly notorious among all the slaves; and his hopeful offspring, Renty, alluding very unmistakably to his superior birth on one occasion when he applied for permission to have a gun, observed that, though the people in general on the plantation were not allowed firearms, he thought he might, *on account of his color,* and added that he thought Mr. K[ing] might have left him his. This precious sample of the mode in which the vices of the whites procure the intellectual progress of the blacks to their own endangerment was, as you will easily believe, a significant chapter to me in the black history of oppression which is laid before my eyes in this place.

an hour; as usual, too, the causes of this unworthiness or incapacity
for a confidential servant's occupation were ignored, and the fact
laid to the natural defects of the Negro race. I am sick and weary
of this cruel and ignorant folly. This afternoon I went out to refresh myself with a row on the broad Altamaha and the conversation of my slave Jack, which is, I assure you, by no means devoid
of interest of various kinds, pathetic and humorous. I do not know
that Jack's scientific information is the most valuable in the world,
and I sometimes marvel with perhaps unjust incredulity at the facts
in natural history which he imparts to me; for instance, today he
told me, as we rowed past certain mud islands, very like children's
mud puddings on a rather larger scale than usual, that they were
inaccessible, and that it would be quite impossible to land on one
of them even for the shortest time. Not understanding why people
who did not mind being up to their knees in mud should not land
there if they pleased, I demurred to his assertion, when he followed
it up by assuring me that there were what he called sand sinks under
the mud, and that whatever was placed on the surface would not
only sink through the mud, but also into a mysterious quicksand of
unknown depth and extent below it. This may be true, but sounds
very strange, although I remember that the frequent occurrence of
large patches of quicksand was found to be one of the principal
impediments in the way of the canal speculators at Brunswick. I
did not, however, hear that these sinks, as Jack called them, were
found below a thick stratum of heavy mud.

In remonstrating with him upon the want of decent cleanliness
generally among the people, and citing to him one among the many
evils resulting from it, the intolerable quantity of fleas in all the
houses, he met me full with another fact in natural history which,
if it be fact and not fiction, certainly gave him the best of the
argument: he declared, with the utmost vehemence, that the sand
of the pinewoods on the mainland cross the river literally swarmed
with fleas; that, in the uninhabited places, the sand itself was full
of them; and that, so far from being a result of human habitation,

they were found in less numbers round the Negro huts on the mainland than in the lonely woods around them.

The plowing is at length fully inaugurated, and there is a regular jubilee among the Negroes thereat. After discoursing fluently on the improvements likely to result from the measure, Jack wound up by saying he had been afraid it would not be tried on account of the greater scarcity, and consequently greater value, of horses over men in these parts—a modest and slavelike conclusion.

XV

The Pine Barrens

[February 14, 1839]

Dearest E[lizabeth],

I walked up today, February 14, to see that land of promise, the plowed field: it did not look to me anything like as heavy soil as the cold, wet, sour, stiff clay I have seen turned up in some of the swampy fields round Lenox; and as for the cypress roots which were urged as so serious an impediment, they are not much more frequent, and certainly not as resisting, as the granite knees and elbows that stick out through the scanty covering of the said clay, which mother earth allows herself as sole garment for her old bones in many a Berkshire patch of corn. After my survey, as I walked home, I came upon a gang of lusty women, as the phrase is here for women in the family way; they were engaged in burning stubble, and I was nearly choked while receiving the multitudinous complaints and compliments with which they overwhelmed me. After leaving them, I wandered along the river side of the dike homeward, rejoicing in the buds and green things putting forth their tender shoots on every spray, in the early bees and even the less amiable wasps busy in the sunshine with flowers (weeds I suppose they should be called), already opening their sweet temptations to them, and giving the earth a spring aspect, such as it does not wear with you in Massachusetts till late in May.

In the afternoon I took my accustomed row: there had been a tremendous ebb tide, the consequence of which was to lay bare portions of the banks which I had not seen before. The cypress roots form a most extraordinary mass of intertwined woodwork, so closely matted and joined together that the separate roots, in spite of their individual peculiarities, appeared only like divisions of a continuous body; they presented the appearance in several places of jagged pieces of splintered rock, with their huge teeth pointing downward into the water. Their decay is so slow that the protection they afford the soft spongy banks against the action of the water is likely to be prolonged until the gathering and deposit of successive layers of alluvium will remove them from the margin of which they are now most useful supports. On my return home I was met by a child (as she seemed to me) carrying a baby, in whose behalf she begged me for some clothes. On making some inquiry, I was amazed to find that the child was her own: she said she was married, and fourteen years old; she looked much younger even than that, poor creature. Her mother, who came up while I was talking to her, said she did not herself know the girl's age; how horridly brutish it all did seem, to be sure.

The spring is already here with her hands full of flowers. I do not know who planted some straggling Pyrus *japonica* near the house, but it is blessing my eyes with a hundred little flamelike buds, which will presently burst into a blaze; there are clumps of narcissus roots sending up sheaves of ivory blossoms, and I actually found a monthly rose in bloom on the sunny side of one of the dikes; what a delight they are in the slovenly desolation of this abode of mine! what a garden one might have on the banks of these dikes, with the least amount of trouble and care!

In the afternoon I rowed over to Darien, and there procuring the most miserable vehicle calling itself a carriage that I had ever seen (the dirtiest and shabbiest London hackney coach were a chariot of splendor and ease to it), we drove some distance into the sandy wilderness that surrounds the little town, to pay a visit to some of the resident gentry who had called upon us. The road was a deep, wearisome sandy track, stretching wearisomely into the wearisome pine forest—a species of wilderness more oppressive a thousand times to the senses and imagination than any extent of monotonous prairie, barren steppe, or boundless desert can be; for the horizon there at least invites and detains the eye, suggesting beyond its limit possible change; the lights, and shadows, and enchanting colors of the sky afford some variety in their movement and change, and the reflections of their tints; while in this hideous and apparently boundless pine barren you are deprived alike of horizon before you and heaven above you: nor sun nor star appears through the thick covert, which, in the shabby dinginess of its dark blue-green expanse, looks like a gigantic cotton umbrella stretched immeasurably over you. It is true that over that sandy soil a dark green cotton umbrella is a very welcome protection from the sun, and when the wind makes music in the tall pine tops and refreshment in the air beneath them. The comparison may seem ungrateful enough: today, however, there was neither sound above nor motion below, and the heat was perfectly stifling, as we plowed our way through the resinous-smelling sand solitudes.

From time to time a thicket of exquisite evergreen shrubs broke the monotonous lines of the countless pine shafts rising round us, and still more welcome were the golden garlands of the exquisite wild jasmine, hanging, drooping, trailing, clinging, climbing through the dreary forest, joining to the warm aromatic smell of the fir trees a delicious fragrance as of acres of heliotrope in bloom. I wonder if this delightful creature is very difficult of cultivation out of its natural region; I never remember to have seen it, at least not in blossom, in any collection of plants in the Northern states or in Europe, where it certainly deserves an honorable place for its grace, beauty, and fragrance.

On our drive we passed occasionally a tattered man or woman, whose yellow mud complexion, straight features, and singularly sinister countenance bespoke an entirely different race from the Negro population in the midst of which they lived. These are the so-called pinelanders of Georgia, I suppose the most degraded race of human beings claiming an Anglo-Saxon origin that can be found on the face of the earth—filthy, lazy, ignorant, brutal, proud, penniless savages, without one of the nobler attributes which have been found occasionally allied to the vices of savage nature. They own no slaves, for they are almost without exception abjectly poor; they will not work, for that, as they conceive, would reduce them to an equality with the abhorred Negroes; they squat, and steal, and starve, on the outskirts of this lowest of all civilized societies, and their countenances bear witness to the squalor of their condition and the utter degradation of their natures. To the crime of slavery, though they have no profitable part or lot in it, they are fiercely accessory, because it is the barrier that divides the black and white races, at the foot of which they lie wallowing in unspeakable degradation, but immensely proud of the base freedom which still separates them from the lash-driven tillers of the soil.*

The house at which our call was paid was set down in the midst

---

* Of such is the white family so wonderfully described in Mrs. Stowe's *Dred*, whose only slave brings up the orphaned children of his masters with such exquisitely grotesque and pathetic tenderness. From such the conscription which has fed the Southern army in the deplorable civil conflict now raging in America has drawn its rank and file. Better "food for powder" the world could scarcely supply. Fierce and idle, with hardly one of the necessities or amenities that belong to civilized existence, they are hardy endurers of hardship, and reckless to a savage degree of the value of life, whether their own or others. The soldier's pay, received or promised, exceeds in amount per month anything they ever earned before per year, and the war they wage is one that enlists all their proud and ferocious instincts. It is against the Yankees, the Northern sons of free soil, free toil and intelligence, the hated abolitionists whose success would sweep away slavery and reduce the Southern white men to work. No wonder they are ready to fight to the death against this detestable alternative, especially as they look to victory as the certain promotion of the refuse of the "poor white" population of the South, of which they are one and all members, to the coveted dignity of slaveholders.

of the Pine Barren, with half-obliterated roads and paths round it, suggesting that it might be visited and was inhabited.[1] It was large and not unhandsome, though curiously dilapidated, considering that people were actually living in it; certain remnants of carving on the cornices and paint on the panels bore witness to some former stage of existence less neglected and deteriorated than the present. The old lady mistress of this most forlorn abode amiably inquired if so much exercise did not fatigue me; at first I thought she imagined I must have walked through the pine forest all the way from Darien, but she explained that she considered the drive quite an effort; and it is by no means uncommon to hear people in America talk of being dragged over bad roads in uneasy carriages as exercise, showing how very little they know the meaning of the word, and how completely they identify it with the idea of mere painful fatigue instead of pleasurable exertion.

Returning home, my reflections ran much on the possible future destiny of these vast tracts of sandy soil. It seems to me that the ground capable of supporting the evergreen growth, the luxuriant Gardenia bushes, the bay myrtle, the beautiful Magnolia *grandiflora,* and the powerful and gnarled live oaks, that find their sustenance in this earth and under this same sky as the fir trees, must be convertible into a prosperous habitation for other valuable vegetable growth that would add immensely to the wealth of the Southern states. The orange thrives and bears profusely along this part of the seaboard of Georgia; and I cannot conceive that the olive, the mulberry, and the vine might not be acclimated, and successfully and profitably cultivated throughout the whole of this region, the swampy lower lands alone remaining as rice plantations. The produce of these already exceeds in value that of the once gold-growing cotton fields; and I cannot help believing that silk, and wine, and oil may, and will, hereafter become, with the present

[1] This was Ashantilly, the winter home of Sarah Leake and Thomas Spalding. When Fanny Kemble visited her "the old lady mistress" of Ashantilly was sixty-one years of age. We shall find Mrs. Spalding returning this visit in the following chapter.

solitary cotton crop, joint possessors of all this now but half-reclaimed wilderness. The soil all round Sorrento is very nearly as light, and dry, and sandy as this, and vineyards, and olive orchards, and cocooneries are part of the agricultural wealth there. Our neighbor, Mr. C[ouper], has successfully cultivated the date palm in his garden on the edge of the sea at St. Simons, and certainly the ilex, orange, and myrtle abounding here suggest natural affinities between the Italian soil and climate and this.

I must tell you something funny which occurred yesterday at dinner, which will give you some idea of the strange mode in which we live. We have now not infrequently had mutton at table, the flavor of which is quite excellent, as indeed it may well be, for it is raised under all the conditions of the famous *pré salé* [2] that the French gourmands especially prize, and which are reproduced on our side of the Channel in the peculiar qualities of our best South Down. The mutton we have here grazes on the short sweet grass at St. Simons within sea-salt influence, and is some of the very best I have ever tasted, but it is invariably brought to table in lumps or chunks of no particular shape or size, and in which it is utterly impossible to recognize any part of the quadruped creature sheep with which my eyes have hitherto become acquainted. Eat it, one may and does thankfully; name it, one could not by any possibility. Having submitted to this for some time, I at length inquired why a decent usual Christian joint of mutton—leg, shoulder, or saddle—was never brought to table: the reply was that the *carpenter* always cut up the meat, and that he did not know how to do it otherwise than by dividing it into so many thick square pieces, and proceeding to chop it up on that principle; and the consequence of this is, that *four lumps* or *chunks* are all that a whole sheep ever furnishes to our table by this artistic and economical process.

This morning I have been to the hospital to see a poor woman who has just enriched Mr. [Butler] by *borning* him another slave.

[2] Salt marsh.

The poor little pickaninny, as they called it, was not one bit uglier than white babies under similarly novel circumstances, except in one particular, that it had a head of hair like a trunk, in spite of which I had all the pains in the world in persuading its mother not to put a cap upon it. I bribed her finally by the promise of a pair of socks instead, with which I undertook to endow her child, and, moreover, actually prevailed upon her to forego the usual swaddling and swathing process, and let her poor baby be dressed at its first entrance into life as I assured her both mine had been.

On leaving the hospital I visited the huts all along the street, confiscating sundry refractory baby caps among shrieks and outcries, partly of laughter and partly of real ignorant alarm for the consequences. I think, if this infatuation for hot headdresses continues, I shall make shaving the children's heads the only condition upon which they shall be allowed to wear caps.

On Sunday morning [February 10] I went over to Darien to church. Our people's church was closed, the minister having gone to officiate elsewhere. With laudable liberality, I walked into the opposite church of a different, not to say opposite sect: here I heard a sermon, the opening of which will probably edify you as it did me, viz., that if a man was *just in all his dealings,* he was apt to think he did all that could be required of him—and no wide mistake either, one might suppose. But is it not wonderful how such words can be spoken here, with the most absolute unconsciousness of their tremendous bearing upon the existence of every slaveholder who hears them? Certainly the use that is second nature has made the awful injustice in the daily practice of which these people live a thing of which they are as little aware as you or I of the atmospheric air that we inhale each time we breathe. The bulk of the congregation in this church was white. The Negroes are, of course, not allowed to mix with their masters in the house of God, and there is no special place set apart for them. Occasionally one or two are to be seen in the corners of the singing gallery, but any more open pollution by them of their owners' church could not be tolerated. Mr. [Butler]'s people have petitioned very vehemently that he would build a church for them on the island. I doubt, however, his allowing them such a luxury as a place of worship all to themselves. Such a privilege might not be thought well of by the neighboring planters; indeed, it is almost what one might call a whity-brown idea, dangerous, demoralizing, inflammatory, incendiary. I should not wonder if I should be suspected of being the chief cornerstone of it, and yet I am not: it is an old hope and entreaty of these poor people, which I am afraid they are not destined to see fulfilled.

XVI

The Move to St. Simons Island

[February 14–17, 1839]

Dearest E[lizabeth],

Passing the rice mill this morning in my walk, I went in to look at the machinery, the large steam mortars which shell the rice, and which work under the intelligent and reliable supervision of engineer Ned. I was much surprised, in the course of conversation with him this morning, to find how much older a man he was than he appeared. Indeed, his youthful appearance had hitherto puzzled me much in accounting for his very superior intelligence and the important duties confided to him. He is, however, a man upward of forty years old, although he looks ten years younger. He attributed his own uncommonly youthful appearance to the fact of his never having done what he called field work, or been exposed, as the common gang Negroes are, to the hardships of their all but brutish existence. He said his former master had brought him up very kindly, and he had learned to tend the engines, and had never been put to any other work, but he said this was not the case with his poor wife. He wished she was as well off as he was, but she had to work in the rice fields, and was "most broke in two" with labor, and exposure, and hard work while with child, and hard work just directly after childbearing; he said she could hardly crawl, and he urged me very much to speak a kind word for her to massa. She was almost all the time in the hospital, and he thought she could not live long.

Now E[lizabeth], here is another instance of the horrible injustice of this system of slavery. In my country or in yours, a man endowed with sufficient knowledge and capacity to be an engineer would, of course, be in the receipt of considerable wages; his wife would, together with himself, reap the advantages of his ability, and share the well-being his labor earned; he would be able to procure for her comfort in sickness or in health, and beyond the necessary household work, which the wives of most artisans are inured to, she would have no labor to encounter; in case of sickness even these would be alleviated by the assistance of some stout girl of all work or kindly neighbor, and the tidy parlor or snug bedroom would be her retreat if unequal to the daily duties of her own kitchen. Think of such a lot compared with that of the head engineer of Mr. [Butler]'s plantation, whose sole wages are his coarse food and raiment and miserable hovel, and whose wife, covered with one filthy garment of ragged texture and dingy color, barefooted and bareheaded, is daily driven afield to labor with aching pain-racked joints, under the lash of a driver, or lies languishing on the earthen floor of the dismal plantation hospital in a condition of utter physical destitution and degradation such as the most miserable dwelling of the poorest inhabitant of your free Northern villages never beheld the like of. Think of the rows of tidy tiny houses in the long suburbs of Boston and Philadelphia, inhabited by artisans of just the same grade as this poor Ned, with their white doors and steps, their hydrants of inexhaustible fresh flowing water, the innumerable appliances for decent comfort of their cheerful rooms, the gay wardrobe of the wife, her cotton prints for daily use, her silk for Sunday churchgoing; the careful comfort of the children's clothing, the books and newspapers in the little parlor, the daily district school, the weekly parish church: imagine if you can—but you are happy that you cannot—the contrast between such an existence and that of the best mechanic on a Southern plantation.

Did you ever read (but I am sure you never did, and no more did I) an epic poem on fresh-water fish? Well, such a one was once written, I have forgotten by whom, but assuredly the heroine of it ought to have been the Altamaha shad—a delicate creature, so superior to the animal you Northerners devour with greedy thankfulness when the spring sends back their finny drove to your colder waters, that one would not suppose these were of the same family, instead of being, as they really are, precisely the same fish. Certainly the mud of the Altamaha must have some most peculiar virtues; and, by-the-by, I have never anywhere tasted such delicious tea as that which we make with this same turbid stream, the water of which, duly filtered of course, has some peculiar softness which affects the tea (and it is the same we always use) in a most curious and agreeable manner.

On my return to the house I found a terrible disturbance in consequence of the disappearance from undercook John's safe-keeping of a ham Mr. [Butler] had committed to his charge. There was no doubt whatever that the unfortunate culinary slave had made away in some inscrutable manner with the joint intended for our table: the very lies he told about it were so curiously shallow, childlike, and transparent, that while they confirmed the fact of his theft quite as much, if not more, than an absolute confession would have done, they provoked at once my pity and my irrepressible mirth to a most painful degree. Mr. [Butler] was in a state of towering anger and indignation, and, besides a flogging, sentenced the unhappy cook to degradation from his high and dignified position (and, alas! all its sweets of comparatively easy labor and good living from the remains of our table) to the hard toil, coarse scanty fare, and despised position of a common field hand. I suppose some punishment was inevitably necessary in such a plain case of deliberate theft as this, but, nevertheless, my whole soul revolts at the injustice of visiting upon these poor wretches a moral darkness which all possible means are taken to increase and perpetuate.

In speaking of this and the whole circumstance of John's trespass to Mr. [Butler] in the evening, I observed that the ignorance of these poor people ought to screen them from punishment. He replied that they knew well enough what was right and wrong. I asked how they could be expected to know it? He replied, by the means of cooper London, and the religious instruction he gave them. So that, after all, the appeal is to be made against themselves to that moral and religious instruction which is withheld from them, and which, if they obtain it at all, is the result of their own unaided and unencouraged exertion. The more I hear, and see, and learn, and ponder the whole of this system of slavery, the more impossible I find it to conceive how its practicers and upholders are to justify their deeds before the tribunal of their own conscience or God's law. It is too dreadful to have those whom we love accomplices to this wickedness; it is too intolerable to find myself an involuntary accomplice to it.

I had a conversation the next morning with Abraham, cook John's brother, upon the subject of his brother's theft; and only think of the *slave* saying that "this action had brought disgrace upon the family." Does not that sound very like the very best sort of free pride, the pride of character, the honorable pride of honesty, integrity, and fidelity? But this was not all, for this same Abraham, a clever carpenter and much valued *hand* on the estate, went on, in answer to my questions, to tell me such a story that I declare to you I felt as if I could have howled with helpless indignation and grief when he departed and went to resume his work. His grandfather had been an old slave in Darien, extremely clever as a carpenter, and so highly valued for his skill and good character that his master allowed him to purchase his liberty by money which he earned by working for himself at odd times, when his task work was over. I asked Abraham what sum his grandfather paid for his freedom: he said he did not know, but he supposed a large one, because of his being a "skilled carpenter," and so a peculiarly valuable chattel. I presume, from what I remember Major M—— and Dr. H[olmes] saying on the subject of the market value of Negroes in Charleston and Savannah, that such a man in the prime of life would have been worth from fifteen hundred to two thousand dollars. However, whatever the man paid for his ransom, by his grandson's account, fourteen years after he became free, when he died, he had again amassed money to the amount of seven hundred dollars, which he left among his wife and children, the former being a slave on Major [Butler]'s estate, where the latter remained by virtue of that fact slaves also. So this man not only bought his own freedom at a cost of *at least* a thousand dollars, but left a little fortune of seven hundred more at his death; and then we are told of the universal idleness, incorrigible sloth, and brutish incapacity of this inferior race of creatures, whose only fitting and Heaven-appointed condition is that of beasts of burden to the whites. I do not believe the whole low white population of the State of Georgia could furnish such an instance of energy, industry, and thrift as the amassing of this laborious little fortune by this poor slave, who left, nevertheless, his children and grandchildren to the lot from which he had so heroically ransomed himself; and yet the white men with whom I live and talk tell me, day after day, that there is neither cruelty nor injustice in this accursed system.

About half past five I went to walk on the dikes, and met a gang of the field hands going to the tide mill, as the water served them for working then. I believe I have told you that besides the great steam mill there is this, which is dependent on the rise and fall of the tide in the river, and where the people are therefore obliged to work by day or night, at whatever time the water serves to impel the wheel. They greeted me with their usual profusion of exclamations, petitions, and benedictions, and I parted from them to come and oversee my slave Jack, for whom I had bought a spade, and to whom I had intrusted the task of turning up some ground for me, in which I wanted to establish some of the narcissus and other flowers I had remarked about the ground and the house. Jack, however, was a worse digger than Adam could have been when first he turned his hand to it, after his expulsion from Paradise. I think I could have managed a spade with infinitely more efficiency, or rather less incapacity, than he displayed. Upon my expressing my amazement at his performance, he said the people here never used spades, but performed all their agricultural operations with the hoe. Their soil must be very light and their agriculture very superficial, I should think. However, I was obliged to terminate Jack's spooning process, and abandon, for the present, my hopes of a flower bed created by his industry, being called into the house to receive the return visit of old Mrs. S[palding]. As usual, the appearance, health, vigor, and good management of the children were the theme of wondering admiration; as usual, my possession of a white nurse the theme of envious congratulation; as usual, I had to hear the habitual senseless complaints of the inefficiency of colored nurses. If you are half as tired of the sameness and stupidity of the conversation of my Southern female neighbors as I am, I pity you; but not as much as I pity them for the stupid sameness of their most vapid existence, which would deaden any amount of intelligence, obliterate any amount of instruction, and render torpid and stagnant any amount of natural energy and vivacity. I would rather die—rather a thousand times—than live the lives of these Georgia planters' wives and daughters.

Mrs. S[palding] had brought me some of the delicious wild jasmine that festoons her dreary pine-wood drive, and most grateful I was for the presence of the sweet wild nosegay in my highly unornamental residence. When my visitors had left me, I took the refreshment of a row over to Darien; and as we had the tide against us coming back, the process was not so refreshing for the rowers. The evening was so extremely beautiful, and the rising of the moon so exquisite, that instead of retreating to the house when I reached the island, I got into the *Dolphin,* my special canoe, and made Jack paddle me down the great river to meet the *Lily,* which was coming back from St. Simons with Mr. [Butler], who has been preparing all things for our advent thither.

[February 17]

My letter has been interrupted, dear E[lizabeth], by the breaking up of our residence on the rice plantation, and our arrival at St. Simons, whence I now address you. We came down yesterday afternoon, and I was thankful enough of the fifteen miles' row to rest in, from the labor of leave-taking, with which the whole morning was taken up, and which, combined with packing and preparing all our own personalities and those of the children, was no sinecure. At every moment one or other of the poor people rushed in upon me to bid me good-by; many of their farewells were grotesque enough, some were pathetic, and all of them made me very sad. Poor people! how little I have done, how little I can do for them.

I had a long talk with that interesting and excellent man, cooper London, who made an earnest petition that I would send him from the North a lot of Bibles and Prayer Books; certainly the science of reading must be much more common among the Negroes than I supposed, or London must look to a marvelously increased spread of the same hereafter. There is, however, considerable reticence upon this point, or else the poor slaves must consider the mere possession of the holy books as good for salvation and as effectual for spiritual assistance to those who cannot as to those who can comprehend them. Since the news of our departure has spread, I have had repeated eager entreaties for presents of Bibles and Prayer Books, and to my demurrer of "But you can't read, can you?" have generally received for answer a reluctant acknowledgment of ignorance, which, however, did not always convince me of the fact. In my farewell conversation with London I found it impossible to get him to tell me how he had learned to read: the penalties for teaching them are very severe—heavy fines, increasing in amount for the first and second offense, and imprisonment for the third.* Such a man as London is certainly aware that to teach the slaves to read is an illegal act, and he may have been unwilling to betray whoever had been his preceptor even to my knowledge; at any rate, I got no answers from him but: "Well, missis, me learn; well, missis, me try"; and finally: "Well, missis, me 'spose Heaven help me"; to which I could only reply that I knew Heaven was helpful, but very hardly to the tune of teaching folks their letters. I got no satisfaction.

Old Jacob, the father of Abraham, cook John, and poor Psyche's husband, took a most solemn and sad leave of me, saying he did not expect ever to see me again. I could not exactly tell why, because, though he is aged and infirm, the fifteen miles between the rice plantation and St. Simons do not appear so insuperable a barrier between the inhabitants of the two places, which I represented to him as a suggestion of consolation.

I have worked my fingers nearly off with making, for the last day or two, innumerable rolls of coarse little baby clothes, layettes for the use of small newborn slaves; M[argery] diligently cutting and shaping, and I as diligently stitching. We leave a good supply for the hospitals, and for the individual clients besides who have besieged me ever since my departure became imminent.

Our voyage from the rice to the cotton plantation was performed in the *Lily,* which looked like a soldier's baggage wagon and an emigrant transport combined. Our crew consisted of eight men. Forward in the bow were miscellaneous livestock, pots, pans, household furniture, kitchen utensils, and an indescribable variety of heterogeneous necessaries. Enthroned upon beds, bedding, tables, and other chattels, sat that poor pretty chattel Psyche, with

* These laws have been greatly increased in stringency and severity since these letters were written, and *death* has not been reckoned too heavy a penalty for those who should venture to offer these unfortunate people the fruit of that forbidden tree of knowledge, their access to which has appeared to their owners the crowning danger of their own precarious existence among their terrible dependents.

her small chattel children. Midships sat the two tiny free women [1] and myself, and in the stern Mr. [Butler] steering. And "all in the blue unclouded weather" we rowed down the huge stream, the men keeping time and tune to their oars with extemporaneous chants of adieu to the rice island and its denizens. Among other poetical and musical comments on our departure recurred the assertion, as a sort of burden, that we were "parted in body, but not in mind," from those we left behind. Having relieved one set of sentiments by this reflection, they very wisely betook themselves to the consideration of the blessings that remained to them, and performed a spirited chant in honor of Psyche and our bouncing black housemaid, Mary.

At the end of a fifteen miles' row we entered one among a perfect labyrinth of arms or branches, into which the broad river ravels like a fringe as it reaches the sea, a dismal navigation along a dismal tract, called Five Pound, [2] through a narrow cut or channel of water divided from the main stream. The conch was sounded, as at our arrival at the rice island, and we made our descent on the famous long-staple cotton island of St. Simons, where we presently took up our abode in what had all the appearance of an old, half-decayed, rattling farmhouse.

This morning, Sunday, I peeped round its immediate neighborhood, and saw, to my inexpressible delight, within hail, some noble-looking evergreen oaks, and close to the house itself a tiny would-be garden, a plot of ground with one or two peach trees in full blossom, tufts of silver narcissus and jonquils, a quantity of violets and an exquisite myrtle bush; wherefore I said my prayers with especial gratitude.

[1] Fanny's little girls, Sally and Fan.

[2] Five Pound was a remote settlement at the extreme western end of Little St. Simons Island. A narrow strip of cultivation wrested from the swamp, it got its name from the fact that it was divided into five main fields, or pounds. How much Five Pound contributed to the estate's rice output is not known, nor the number of slaves who labored there. But it was an integral part of the rice economy.

ST. SIMONS ISLAND.

February 16—

April 19, 1839

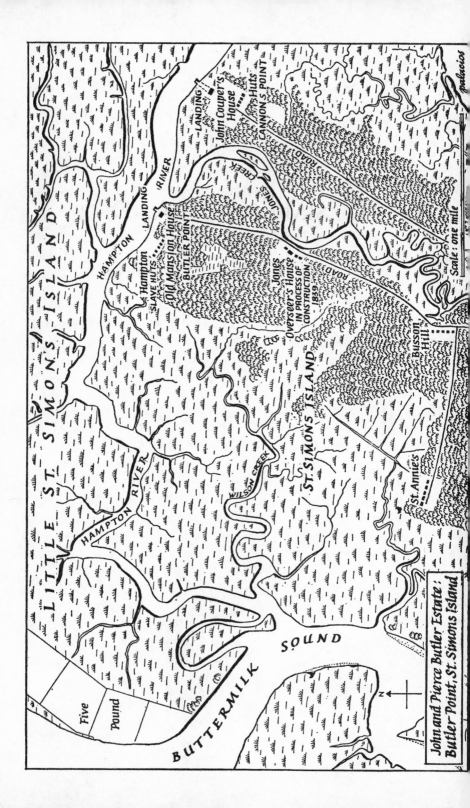

John and Pierce Butler Estate;
Butler Point, St. Simons Island

XVII

Hampton Point

[February 18, 1839]

Dearest E[lizabeth],

The fame of my peculiar requisitions has, I find, preceded me here, for the babies that have been presented to my admiring notice have all been without caps; also, however, without socks to their opposite little wretched extremities, but that does not signify quite so much. The people, too, that I saw yesterday were remarkably clean and tidy; to be sure, it was Sunday. The whole day, till quite late in the afternoon, the house was surrounded by a crowd of our poor dependents, waiting to catch a glimpse of Mr. [Butler], myself, or the children; and until, from sheer weariness, I was obliged to shut the doors, an incessant stream poured in and out, whose various modes of salutation, greeting, and welcome were more grotesque and pathetic at the same time than anything you can imagine. In the afternoon I walked with [Mr. Butler] to see a new house in process of erection, which, when it is finished, is to be the overseer's abode and our residence during any future visits we may pay to the estate.[1] I was horrified at the dismal site

[1] The new overseer's house was strategically located at the Jones's Creek settlement, nearly midway between the Hampton fields on the north and the Busson Hill and St. Annie's fields on the south. This house was marked on the government survey of the area made in 1868, but no trace of it now remains.

selected, and the hideous house erected on it. It is true that the central position is the principal consideration in the overseer's location; but both position and building seemed to me to witness to an inveterate love of ugliness, or, at any rate, a deadness to every desire of beauty, nothing short of horrible; and, for my own part, I think it is intolerable to have to leave the point where the waters meet, and where a few fine picturesque old trees are scattered about, to come to this place even for the very short time I am ever likely to spend here.

In every direction our view, as we returned, was bounded by thickets of the most beautiful and various evergreen growth, which beckoned my inexperience most irresistibly. [Mr. Butler] said, to my unutterable horror, that they were perfectly infested with rattlesnakes, and I must on no account go "beating about the bush" in these latitudes, as the game I should be likely to start would be anything but agreeable to me. We saw quantities of wild plum trees all silvery with blossoms, and in lovely companionship and contrast with them a beautiful shrub covered with delicate pink bloom like flowering peach trees. After that life in the rice swamp, where the Altamaha kept looking over the dike at me all the time as I sat in the house writing or working, it is pleasant to be on terra firma again, and to know that the river is at the conventional, not to say natural, depth below its banks, and under my feet instead of over my head. The two plantations are of diametrically opposite dispositions—that is all swamp, and this all sand; or, to speak more accurately, that is all swamp, and all of this that is not swamp is sand.

On our way home we met a most extraordinary creature of the Negro kind, who, coming toward us, halted, and caused us to halt straight in the middle of the path, when, bending himself down till his hands almost touched the ground, he exclaimed to Mr. [Butler], "Massa [Butler], your most obedient"; and then, with a kick and a flourish altogether indescribable, he drew to the side of the path to let us pass, which we did perfectly shouting with laughter, which broke out again every time we looked at each other and stopped to take breath: so sudden, grotesque, uncouth, and yet dexterous a gambado [2] never came into the brain or out of the limbs of anything but a "niggar."

I observed, among the numerous groups that we passed or met, a much larger proportion of mulattoes than at the rice island; upon asking Mr. [Butler] why this was so, he said that there no white person could land without his or the overseer's permission, whereas on St. Simons, which is a large island containing several plantations belonging to different owners, of course the number of whites, both residing on and visiting the place, was much greater, and the opportunity for intercourse between the blacks and whites much more frequent. While we were still on this subject, a horrid-looking filthy woman met us with a little child in her arms, a very light mulatto, whose extraordinary resemblance to driver Bran (one of the officials who had been duly presented to me on my arrival, and who was himself a mulatto) struck me directly. I pointed it out to Mr. [Butler], who merely answered: "Very likely his child."

"And," said I, "did you never remark that driver Bran is the exact image of Mr. K[ing]?"

"Very likely his brother," was the reply: all which rather unpleasant state of relationships seemed accepted as such a complete matter of course, that I felt rather uncomfortable, and said no more about who was like who, but came to certain conclusions in my own mind as to a young lad who had been among our morning visitors, and whose extremely light color and straight, handsome features and striking resemblance to Mr. K[ing] had suggested suspicions of a rather unpleasant nature to me, and whose sole acknowledged parent was a very black Negress of the name of Minda. I have no doubt at all, now, that he is another son of Mr. K[ing], Mr. [Butler]'s paragon overseer.

As we drew near the house again we were gradually joined by

[2] An antic.

such a numerous escort of Mr. [Butler]'s slaves that it was almost with difficulty we could walk along the path. They buzzed, and hummed, and swarmed round us like flies, and the heat and dust consequent upon this friendly companionship were a most unpleasant addition to the labor of walking in the sandy soil through which we were plowing. I was not sorry when we entered the house and left our bodyguard outside. In the evening I looked over the plan of the delightful residence I had visited in the morning, and could not help suggesting to Mr. [Butler] the advantage to be gained in point of picturesqueness by merely turning the house round. It is but a wooden frame one after all, and your folks "down East" would think no more of inviting it to face about than if it was built of cards; but the fact is, here nothing signifies except the cotton crop, and whether one's nose is in a swamp and one's eyes in a sand heap is of no consequence whatever either to one's self (if one's self was not I) or anyone else.

I find here an immense proportion of old people; the work and the climate of the rice plantation require the strongest of the able-bodied men and women of the estate. The cotton crop is no longer by any means as paramount in value as it used to be, and the climate, soil, and labor of St. Simons are better adapted to old, young and feeble cultivators than the swamp fields of the rice island. I wonder if I ever told you of the enormous decrease in value of this same famous sea-island, long-staple cotton. When Major [Butler], Mr. [Butler]'s grandfather, first sent the produce of this plantation where we now are to England, it was of so fine a quality that it used to be quoted by itself in the Liverpool cotton market, and was then worth half a guinea a pound; it is now not worth a shilling a pound. This was told me by the gentleman in Liverpool who has been factor for this estate for thirty years. Such a decrease as this in the value of one's crop, and the steady increase at the same time of a slave population, now numbering between seven hundred and eight hundred bodies to clothe and house, mouths to feed, while the land is being exhausted by the careless and wasteful nature of the agriculture itself, suggests a pretty serious prospect of declining prosperity; and, indeed, unless these Georgia cotton planters can command more land, or lay abundant capital (which they have not, being almost all of them over head and ears in debt) upon that which has already spent its virgin vigor, it is a very obvious thing that they must all very soon be eaten up by their own property. The rice plantations are a great thing to fall back upon under these circumstances, and the rice crop is now quite as valuable, if not more so, than the cotton one on Mr. [Butler]'s estates, once so famous and prosperous through the latter [i.e., cotton].

I find any number of all but superannuated men and women here, whose tales of the former grandeur of the estate and family are like things one reads of in novels. One old woman, who crawled to see me, and could hardly lift her poor bowed head high enough to look in my face, had been in Major [Butler]'s establishment in Philadelphia, and told with infinite pride of having waited upon his daughters and granddaughters, Mr. [Butler]'s sisters. Yet here she is, flung by like an old rag, crippled with age and disease, living, or rather dying by slow degrees in a miserable hovel, such as no decent household servant would at the North, I suppose, ever set their foot in. The poor old creature complained bitterly to me of all her ailments and all her wants. I can do little, alas! for either.

I had a visit from another tottering old crone called Dorcas, who all but went on her knees as she wrung and kissed my hands; with her came my friend Molly, the grandmother of the poor runaway girl Louisa, whose story I wrote you some little time ago. I had to hear it all over again, it being the newest event evidently in Molly's life; and it ended as before with the highly reasonable proposition: "Me say, missis, what for massa's niggar run away? Snake eat 'em up, or dey starve to def in a swamp. Massa's niggars dey don't neber run away." If I was "massa's niggars," I "spose" I shouldn't run away either, with only those alternatives; but when I look at these wretches and at the sea that rolls round this island, and think how near the English West Indies and freedom are, it gives me a pretty severe twinge at the heart.

XVIII

A Furious Wind and Sea

[February 19–27, 1839]

Dearest E[lizabeth],

I am afraid my letters must be becoming very wearisome to you; for if, as the copybook runs, "Variety is charming," they certainly cannot be so unless monotony is also charming, a thing not impossible to some minds, but of which the copybook makes no mention. But what will you? as the French say; my days are no more different from one another than peas in a dish, or sands on the shore: it is a pleasant enough life to live for one who, like myself, has a passion for dullness, but it affords small matter for epistolary correspondence. I suppose it is the surfeit of excitement that I had in my youth that has made a life of quiet monotony so extremely agreeable to me; it is like stillness after loud noise, twilight after glare, rest after labor. There is enough strangeness, too, in everything that surrounds me here to interest and excite me agreeably and sufficiently, and I should like the wild savage loneliness of the faraway existence extremely if it were not for the one small item of "the slavery."

I had a curious visit this morning from half-a-dozen of the women, among whom were driver Morris's wife and Venus (a hideous old goddess she was, to be sure), driver Bran's mother.

They came especially to see the children, who are always eagerly asked for, and hugely admired by their sooty dependents. These poor women went into ecstasies over the little white "pickaninnies," and were loud and profuse in their expressions of gratitude to Massa [Butler] for getting married and having children, a matter of thankfulness which, though it always makes me laugh very much, is a most serious one to them; for the continuance of the family keeps the estate and slaves from the hammer, and the poor wretches, besides seeing in every new child born to their owners a security against their own banishment from the only home they know, and separation from all ties of kindred and habit, and dispersion to distant plantations, not unnaturally look for a milder rule from masters who are the children of their fathers' masters. The relation of owner and slave may be expected to lose some of its harsher features, and, no doubt, in some instances, does so, when it is on each side the inheritance of successive generations. And so [Mr. Butler]'s slaves laud, and applaud, and thank, and bless him for having married, and endowed their children with two little future mistresses. One of these women, a Diana by name, went down on her knees, and uttered in a loud voice a sort of extemporaneous prayer of thanksgiving at our advent, in which the sacred and the profane were most ludicrously mingled: her "tanks to de good Lord God Almighty that missus had come, what give de poor niggar sugar and flannel," and dat "Massa [Butler], him hab brought de missis and de two little misses down among de people," were really too grotesque, and yet certainly more sincere acts of thanksgiving are not often uttered among the solemn and decorous ones that are offered up to heaven for "benefits received."

I find the people here much more inclined to talk than those on the rice island; they have less to do and more leisure, and bestow it very liberally on me; moreover, the poor old women, of whom there are so many turned out to grass here, and of whom I have spoken to you before, though they are past work, are by no means past gossip, and the stories they have to tell of the former government of the estate under old Massa K[ing] are certainly pretty tremendous illustrations of the merits of slavery as a moral institution. This man, the father of the late overseer, Mr. R[oswell] K[ing], was Major [Butler]'s agent in the management of this property, and a more cruel and unscrupulous one as regards the slaves themselves, whatever he may have been in his dealings with the master, I should think it would be difficult to find, even among the cruel and unscrupulous class to which he belonged.

In a conversation with old "House Molly," as she is called, to distinguish her from all other Mollies on the estate, she having had the honor of being a servant in Major [Butler]'s house for many years, I asked her if the relation between men and women who are what they call married, i.e., who have agreed to live together as man and wife (the only species of marriage formerly allowed on the estate, I believe now London may read the Marriage Service to them), was considered binding by the people themselves and by the overseer. She said "not much formerly," and that the people couldn't be expected to have much regard to such an engagement, utterly ignored as it was by Mr. K[ing], whose invariable rule, if he heard of any disagreement between a man and woman calling themselves married, was immediately to bestow them in "marriage" on other parties, whether they chose it or not, by which summary process the slightest "incompatibility of temper" received the relief of a divorce more rapid and easy than even Germany could afford, and the estate lost nothing by any prolongation of celibacy on either side. Of course, the misery consequent upon such arbitrary destruction of voluntary and imposition of involuntary ties was nothing to Mr. K[ing].

I was very sorry to hear today that Mr. O——, the overseer at the rice island, of whom I have made mention to you more than once in my letters, had had one of the men flogged very severely for getting his wife baptized. I was quite unable, from the account I received, to understand what his objection had been to the poor man's desire to make his wife at least a formal Christian; but it does seem dreadful that such an act should be so visited. I almost wish I was back again at the rice island; for, though this is every way the pleasanter residence, I hear so much more that is intolerable of the treatment of the slaves from those I find here, that my life is really made wretched by it. There is not a single natural right that is not taken away from these unfortunate people, and the worst of all is, that their condition does not appear to me, upon farther observation of it, to be susceptible of even partial alleviation as long as the fundamental evil, the slavery itself, remains.

My letter was interrupted as usual by clamors for my presence at the door, and petitions for sugar, rice, and baby clothes from a group of women who had done their tasks at three o'clock in the afternoon, and had come to say: "Ha do, missis?" (How do you do?), and beg something on their way to their huts. Observing one among them whose hand was badly maimed, one finger being reduced to a mere stump, she told me it was in consequence of the bite of a rattlesnake, which had attacked and bitten her child, and then struck her as she endeavored to kill it; her little boy had died, but one of the drivers cut off her finger, and so she had escaped with the loss of that member only. It is yet too early in the season for me to make acquaintance with these delightful animals, but the accounts the Negroes give of their abundance is full of agreeable promise for the future. It seems singular, considering how very common they are, that there are not more frequent instances of the slaves being bitten by them; to be sure, they seem to me to have a holy horror of ever setting their foot near either tree or bush, or anywhere but on the open road and the fields where they labor; and, of course, the snakes are not so frequent in open and frequented places as in their proper coverts. The Red Indians are said to use successfully some vegetable cure for the bite, I believe the leaves of the slippery ash or elm; the only infallible remedy, however, is suction, but of this the ignorant Negroes are so afraid that they never can be induced to have recourse to it, being, of course, immovably persuaded that the poison which is so fatal to the blood must be equally so to the stomach. They tell me that the cattle wandering into the brakes and bushes are often bitten to death by these deadly creatures; the pigs, whose fat, it seems, does not accept the venom into its tissues with the same effect, escape unhurt for the most part—so much for the antivenomous virtue of adipose matter—a consolatory consideration for such of us as are inclined to take on flesh more than we think graceful.

This letter has been long on the stocks, dear E[lizabeth]. I have been busy all day, and tired, and lazy in the evening latterly, and, moreover, feel as if such very dull matter was hardly worth sending all the way off to where you are happy to be. However, that is nonsense; I know well enough that you are glad to hear from me, be it what it will, and so I resume my chronicle. Some of my evenings have been spent in reading Mr. Clay's antiabolition speech,[1] and making notes on it, which I will show you when we meet. What a cruel pity and what a cruel shame it is that such a man should either know no better or do no better for his country than he is doing now!

Yesterday [February 24] I for the first time bethought me of the riding privileges of which Jack used to make such magnificent mention when he was fishing with me at the rice island; and desiring to visit the remoter parts of the plantation and the other end of the island, I inquired into the resources of the stable. I was told I could have a mare with foal; but I declined adding my weight to what the poor beast already carried, and my only choice then was between one who had just foaled, or a fine stallion used

---

[1] At this time a debate was raging in Congress on the question of the people's right to petition their representatives for the abolition of slavery in the District of Columbia. Henry Clay's contribution to this debate, here referred to, was delivered in the Senate on February 7, 1839. His remarks consisted of a full and systematic denunciation of the abolition movement in all its phases; they were construed at the time as a move to win the Whig nomination and Southern support in the 1840 presidential campaign.

as a plow horse on the plantation. I determined for the latter, and shall probably be handsomely shaken whenever I take my rides abroad.

My dearest E[lizabeth], I write to you today [February 26] in great depression and distress. I have had a most painful conversation with Mr. [Butler], who has declined receiving any of the people's petitions through me. Whether he is wearied with the number of these prayers and supplications, which he would escape but for me, as they probably would not venture to come so incessantly to him, and I, of course, feel bound to bring every one confided to me to him, or whether he has been annoyed at the number of pitiful and horrible stories of misery and oppression under the former rule of Mr. K[ing], which have come to my knowledge since I have been here, and the grief and indignation caused, but which cannot, by any means, always be done away with, though their expression may be silenced by his angry exclamations of: "Why do you listen to such stuff?" or "Why do you believe such trash? don't you know the niggers are all d—d liars?" etc., I do not know; but he desired me this morning to bring him no more complaints or requests of any sort, as the people had hitherto had no such advocate, and had done very well without, and I was only kept in an incessant state of excitement with all the falsehoods they "found they could make me believe." How well they have done without my advocacy, the conditions which I see with my own eyes, even more than their pitiful petitions, demonstrate; it is indeed true that the sufferings of those who come to me for redress, and, still more, the injustice done to the great majority who cannot, have filled my heart with bitterness and indignation that have overflowed my lips, till, I suppose, [Mr. Butler] is weary of hearing what he has never heard before, the voice of passionate expostulation and importunate pleading against wrongs that he will not even acknowledge, and for creatures whose common humanity with his own I half think he does not believe; but I must return to the North, for my condition would be almost worse than theirs—condemned to hear and see so much wretchedness, not only without the means of alleviating it, but without permission even to represent it for alleviation: this is no place for me, since I was not born among slaves, and cannot bear to live among them.

Perhaps, after all, what he says is true: when I am gone they will fall back into the desperate uncomplaining habit of suffering, from which my coming among them, willing to hear and ready to help, has tempted them. He says that bringing their complaints to me, and the sight of my credulous commiseration, only tend to make them discontented and idle, and brings renewed chastisement upon them; and that so, instead of really befriending them, I am only preparing more suffering for them whenever I leave the place, and they can no more cry to me for help. And so I see nothing for it but to go and leave them to their fate; perhaps, too, he is afraid of the mere contagion of freedom which breathes from the very existence of those who are free; my way of speaking to the people, of treating them, or living with them, the appeals I make to their sense of truth, of duty, of self-respect, the infinite compassion and the human consideration I feel for them—all this, of course, makes my intercourse with them dangerously suggestive of relations far different from anything they have ever known; and, as Mr. O—— once almost hinted to me, my existence among slaves was an element of danger to the "institution." If I should go away, the human sympathy that I have felt for them will certainly never come near them again.

I was too unhappy to write any more, my dear friend, and you have been spared the rest of my paroxysm, which hereabouts culminated in the blessed refuge of abundant tears. God will provide. He has not forgotten, nor will He forsake these His poor children; and if I may no longer minister to them, they yet are in His hand, who cares for them more and better than I can.

Toward the afternoon yesterday I rowed up the river to the rice island by way of refreshment to my spirits, and came back today,

[February 27], through rather a severe storm. Before going to bed last night I finished Mr. Clay's speech, and ground my teeth over it. Before starting this morning I received from headman Frank a lesson on the various qualities of the various sorts of rice, and should be (at any rate till I forget all he told me, which I "feel in my bones" will be soon) a competent judge and expert saleswoman. The dead white speck, which shows itself sometimes in rice as it does in teeth, is in the former, as in the latter, a sign of decay; the finest quality of rice is what may be called flinty, clear and unclouded, and a pretty, clean, sparkling-looking thing it is.

I will tell you something curious and pleasant about my row back. The wind was so high and the river so rough when I left the rice island, that just as I was about to get into the boat I thought it might not be amiss to carry my life preserver with me, and ran back to the house to fetch it. Having taken that much care for my life, I jumped into the boat, and we pushed off. The fifteen miles' row with a furious wind, and part of the time the tide against us, and the huge broad, turbid river broken into a foaming sea of angry waves, was a pretty severe task for the men. They pulled with a will, however, but I had to forego the usual accompaniment of their voices, for the labor was tremendous, especially toward the end of our voyage, where, of course, the nearness of the sea increased the roughness of the water terribly. The men were in great spirits, however (there were eight of them rowing, and one behind was steering); one of them said something which elicited an exclamation of general assent, and I asked what it was; the steerer said they were pleased because there was not another planter's lady in all Georgia who would have gone through the storm all alone with them in a boat; i.e., without the protecting presence of a white man. "Why," said I, "my good fellows, if the boat capsized, or anything happened, I am sure I should have nine chances for my life instead of one"; at this there was one shout of "So you would, missis; true for dat, missis"; and in great mutual good humor we reached the landing at Hampton Point.

As I walked home I pondered over this compliment of Mr. [Butler]'s slaves to me, and did not feel quite sure that the very absence of the fear which haunts the Southern women in their intercourse with these people, and prevents them from trusting themselves ever with them out of reach of white companionship and supervision, was not one of the circumstances which makes my intercourse with them unsafe and undesirable. The idea of apprehending any mischief from them never yet crossed my brain; and in the perfect confidence with which I go among them, they must perceive a curious difference between me and my lady neighbors in these parts; all have expressed unbounded astonishment at my doing so.

The spring is fast coming on, and we shall, I suppose, soon leave Georgia. How new and sad a chapter of my life this winter here has been!

XIX

Women in Slavery

[February 28–March 2, 1839]

Dear E[lizabeth],

I cannot give way to the bitter impatience I feel at my present position, and come back to the North without leaving my babies; and though I suppose their stay will not in any case be much prolonged in these regions of swamp and slavery, I must, for their sakes, remain where they are, and learn this dreary lesson of human suffering to the end. The record, it seems to me, must be utterly wearisome to you, as the instances themselves, I suppose, in a given time (thanks to that dreadful reconciler to all that is evil—habit), would become to me.

This morning [February 28] I had a visit from two of the women, Charlotte and Judy, who came to me for help and advice for a complaint, which it really seems to me every other woman on the estate is cursed with, and which is a direct result of the conditions of their existence; the practice of sending women to labor in the fields in the third week after their confinement is a specific for causing this infirmity, and I know no specific for curing it under these circumstances. As soon as these poor things had departed with such comfort as I could give them, and the bandages they especially begged for, three other sable graces introduced themselves, Edie, Louisa, and Diana; the former told me she had had a family of seven children, but had lost them all through "ill luck," as she denominated the ignorance and ill-treatment which were answerable for the loss of these, as of so many other poor little creatures their fellows. Having dismissed her and Diana with the sugar and rice they came to beg, I detained Louisa, whom I had never seen but in the presence of her old grandmother, whose version of the poor child's escape to, and hiding in the woods, I had a desire to compare with the heroine's own story.

She told it very simply, and it was most pathetic. She had not finished her task one day, when she said she felt ill, and unable to do so, and had been severely flogged by driver Bran, in whose "gang" she then was. The next day, in spite of this encouragement to labor, she had again been unable to complete her appointed work; and Bran having told her that he'd tie her up and flog her if she did not get it done, she had left the field and run into the swamp.

"Tie you up, Louisa!" said I; "what is that?"

She then described to me that they were fastened up by their wrists to a beam or a branch of a tree, their feet barely touching the ground, so as to allow them no purchase for resistance or evasion of the lash, their clothes turned over their heads, and their backs scored with a leather thong, either by the driver himself, or, if he pleases to inflict their punishment by deputy, any of the men he may choose to summon to the office; it might be father, brother, husband, or lover, if the overseer so ordered it. I turned sick, and my blood curdled listening to these details from the slender young slip of a lassie, with her poor piteous face and murmuring, pleading voice.

"Oh," said I, "Louisa; but the rattlesnakes—the dreadful rattlesnakes in the swamps; were you not afraid of those horrible creatures?"

"Oh, missis," said the poor child, "me no tink of dem; me forget all 'bout dem for de fretting."

"Why did you come home at last?"

"Oh, missis, me starve with hunger, me most dead with hunger before me come back."

"And were you flogged, Louisa?" said I, with a shudder at what the answer might be.

"No, missis, me go to hospital; me almost dead and sick so long, 'spec driver Bran him forgot 'bout de flogging."

I am getting perfectly savage over all these doings, E[lizabeth], and really think I should consider my own throat and those of my children well cut if some night the people were to take it into their heads to clear off scores in that fashion.

The Calibanish wonderment of all my visitors at the exceedingly coarse and simple furniture and rustic means of comfort of my abode is very droll. I have never inhabited any apartment so perfectly devoid of what we should consider the common decencies of life; but to them, my rude chintz-covered sofa and common pine-wood table, with its green baize cloth, seem the adornings of a palace; and often in the evening, when my bairns are asleep, and M[argery] upstairs keeping watch over them, and I sit writing this daily history for your edification, the door of the great barnlike room is opened stealthily, and one after another, men and women come trooping silently in, their naked feet falling all but inaudibly on the bare boards as they betake themselves to the hearth, where they squat down on their hams in a circle, the bright blaze from the huge pine logs, which is the only light of this half of the room, shining on their sooty limbs and faces, and making them look like a ring of ebony idols surrounding my domestic hearth. I have had as many as fourteen at a time squatting silently there for nearly half an hour, watching me writing at the other end of the room. The candles on my table give only light enough for my own occupation, the firelight illuminates the rest of the apartment; and you cannot imagine anything stranger than the effect of all these glassy whites of eyes and grinning white teeth turned toward me, and shining in the flickering light. I very often take no notice of them at all, and they seem perfectly absorbed in contemplating me. My evening dress probably excites their wonder and admiration no less than my rapid and continuous writing, for which they have sometimes expressed compassion, as if they thought it must be more laborious than hoeing; sometimes at the end of my day's journal I look up and say suddenly: "Well, what do you want?" when each black figure springs up at once, as if moved by machinery; they all answer: "Me come say ha do (how d'ye do), missis"; and then they troop out as noiselessly as they entered, like a procession of sable dreams, and I go off in search, if possible, of whiter ones.

Two days ago I had a visit of great interest to me from several lads from twelve to sixteen years old, who had come to beg me to give them work. To make you understand this, you must know that, wishing very much to cut some walks and drives through the very picturesque patches of woodland not far from the house, I announced, through Jack, my desire to give employment in the wood-cutting line to as many lads as chose, when their unpaid task was done, to come and do some work for me, for which I engaged to pay them. At the risk of producing a most dangerous process of reflection and calculation in their brains, I have persisted in paying what I considered wages to every slave that has been my servant; and these my laborers must, of course, be free to work or no, as they like, and if they work for me must be paid by me. The proposition met with unmingled approbation from my "gang"; but I think it might be considered dangerously suggestive of the rightful relation between work and wages; in short, very involuntarily no doubt, but, nevertheless, very effectually I am disseminating ideas among Mr. [Butler]'s dependents, the like of which have certainly never before visited their wool-thatched brains.

Last night, after writing so much to you, I felt weary, and went out into the air to refresh my spirit. The scene just beyond the house was beautiful; the moonlight slept on the broad river, which here is almost the sea, and on the masses of foliage of the great Southern oaks; the golden stars of German poetry shone in the purple curtains of the night, and the measured rush of the Atlantic unfurling its huge skirts upon the white sands of the beach (the sweetest and most awful lullaby in nature) resounded through the silent air.

I have not felt well, and have been much depressed for some days past. I think I should die if I had to live here. This morning [March 1], in order not to die yet, I thought I had better take a ride, and accordingly mounted the horse which I told you was one of the equestrian alternatives offered me here; but no sooner did he feel my weight, which, after all, is mere levity and frivolity to him, than he thought proper to rebel, and find the grasshopper a burden, and rear and otherwise demonstrate his disgust. I have not ridden for a long time now; but Montreal's opposition very presently aroused the Amazon which is both natural and acquired in me, and I made him comprehend that, though I object to slaves, I expect obedient servants; which views of mine being imparted by a due administration of both spur and whip, attended with a judicious combination of coaxing pats on his great crested neck, and endearing commendations of his beauty, produced the desired effect. Montreal accepted me as inevitable, and carried me very wisely and well up the island to another of the slave settlements on the plantation, called Jones's Creek.

On my way I passed some magnificent evergreen oaks,* and some thickets of exquisite evergreen shrubs, and one or two beautiful sites for a residence, which made me gnash my teeth when I thought of the one we had chosen. To be sure, these charming spots, instead of being conveniently in the middle of the plantation, are at an out-of-the-way end of it, and so hardly eligible for the one quality desired for the overseer's abode, viz., being central.

* The only ilex trees which I have seen comparable in size and beauty with those of the seaboard of Georgia are some to be found in the Roman Campagna, at Passerano, Lun- ghegna, Castel Fusano, and other of its great princely farms, but especially in the magnificent woody wilderness of Valerano.

All the slaves' huts on St. Simons are far less solid, comfortable, and habitable than those at the rice island. I do not know whether the laborer's habitation bespeaks the alteration in the present relative importance of the crops, but certainly the cultivators of the once far-famed long-staple, sea-island cotton of St. Simons are far more miserably housed than the rice raisers of the other plantation. These ruinous shielings,[1] that hardly keep out wind or weather, are deplorable homes for young or aged people, and poor shelters for the hard-working men and women who cultivate the fields in which they stand.

Riding home I passed some beautiful woodland, with charming pink and white blossoming peach and plum trees, which seemed to belong to some orchard that had been attempted, and afterward delivered over to wildness. On inquiry, I found that no fruit worth eating was ever gathered from them. What a pity it seems! for in this warm, delicious winter climate any and every species of fruit might be cultivated with little pains and to great perfection.

As I was cantering along the side of one of the cotton fields I suddenly heard some inarticulate vehement cries, and saw what seemed to be a heap of black limbs tumbling and leaping toward me, renewing the screams at intervals as it approached. I stopped my horse, and the black ball bounded almost into the road before me, and, suddenly straightening itself up into a haggard hag of a half-naked Negress exclaimed, with panting, eager breathlessness: "Oh, missis, missis, you no hear me cry, you no hear me call. Oh, missis, me call, me cry, and me run; make me a gown like dat. Do, for massy's sake, only make me a gown like dat." This modest request for a riding habit in which to hoe the cotton fields served for an introduction to sundry other petitions for rice, and sugar, and flannel, all which I promised the petitioner, but not the "gown like dat"; whereupon I rode off, and she flung herself down in the middle of the road to get her wind and rest.

The passion for dress is curiously strong in these people, and

[1] Scottish term for a shepherd's hut.

seems as though it might be made an instrument in converting them, outwardly at any rate, to something like civilization; for, though their own native taste is decidedly both barbarous and ludicrous, it is astonishing how very soon they mitigate it in imitation of their white models. The fine figures of the mulatto women in Charleston and Savannah are frequently as elegantly and tastefully dressed as those of any of their female superiors; and here on St. Simons, owing, I suppose, to the influence of the resident lady proprietors of the various plantations, and the propensity to imitate in their black dependents, the people that I see all seem to me much tidier, cleaner, and less fantastically dressed than those on the rice plantation, where no such influences reach them.

On my return from my ride I had a visit from Captain F[raser], the manager of a neighboring plantation,[2] with whom I had a long conversation about the present and past condition of the estate, the species of feudal magnificence in which its original owner, Major [Butler], lived, the iron rule of old overseer K[ing] which succeeded to it, and the subsequent sovereignty of his son, Mr. R[oswell] K[ing], the man for whom Mr. [Butler] entertains such a cordial esteem, and of whom every account I receive from the Negroes seems to me to indicate a merciless sternness of disposition that may be a virtue in a slave driver, but is hardly a Christian grace. Captain F[raser] was one of our earliest visitors at the rice plantation on our arrival, and I think I told you of his mentioning, in speaking to me of the orange trees which formerly grew all round the dikes there, that he had taken Basil Hall there once in their blossoming season, and that he had said the sight was as well worth crossing the Atlantic for as Niagara. Today he referred to that again. He has resided for a great many years on a plantation here, and is connected with our neighbor, old Mr.

[2] Captain John Fraser has already been referred to—above—as the person who acted as guide to the Basil Halls on their visit to the Sea Islands in 1828. At the time of Fanny Kemble's residence, Captain Fraser was acting as manager of Hamilton Plantation, one of the largest estates on the island, located at Gascoigne's Bluff, its southwestern extremity.

C[ouper], whose daughter, I believe, he married. He interested me extremely by his description of the house Major [Butler] had many years ago on a part of the island called Sinclair. As far as I can understand, there must have been an indefinite number of "masters' " residences on this estate in the old Major's time; for, what with the one we are building, and the ruined remains of those not quite improved off the face of the earth, and the tradition of those that have ceased to exist, even as ruins, I make out no fewer than seven. How gladly would I exchange all that remain and all that do not for the smallest tenement in your blessed Yankee mountain village!

Captain F[raser] told me that at Sinclair General Oglethorpe, the good and brave English governor of the State of Georgia in its colonial days, had his residence, and that among the magnificent live oaks which surround the site of the former settlement, there was one especially venerable and picturesque, which in his recollection always went by the name of General Oglethorpe's Oak.[3] If you remember the history of the colony under his benevolent rule, you must recollect how absolutely he and his friend and counselor, Wesley, opposed the introduction of slavery in the colony. How wrathfully the old soldier's spirit ought to haunt these cotton fields and rice swamps of his old domain, with their population of wretched slaves! I will ride to Sinclair and see his oak; if I should see him, he cannot have much to say to me on the subject that I should not cry amen to.

I have made a gain, no doubt, in one respect in coming here, dear E[lizabeth], for, not being afraid of a rearing stallion, I can ride; but, on the other hand, my aquatic diversions are all likely, I

[3] Sinclair or St. Clair was an estate on the eastern shore of the island. At one time it was owned by Major Butler, but was not part of the Butler Point estate. General Oglethorpe never had a residence there. The old house whose ruins Fanny Kemble refers to was built by Sinclair and then occupied by Major William McIntosh. Mrs. Margaret Davis Cate, from whom this information comes, writes that "the old timers here still talk about the great oak at Sinclair, which was called 'Old England,' not 'Oglethorpe Oak.' "

fear, to be much curtailed. Well may you, or any other Northern abolitionist, consider this a heaven-forsaken region—why, I cannot even get worms to fish with, and was solemnly assured by Jack this morning [March 2] that the whole "Point," i.e., neighborhood of the house, had been searched in vain for these useful and agreeable animals. I must take to some more sportsmanlike species of bait; but, in my total ignorance of even the kind of fish that inhabit these waters, it is difficult for me to adapt my temptations to their taste.

Yesterday evening I had a visit that made me very sorrowful, if anything connected with these poor people can be called more especially sorrowful than their whole condition; but Mr. [Butler]'s declaration, that he will receive no more statements of grievances or petitions for redress through me, makes me as desirous now of shunning the vain appeals of these unfortunates as I used to be of receiving and listening to them. The imploring cry: "Oh missis!" that greets me whichever way I turn, makes me long to stop my ears now; for what can I say or do any more for them? The poor little favors—the rice, the sugar, the flannel—that they beg for with such eagerness, and receive with such exuberant gratitude, I can, it is true, supply, and words and looks of pity, and counsel of patience, and such instruction in womanly habits of decency and cleanliness as may enable them to better, in some degree, their own hard lot; but to the entreaty: "Oh, missis, you speak to massa for us! Oh, missis, you beg massa for us! Oh, missis, you tell massa for we, he sure do as you say!" I cannot now answer as formerly, and I turn away choking and with eyes full of tears from the poor creatures, not even daring to promise any more the faithful transmission of their prayers.

The women who visited me yesterday evening were all in the family way, and came to entreat of me to have the sentence (what else can I call it?) modified which condemns them to resume their labor of hoeing in the fields three weeks after their confinement. They knew, of course, that I cannot interfere with their appointed labor, and therefore their sole entreaty was that I would use my influence with Mr. [Butler] to obtain for them a month's respite from labor in the field after childbearing. Their principal spokeswoman, a woman with a bright sweet face, called Mary, and a very sweet voice, which is by no means an uncommon excellence among them, appealed to my own experience; and while she spoke of my babies, and my carefully tended, delicately nursed, and tenderly watched confinement and convalescence, and implored me to have a kind of labor given to them less exhausting during the month after their confinement, I held the table before me so hard in order not to cry that I think my fingers ought to have left a mark on it. At length I told them that Mr. [Butler] had forbidden me to bring him any more complaints from them, for that he thought the ease with which I received and believed their stories only tended to make them discontented, and that, therefore, I feared I could not promise to take their petitions to him; but that he would be coming down to "the Point" soon, and that they had better come then sometime when I was with him, and say what they had just been saying to me; and with this, and various small bounties, I was forced, with a heavy heart, to dismiss them; and when they were gone, with many exclamations of: "Oh yes, missis, you will, you will speak to massa for we; God bless you, missis, we sure you will!" I had my cry out for them, for myself, for *us*. All these women had had large families, and *all* of them had lost half their children, and several of them had lost more. How I do ponder upon the strange fate which has brought me here, from so far away, from surroundings so curiously different—how my own people in that blessed England of my birth would marvel if they could suddenly have a vision of me as I sit here, and how sorry some of them would be for me!

I am helped to bear all that is so very painful to me here by my constant enjoyment of the strange, wild scenery in the midst of which I live, and which my resumption of my equestrian habits gives me almost daily opportunity of observing. I rode today to some new-cleared and plowed ground that was being prepared for the precious cotton crop. I crossed a salt marsh upon a raised causeway that was perfectly alive with land crabs, whose desperately active endeavors to avoid my horse's hoofs were so ludicrous that I literally laughed alone and aloud at them. The sides of this road across the swamp were covered with a thick and close embroidery of creeping moss, or rather lichens of the most vivid green and red: the latter made my horse's path look as if it was edged with an exquisite pattern of coral; it was like a thing in a fairy tale, and delighted me extremely.

I suppose, E[lizabeth], one secret of my being able to suffer as acutely as I do, without being made either ill or absolutely miserable, is the childish excitability of my temperament, and the sort of ecstasy which any beautiful thing gives me. No day, almost no hour, passes without some enjoyment of the sort this coral-bordered road gave me, which not only charms my senses completely at the time, but returns again and again before my memory, delighting my fancy, and stimulating my imagination. I sometimes despise myself for what seems to me an inconceivable rapidity of emotion, that almost makes me doubt whether anyone who feels so many things can really be said to feel anything; but I generally recover from this perplexity by remembering whither invariably every impression of beauty leads my thoughts, and console myself for my contemptible facility of impression by the reflection that it is, upon the whole, a merciful system of compensation by which my whole nature, tortured as it was last night, can be absorbed this morning in a perfectly pleasurable contemplation of the capers of crabs and the color of mosses as if nothing else existed in creation. One thing, however, I think, is equally certain, and that is, that I need never expect much sympathy, and perhaps this special endowment will make me, to some degree, independent of it; but I have no doubt that to follow me through half a day with any species of lively participation in my feelings would be a severe breathless moral calisthenic to most of my friends—what Shakespeare calls "sweating labor." As far as I have hitherto had opportunities of observing, children and maniacs are the only creatures who would be capable of sufficiently rapid transitions of thought and feeling to keep pace with me.

And so I rode through the crabs and the coral. There is one thing, however, I beg to commend to your serious consideration as a trainer of youth, and that is, the expediency of cultivating in all the young minds you educate an equal love of the good, the beautiful, and the absurd (not an easy task, for the latter is apt in its development to interfere a little with the two others): doing this, you command all the resources of existence. The love of the good and beautiful, of course, you are prepared to cultivate—that goes without saying, as the French say; the love of the ludicrous will not appear to you as important, and yet you will be wrong to undervalue it. In the first place, I might tell you that it was almost like cherishing the love of one's fellow creatures—at which, no doubt, you shake your head reprovingly; but, leaving aside the enormous provision for the exercise of this natural faculty which we offer to each other, why should crabs scuttle from under my horse's feet in such a way as to make me laugh again every time I think of it, if there is not an inherent propriety in laughter, as the only emotion which certain objects challenge—an emotion wholesome for the soul and body of man? After all, *why* are we contrived to laugh at all, if laughter is not essentially befitting and beneficial? and most people's lives are too lead-colored to afford to lose one sparkle on them, even the smallest twinkle of light gathered from a flash of nonsense. Hereafter point out for the "appreciative" study of your pupils all that is absurd in themselves, others, and the universe in general; it is an element largely provided, of course, to meet a corresponding and grateful capacity for its enjoyment.

After my crab and coral causeway I came to the most exquisite thickets of evergreen shrubbery you can imagine. If I wanted to paint Paradise I would copy this undergrowth, passing through which I went on to the settlement at St. Annie's, traversing another swamp on another raised causeway. The thickets through which I next rode were perfectly draped with the beautiful wild jasmine of these woods. Of all the parasitical plants I ever saw, I do think it is the most exquisite in form and color, and its perfume is like the most delicate heliotrope.

I stopped for some time before a thicket of glittering evergreens, over which hung, in every direction, streaming garlands of these fragrant golden cups, fit for Oberon's banqueting service. These beautiful shrubberies were resounding with the songs of mockingbirds. I sat there on my horse in a sort of dream of enchantment, looking, listening, and inhaling the delicious atmosphere of those flowers; and suddenly my eyes opened, as if I had been asleep, on some bright red bunches of spring leaves on one of the winter-stripped trees, and I as suddenly thought of the cold Northern skies and earth, where the winter was still inflexibly tyrannizing over you all, and, in spite of the loveliness of all that was present, and the harshness of all that I seemed to see at that moment, no first tokens of the spring's return were ever more welcome to me than those bright leaves that reminded me how soon I should leave this scene of material beauty and moral degradation, where the beauty itself is of an appropriate character to the human existence it surrounds: above all, loveliness, brightness, and fragrance; but below! it gives one a sort of Melusina [4] feeling of horror—all swamp and poisonous stagnation, which the heat will presently make alive with venomous reptiles.

I rode on, and the next object that attracted my attention was a very startling and by no means agreeable one—an enormous cypress tree which had been burned, stood charred and blackened, and leaning toward the road so as to threaten a speedy fall across it, and on one of the limbs of this great charcoal giant hung a dead

---

[4] In medieval French legend, Melusina was a water fairy who married Raymond of Lusignan, in Poitou. According to local superstition Melusina would appear on the highest tower of the castle of Lusignan and shriek three times whenever the head of the family or the king of France lay dying.

rattlesnake. If I tell you that it looked to me at least six feet long, you will say you only wonder I did not say twelve; it was a hideous-looking creature, and some Negroes I met soon after told me they had found it in the swamp, and hung it dead on the burning tree. Certainly the two together made a dreadful trophy, and a curious contrast to the lovely bowers of bloom I had just been contemplating with such delight.

This settlement at St. Annie's is the remotest on the whole plantation, and I found there the wretchedest huts, and most miserably squalid, filthy, and forlorn creatures I had yet seen here —certainly the condition of the slaves on this estate is infinitely more neglected and deplorable than that on the rice plantation. Perhaps it may be that the extremely unhealthy nature of the rice cultivation makes it absolutely necessary that the physical condition of the laborers should be maintained at its best to enable them to abide it; and yet it seems to me that even the process of soaking the rice can hardly create a more dangerous miasma than the poor creatures must inhale who live in the midst of these sweltering swamps, half sea, half river slime. Perhaps it has something to do with the fact that the climate on St. Simons is generally considered peculiarly mild and favorable, and so less protection of clothes and shelter is thought necessary here for the poor residents; perhaps, too, it may be because the cotton crop is now, I believe, hardly as valuable as the rice crop, and the plantation here, which was once the chief source of its owner's wealth, is becoming a secondary one, and so not worth so much care or expense in repairing and constructing Negro huts and feeding and clothing the slaves. More pitiable objects than some of those I saw at the St. Annie's settlement today I hope never to see: there was an old crone called Hannah, a sister, as well as I could understand what she said, of old House Molly, whose face and figure, seamed with wrinkles, and bowed and twisted with age and infirmity, really hardly retained the semblance of those of a human creature, and as she crawled to me almost half her naked body was exposed through the miserable tatters that she held on with one hand, while the other eagerly clutched my hand, and her poor blear eyes wandered all over me as if she was bewildered by the strange aspect of any human being but those whose sight was familiar to her. One or two forlorn creatures like herself, too old or too infirm to be compelled to work, and the half-starved and more than half-naked children apparently left here under their charge, were the only inmates I found in these wretched hovels.

I came home without stopping to look at anything, for I had no heart any longer for what had so charmed me on my way to this place. Galloping along the road after leaving the marshes, I scared an ox who was feeding leisurely, and, to my great dismay, saw the foolish beast betake himself with lumbering speed into the "bush": the slaves will have to hunt after him, and perhaps will discover more rattlesnakes six or twelve feet long.

After reaching home I went to the house of the overseer to see his wife, a tidy, decent, kindhearted little woman, who seems to me to do her duty by the poor people she lives among as well as her limited intelligence and still more limited freedom allow. The house her husband lives in is the former residence of Major [Butler], which was the great mansion of the estate. It is now in a most ruinous and tottering condition, and they inhabit but a few rooms in it; the others are gradually moldering to pieces, and the whole edifice will, I should think, hardly stand long enough to be carried away by the river, which in its yearly inroads on the bank on which it stands has already approached within a perilous proximity to the old dilapidated planter's palace. Old Molly, of whom I have often before spoken to you, who lived here in the days of the prosperity and grandeur of "Hampton," still clings to the relics of her old master's former magnificence, and with a pride worthy of old Caleb of Ravenswood [5] showed me through the dismantled decaying rooms and over the remains of the dairy, displaying a capacious

[5] Caleb was the Ravenswood family's old retainer in Sir Walter Scott's *Bride of Lammermoor.*

fish box or well, where, in the good old days, the master's supply was kept in fresh salt water till required for table. Her prideful lamentations over the departure of all this quondam glory were ludicrous and pathetic; but, while listening with some amusement to the jumble of grotesque descriptions, through which her impression of the immeasurable grandeur and nobility of the house she served was the predominant feature, I could not help contrasting the present state of the estate with that which she described, and wondering why it should have become, as it undoubtedly must have done, so infinitely less productive a property than in the old Major's time.

Before closing this letter, I have a mind to transcribe to you the entries for today recorded in a sort of daybook, where I put down very succinctly the number of people who visit me, their petitions and ailments, and also such special particulars concerning them as seem to me worth recording. You will see how miserable the physical condition of many of these poor creatures is; and their physical condition, it is insisted by those who uphold this evil system, is the only part of it which is prosperous, happy, and compares well with that of Northern laborers. Judge from the details I now send you; and never forget, while reading them, that the people on this plantation are well off, and consider themselves well off, in comparison with the slaves on some of the neighboring estates.

Fanny has had six children; all dead but one. She came to beg to have her work in the field lightened.

Nanny has had three children; two of them are dead. She came to implore that the rule of sending them into the field three weeks after their confinement might be altered.

Leah, Caesar's wife, has had six children; three are dead.

Sophy, Lewis's wife, came to beg for some old linen. She is suffering fearfully; has had ten children; five of them are dead. The principal favor she asked was a piece of meat, which I gave her.

Sally, Scipio's wife, has had two miscarriages and three children born, one of whom is dead. She came complaining of incessant pain and weakness in her back. This woman was a mulatto daughter of a slave called Sophy, by a white man of the name of Walker, who visited the plantation.

Charlotte, Renty's wife, had had two miscarriages, and was with child again. She was almost crippled with rheumatism, and showed me a pair of poor swollen knees that made my heart ache. I have promised her a pair of flannel trousers, which I must forthwith set about making.

Sarah, Stephen's wife; this woman's case and history were alike deplorable. She had had four miscarriages, had brought seven children into the world, five of whom were dead, and was again with child. She complained of dreadful pains in the back, and an internal tumor which swells with the exertion of working in the fields; probably, I think, she is ruptured. She told me she had once been mad and had run into the woods, where she contrived to elude discovery for some time, but was at last tracked and brought back, when she was tied up by the arms, and heavy logs fastened to her feet, and was severely flogged. After this she contrived to escape again, and lived for some time skulking in the woods, and she supposes mad, for when she was taken again she was entirely naked. She subsequently recovered from this derangement, and seems now just like all the other poor creatures who come to me for help and pity. I suppose her constant childbearing and hard labor in the fields at the same time may have produced the temporary insanity.

Sukey, Bush's wife, only came to pay her respects. She had had four miscarriages; had brought eleven children into the world, five of whom are dead.

Molly, Quambo's wife, also only came to see me. Hers was the best account I have yet received; she had had nine children, and six of them were still alive.

This is only the entry for today, in my diary, of the people's complaints and visits. Can you conceive a more wretched picture than that which it exhibits of the conditions under which these women live? Their cases are in no respect singular, and though they come with pitiful entreaties that I will help them with some alleviation of their pressing physical distresses, it seems to me marvelous with what desperate patience (I write it advisedly, patience of utter despair) they endure their sorrow-laden existence. Even the poor wretch who told that miserable story of insanity, and lonely hiding in the swamps, and scourging when she was found, and of her renewed madness and flight, did so in a sort of low, plaintive, monotonous murmur of misery, as if such sufferings were "all in the day's work."

I ask these questions about their children because I think the number they bear as compared with the number they rear a fair gauge of the effect of the system on their own health and that of their offspring. There was hardly one of these women, as you will see by the details I have noted of their ailments, who might not have been a candidate for a bed in a hospital, and they had come to me after working all day in the fields.

XX

Sally, Auber, and Judy

[March 3–4, 1839]

Dearest E[lizabeth],

When I told you in my last letter of the encroachments which the waters of the Altamaha are daily making on the bank at Hampton Point and immediately in front of the imposing-looking old dwelling of the former master, I had no idea how rapid this crumbling process has been of late years; but today, standing there with Mrs. G[owen], whom I had gone to consult about the assistance we might render to some of the poor creatures whose cases I sent you in my last letter, she told me that within the memory of many of the slaves now living on the plantation, a grove of orange trees had spread its fragrance and beauty between the house and the river. Not a vestige remains of them. The earth that bore them was gradually undermined, slipped, and sank down into the devouring flood; and when she saw the astonished incredulity of my look, she led me to the ragged and broken bank, and there, immediately below it, and just covered by the turbid waters of the inrushing tide, were the heads of the poor drowned orange trees, swaying like black twigs in the briny flood, which had not yet dislodged all of them from their hold upon the soil which had gone down beneath the water wearing its garland of bridal blossom.

As I looked at those trees a wild wish rose in my heart that the river and the sea would swallow up and melt in their salt waves the whole of this accursed property of ours. I am afraid the horror of slavery with which I came down to the South, the general theoretic abhorrence of an Englishwoman for it, has gained, through the intensity it has acquired, a morbid character of mere desire to be delivered from my own share in it. I think so much of these wretches that I see, that I can hardly remember any others; and my zeal for the general emancipation of the slave has almost narrowed itself to this most painful desire that I and mine were freed from the responsibility of our share in this huge misery; and so I thought: "Beat, beat, the crumbling banks and sliding shores, wild waves of the Atlantic and the Altamaha! Sweep down and carry hence this evil earth and these homes of tyranny, and roll above the soil of slavery, and wash my soul and the souls of those I love clean from the blood of our kind!" But I have no idea that Mr. [Butler] and his brother would cry amen to any such prayer. Sometimes, as I stand and listen to the roll of the great ocean surges on the farther side of Little St. Simons Island, a small green screen of tangled wilderness that interposes between this point and the Atlantic, I think how near our West Indian Islands and freedom are to these unfortunate people, many of whom are expert and hardy boatmen, as far as the mere mechanical management of a boat goes; but, unless Providence were compass and steersman too, it avails nothing that they should know how near their freedom might be found, nor have I any right to tell them if they could find it, for the slaves are not mine, they are Mr. [Butler]'s.

The mulatto woman, Sally, accosted me again today [March 3], and begged that she might be put to some other than field labor. Supposing she felt herself unequal to it, I asked her some questions, but the principal reason she urged for her promotion to some less laborious kind of work was, that hoeing in the field was so hard to her *"on account of her color,"* and she therefore petitions to be allowed to learn a trade. I was much puzzled at this reason for her petition, but was presently made to understand that, being a mulatto, she considered field labor a degradation; her white bastardy appearing to her a title to consideration in my eyes. The degradation of these people is very complete, for they have accepted the contempt of their masters to that degree that they profess, and really seem to feel it for themselves, and the faintest admixture of white blood in their black veins appears at once, by common consent of their own race, to raise them in the scale of humanity. I had not much sympathy for this petition. The woman's father had been a white man who was employed for some purpose on the estate. In speaking upon this subject to Mrs. G[owen], she said that, as far as her observation went, the lower class of white men in the South lived with colored women precisely as they would at the North with women of their own race; the outcry that one hears against amalgamation appears therefore to be something educated and acquired rather than intuitive. I cannot perceive, in observing my children, that they exhibit the slightest repugnance or dislike to these swarthy dependents of theirs, which they surely would do if, as is so often pretended, there is an inherent, irreconcilable repulsion on the part of the white toward the Negro race. All the Southern children that I have seen seem to have a special fondness for these good-natured, childish human beings, whose mental condition is kin in its simplicity and proneness to impulsive emotion to their own, and I can detect in them no trace of the abhorrence and contempt for their dusky skins which all questions of treating them with common justice is so apt to elicit from American men and women.

Today, for the first time since I left the rice island, I went out fishing, but had no manner of luck. Jack rowed me up Jones's Creek, a small stream which separates St. Simons from the main, on the opposite side from the great waters of the Altamaha. The day was very warm. It is becoming almost too hot to remain here much longer, at least for me, who dread and suffer from heat so much. The whole summer, however, is passed by many members of the

Georgia families on their estates by the sea. When the heat is intense, the breeze from the ocean and the salt air, I suppose, prevent it from being intolerable or hurtful. Our neighbor, Mr. C[ouper], and his family reside entirely, the year round, on their plantations here without apparently suffering in their health from the effects of the climate. I suppose it is the intermediate region between the seaboard and the mountains that becomes so pestilential when once the warm weather sets in. I remember the Belgian minister, M. de———, telling me that the mountain country of Georgia was as beautiful as Paradise, and that the climate, as far as his experience went, was perfectly delicious. He was, however, only there on an exploring expedition, and, of course, took the most favorable season of the year for the purpose.

I have had several women with me this afternoon more or less disabled by chronic rheumatism. Certainly, either their labor or the exposure it entails must be very severe, for this climate is the last that ought to engender rheumatism. This evening I had a visit from a bright young woman, calling herself Minda, who came to beg for a little rice or sugar. I inquired from which of the settlements she had come down, and found that she has to walk three miles every day to and from her work. She made no complaint whatever of this, and seemed to think her laborious tramp down to the Point after her day of labor on the field well rewarded by the pittance of rice and sugar she obtained. Perhaps she consoled herself for the exertion by the reflection which occurred to me while talking to her, that many women who have borne children, and many women with child, go the same distance to and from their task ground—that seems dreadful!

I have let my letter lie from a stress of small interruptions. Yesterday [March 3], old Auber, a stooping, halting hag, came to beg for flannel and rice. As usual, of course, I asked various questions concerning her condition, family, etc.; she told me she had never been married, but had had five children, two of whom were dead. She complained of flooding, of intolerable backache, and said that with all these ailments she considered herself quite recovered, having suffered horribly from an abscess in her neck, which was now nearly well. I was surprised to hear of her other complaints, for she seemed to me like quite an old woman; but constant childbearing, and the life of labor, exposure, and privation which they lead, ages these poor creatures prematurely.

Dear E[lizabeth], how I do defy you to guess the novel accomplishment I have developed within the last two days; what do you say to my turning butcher's boy, and cutting up the carcass of a sheep for the instruction of our butcher and cook, and benefit of our table? You know, I have often written you word that we have mutton here—thanks to the short salt grass on which it feeds —that compares with the best South Down or *pré salé;* but such is the barbarous ignorance of the cook, or rather the butcher who furnishes our kitchen supplies, that I defy the most expert anatomist to pronounce on any piece (joints they cannot be called) of mutton brought to our table to what part of the animal sheep it originally belonged. I have often complained bitterly of this, and in vain implored Abraham the cook to send me some dish of mutton to which I might with safety apply the familiar name of leg, shoulder, or haunch. These remonstrances and expostulations have produced no result whatever, however, but an increase of eccentricity in the *chunks* of sheeps' flesh placed upon the table; the squares, diamonds, cubes, and rhomboids of mutton have been more ludicrously and hopelessly unlike anything we see in a Christian butcher's shop, with every fresh endeavor Abraham has made to find out "zackly wot de missis do want"; so the day before yesterday, while I was painfully dragging S[ally] through the early intellectual science of the alphabet and first reading lesson, Abraham appeared at the door of the room brandishing a very long thin knife, and with many bows, grins, and apologies for disturbing me, begged that I would go and cut up a sheep for him. My first impulse, of course, was to decline the very unusual task offered me with mingled horror and amusement. Abraham, however, insisted and besought, extolled the fineness of his sheep, declared his misery at being unable to cut it as I wished, and his readiness to conform for the future to whatever *patterns* of mutton "de missis would only please to give him." Upon reflection, I thought I might very well contrive to indicate upon the sheep the size and form of the different joints of civilized mutton, and so, for the future, save much waste of good meat; and, moreover, the lesson, once taught, would not require to be repeated, and I have ever held it expedient to accept every opportunity of learning to do anything, no matter how unusual, which presented itself to be done; and so I followed Abraham to the kitchen, when, with a towel closely pinned over my silk dress, and knife in hand, I stood for a minute or two meditating profoundly before the rather unsightly object which Abraham had pronounced "de beautifullest sheep de missis eber saw." The sight and smell of raw meat are especially odious to me, and I have often thought that if I had had to be my own cook, I should inevitably become a vegetarian, probably, indeed, return entirely to my green and salad days. Nathless, I screwed my courage to the sticking point, and slowly and delicately traced out with the point of my long carving knife two shoulders, two legs, a saddle, and a neck of mutton; not probably in the most thoroughly artistic and butcherly style, but as nearly as my memory and the unassisted light of nature would enable me; and having instructed Abraham in the various boundaries, sizes, shapes, and names of the several joints, I returned to S[ally] and her belles-lettres, rather elated, upon the whole, at the creditable mode in which I flattered myself I had accomplished my unusual task, and the hope of once more seeing roast mutton of my acquaintance. I will confess to you, dear E[lizabeth], that the *neck* was not a satisfactory part of the performance, and I have spent some thoughts since in trying to adjust in my own mind its proper shape and proportions.

As an accompaniment to "de beautifullest mutton de missis eber see," we have just received from my neighbor Mr. C[ouper] the most magnificent supply of fresh vegetables, green peas, salad, etc.

He has a garden, and a Scotchman's real love for horticulture, and I profit by them in this very agreeable manner.

I have been interrupted by several visits, my dear E[lizabeth], among other, one from a poor creature called Judy, whose sad story and condition affected me most painfully. She had been married, she said, some years ago to one of the men called Temba, who, however, now has another wife, having left her because she went mad. While out of her mind she escaped into the jungle, and contrived to secrete herself there for some time, but was finally tracked and caught, and brought back and punished by being made to sit, day after day, for hours in the stocks—a severe punishment for a man, but for a woman perfectly barbarous. She complained of chronic rheumatism, and other terrible ailments, and said she suffered such intolerable pain while laboring in the fields, that she had come to entreat me to have her work lightened. She could hardly crawl, and cried bitterly all the time she spoke to me.

She told me a miserable story of her former experience on the plantation under Mr. K[ing]'s overseership. It seems that Jem Valiant (an extremely difficult subject, a mulatto lad, whose valor is sufficiently accounted for now by the influence of the mutinous white blood) was her first-born, the son of Mr. K[ing], who forced her, flogged her severely for having resisted him, and then sent her off, as a farther punishment, to Five Pound—a horrible swamp in a remote corner of the estate, to which the slaves are sometimes banished for such offenses as are not sufficiently atoned for by the lash. The dismal loneliness of the place to these poor people, who are as dependent as children upon companionship and sympathy, makes this solitary exile a much-dreaded infliction; and this poor creature said that, bad as the flogging was, she would sooner have taken that again than the dreadful lonely days and nights she spent on the penal swamp of Five Pound.

I make no comment on these terrible stories, my dear friend, and tell them to you as nearly as possible in the perfectly plain, unvarnished manner in which they are told to me. I do not wish to add to, or perhaps I ought to say take away from, the effect of such narrations by amplifying the simple horror and misery of their bare details.

XXI

No Trace of Pity

[March 4, 1839]

My dearest E[lizabeth],

I have had an uninterrupted stream of women and children flowing in the whole morning to say "Ha de, missis?" Among others, a poor woman called Mile, who could hardly stand for pain and swelling in her limbs; she had had fifteen children and two miscarriages; nine of her children had died; for the last three years she had become almost a cripple with chronic rheumatism, yet she is driven every day to work in the field. She held my hands, and stroked them in the most appealing way while she exclaimed: "Oh my missis! my missis! me neber sleep till day for de pain," and with the day her labor must again be resumed. I gave her flannel and *sal volatile* to rub her poor swelled limbs with; rest I could not give her—rest from her labor and her pain—this mother of fifteen children.

Another of my visitors had a still more dismal story to tell; her name was Die; she had had sixteen children, fourteen of whom were dead; she had had four miscarriages: one had been caused with falling down with a very heavy burden on her head, and one from having her arms strained up to be lashed. I asked her what she meant by having her arms tied up. She said their hands were first tied together, sometimes by the wrists, and sometimes, which was worse, by the thumbs, and they were then drawn up to a tree or post, so as almost to swing them off the ground, and then their clothes rolled round their waist, and a man with a cowhide stands and stripes them. I give you the woman's words. She did not speak of this as of anything strange, unusual, or especially horrid and abominable; and when I said: "Did they do that to you when you were with child?" she simply replied: "Yes, missis." And to all this I listen—I, an Englishwoman, the wife of the man who owns these wretches, and I cannot say: "That thing shall not be done again; that cruel shame and villainy shall never be known here again." I gave the woman meat and flannel, which were what she came to ask for, and remained choking with indignation and grief long after they had all left me to my most bitter thoughts.

I went out to try and walk off some of the weight of horror and depression which I am beginning to feel daily more and more, surrounded by all this misery and degradation that I can neither help nor hinder. The blessed spring is coming very fast, the air is full of delicious wildwood fragrances, and the wonderful songs of Southern birds; the wood paths are as tempting as paths into Paradise, but Jack is in such deadly terror about the snakes, which are now beginning to glide about with a freedom and frequency certainly not pleasing, that he will not follow me off the open road, and twice today scared me back from charming wood paths I ventured to explore with his exclamations of terrified warning.

I gathered some exquisite pink blossoms, of a sort of waxen texture, off a small shrub which was strange to me, and for which Jack's only name was dye bush; but I could not ascertain from him whether any dyeing substance was found in its leaves, bark, or blossoms.

I returned home along the riverside, stopping to admire a line of noble live oaks beginning, alas! to be smothered with the treacherous white moss under whose pale trailing masses their verdure gradually succumbs, leaving them, like huge hoary ghosts, perfect mountains of parasitical vegetation, which, strangely enough, appears only to hang upon and swing from their boughs without adhering to them. The mixture of these streams of gray-white filaments with the dark foliage is extremely beautiful as long as the leaves of the tree survive in sufficient masses to produce the rich contrast of color; but when the moss has literally conquered the whole tree, and, after stripping its huge limbs bare, clothed them with its own wan masses, they always looked to me like so many gigantic Druid ghosts, with flowing robes and beards, and locks all of one ghastly gray, and I would not have broken a twig off them for the world, lest a sad voice, like that which reproached Dante, should have moaned out of it to me,

'Non hai tu spirto di pietate alcuno?' [1]

A beautiful mass of various woodland skirted the edge of the stream, and mingled in its foliage every shade of green, from the pale, stiff spikes and fans of the dwarf palmetto to the dark canopy of the magnificent ilex—bowers and brakes of the loveliest wildness, where one dare not tread three steps for fear. What a tantalization! it is like some wicked enchantment.

[1] *Inferno,* Canto XIII, line 36. Dante finds himself in the seventh circle of hell, where people who have committed suicide have been turned into trees. Thrusting out his hand he plucked a twig from one of these, which screeched: "Why do you tear me?" And, as the dark blood oozed from the wound, the tree began to wail again *Perchè mi scerpi? Non hai tu spirto di pietate alcuno?* "Why do you rend me? Have you no trace of pity?"

XXII

Visitors and Petitioners

Dearest E[lizabeth],

I have found growing along the edge of the dreary enclosure
where the slaves are buried such a lovely wild flower; it is a little
like the Euphrasia or eyebright of the English meadows, but grows
quite close to the turf, almost into it, and consists of clusters of tiny
white flowers that look as if they were made of the finest porcelain.
I took up a root of it yesterday, with a sort of vague idea that I
could transplant it to the North; though I cannot say that I should
care to transplant anything thither that could renew to me the
associations of this place—not even the delicious wild flowers, if
I could.

The woods here are full of wild plum trees, the delicate white
blossoms of which twinkle among the evergreen copses, and,
besides illuminating them with a faint starlight, suggest to my mind
a possible liqueur like kirsch, which I should think could quite as
well be extracted from wild plums as wild cherries, and the trees
are so numerous that there ought to be quite a harvest from them.
You may, and, doubtless, have seen palmetto plants in Northern
green- and hothouses, but you never saw palmetto roots; and what
curious things they are! huge, hard, yellowish-brown stems, as

thick as my arm, or thicker, extending and ramifying under the ground in masses that seem hardly justified or accounted for by the elegant, light, spiky fans of dusky green foliage with which they fill the under part of the woods here. They look very tropical and picturesque, but both in shape and color suggest something metallic rather than vegetable; the bronze-green hue and lancelike form of their foliage has an arid, hard character, that makes one think they could be manufactured quite as well as cultivated. At first I was extremely delighted with the novelty of their appearance; but now I feel thirsty when I look at them, and the same with their kinsfolk, the Yuccas and their intimate friends, if not relations, the prickly pears, with all of which once strange growth I have grown contemptuously familiar now.

Did it ever occur to you what a strange affinity there is between the texture and color of the wild vegetables of these sandy Southern soils, and the texture and color of shells? The prickly pear, and especially the round little cactus plants all covered with hairy spikes, are curiously suggestive of a family of round spiked shells, with which you, as well as myself, are doubtless familiar; and though the splendid flame-color of some cactus blossoms never suggests any nature but that of flowers, I have seen some of a peculiar shade of yellow-pink, that resembles the mingled tint on the inside of some elaborately colored shell, and the pale white and rose flowers of another kind have the coloring and almost texture of shell, much rather than of any vegetable substance.

Today I walked out without Jack, and, in spite of the terror of snakes with which he has contrived slightly to inoculate me, I did make a short exploring journey into the woods. I wished to avoid a plowed field, to the edge of which my wanderings had brought me; but my dash into the woodland, though unpunished by an encounter with snakes, brought me only into a marsh as full of land crabs as an anthill is of ants, and from which I had to retreat ingloriously, finding my way home at last by the beach.

I have had, as usual, a tribe of visitors and petitioners ever since

I came home. I will give you an account of those cases which had anything beyond the average of interest in their details. One poor woman, named Molly, came to beg that I would, if possible, get an extension of their exemption from work after childbearing. The close of her argument was concise and forcible. "Missis, we hab um pickanniny—tree weeks in de ospital, and den right out upon the hoe again—*can we strong* dat way, missis? No!" And truly I do not see that they can. This poor creature has had eight children and two miscarriages. All her children were dead but one.

Another of my visitors was a divinely named but not otherwise divine Venus; it is a favorite name among these sable folk, but, of course, must have been given originally in derision. The Aphrodite in question was a dirt-colored (convenient color I should say for these parts) mulatto. I could not understand how she came on this property, for she was the daughter of a black woman and the overseer of an estate to which her mother formerly belonged, and from which I suppose she was sold, exchanged, or given, as the case may be, to the owners of this plantation. She was terribly crippled with rheumatism, and came to beg for some flannel. She had had eleven children, five of whom had died, and two miscarriages.

As she took her departure, the vacant space she left on the other side of my writing table was immediately filled by another black figure with a bowed back and piteous face, one of the thousand "Mollies" on the estate, where the bewildering redundancy of their name is avoided by adding that of their husband; so when the question: "Well, who are you?" was answered with the usual genuflexion, and "I'se Molly, missis!" I, of course, went on with "whose Molly," and she went on to refer herself to the ownership (under Mr. [Butler] and heaven) of one Tony, but proceeded to say that he was not her *real* husband. This appeal to an element of reality in the universally accepted fiction which passes here by the title of marriage surprised me; and on asking her what she meant, she replied that her real husband had been sold from the estate for repeated attempts to run away. He had made his escape several times, and skulked starving in the woods and morasses, but had always been tracked and brought back, and flogged almost to death, and finally sold as an incorrigible runaway. What a spirit of indomitable energy the wretched man must have had, to have tried so often that hideously hopeless attempt to fly! I do not write you the poor woman's jargon, which was ludicrous; for I cannot write you the sighs, and tears, and piteous looks, and gestures, that made it pathetic; of course she did not know whither or to whom her *real* husband had been sold; but in the meantime Mr. K[ing], that merciful Providence of the estate, had provided her with the above-named Tony, by whom she had had nine children, six of whom were dead; she, too, had miscarried twice. She came to ask me for some flannel for her legs, which were all swollen with constant rheumatism, and to beg me to give her something to cure some bad sores and ulcers, which seemed to me dreadful enough in their present condition, but which she said break out afresh and are twice as bad every summer.

I have let my letter lie since the day before yesterday, dear E[lizabeth], having had no leisure to finish it. Yesterday morning I rode out to Sinclair's, where there used formerly to be another Negro settlement, and another house of Major [Butler]'s. I had been persuaded to try one of the mares I had formerly told you of, and to be sure a more "curst" quadruped, and one more worthy of a Petruchio for a rider I did never back. Her temper was furious, her gait intolerable, her mouth the most obdurate that ever tugged against bit and bridle. It is not wise anywhere—here it is less wise than anywhere else in the world—to say *jamais de cette eau je ne boirai;* but I *think* I will never ride that delightful creature Miss Kate again.

I wrote you of my having been to a part of the estate called Sinclair's, where there was formerly another residence of Major [Butler]'s; nothing remains now of it but a ruined chimney of some of the offices, which is standing yet in the middle of what has become a perfect wilderness. At the best of times, with a large house, numerous household, and paths, and drives of approach, and the usual external conditions of civilization about it, a residence here would have been the loneliest that can well be imagined; now it is the shaggiest desert of beautiful wood that I ever saw. The magnificent old oaks stand round the place in silent solemn grandeur; and among them I had no difficulty in recognizing, by the description Captain F[raser] had given me of it, the crumbling, shattered relic of a tree called Oglethorpe's Oak. That worthy, valiant old governor had a residence here himself in the early days of the colony, when, under the influence of Wesley, he vainly made such strenuous efforts to keep aloof from his infant province the sore curse of slavery.

I rode almost the whole way through a grove of perfect evergreen. I had with me one of the men of the name of Hector, who has a good deal to do with the horses, and so had volunteered to accompany me, being one of the few Negroes on the estate who can sit a horse. In the course of our conversation, Hector divulged certain opinions relative to the comparative gentility of driving in a carriage and the vulgarity of walking, which sent me into fits of laughing; at which he grinned sympathetically, and opened his eyes very wide, but certainly without attaining the least insight into what must have appeared to him my very unaccountable and unreasonable merriment. Among various details of the condition of the people on the several estates in the island, he told me that a great number of the men on all the different plantations had *wives* on the neighboring estates as well as on that to which they properly belonged. "Oh, but," said I, "Hector, you know that cannot be; a man has but one lawful wife." Hector knew this, he said, and yet seemed puzzled himself, and rather puzzled me to account for the fact, that this extensive practice of bigamy was perfectly well known to the masters and overseers, and never in any way found fault with or interfered with. Perhaps this promiscuous mode of keeping up the slave population finds favor with the owners of creatures who are valued in the market at so much per head. This was a solution which occurred to me, but which I left my Trojan hero to discover, by dint of the profound pondering into which he fell.

Not far from the house, as I was cantering home, I met S[ally], and took her up on the saddle before me, an operation which seemed to please her better than the vicious horse I was riding, whose various demonstrations of dislike to the arrangement afforded my small equestrian extreme delight and triumph. My whole afternoon was spent in shifting my bed and bedroom furniture from a room on the ground floor to one above; in the course of which operation a brisk discussion took place between M[argery] and my boy Jack, who was nailing on the valance of the bed, and whom I suddenly heard exclaim, in answer to something she had said: "Well, den, I do tink so; and dat's the speech of a man, whether um bond or free." A very trifling incident, and insignificant speech; and yet it came back to my ears very often afterward— "the speech of a *man,* whether bond or free." They might be made conscious—some of them are evidently conscious—of an inherent element of manhood superior to the bitter accident of slavery, and to which, even in their degraded condition, they might be made to refer that vital self-respect which can survive all external pressure of mere circumstance, and give their souls to that service of God, which is perfect freedom, in spite of the ignoble and cruel bondage of their bodies.

My new apartment is what I should call decidedly airy; the window, unless when styled by courtesy shut, which means admitting of draught enough to blow a candle out, must be wide open, being incapable of any intermediate condition; the latch of the door, to speak the literal truth, does shut; but it is the only part of it that does—that is, the latch and the hinges; everywhere else its configuration is traced by a distinct line of light and air. If what old Dr. Physic used to say be true, that a draught which will not blow out a candle will blow out a man's life (a Spanish proverb originally I believe), my life is threatened with extinction in almost every part of this new room of mine, wherein, moreover, I now discover to my dismay, having transported every other article of bedroom furniture to it, it is impossible to introduce the wardrobe for my clothes. Well, our stay here is drawing to a close, and therefore these small items of discomfort cannot afflict me much longer.

Among my visitors today was a poor woman named Oney, who told me her husband had gone away from her now for four years; it seems he was the property of Mr. K[ing], and when that gentleman went to slave driving on his own account, and ceased to be the overseer of this estate, he carried her better half, who was his chattel, away with him, and she never expects to see him again. After her departure I had a most curious visitor, a young lad of the name of Renty, whose very decidedly mulatto tinge accounted, I suppose, for the peculiar *disinvoltura* [1] of his carriage and manner; he was evidently, in his own opinion, a very superior creature, and yet, as his conversation with me testified, he was conscious of some flaw in the honor of his "yellow" complexion.

"Who is your mother, Renty?" said I (I give you our exact dialogue).

"Betty, headman Frank's wife."

I was rather dismayed at the promptness of this reply, and hesitated a little at my next question: "Who is your father?"

My sprightly young friend, however, answered, without an instant's pause: "Mr. K[ing]."

Here I came to a halt, and, willing to suggest some doubt to the lad, because for many peculiar reasons this statement seemed to me shocking, I said: "What, old Mr. K[ing]?"

"No, Massa R[oswell]."

"Did your mother tell you so?"

"No, missis, me ashamed to ask her; Mr. C[ouper]'s children told me so, and I 'spect they know it."

[1] Air of superiority, easy condescension.

Renty, you see, did not take Faulconbridge's [2] view of such matters; and as I was by no means sorry to find that he considered his relation to Mr. K[ing] a disgrace to his mother, which is an advance in moral perception not often met with here, I said no more upon the subject.

This morning [March 5], old House Molly, coming from Mr. G[owen]'s upon some errand to me, I asked her if Renty's statement was true; she confirmed the whole story, and, moreover, added that this connection took place after Betty was married to headman Frank. Now he, you know, E[lizabeth], is the chief man at the rice island, second in authority to Mr. O——, and, indeed, for a considerable part of the year, absolute master and guardian during the night of all the people and property at the rice plantation; for, after the early spring, the white overseer himself is obliged to betake himself to the mainland to sleep, out of the influence of the deadly malaria of the rice swamp, and Frank remains sole sovereign of the island from sunset to sunrise—in short, during the whole period of his absence. Mr. [Butler] bestowed the highest commendations upon his fidelity and intelligence, and, during the visit Mr. R[oswell] K[ing] paid us at the island, he was emphatic in his praise of both Frank and his wife, the latter having, as he declared, by way of climax to his eulogies, quite the principles of a white woman. Perhaps she imbibed them from his excellent influence over her. Frank is a serious, sad, sober-looking, very intelligent man; I should think he would not relish having his wife borrowed from him even by the white gentleman who admired her principles so much; and it is quite clear, from poor Renty's speech about his mother, that by some of these people (and if by any, then very certainly by Frank) the disgrace of such an injury is felt and appreciated much after the fashion of white men.

This old woman Molly is a wonderfully intelligent, active,

---

[2] Philip Faulconbridge, in Shakespeare's *King John*, openly acknowledges himself the bastard son of Richard Coeur de Lion for reasons of personal advancement.

energetic creature, though considerably over seventy years old; she was talking to me about her former master, Major [Butler], and what she was pleased to call the *revelation* war (i.e., revolution war), during which that gentleman, having embraced the side of the rebellious colonies in their struggle against England, was by no means on a bed of roses. He bore King George's commission, and was a major in the British army; but having married a great Carolina heiress, and become proprietor of these plantations,[3] sided with the country of his adoption, and not that of his birth, in the war between them, and was a special object of animosity on that account to the English officers who attacked the seaboard of Georgia, and sent troops on shore and up the Altamaha to fetch off the Negroes, or incite them to rise against their owners. "De British," said Molly, "make old massa run about bery much in de great revelation war." He ran effectually, however, and contrived to save both his life and property from the invader.

Molly's account was full of interest, in spite of the grotesque lingo in which it was delivered, and which once or twice nearly sent me into convulsions of laughing, whereupon she apologized with great gravity for her mispronunciation, modestly suggesting that *white words* were impossible to the organs of speech of black folks. It is curious how universally any theory, no matter how absurd, is accepted by these people; for anything in which the contemptuous supremacy of the dominant race is admitted, and their acquiescence in the theory of their own incorrigible baseness is so complete, that this, more than any other circumstance in their condition, makes me doubtful of their rising from it.

[3] Major Pierce Butler did not acquire Hampton Point or Butler Island until 1793–1800. Molly was probably confusing the Revolutionary War with the War of 1812; it was during the latter struggle that the British occupied St. Simons Island and took away with them three hundred slaves, some of which, no doubt, were Major Butler's. During the Revolutionary War Molly would have been a child of ten years or more; it is possible that she was relating to Fanny Kemble events that occurred on the Butler-Middleton estates in Berkeley county, South Carolina.

In order to set poor dear old Molly's notions straight with regard to the Negro incapacity for speaking plain the noble white words, I called S[ally] to me and set her talking; and having pointed out to Molly how very imperfect her mode of pronouncing many words was, convinced the worthy old Negress that want of training, and not any absolute original impotence, was the reason why she disfigured the *white words,* for which she had such a profound respect. In this matter, as in every other, the slaves pay back to their masters the evil of their own dealings with usury, though unintentionally. No culture, however slight, simple, or elementary, is permitted to these poor creatures, and the utterance of many of them is more like what Prospero describes Caliban's to have been, than the speech of men and women in a Christian and civilized land: the children of their owners, brought up among them, acquire their Negro mode of talking—slavish speech surely it is—and it is distinctly perceptible in the utterances of all Southerners, particularly of the women, whose avocations, taking them less from home, are less favorable to their throwing off this ignoble trick of pronunciation than the more varied occupation and the more extended and promiscuous business relations of men. The Yankee twang of the regular down-Easter is not more easily detected by any ear, nice in enunciation and accent, than the thick Negro speech of the Southerners: neither is lovely or melodious; but, though the Puritan snuffle is the harsher of the two, the slave *slobber* of the language is the more ignoble, in spite of the softer voices of the pretty Southern women who utter it.

I rode out today upon Miss Kate again, with Jack for my esquire. I made various vain attempts to ride through the woods, following the cattle tracks; they turned round and round into each other, or led out into the sandy pine barren, the eternal frame in which all nature is set here, the inevitable limit to the prospect, turn landward which way you will. The wood paths which I followed between evergreen thickets, though little satisfactory in their ultimate result, were really more beautiful than the most perfect arrangement of artificial planting that I ever saw in an English park; and I thought, if I could transplant the region which I was riding through bodily into the midst of some great nobleman's possessions on the other side of the water, how beautiful an accession it would be thought to them. I was particularly struck with the elegant growth of a profuse wild shrub I passed several times today, the leaves of which were pale green underneath, and a deep red, varnished brown above.

I must give you an idea of the sort of service one is liable to obtain from one's most intelligent and civilized servants hereabouts, and the consequent comfort and luxury of one's daily existence. Yesterday Aleck, the youth who fulfills the duties of what you call a waiter, and we in England a footman, gave me a salad for dinner, mixed with so large a portion of the soil in which it had grown that I requested him today to be kind enough to wash the lettuce before he brought it to table. M[argery] later in the day told me that he had applied to her very urgently for soap and a brush, "as missis wished de lettuce scrubbed," a fate from which my second salad was saved by her refusal of these desired articles, and further instructions upon the subject.

XXIII

Visits to the Old and Sick

Dearest E[lizabeth],

I have been long promising poor old House Molly to visit her in her own cabin, and so the day before yesterday I walked round the settlement to her dwelling, and a most wretched hovel I found it. She has often told me of the special directions left by her old master for the comfort and well-being of her old age, and certainly his charge has been but little heeded by his heirs, for the poor faithful old slave is most miserably off in her infirm years. She made no complaint, however, but seemed overjoyed at my coming to see her. She took me to the hut of her brother, old Jacob, where the same wretched absence of every decency and every comfort prevailed; but neither of them seemed to think the condition that appeared so wretched to me one of peculiar hardship—though Molly's former residence in her master's house might reasonably have made her discontented with the lot of absolute privation to which she was now turned over—but, for the moment, my visit seemed to compensate for all sublunary sorrows, and she and poor old Jacob kept up a duet of rejoicing at my advent, and that I had brought "de little missis among um people afore they die."

Leaving them, I went on to the house of Jacob's daughter

Hannah, with whom Psyche, the heroine of the rice island story, and wife of his son Joe, lives. I found their cabin as tidy and comfortable as it could be made, and their children, as usual, neat and clean; they are capital women, both of them, with an innate love of cleanliness and order most uncommon among these people. On my way home I overtook two of my daily suppliants, who were going to the house in search of me, and meat, flannel, rice, and sugar, as the case might be; they were both old and infirm-looking women, and one of them, called Scylla, was extremely lame, which she accounted for by an accident she had met with while carrying a heavy weight of rice on her head; she had fallen on a sharp stake, or snag, as she called it, and had never recovered the injury she had received. She complained also of falling of the womb. Her companion (who was not Charybdis, however, but Phœbe) was a cheery soul who complained of nothing, but begged for flannel. I asked her about her family and children; she had no children left, nothing but grandchildren; she had had nine children, and seven of them died quite young; the only two who grew up left her to join the British when they invaded Georgia in the last war, and their children, whom they left behind, were all her family now.

In the afternoon I made my first visit to the hospital of the estate, and found it, as indeed I find everything else here, in a far worse state even than the wretched establishments on the rice island, dignified by that name; so miserable a place for the purpose to which it was dedicated I could not have imagined on a property belonging to Christian owners. The floor (which was not boarded, but merely the damp hard earth itself) was strewn with wretched women, who, but for their moans of pain, and uneasy, restless motions, might very well each have been taken for a mere heap of filthy rags; the chimney refusing passage to the smoke from the pine-wood fire, it puffed out in clouds through the room, where it circled and hung, only gradually oozing away through the windows, which were so far well-adapted to the purpose that there was not a single whole pane of glass in them. My eyes, unaccustomed to the turbid atmosphere, smarted and watered, and refused to distinguish at first the different dismal forms, from which cries and wails assailed me in every corner of the place. By degrees I was able to endure for a few minutes what they were condemned to live their hours and days of suffering and sickness through; and, having given what comfort kind words and promises of help in more substantial forms could convey, I went on to what seemed a yet more wretched abode of wretchedness.

This was a room where there was no fire because there was no chimney, and where the holes made for windows had no panes or glasses in them. The shutters being closed, the place was so dark that, on first entering it, I was afraid to stir lest I should fall over some of the deplorable creatures extended upon the floor. As soon as they perceived me, one cry of "Oh missis!" rang through the darkness; and it really seemed to me as if I was never to exhaust the pity, and amazement, and disgust which this receptacle of suffering humanity was to excite in me. The poor dingy supplicating sleepers upraised themselves as I cautiously advanced among them; those who could not rear their bodies from the earth held up piteous beseeching hands, and as I passed from one to the other I felt more than one imploring clasp laid upon my dress, to solicit my attention to some new form of misery. One poor woman, called Tressa, who was unable to speak above a whisper from utter weakness and exhaustion, told me she had had nine children, was suffering from incessant flooding, and felt "as if her back would split open." There she lay, a mass of filthy tatters, without so much as a blanket under her or over her, on the bare earth in this chilly darkness. I promised them help and comfort, beds and blankets, and light and fire—that is, I promised to ask Mr. [Butler] for all this for them; and, in the very act of doing so, I remembered with a sudden pang of anguish that I was to urge no more petitions from his slaves to their master. I groped my way out, and, emerging on the piazza, all the choking tears and sobs I had controlled broke forth, and I leaned there crying over the lot of these unfortunates till I heard a feeble voice of "Missis, you no cry; missis, what for you cry?" and, looking up, saw that I had not yet done with this intolerable infliction. A poor crippled old man, lying in the corner of the piazza, unable even to crawl toward me, had uttered this word of consolation, and by his side (apparently too idiotic, as he was too impotent, to move) sat a young woman, the expression of whose face was the most suffering, and, at the same time, the most horribly repulsive I ever saw. I found she was, as I supposed, half-witted; and, on coming nearer to inquire into her ailments and what I could do for her, found her suffering from that horrible disease—I believe some form of scrofula—to which the Negroes are subject, which attacks and eats away the joints of their hands and fingers—a more hideous and loathsome object I never beheld; her name was Patty, and she was granddaughter to the old crippled creature by whose side she was squatting.

I wandered home, stumbling with crying as I went, and feeling so utterly miserable that I really hardly saw where I was going, for I as nearly as possible fell over a great heap of oyster shells left in the middle of the path. This is a horrid nuisance, which results from an indulgence which the people here have and value highly; the waters round the island are prolific in shellfish, oysters, and the most magnificent prawns I ever saw. The former are a considerable article of the people's diet, and the shells are allowed to accumulate, as they are used in the composition of which their huts are built, and which is a sort of combination of mud and broken oyster shells, which forms an agglomeration of a kind very solid and durable for such building purposes; but, instead of being all carried to some specified place out of the way, these great heaps of oyster shells are allowed to be piled up anywhere and everywhere, forming the most unsightly obstructions in every direction. Of course, the cultivation of order for the sake of its own seemliness and beauty is not likely to be an element of slave existence; and as masters have been scarce on this plantation for many years now, a mere unsightliness is not a matter likely to trouble anybody much; but, after my imminent overthrow by one of these disorderly heaps of refuse, I think I may make bold to request that the paths along which I am likely to take my daily walks may be kept free from them.

On my arrival at home—at the house—I cannot call any place here my home!—I found Renty waiting to exhibit to me an extremely neatly-made leather pouch, which he has made by my order, of fitting size and dimensions to receive Jack's hatchet and saw. Jack and I have set up a sort of Sir Walter and Tom Purdie [1] companionship of clearing and cutting paths through the woods nearest to the house; thinning the overhanging branches, clearing the small evergreen thickets which here and there close over and across the grassy track. To me this occupation was especially delightful until quite lately, since the weather began to be rather warmer and the snakes to slide about. Jack has contrived to inoculate me with some portion of his terror of them; but I have still a daily hankering after the lovely green wood walks; perhaps, when once I have seen a live rattlesnake, my enthusiasm for them will be modified to the degree that his is.

[1] Tom Purdie was a shepherd and old retainer of Sir Walter Scott's, highly praised by the latter for his fidelity and devotion.

XXIV

Negro Boat Songs

[March 16, 1839]

Dear E[lizabeth],

This letter has remained unfinished, and my journal interrupted for more than a week. Mr. [Butler] has been quite unwell, and I have been traveling to and fro daily between Hampton and the rice island in the long boat to visit him; for the last three days I have remained at the latter place, and only returned here this morning early. My daily voyages up and down the river have introduced me to a great variety of new musical performances of our boatmen, who invariably, when the rowing is not too hard, moving up or down with the tide, accompany the stroke of their oars with the sound of their voices. I told you formerly that I thought I could trace distinctly some popular national melody with which I was familiar in almost all their songs; but I have been quite at a loss to discover any such foundation for many that I have heard lately, and which have appeared to me extraordinarily wild and unaccountable. The way in which the chorus strikes in with the burden, between each phrase of the melody chanted by a single voice, is very curious and effective, especially with the rhythm of the rowlocks for accompaniment. The high voices all in unison, and the admirable time and true accent with which their responses are made, always make me wish that some great musical composer could hear these semisavage performances. With a very little skillful adaptation and instrumentation, I think one or two barbaric chants and choruses might be evoked from them that would make the fortune of an opera.

The only exception that I have met with yet among our boat voices to the high tenor which they seem all to possess is in the person of an individual named Isaac, a basso profundo of the deepest dye, who nevertheless never attempts to produce with his different register any different effects in the chorus by venturing a second, but sings like the rest in unison, perfect unison, of both time and tune. By-the-by, this individual *does* speak, and therefore I presume he is not an ape, orangoutang, chimpanzee, or gorilla; but I could not, I confess, have conceived it possible that the presence of articulate sounds, and the absence of an articulate tail, should make, externally at least, so completely the only appreciable difference between a man and a monkey, as they appear to do in this individual "black brother." Such stupendous long thin hands, and long flat feet, I did never see off a large quadruped of the ape species. But, as I said before, Isaac *speaks,* and I am much comforted thereby.

You cannot think (to return to the songs of my boatmen) how strange some of their words are: in one, they repeatedly chanted the "sentiment" that "God made man, and man makes"—what do you think?—"money!" Is not that a peculiar poetical proposition? Another ditty to which they frequently treat me they call Caesar's song; it is an extremely spirited war song, beginning "The trumpets blow, the bugles sound—Oh, stand your ground!" It has puzzled me not a little to determine in my own mind whether this title of Caesar's song has any reference to the great Julius, and, if so, what may be the Negro notion of him, and whence and how derived. One of their songs displeased me not a little, for it embodied the opinion that "twenty-six black girls not make mulatto yellow girl"; and as I told them I did not like it, they have omitted it since. This desperate tendency to despise and undervalue their own race and color, which is one of the very worst results of their abject condition, is intolerable to me.

While rowing up and down the broad waters of the Altamaha to the music of these curious chants, I have been reading Mr. Moore's [1] speech about the abolition of slavery in the District of Columbia, and I confess I think his the only defensible position yet taken, and the only consistent argument yet used in any of the speeches I have hitherto seen upon the subject.

I have now settled down at Hampton again; Mr. [Butler] is quite recovered, and is coming down here in a day or two for change of air; it is getting too late for him to stay on the rice plantation even in the day, I think. You cannot imagine anything so exquisite as the perfect curtains of jellow jasmine with which this whole island is draped; and as the boat comes sweeping down toward the Point, the fragrance from the thickets hung with their golden garlands greets one before one can distinguish them; it is really enchanting.

I have now to tell you of my hallowing last Sunday [probably March 10] by gathering a congregation of the people into my big sitting room, and reading prayers to them. I had been wishing very much to do this for some time past, and obtained Mr. [Butler]'s leave while I was with him at the rice island, and it was a great pleasure to me. Some of the people are allowed to go up to Darien once a month to church; but, with that exception, they have no religious service on Sunday whatever for them. There is a church on the island of St. Simons, but they are forbidden to frequent it, as it leads them off their own through neighboring plantations,

[1] Ely Moore of New York made his contribution on February 4, 1839, to the debate in Congress on the question of the people's right to petition for the abolition of slavery in the District of Columbia. Moore took the position that slavery in the District was a purely local concern, in which the people of the country as a whole should have no voice. Fanny's approval of this speech underlines the fact that her view on the right of petition was in 1839 different from that of probably a majority of antislavery people.

and gives opportunities for meetings between the Negroes of the different estates, and very likely was made the occasion of abuses and objectionable practices of various kinds; at any rate, Mr. K[ing] forbade the Hampton slaves resorting to the St. Simons church, and so for three Sundays in the month they are utterly without Christian worship or teaching, or any religious observance of God's day whatever.

I was very anxious that it should not be thought that I *ordered* any of the people to come to prayers, as I particularly desired to see if they themselves felt the want of any Sabbath service, and would of their own accord join in any such ceremony; I therefore merely told the house servants that if they would come to the sitting room at eleven o'clock, I would read prayers to them, and that they might tell any of their friends or any of the people that I should be very glad to see them if they liked to come. Accordingly, most of those who live at the Point, i.e., in the immediate neighborhood of the house, came, and it was encouraging to see the very decided efforts at cleanliness and decorum of attire which they had all made. I was very much affected and impressed myself by what I was doing, and I suppose must have communicated some of my own feeling to those who heard me. It is an extremely solemn thing to me to read the Scriptures aloud to anyone, and there was something in my relation to the poor people by whom I was surrounded that touched me so deeply while thus attempting to share with them the best of my possessions, that I found it difficult to command my voice, and had to stop several times in order to do so. When I had done, they all with one accord uttered the simple words: "We thank you, missis," and instead of overwhelming me as usual with petitions and complaints, they rose silently and quietly, in a manner that would have become the most orderly of Christian congregations accustomed to all the impressive decorum of civilized church privileges. Poor people! They are said to have what a very irreligious young English clergyman once informed me I had—a *"turn"* for religion." They seem to me to have a "turn" for instinctive good manners too; and certainly their mode of withdrawing from my room after our prayers bespoke either a strong feeling of their own, or a keen appreciation of mine.

I have resumed my explorations in the woods with renewed enthusiasm, for during my week's absence they have become more lovely and enticing than ever: unluckily, however, Jack seems to think that fresh rattlesnakes have budded together with the tender spring foliage, and I see that I shall either have to give up my wood walks and rides, or go without a guide. Lovely blossoms are springing up everywhere—weeds, of course, wild things, impertinently so called. Nothing is cultivated here but cotton; but in some of the cotton fields beautiful creatures are peeping into blossom, which I suppose will all be duly hoed off the surface of the soil in proper season; meantime I rejoice in them, and in the splendid, magnificent thistles, which would be in flower gardens in other parts of the world, and in the wonderful, strange, beautiful butterflies that seem to me almost as big as birds, that go zigzagging in the sun. I saw yesterday a lovely monster, who thought proper, for my greater delectation, to alight on a thistle I was admiring, and as the flower was purple, and he was all black velvet fringed with gold, I was exceedingly pleased with his good inspiration.

This morning I drove up to the settlement at St. Annie's, having various bundles of benefaction to carry in the only equipage my estate here affords—an exceedingly small, rough, and uncomfortable cart, called the sick-house wagon, inasmuch as it is used to convey to the hospital such of the poor people as are too ill to walk there. Its tender mercies must be terrible indeed for the sick, for I, who am sound, could very hardly abide them; however, I suppose Montreal's pace is moderated for them: today he went rollicking along with us behind him, shaking his fine head and mane, as if he thought the more we were jolted the better we should like it. We found, on trying to go on to Cartwright's Point, that the state of the tide would not admit of our getting thither, and so had to return, leaving it unvisited. It seems to me strange that, where the labor of so many hands might be commanded, piers, and wharves, and causeways are not thrown out (wooden ones, of course, I mean) wherever the common traffic to or from different parts of the plantation is thus impeded by the daily rise and fall of the river; the trouble and expense would be nothing, and the gain in convenience very considerable. However, perhaps the nature of the tides, and of the banks and shores themselves, may not be propitious for such constructions, and I rather incline, upon reflection, to think this may be so, because to go from Hampton to our neighbor Mr. C[ouper]'s plantation, it is necessary to consult the tide in order to land conveniently. Driving home today by Jones's Creek, we saw an immovable row of white cranes, all standing with imperturbable gravity upon one leg. I thought of Boccaccio's cook, and had a mind to say ha! at them, to try if they had two. I have been over to Mr. C[ouper]'s, and was very much pleased with my visit, but will tell you of it in my next.

XXV

Rides and Visits

[March 17–22, 1839]

Dear E[lizabeth],

I promised to tell you of my visit to my neighbor Mr. C[ouper],
which pleased and interested me very much. He is an old Glasgow
man, who has been settled here many years.[1] It is curious how
many of the people round this neighborhood have Scotch names; it
seems strange to find them thus gathered in the vicinity of a new
Darien; but those in our immediate neighborhood seem to have
found it a far less fatal region than their countrymen did its name-
sake of the Isthmus. Mr. C[ouper]'s house is a roomy, comfortable, handsomely laid-out mansion, to which he received me with
very cordial kindness, and where I spent part of a very pleasant
morning, talking with him, hearing all he could tell me of the former history of Mr. [Butler]'s plantation. His description of its
former master, old Major [Butler], and of his agent and overseer
Mr. K[ing], and of that gentleman's worthy son and successor the

---

[1] Fanny here records the first of
four visits to John Couper, who was
her immediate neighbor at Cannon's
Point. The son of the pastor of
Lochwinnoch, a small village west
of Glasgow, Couper had been settled
in Georgia for sixty-four years when
Fanny called upon him, and was in
1839 eighty years old.

late overseer, interested me very much; of the two latter function-
aries his account was terrible, and much what I had supposed any
impartial account of them would be; because, let the propensity to
lying of the poor wretched slaves be what it will, they could not in-
vent, with a common consent, the things that they one and all tell
me with reference to the manner in which they have been treated
by the man who has just left the estate, and his father, who for the
last nineteen years have been sole sovereigns of their bodies and
souls. The crops have satisfied the demands of the owners, who,
living in Philadelphia, have been perfectly contented to receive a
large income from their estate without apparently caring how it
was earned. The stories that the poor people tell me of the cruel
tyranny under which they have lived are not complaints, for they
are of things past and gone, and very often, horridly as they shock
and affect me, they themselves seem hardly more than half-con-
scious of the misery their condition exhibits to me, and they speak
of things which I shudder to hear of almost as if they had been
matters of course with them.

Old Mr. C[ouper] spoke with extreme kindness of his own people, and had evidently bestowed much humane and benevolent
pains upon endeavors to better their condition. I asked him if he
did not think the soil and climate of this part of Georgia admirably
suited to the cultivation of the mulberry and the rearing of the silkworm; for it has appeared to me that hereafter silk may be made
one of the most profitable products of this whole region. He said
that that had long been his opinion, and he had at one time had it
much at heart to try the experiment, and had proposed to Major
[Butler] to join him in it, on a scale large enough to test it satisfactorily; but he said Mr. K[ing] opposed the scheme so persistently
that of course it was impossible to carry it out, as his agency and
co-operation were indispensable; and that in like manner he had
suggested sowing turnip crops, and planting peach trees for the
benefit and use of the people on the Hampton estate, experiments
which he had tried with excellent success on his own. But all these

plans for the amelioration and progress of the people's physical condition had been obstructed and finally put entirely aside by old Mr. K[ing] and his son, who, as Mr. C[ouper] said, appeared to give satisfaction to their employers, so it was not his business to find fault with them; he said, however, that the whole condition and treatment of the slaves had changed from the time of Major [Butler]'s death, and that he thought it providential for the poor people that Mr. K[ing] should have left the estate, and the young gentleman, the present owner, come down to look after the people.

He showed me his garden, from whence come the beautiful vegetables he had more than once supplied me with; in the midst of it was a very fine and flourishing date palm tree, which he said bore its fruit as prosperously here as it would in Asia. After the garden we visited a charming, nicely kept poultry yard, and I returned home much delighted with my visit and the kind good humor of my host.

In the afternoon I sat as usual at the receipt of custom, hearing of aches and pains till I ached myself sympathetically from head to foot.

Yesterday morning [March 18], dear E[lizabeth], I went on horseback to St. Annie's, exploring on my way some beautiful woods, and in the afternoon I returned thither in a wood wagon, with Jack to drive and a mule to draw me, Montreal being quite beyond his management; and then and there, the hatchet and saw being in company, I compelled my slave Jack, all the rattlesnakes in creation to the contrary notwithstanding, to cut and clear a way for my chariot through the charming copse.

My letter has been lying unfinished for the last three days. I have been extraordinarily busy, having emancipated myself from the trammels of Jack and all his terror, and as I fear no serpents on horseback, have been daily riding through new patches of woodland without any guide, taking my chance of what I might come to in the shape of impediments. Last Tuesday [March 19] I rode through a whole wood of burned and charred trees, cypresses and oaks, that looked as if they had been each of them blasted by a special thunderbolt, and whole thickets of young trees and shrubs perfectly black and brittle from the effect of fire, I suppose the result of some carelessness of the slaves. As this charcoal woodland extended for some distance, I turned out of it, and round the main road through the plantation, as I could not ride through the blackened boughs and branches without getting begrimed. It had a strange, wild, desolate effect, not without a certain gloomy picturesqueness.

In the afternoon I made Israel drive me through Jack's new-made path to break it down and open it still more, and Montreal's powerful trampling did good service to that effect, though he did not seem to relish the narrow wood road with its grass path by any means as much as the open way of what may be called the high road. After this operation I went on to visit the people at the Busson Hill settlement. I here found, among other noteworthy individuals, a female named Judy, whose two children belong to an individual called Joe, who has another wife, called Mary, at the rice island. In one of the huts I went to leave some flannel, and rice, and sugar for a poor old creature called Nancy, to whom I had promised such indulgences: she is exceedingly infirm and miserable, suffering from sore limbs and an ulcerated leg so cruelly that she can hardly find rest in any position from the constant pain she endures, and is quite unable to lie on her hard bed at night. As I bent over her today, trying to prop her into some posture where she might find some ease, she took hold of my hand, and with the tears streaming over her face, said: "I have worked every day through dew and damp, and sand and heat, and done good work; but oh, missis, me old and broken now; no tongue can tell how much I suffer." In spite of their curious thick utterance and comical jargon, these people sometimes use wonderfully striking and pathetic forms of speech.

In the next cabin, which consisted of an enclosure called by courtesy a room, certainly not ten feet square, and owned by a woman called Dice—that is, not owned, of course, but inhabited by her—three grown-up human beings and eight children stow themselves by day and night, which may be called close packing, I think. I presume that they must take turns to be inside and outside the house, but they did not make any complaint about it, though I should think the aspect of my countenance, as I surveyed their abode and heard their numbers, might have given them a hint to that effect; but I really do find these poor creatures patient of so much misery, that it inclines me the more to heed as well as hear their petitions and complaints when they bring them to me.

After my return home I had my usual evening reception, and, among other pleasant incidents of plantation life, heard the following agreeable anecdote from a woman named Sophy, who came to beg for some rice. In asking her about her husband and children, she said she had never had any husband; that she had had two children by a white man of the name of Walker, who was employed at the mill on the rice island; she was in the hospital after the birth of the second child she bore this man, and at the same time two women, Judy and Scylla, of whose children Mr. K[ing] was the father, were recovering from their confinements. It was not a month since any of them had been delivered, when Mrs. K[ing] came to the hospital, had them all three severely flogged, a process which *she* personally superintended, and then sent them to Five Pound—the swamp Botany Bay of the plantation, of which I have told you—with further orders to the drivers to flog them every day for a week. Now, E[lizabeth], if I make you sick with these disgusting stories, I cannot help it; they are the life itself here; hitherto I have thought these details intolerable enough, but this apparition of a female fiend in the middle of this hell I confess adds an element of cruelty which seems to me to surpass all the rest. Jealousy is not an uncommon quality in the feminine temperament; and just conceive the fate of these unfortunate women between the passions of their masters and mistresses, each alike armed with power to oppress and torture them.

Sophy went on to say that Isaac was her son by driver Morris, who had forced her while she was in her miserable exile at Five Pound. Almost beyond my patience with this string of detestable details, I exclaimed—foolishly enough, heaven knows: "Ah! but don't you know—did nobody ever tell or teach any of you that it is a sin to live with men who are not your husbands?"

Alas! E[lizabeth], what could the poor creature answer but what she did, seizing me at the same time vehemently by the wrist: "Oh yes, missis, we know—we know all about dat well enough; but we do anything to get our poor flesh some rest from de whip; when he made me follow him into de bush, what use me tell him no? he have strength to make me."

I have written down the woman's words; I wish I could write down the voice and look of abject misery with which they were spoken. Now you will observe that the story was not told to me as a complaint; it was a thing long past and over, of which she only spoke in the natural course of accounting for her children to me. I make no comment; what need, or can I add, to such stories? But how is such a state of things to endure? And again, how is it to end?

While I was pondering, as it seemed to me, at the very bottom of the Slough of Despond, on this miserable creature's story, another woman came in (Tema), carrying in her arms a child the image of the mulatto Bran; she came to beg for flannel. I asked her who was her husband. She said she was not married. Her child is the child of bricklayer Temple, who has a wife at the rice island. By this time, what do you think of the moralities, as well as the amenities, of slave life? These are the conditions which can only be known to one who lives among them; flagrant acts of cruelty may be rare, but this ineffable state of utter degradation, this really *beastly* existence, is the normal condition of these men and women, and of that no one seems to take heed, nor have I ever heard it described, so as to form any adequate conception of it, till I found myself plunged into it; where and how is one to begin the cleansing of this horrid pestilential *immondezza* ² of an existence?

It is Wednesday, the 20th of March; we cannot stay here much longer; I wonder if I shall come back again! and whether, when I do, I shall find the trace of one idea of a better life left in these poor people's minds by my sojourn among them.

One of my industries this morning has been cutting out another dress for one of our women, who had heard of my tailoring prowess at the rice island. The material, as usual, was a miserable cotton, many-colored like the scarf of Iris. While shaping it for my client, I ventured to suggest the idea of the possibility of a change of the nethermost as well as the uppermost garment. This, I imagine, is a conception that has never dawned upon the female slave mind on this plantation. They receive twice a year a certain supply of clothing, and wear them (as I have heard some nasty fine ladies do their stays, for fear they should get out of shape), without washing, till they receive the next suit. Under these circumstances I think it is unphilosophical, to say the least of it, to speak of the Negroes as a race whose unfragrance is heaven-ordained, and the result of special organization.

I must tell you that I have been delighted, surprised, and the very least perplexed, by the sudden petition on the part of our young waiter, Aleck, that I will teach him to read. He is a very intelligent lad of about sixteen, and preferred his request with an urgent humility that was very touching. I told him I would think about it. I mean to do it. I will do it; and yet, it is simply breaking the laws of the government under which I am living. Unrighteous laws are made to be broken—*perhaps*—but then, you see, I am a woman, and Mr. [Butler] stands between me and the penalty. If I were a man, I would do that and many a thing besides, and doubtless should be shot some fine day from behind a tree by some good neighbor, who would do the community a service by quietly

² Foulness.

getting rid of a mischievous incendiary; and I promise you, in such a case, no questions would be asked, and my lessons would come to a speedy and silent end; but teaching slaves to read is a finable offense, and I am *feme couverte*,[3] and my fines must be paid by my legal owner, and the first offense of the sort is heavily fined, and the second more heavily fined, and for the third, one is sent to prison. What a pity it is I can't begin with Aleck's third lesson, because going to prison can't be done by proxy, and that penalty would light upon the right shoulders! I certainly intend to teach Aleck to read. I certainly won't tell Mr. [Butler] anything about it. I'll leave him to find it out, as slaves, and servants, and children, and all oppressed, and ignorant, and uneducated, and unprincipled people do; then, if he forbids me, I can stop—perhaps before then the lad may have learned his letters. I begin to perceive one most admirable circumstance in this slavery: you are absolute on your own plantation. No slaves' testimony avails against you, and no white testimony exists but such as you choose to admit. Some owners have a fancy for maiming their slaves, some brand them, some pull out their teeth, some shoot them a little here and there (all details gathered from advertisements of runaway slaves in Southern papers); now they do all this on their plantations, where nobody comes to see, and I'll teach Aleck to read, for nobody is here to see, at least nobody whose seeing I mind; and I'll teach every other creature that wants to learn. I haven't much more than a week to remain in this blessed purgatory; in that last week perhaps I may teach the boy enough to go on alone when I am gone.

I took a long ride today [March 21] all through some new woods and fields, and finally came upon a large space sown with corn for the people. Here I was accosted by such a shape as I never beheld in the worst of my dreams; it looked at first, as it came screaming toward me, like a live specimen of the arms of the Isle of Man, which, as you may or may not know, are three legs joined together, and kicking in different directions. This uncouth device is

[3] A married woman.

not an invention of the Manxmen, for it is found on some very ancient coins—Greek, I believe; but, at any rate, it is now the device of our subject Island of Man, and, like that set in motion, and nothing else, was the object that approached me, only it had a head where the three legs were joined, and a voice came out of the head to this effect: "Oh, missis, you hab to take me out of dis here bird field; me no able to run after birds, and ebery night me lick because me no run after dem." When this apparition reached me and stood as still as it could, I perceived it consisted of a boy who said his name was "Jack de bird driver." I suppose some vague idea of the fitness of things had induced them to send this living scarecrow into the cornfield, and if he had been set up in the midst of it, nobody, I am sure, would have imagined he was anything else; but it seems he was expected to run after the feathered fowl who alighted on the grainfield, and I do not wonder that he did not fulfill this expectation. His feet, legs, and knees were all maimed and distorted, his legs were nowhere thicker than my wrist, his feet were a yard apart from each other, and his knees swollen and knocking together. What a creature to run after birds! He implored me to give him some meat, and have him sent back to Little St. Simons Island, from which he came, and where he said his poor limbs were stronger and better.

Riding home, I passed some sassafras trees, which are putting forth deliciously fragrant tassels of small leaves and blossoms, and other exquisite flowering shrubs, which are new to me, and enchant me perhaps all the more for their strangeness. Before reaching the house I was stopped by one of our multitudinous Jennies with a request for some meat, and that I would help her with some clothes for Ben and Daphne, of whom she had the sole charge; these are two extremely pretty and interesting-looking mulatto children, whose resemblance to Mr. K[ing] had induced me to ask Mr. [Butler], when first I saw them, if he did not think they must be his children. He said they were certainly like him, but Mr. K[ing] did not acknowledge the relationship.

I asked Jenny who their mother was.

"Minda."

"Who their father?"

"Mr. K[ing]."

"What! old Mr. K[ing]?"

"No, Mr. R[oswell] K[ing]."

"Who told you so?"

"Minda, who ought to know."

"Mr. K[ing] denies it."

"That's because he never has looked upon them, nor done a thing for them."

"Well, but he acknowledged Renty as his son, why should he deny these?"

"Because old master was here then when Renty was born, and he made Betty tell all about it, and Mr. K[ing] had to own it; but nobody knows anything about this, and so he denies it"—with which information I rode home.

I always give you an exact report of any conversation I may have with any of the people, and you see from this that the people on the plantation themselves are much of my worthy neighbor Mr. C[ouper]'s mind, that the death of Major [Butler] was a great misfortune for the slaves on his estate.

I went to the hospital this afternoon to see if the condition of the poor people was at all improved since I had been last there; but nothing had been done. I suppose Mr. G[owen] is waiting for Mr. [Butler] to come down in order to speak to him about it. I found some miserable new cases of women disabled by hard work. One poor thing, called Priscilla, had come out of the fields today scarcely able to crawl; she has been losing blood for a whole fortnight without intermission, and, until today, was laboring in the fields. Leah, another new face since I visited the hospital last, is lying quite helpless from exhaustion; she is advanced in her pregnancy, and doing taskwork in the fields at the same time. What piteous existences, to be sure! I do wonder, as I walk among them, well-fed, well-clothed, young, strong, idle, doing nothing but ride and drive about all day, a woman, a creature like themselves, who have borne children too, what sort of feeling they have toward me. I wonder it is not one of murderous hate—that they should lie here almost dying with unrepaid labor for me. I stand and look at them, and these thoughts work in my mind and heart, till I feel as if I must tell them how dreadful and how monstrous it seems to me myself, and how bitterly ashamed and grieved I feel for it all.

Today [March 22] I rode in the morning round poor Cripple Jack's bird field again, through the sweet, spicy-smelling pineland, and home by my new road cut through Jones's wood, of which I am as proud as if I had made instead of found it—the grass, flowering shrubs, and all. In the afternoon I drove in the wood wagon back to Jones's, and visited Busson Hill on the way, with performances of certain promises of flannel, quarters of dollars, etc., etc. At Jones's, the women today had all done their work at a quarter past three, and had swept their huts out very scrupulously for my reception. Their dwellings are shockingly dilapidated and over-crammed—poor creatures!—and it seems hard that, while exhorting them to spend labor in cleaning and making them tidy, I cannot promise them that they shall be repaired and made habitable for them.

In driving home through my new wood cut, Jack gave me a terrible account of a flogging that a Negro called Glasgow had received yesterday. He seemed awfully impressed with it, so I suppose it must have been an unusually severe punishment; but he either would not or could not tell me what the man had done. On my return to the house I found Mr. [Butler] had come down from the rice plantation, whereat I was much delighted on all accounts. I am sure it is getting much too late for him to remain in that pestilential swampy atmosphere; besides, I want him to see my improvements in the new wood paths, and I want him to come and hear all these poor people's complaints and petitions himself. They have been flocking in to see him ever since it was known he had arrived. I met coming on that errand Dandy, the husband of the woman for whom I cut out the gown the other day; and asking him how it had answered, he gave a piteous account of its tearing all to pieces the first time she put it on; it had appeared to me perfectly rotten and good for nothing, and, upon questioning him as to where he bought it and what he paid for it, I had to hear a sad account of hardship and injustice. I have told you that the people collect moss from the trees and sell it to the shopkeepers in Darien for the purpose of stuffing furniture; they also raise poultry, and are allowed to dispose of the eggs in the same way. It seems that poor Dandy had taken the miserable material Edie's gown was made of as payment for a quantity of moss and eggs furnished by him at various times to one of the Darien storekeepers, who refused him payment in any other shape, and the poor fellow had no redress; and this, he tells me, is a frequent experience with all the slaves both here and at the rice island. Of course, the rascally shopkeepers can cheat these poor wretches to any extent they please with perfect impunity.

Mr. [Butler] told me of a visit Renty paid him, which was not a little curious in some of its particulars. You know none of the slaves are allowed the use of firearms; but Renty put up a petition to be allowed Mr. K[ing]'s gun, which it seems that gentleman left behind him. Mr. [Butler] refused this petition, saying at the same time to the lad that he knew very well that none of the people were allowed guns. Renty expostulated on the score of his *white blood,* and finding his master uninfluenced by that consideration, departed with some severe reflections on Mr. K[ing], his father, for not having left him his gun as a keepsake, in token of paternal affection, when he left the plantation.

It is quite late, and I am very tired, though I have not done much more than usual today, but the weather is beginning to be oppressive to me, who hate heat; but I find the people, and especially the sick in the hospital, speak of it as cold. I will tell you hereafter of a most comical account Mr. [Butler] has given me of the prolonged and still protracted pseudopregnancy of a woman called Markie, who for many more months than are generally required for the process of continuing the human species, pretended to be what the Germans pathetically and poetically call "in good hope," and continued to reap increased rations as the reward of her expectation, till she finally had to disappoint the estate and receive a flogging. He told me, too, what interested me very much, of a conspiracy among Mr. C[ouper]'s slaves some years ago. I cannot tell you about it now; I will some other time. It is wonderful to me that such attempts are not being made the whole time among these people to regain their liberty; probably because many are made ineffectually, and never known beyond the limits of the plantation where they take place.

XXVI

Broughton Island and Hamilton Estate

[March 24–28, 1839]

Dear E[lizabeth],

We have been having something like Northern March weather —blinding sun, blinding wind, and blinding dust, through all which, the day before yesterday [March 23], Mr. [Butler] and I rode together round most of the fields, and over the greater part of the plantation. It was a detestable process, the more so that he rode Montreal and I Miss Kate, and we had no small difficulty in managing them both. In the afternoon we had an equally detestable drive through the new wood paths to St. Annie's, and having accomplished all my errands among the people there, we crossed over certain sounds, and seas, and separating waters, to pay a neighborly visit to the wife of one of our adjacent planters.[1]

How impossible it would be for you to conceive, even if I could describe, the careless desolation which pervaded the whole place;

[1] Florida Troup, daughter of George Michael Troup, married Thomas Bryan, the owner of Broughton Island, in 1835. Florida bore five children and died young. For the location of Bryan's house on Broughton Island, see map, page xl.

the shaggy unkempt grounds we passed through to approach the house; the ruinous, rackrent, tumble-down house itself; the untidy, slatternly, all but beggarly appearance of the mistress of the mansion herself. The smallest Yankee farmer has a tidier estate, a tidier house, and a tidier wife than this member of the proud Southern chivalry, who, however, inasmuch as he has slaves, is undoubtedly a much greater personage in his own estimation than those capital fellows W—— and B——, who walk in glory and in joy behind their plows upon your mountain sides. The Brunswick Canal project was descanted upon, and pronounced, without a shadow of dissent, a scheme the impracticability of which all but convicted its projectors of insanity. Certainly, if, as I hear, the moneyed men of Boston have gone largely into this speculation, their habitual sagacity must have been seriously at fault, for here on the spot nobody mentions the project but as a subject of utter derision.

While the men discussed about this matter, Mrs. B[ryan] favored me with the congratulations I have heard so many times on the subject of my having a white nurserymaid for my children. Of course, she went into the old subject of the utter incompetency of Negro women to discharge such an office faithfully; but, in spite of her multiplied examples of their utter inefficiency, I believe the discussion ended by simply our both agreeing that ignorant Negro girls of twelve years old are not as capable or trustworthy as well-trained white women of thirty.

Returning home, our route was changed, and Quash the boatman took us all the way round by water to Hampton. I should have told you that our exit was as wild as our entrance to this estate, and was made through a broken wooden fence, which we had to climb partly over and partly under, with some risk and some obloquy, in spite of our dexterity, as I tore my dress, and very nearly fell flat on my face in the process. Our row home was perfectly enchanting; for, though the morning's wind and (I suppose) the state of the tide had roughened the waters of the great river, and our passage was not as smooth as it might have been, the wind had died away, the evening air was deliciously still, and mild, and soft. A young slip of a moon glimmered just above the horizon, and "the stars climbed up the sapphire steps of heaven," while we made our way over the rolling, rushing, foaming waves, and saw to right and left the marsh fires burning in the swampy meadows, adding another colored light in the landscape to the amber-tinted lower sky and the violet arch above, and giving wild picturesqueness to the whole scene by throwing long flickering rays of flame upon the distant waters.

[Sunday, March 24] I read service again today to the people. You cannot conceive anything more impressive than the silent devotion of their whole demeanor while it lasted, nor more touching than the profound thanks with which they rewarded me when it was over, and they took their leave; and today they again left me with the utmost decorum of deportment, and without pressing a single petition or complaint such as they ordinarily thrust upon me on all other occasions, which seems to me an instinctive feeling of religious respect for the day and the business they have come upon, which does them infinite credit.

In the afternoon I took a long walk with the chicks in the woods—long at least for the little legs of S[ally] and M[argery], who carried baby. We came home by the shore, and I stopped to look at a jutting point, just below which a sort of bay would have afforded the most capital position for a bathing house. If we stayed here late in the season, such a refreshment would become almost a necessary of life, and anywhere along the bank just where I stopped to examine it today an establishment for that purpose might be prosperously founded.

I am amused, but by no means pleased, at an entirely new mode of pronouncing which S[ally] has adopted. Apparently the Negro jargon has commended itself as euphonious to her infantile ears, and she is now treating me to the most ludicrous and accurate imitations of it every time she opens her mouth. Of course I shall not allow this, comical as it is, to become a habit. This is the way the Southern ladies acquire the thick and inelegant pronunciation which distinguishes their utterances from the Northern snuffle, and I have no desire that S[ally] should adorn her mother tongue with either peculiarity.

It is a curious and sad enough thing to observe, as I have frequent opportunities of doing, the unbounded insolence and tyranny (of manner, of course it can go no farther) of the slaves toward each other. "Hi! you boy!" and "Hi! you girl!" shouted in an imperious scream, is the civilest mode of apostrophizing those at a distance from them; more frequently it is "You niggar, you hear? hi! you niggar!" And I assure you no contemptuous white intonation ever equaled the *prepotenza*[2] of the despotic insolence of this address of these poor wretches to each other.

I have left my letter lying for a couple of days, dear E[lizabeth]. I have been busy and tired; my walking and riding is becoming rather more laborious to me, for, though nobody here appears to do so, I am beginning to feel the relaxing influence of the spring. The day before yesterday [March 25] I took a disagreeable ride, all through swampy fields, and charred, blackened thickets, to discover nothing either picturesque or beautiful; the woods in one part of the plantation have been on fire for three days, and a whole tract of exquisite evergreens has been burned down to the ground. In the afternoon I drove in the wood wagon to visit the people at St. Annie's. There has been rain these last two nights, and their wretched hovels do not keep out the weather; they are really miserable abodes for human beings. I think pigs who were at all particular might object to some of them. There is a woman at this settlement called Sophy, the wife of a driver, Morris, who is so pretty that I often wonder if it is only by contrast that I admire her so much, or if her gentle, sweet, refined face, in spite of its dusky color, would not approve itself anywhere to anyone with an eye for beauty. Her manner and voice, too, are peculiarly

[2] Arrogance.

soft and gentle; but, indeed, the voices of all these poor people, men as well as women, are much pleasanter and more melodious than the voices of white people in general. Most of the wretched hovels had been swept and tidied out in expectation of my visit, and many were the consequent petitions for rations of meat, flannel, Osnaburgs,[3] etc.; promising all which, in due proportion to the cleanliness of each separate dwelling, I came away. On my way home I called for a moment at Jones's settlement to leave money and presents promised to the people there for similar improvement in the condition of their huts. I had not time to stay and distribute my benefactions myself, and so appointed a particularly bright, intelligent-looking woman, called Jenny, paymistress in my stead, and her deputed authority was received with the utmost cheerfulness by them all.

I have been having a long talk with Mr. [Butler] about Ben and Daphne, those two young mulatto children of Mr. K[ing]'s, whom I mentioned to you lately. Poor pretty children! they have refined and sensitive faces as well as straight, regular features; and the expression of the girl's countenance, as well as the sound of her voice, and the sad humility of her deportment, are indescribably touching. Mr. B[utler] expressed the strongest interest in and pity for them, *because of their color:* it seems unjust almost to the rest of their fellow unfortunates that this should be so, and yet it is almost impossible to resist the impression of the unfitness of these two forlorn young creatures for the life of coarse labor and dreadful degradation to which they are destined. In any of the Southern cities the girl would be pretty sure to be reserved for a worse fate; but even here, death seems to me a thousand times preferable to the life that is before her.

In the afternoon [March 26] I rode with Mr. [Butler] to look at the fire in the woods. We did not approach it, but stood where the great volumes of smoke could be seen rising steadily above the

---

[3] Coarse cotton clothing which took its name from the manufacturing center of Osnabrück in the German province of Hanover.

pines, as they have now continued to do for upward of a week; the destruction of the pine timber must be something enormous. We then went to visit Dr. and Mrs. G[rant], and wound up these exercises of civilized life by a call on dear old Mr. C[ouper], whose nursery and kitchen garden are a real refreshment to my spirits. How completely the national character of the worthy canny old Scot is stamped on the care and thrift visible in his whole property, the judicious, successful culture of which has improved and adorned his dwelling in this remote corner of the earth! The comparison, or rather contrast, between himself and his quondam neighbor, Major [Butler], is curious enough to contemplate. The Scotch tendency of the one to turn everything to good account, the Irish propensity of the other to leave everything to ruin, to disorder, and neglect; the careful economy and prudent management of the mercantile man, the reckless profusion and careless extravagance of the soldier. The one made a splendid fortune and spent it in Philadelphia, where he built one of the finest houses that existed there in the old-fashioned days, when fine old family mansions were still to be seen breaking the monotonous uniformity of the Quaker city. The other has resided here on his estate, ameliorating the condition of his slaves and his property, a benefactor to the people and the soil alike—a useful and a good existence, an obscure and tranquil one.

Last Wednesday [March 27] we drove to Hamilton, by far the finest estate on St. Simons Island. The gentleman to whom it belongs lives, I believe, habitually in Paris; but Captain F[raser] resides on it, and, I suppose, is the real overseer of the plantation. All the way along the road (we traversed nearly the whole length of the island) we found great tracts of wood all burned or burning; the destruction had spread in every direction, and against the sky we saw the slow rising of the smoky clouds that showed the pine forest to be on fire still. What an immense quantity of property such a fire must destroy! The Negro huts on several of the plantations that we passed through were the most miserable human habitations I ever beheld. The wretched hovels at St. Annie's, on the Hampton estate, that had seemed to me the *ne plus ultra* of misery, were really palaces to some of the dirty, desolate, dilapidated dog kennels which we passed today, and out of which the Negroes poured like black ants at our approach, and stood to gaze at us as we drove by.

The planters' residences we passed were only three. It makes one ponder seriously when one thinks of the mere handful of white people on this island. In the midst of this large population of slaves, how absolutely helpless they would be if the blacks were to become restive! They could be destroyed to a man before human help could reach them from the main, or the tidings even of what was going on be carried across the surrounding waters. As we approached the southern end of the island we began to discover the line of the white sea sands beyond the bushes and fields, and presently, above the sparkling, dazzling line of snowy white—for the sands were as white as our English chalk cliffs—stretched the deep blue sea line of the great Atlantic Ocean.

We found that there had been a most terrible fire in the Hamilton woods—more extensive than that on our own planta-tion. It seems as if the whole island had been burning at different points for more than a week. What a cruel pity and shame it does seem to have these beautiful masses of wood so destroyed! I suppose it is impossible to prevent it. The field hands make fires to cook their midday food wherever they happen to be working, and sometimes through their careless neglect, but sometimes, too, undoubtedly on purpose, the woods are set fire to by these means. One benefit they consider that they derive from the process is the destruction of the dreaded rattlesnakes that infest the woodland all over the island; but really the funeral pyre of these hateful reptiles is too costly at this price.

Hamilton struck me very much—I mean the whole appearance of the place; the situation of the house, the noble water prospect it commanded, the magnificent old oaks near it, a luxuriant vine trellis, and a splendid hedge of Yucca *gloriosa,* were all objects of great delight to me. The latter was most curious to me, who had never seen any but single specimens of the plant, and not many of these. I think our green house at the North boasts but two; but here they were growing close together, and in such a manner as to form a compact and impenetrable hedge, their spiky leaves striking out on all sides like chevaux-de-frise,[4] and the tall, slender stems, that bear those delicate ivory-colored bells of blossoms, springing up against the sky in a regular row. I wish I could see that hedge in blossom. It must be wonderfully strange and lovely, and must look by moonlight like a whole range of fairy Chinese pagodas carved in ivory.

At dinner we had some delicious green peas, so much in advance of you are we down here with the seasons. Don't you think one might accept the rattlesnakes, or perhaps indeed the slavery, for the sake of the green peas? It is a world of compensations—a life of compromises, you know; and one should learn to set one thing against another if one means to thrive and fare well, i.e., eat green peas on the 28th of March.[5]

After dinner I walked up and down before the house for a long while with Mrs. F[raser], and had a most interesting conversation with her about the Negroes and all the details of their condition. She is a kindhearted, intelligent woman; but, though she seemed to me to acquiesce, as a matter of inevitable necessity, in the social system in the midst of which she was born and lives, she did not appear to me, by several things she said, to be by any means in love with it. She gave me a very sad character of Mr. K[ing], confirming by her general description of him the impression produced by all the details I have received from our own people. As for any care for the moral or religious training of the slaves, that, she said, was a matter that never troubled his thoughts;

[4] A spiked fence.

[5] The Butlers dined with the Frasers and ate their green peas, on Wednesday, March 27, 1839. Fanny wrote up her account of this visit the next day, and this accounts for the transposing of the date.

indeed, his only notion upon the subject of religion, she said, was that it was something *not bad* for white women and children.

We drove home by moonlight; and as we came toward the woods in the middle of the island, the fireflies glittered out from the dusky thickets as if some magical golden veil was every now and then shaken out into the darkness. The air was enchantingly mild and soft, and the whole way through the silvery night delightful.

My dear friend, I have at length made acquaintance with a live rattlesnake. Old Scylla had the pleasure of discovering it while hunting for some wood to burn. Israel captured it, and brought it to the house for my edification. I thought it an evil-looking beast, and could not help feeling rather nervous while contemplating it, though the poor thing had a noose round its neck, and could by no manner of means have extricated itself. The flat head, and vivid, vicious eye, and darting tongue, were none of them lovely to behold; but the sort of threatening whirr produced by its rattle, together with the deepening and fading of the marks on its skin, either with its respiration, or the emotions of fear and anger it was enduring, were peculiarly dreadful and fascinating. It was quite a young one, having only two or three rattles in its tail. These, as you probably know, increase in number by one annually, so that you can always tell the age of the amiable serpent you are examining—if it will let you count the number of joints of its rattle. Captain F[raser] gave me the rattle of one which had as many as twelve joints. He said it had belonged to a very large snake, which had crawled from under a fallen tree trunk on which his children were playing. After exhibiting his interesting captive, Israel killed, stuffed, and presented it to me for preservation as a trophy, and made me extremely happy by informing me that there was a nest of them where this one was found. I think with terror of S[ally] running about with her little socks not reaching halfway up her legs, and her little frocks not reaching halfway down them. However, we shall probably not make acquaintance with many more of these natives of Georgia, as we are to return as soon as possible now to the North. We shall soon be free again.

This morning [March 28] I rode to the burned district, and attempted to go through it at Sinclair's, but unsuccessfully: it was impossible to penetrate through the charred and blackened thickets. In the afternoon I walked round the Point, and visited the houses of the people who are our nearest neighbors. I found poor Edie in sad tribulation at the prospect of resuming her field labor. It is really shameful treatment of a woman just after child labor. She was confined exactly three weeks ago today, and she tells me she is ordered out to field work on Monday. She seems to dread the approaching hardships of her task labor extremely. Her baby was born dead, she thinks in consequence of a fall she had while carrying a heavy weight of water. She is suffering great pain in one of her legs and sides, and seems to me in a condition utterly unfit for any work, much less hoeing in the fields; but I dare not interfere to prevent this cruelty. She says she has already had to go out to work three weeks after her confinement with each of her other children, and does not complain of it as anything special in her case. She says that is now the invariable rule of the whole plantation, though it used not to be so formerly.

I have let my letter lie since I wrote the above, dear E[lizabeth]; but as mine is a story without beginning, middle, or end, it matters extremely little where I leave it off or where I take it up; and if you have not, between my wood rides and sick slaves, come to Falstaff's conclusion that I have "damnable iteration," you are patient of sameness. But the days are like each other; and the rides and the people, and, alas! their conditions, do not vary.

Today, however, my visit to the infirmary was marked by an event which has not occurred before—the death of one of the poor slaves while I was there. I found, on entering the first ward— to use a most inapplicable term for the dark, filthy, forlorn room I have so christened—an old Negro called Friday lying on the ground. I asked what ailed him, and was told he was dying. I approached him, and perceived, from the glazed eyes and the feeble rattling breath, that he was at the point of expiring. His tattered shirt and trousers barely covered his poor body; his appearance was that of utter exhaustion from age and feebleness; he had nothing under him but a mere handful of straw that did not cover the earth he was stretched on; and under his head, by way of pillow for his dying agony, two or three rough sticks just raising his skull a few inches from the ground. The flies were all gathering around his mouth, and not a creature was near him. There he lay—the worn-out slave, whose life had been spent in unrequited labor for me and mine, without one physical alleviation, one Christian solace, one human sympathy, to cheer him in his extremity—panting out the last breath of his wretched existence like some forsaken, overworked, wearied-out beast of burden, rotting where it falls! I bent over the poor awful human creature in the supreme hour of his mortality; and while my eyes, blinded with tears of unavailing pity and horror, were fixed upon him, there was a sudden quivering of the eyelids and falling of the jaw—and he was free. I stood up, and remained long lost in the imagination of the change that creature had undergone, and in the tremendous overwhelming consciousness of the deliverance God had granted the soul whose castoff vesture of decay lay at my feet. How I rejoiced for him; and how, as I turned to the wretches who were calling to me from the inner room, whence they could see me as I stood contemplating the piteous object, I wished they all were gone away with him, the delivered, the freed by death from bitter, bitter bondage.

In the next room I found a miserable, decrepit old Negress, called Charity, lying sick, and I should think near too to die; but she did not think her work was over, much as she looked unfit for farther work on earth; but with feeble voice and beseeching hands implored me to have her work lightened when she was sent back to it from the hospital. She is one of the oldest slaves on the plantation, and has to walk to her field labor, and back again at night, a distance of nearly four miles. There were an unusual number of sick women in the room today; among them quite a young girl, daughter of boatman Quash's, with a sick baby, who has a father, though she has no husband. Poor thing! she looks like a mere child herself. I returned home so very sad and heartsick that I could not rouse myself to the effort of going up to St. Annie's with the presents I had promised the people there. I sent M[argery] up in the wood wagon with them, and remained in the house with my thoughts, which were none of the merriest.

XXVII

A Planter Feud

[April 1, 1839]

Dearest E[lizabeth],

On Friday [March 29] I rode to where the rattlesnake was found, and where I was informed by the Negroes there was a *nest* of them—a pleasing domestic picture of home and infancy that word suggests, not altogether appropriate to rattlesnakes, I think. On horseback I felt bold to accomplish this adventure, which I certainly should not have attempted on foot; however, I could discover no sign of either snake or nest—perhaps it is of the nature of a mare's nest, and undiscoverable; but, having done my duty by myself in endeavoring to find it, I rode off and coasted the estate by the side of the marsh till I came to the causeway. There I found a new-cleared field, and stopped to admire the beautiful appearance of the stumps of the trees scattered all about it, and wreathed and garlanded with the most profuse and fantastic growth of various plants, wild roses being among the most abundant. What a lovely aspect one side of nature presents here, and how hideous is the other!

In the afternoon I drove to pay a visit to old Mrs. A[rmstrong], the lady proprietress whose estate immediately adjoins ours. On my way thither I passed a woman called Margaret walking rapidly and powerfully along the road. She was returning home from the field, having done her task at three o'clock; and told me, with a merry, beaming black face, that she was going "to clean up de house, to please de missis." On driving through my neighbor's grounds, I was disgusted more than I can express with the miserable Negro huts of her people; they were not fit to shelter cattle— they were not fit to shelter anything, for they were literally in holes, and, as we used to say of our stockings at school, too bad to darn. To be sure, I will say, in excuse for their old mistress, her own habitation was but a very few degrees less ruinous and disgusting. What would one of your Yankee farmers say to such abodes? When I think of the white houses, the green blinds, and the flower plots of the villages in New England, and look at these dwellings of lazy filth and inert degradation, it does seem amazing to think that physical and moral conditions so widely opposite should be found among people occupying a similar place in the social scale of the same country. The Northern farmer, however, thinks it no shame to work, the Southern planter does; and there begins and ends the difference. Industry, man's crown of honor elsewhere, is here his badge of utter degradation; and so comes all by which I am here surrounded—pride, profligacy, idleness, cruelty, cowardice, ignorance, squalor, dirt, and ineffable abasement.

When I returned home I found that Mrs. F[raser] had sent me some magnificent prawns. I think of having them served singly, and divided as one does a lobster—their size really suggests no less respect.

I rode [March 30] all through the burned district and the bush to Mrs. W[ylly]'s field, in making my way out of which I was very nearly swamped, and, but for the valuable assistance of a certain sable Scipio who came up and extricated me, I might be floundering hopelessly there still. He got me out of my Slough of Despond, and put me in the way to a charming wood ride which runs between Mrs. W[ylly]'s and Colonel H[azzard]'s grounds.

While going along this delightful boundary of these two neighboring estates, my mind not unnaturally dwelt upon the terms of deadly feud in which the two families owning them are living with each other. A horrible quarrel has occurred quite lately upon the subject of the ownership of this very ground I was skirting, between Dr. H[azzard] and young Mr. W[ylly]; they have challenged each other, and what I am going to tell you is a good sample of the sort of spirit which grows up among slaveholders. So read it, for it is curious to people who have not lived habitually among savages. The terms of the challenge that has passed between them have appeared like a sort of advertisement in the local paper, and are to the effect that they are to fight at a certain distance with certain weapons—firearms, of course; that there is to be on the person of each a white paper, or mark, immediately over the region of the heart, as a point for direct aim; and whoever kills the other is to have the privilege of *cutting off his head, and sticking it up on a pole on the piece of land which was the origin of the debate;* so that, some fine day, I might have come hither as I did today, and found myself riding under the shadow of the gory locks of Dr. H[azzard] or Mr. W[ylly], my peaceful and pleasant neighbors.

I came home through our own pinewoods, which are actually a wilderness of black desolation. The scorched and charred tree trunks are still smoking and smouldering; the ground is a sort of charcoal pavement, and the fire is still burning on all sides, for the smoke was rapidly rising in several directions on each hand of the path I pursued. Across this dismal scene of strange destruction, bright blue and red birds, like living jewels, darted in the brilliant sunshine. I wonder if the fire has killed and scared away many of these beautiful creatures. In the afternoon I took Jack with me to clear some more of the wood paths; but the weather is what I call hot, and what the people here think warm, and the air was literally thick with little black points of insects, which they call sand flies, and which settle upon one's head and face literally like a black net; you hardly see them or feel them at the time, but the irritation occasioned by them is intolerable, and I had to relinquish my work and fly before this winged plague as fast as I could from my new acquaintance the rattlesnakes. Jack informed me, in the course of our expedition, that the woods on the island were sometimes burned away in order to leave the ground in grass for fodder for the cattle, and that the very beautiful ones he and I had been clearing paths through were not unlikely to be so doomed, which strikes me as a horrible idea.

In the evening poor Edie came up to the house to see me, with an old Negress called Sackey, who has been one of the chief nurses on the island for many years. I suppose she has made some application to Mr. G[owen] for a respite for Edie, on finding how terribly unfit she is for work; or perhaps Mr. [Butler], to whom I represented her case, may have ordered her reprieve; but she came with much gratitude to me (who have, as far as I know, had nothing to do with it), to tell me that she is not to be sent into the field for another week. Old Sackey fully confirmed Edie's account of the terrible hardships the women underwent in being thus driven to labor before they had recovered from childbearing. She said that old Major [Butler] allowed the women at the rice island five weeks, and those here four weeks, to recover from a confinement, and then never permitted them for some time after they resumed their work to labor in the fields before sunrise or after sunset; but Mr. K[ing] had altered that arrangement, allowing the women at the rice island only four weeks, and those here only three weeks, for their recovery. "And then, missis," continued the old woman, "out into the field again, through dew and dry, as if nothing had happened; that is why, missis, so many of the women have falling of the womb and weakness in the back; and if he had continued on the estate, he would have utterly destroyed all the breeding women." Sometimes, after sending them back into the field at the expiration of their three weeks, they would work for a day or two, she said, and then fall down in the field with exhaustion, and be brought to the hospital almost at the point of death.

Yesterday, Sunday [March 31], I had my last service [1] at home with these poor people; nearly thirty of them came, all clean, neat, and decent, in their dress and appearance. S[ally] had begged very hard to join the congregation, and upon the most solemn promise of remaining still she was admitted; but, in spite of the perfect honor with which she kept her promise, her presence disturbed my thoughts not a little, and added much to the poignancy of the feeling with which I saw her father's poor slaves gathered round me. The child's exquisite complexion, large gray eyes, and solemn and at the same time eager countenance, was such a wonderful piece of contrast to their sable faces, so many of them so uncouth in their outlines and proportions, and yet all of them so pathetic, and some so sublime in their expression of patient suffering and religious fervor: their eyes never wandered from me and my child, who sat close by my knee, their little mistress, their future providence, my poor baby! Dear E[lizabeth], bless God that you have never reared a child with such an awful expectation: and at the end of the prayers, the tears were streaming over their faces, and one chorus of blessings rose round me and the child—farewell blessings, and prayers that we would return; and thanks so fervent in their incoherency, it was more than I could bear, and I begged them to go away and leave me to recover myself. And then I remained with S[ally], and for quite a long while even her restless spirit was still in wondering amazement at my bitter crying. I am to go next Sunday to the church on the island, where there is to be service; and so this is my last Sunday with the people.

When I had recovered from the emotion of this scene, I walked out with S[ally] a little way, but meeting M[argery] and the baby, she turned home with them, and I pursued my walk alone up the road, and home by the shore. They are threatening to burn

[1] The last of Fanny Kemble's home services actually took place on Sunday, April 14, 1839. See page 327.

down all my woods to make grassland for the cattle, and I have terrified them by telling them that I will never come back if they destroy the woods. I went and paid a visit to Mrs. G[owen]; poor little, well-meaning, helpless woman, what can she do for these poor people, where I, who am supposed to own them, can do nothing? And yet how much may be done, is done, by the brain and heart of one human being in contact with another! We are answerable for incalculable opportunities of good and evil in our daily intercourse with every soul with whom we have to deal; every meeting, every parting, every chance greeting, and every appointed encounter, are occasions open to us for which we are to account. To our children, our servants, our friends, our acquaintances—to each and all every day, and all day long, we are distributing that which is best or worst in existence—influence: with every word, with every look, with every gesture, something is given or withheld of great importance it may be to the receiver, of inestimable importance to the giver.

Certainly the laws and enacted statues on which this detestable system is built up are potent enough; the social prejudice that buttresses it is almost more potent still; and yet a few hearts and brains well bent to do the work would bring within this almost impenetrable dungeon of ignorance, misery, and degradation, in which so many millions of human souls lie buried, that freedom of God which would presently conquer for them their earthly liberty. With some such thoughts I commended the slaves on the plantation to the little overseer's wife; I did not tell my thoughts to her— they would have scared the poor little woman half out of her senses. To begin with, her bread, her husband's occupation, has its root in slavery; it would be difficult for her to think as I do of it. I am afraid her care, even of the bodily habits and sicknesses of the people left in Mrs. G[owen]'s charge, will not be worth much, for nobody treats others better than they do themselves; and she is certainly doing her best to injure herself and her own poor baby, who is two and a half years old, and whom she is still suckling.

This is, I think, the worst case of this extraordinary delusion so prevalent among your women that I have ever met with yet; but they all nurse their children much longer than is good for either baby or mother. The summer heat, particularly when a young baby is cutting teeth, is, I know, considered by young American mothers an exceedingly critical time, and therefore I always hear of babies being nursed till after the second summer; so that a child born in January would be suckled till it was eighteen or nineteen months old, in order that it might not be weaned till its second summer was over. I am sure that nothing can be worse than this system, and I attribute much of the wretched ill-health of young American mothers to overnursing; and of course a process that destroys their health and vigor completely must affect most unfavorably the child they are suckling. It is a grievous mistake. I remember my charming friend F—— D—— [2] telling me that she had nursed her first child till her second was born—a miraculous statement, which I can only believe because she told it me herself. Whenever anything seems absolutely impossible, the word of a true person is the only proof of it worth anything.

[2] Probably Mrs. Dulaney, one of Fanny's Philadelphia intimates.

XXVIII

Rides and Visits

[April 2–4, 1839]

Dear E[lizabeth],

I have been riding into the swamp behind the new house; I
had a mind to survey the ground all round it before going away,
to see what capabilities it afforded for the founding of a garden,
but I confess it looked very unpromising. Trying to return by another way, I came to a morass, which, after contemplating, and
making my horse try for a few paces, I thought it expedient not
to attempt. A woman named Charlotte, who was working in the
field, seeing my dilemma, and the inglorious retreat I was about to
make, shouted to me at the top of her voice: "You no turn back,
missis; if you want to go through, send, missis, send; you hab
slave enough, nigger enough, let 'em come, let 'em fetch planks,
and make de bridge; what you say dey must do—send, missis,
send, missis!" It seemed to me, from the lady's imperative tone in
my behalf, that if she had been in my place, she would presently
have had a corduroy road through the swamp of prostrate "niggers," as she called her family in Ham, and have ridden over the
sand dry-hoofed; and to be sure, if I pleased, so might I, for, as
she very truly said, "what you say, missis, they must do." Instead
of summoning her sooty tribe, however, I backed my horse out

of the swamp, and betook myself to another pretty wood path, which only wants widening to be quite charming. At the end of this, however, I found swamp the second, and out of this having been helped by a grinning, facetious personage, most appropriately named Pun, I returned home in dudgeon, in spite of what dear Miss M[artineau] calls the "moral suitability" of finding a foul bog at the end of every charming wood path or forest ride in this region.

In the afternoon I drove to Busson Hill to visit the people there. I found that both the men and women had done their work at half past three. Saw Tema with her child, that ridiculous image of driver Bran, in her arms, in spite of whose whity-brown skin she still maintains that its father is a man as black as herself —and she (to use a most extraordinary comparison I heard of a Negro girl making with regard to her mother) is as black as "de hinges of hell." Query: did she really mean hinges, or angels? The angels of hell is a polite and pretty paraphrase for devils, certainly. In complimenting a woman called Joan upon the tidy condition of her house, she answered, with that cruel humility that is so bad an element in their character: "Missis no 'spect to find colored folks' house clean as white folks'." The mode in which they have learned to accept the idea of their own degradation and unalterable inferiority is the most serious impediment that I see in the way of their progress, since assuredly "self-love is not so vile a sin as self-neglecting." In the same way yesterday, Abraham the cook, in speaking of his brother's theft at the rice island, said "it was a shame even for a colored man to do such things." I labor hard, whenever any such observation is made, to explain to them that the question is one of moral and mental culture—not the color of an integument—and assure them, much to my own comfort, whatever it may be to theirs, that white people are as dirty and as dishonest as colored folks, when they have suffered the same lack of decent training. If I could but find one of these women on whose mind the idea had dawned that she was neither more nor less than my equal, I think I should embrace her in an ecstasy of hopefulness.

In the evening, while I was inditing my journal for your edification, Tema made her appearance with her Bran-brown baby, having walked all the way down from Busson Hill to claim a little sugar I had promised her. She had made her child perfectly clean, and it looked quite pretty. When I asked her what I should give her the sugar in, she snatched her filthy handkerchief off her head; but I declined this sugar basin, and gave it to her in some paper. Hannah came on the same errand.

After all, dear E[lizabeth], we shall not leave Georgia so soon as I expected; we cannot get off for at least another week. You know, our movements are apt to be both tardy and uncertain. I am getting sick in spirit of my stay here; but I think the spring heat is beginning to affect me miserably, and I long for a cooler atmosphere. Here, on St. Simons, the climate is perfectly healthy, and our neighbors, many of them, never stir from their plantations within reach of the purifying sea influence. But a land that grows Magnolias is not fit for me—I was going to say Magnolias and rattlesnakes; but I remember K[itty]'s [1] adventure with her friend the rattlesnake of Monument Mountain, and the wild wood-covered hill halfway between Lenox and Stockbridge, which your Berkshire farmers have christened Rattlesnake Mountain. These agreeable serpents seem, like the lovely little hummingbirds which are found in your northernmost as well as southernmost states, to have an accommodating disposition with regard to climate.

Not only is the vicinity of the sea an element of salubrity here, but the great masses of pinewood growing in every direction indi-

---

[1] Kitty Sedgwick was the oldest child of Elizabeth Dwight Sedgwick and a dear friend of Fanny's. Kitty accompanied the actress on her Berkshire rambles and visited her in Philadelphia. Her full name was Catharine Maria, after her famous aunt, who bestowed upon her a full measure of love and affection, and addressed to her the beautiful letters which may be read in the Sedgwick Papers of the Massachusetts Historical Society.

cate lightness of soil and purity of air. Wherever these fragrant, dry, aromatic fir forests extend, there can be no inherent malaria, I should think, in either atmosphere or soil. The beauty and profusion of the weeds and wild flowers in the fields now is something, too, enchanting. I wish I could spread one of these enameled tracts on the side of one of your snow-covered hills now, for I dare say they are snow-covered yet.

I must give you an account of Aleck's first reading lesson, which took place at the same time that I gave S[ally] hers this morning. It was the first time he had had leisure to come, and it went off most successfully. He seems to me by no means stupid. I am very sorry he did not ask me to do this before; however, if he can master his alphabet before I go, he may, if chance favor him with the occasional sight of a book, help himself on by degrees. Perhaps he will have the good inspiration to apply to cooper London for assistance; I am much mistaken if that worthy does not contrive that Heaven shall help Aleck, as it formerly did him, in the matter of reading.

I rode with Jack afterward, showing him where I wish paths to be cut and brushwood removed. I passed the new house, and again circumvented it meditatingly to discover its available points of possible future comeliness, but remained as convinced as ever that there are absolutely none. Within the last two days a perfect border of the dark blue *virginica* has burst into blossom on each side of the road, fringing it with purple as far as one can look along it; it is lovely. I must tell you of something which has delighted me greatly. I told Jack yesterday that, if any of the boys liked, when they had done their tasks, to come and clear the paths that I want widened and trimmed, I would pay them a certain small sum per hour for their labor; and behold, three boys have come, having done their tasks early in the afternoon, to apply for *work* and *wages:* so much for a suggestion not barely twenty-four hours old, and so much for a prospect of compensation!

In the evening I attempted to walk out when the air was cool, but had to run precipitately back into the house to escape from the clouds of sand flies that had settled on my neck and arms. The weather has suddenly become intensely hot; at least that is what it appears to me. After I had come in I had a visit from Venus and her daughter, a young girl of ten years old, for whom she begged a larger allowance of food, as, she said, what she received for her was totally inadequate to the girl's proper nourishment. I was amazed, upon inquiry, to find that three quarts of grits a week—that is not a pint a day—was considered a sufficient supply for children of her age. The mother said her child was half-famished on it, and it seemed to me terribly little.

My little workmen have brought me in from the woods three darling little rabbits which they have contrived to catch. They seemed to me slightly different from our English bunnies; and Captain F[raser], who called today, gave me a long account of how they differed from the same animal in the Northern states. I did not like to mortify my small workmen by refusing their present; but the poor little things must be left to run wild again, for we have no conveniences for pets here, besides we are just weighing anchor ourselves. I hope these poor little fluffy things will not meet any rattlesnakes on their way back to the woods.

I had a visit for flannel from one of our Dianas today—who had done her task in the middle of the day, yet came to receive her flannel—the most horribly dirty human creature I ever beheld, unless, indeed, her child, whom she brought with her, may have been half a degree dirtier.

The other day, Psyche (you remember the pretty undernurse, the poor thing whose story I wrote you from the rice plantation) asked me if her mother and brothers might be allowed to come and see her when we are gone away. I asked her some questions about them, and she told me that one of her brothers, who belonged to Mr. K[ing], was hired by that gentleman to a Mr. G——, of Darien, and that, upon the latter desiring to purchase him, Mr. K[ing] had sold the man without apprising him or any member of his family that he had done so—a humane proceeding that makes one's blood boil when one hears of it. He had owned the man ever since he was a boy. Psyche urged me very much to obtain an order permitting her to see her mother and brothers. I will try and obtain it for her; but there seems generally a great objection to the visits of slaves from neighboring plantations, and, I have no doubt, not without sufficient reason. The more I see of this frightful and perilous social system, the more I feel that those who live in the midst of it must make their whole existence one constant precaution against danger of some sort or other.

I have given Aleck a second reading lesson with S[ally], who takes an extreme interest in his newly acquired alphabetical lore. He is a very quick and attentive scholar, and I should think a very short time would suffice to teach him to read; but, alas! I have not even that short time. When I had done with my class I rode off with Jack, who has become quite an expert horseman, and rejoices in being lifted out of the immediate region of snakes by the length of his horse's legs. I cantered through the new wood paths, and took a good sloping gallop through the pineland to St. Annie's. The fire is actually still burning in the woods. I came home quite tired with the heat, though my ride was not a long one.

Just as I had taken off my habit and was preparing to start off with M[argery] and the chicks for Jones's in the wood wagon, old Dorcas, one of the most decrepit, rheumatic, and miserable old Negresses from the farther end of the plantation, called in to beg for some sugar. She had walked the whole way from her own settlement, and seemed absolutely exhausted then, and yet she had to walk all the way back. It was not otherwise than slightly meritorious in me, my dear E[lizabeth], to take her up in the wagon and endure her abominable dirt and foulness in the closest proximity, rather than let her drag her poor old limbs all that way back; but I was glad when we gained her abode and lost her company. I am mightily reminded occasionally in these parts of Trinculo's soliloquy over Caliban.

The people at Jones's had done their work at half past three. Most of the houses were tidy and clean, so were many of the babies. On visiting the cabin of an exceedingly decent woman called Peggy, I found her, to my surprise, possessed of a fine large Bible. She told me her husband, carpenter John, can read, and that she means to make him teach her. The fame of Aleck's literature has evidently reached Jones's, and they are not afraid to tell me that they can read or wish to learn to do so. This poor woman's health is miserable; I never saw a more weakly, sickly-looking creature. She says she has been broken down ever since the birth of her last child. I asked her how soon after her confinement she went out into the field to work again. She answered very quietly, but with a deep sigh: "Three weeks, missis; de usual time." As I was going away, a man named Martin came up, and with great vehemence besought me to give him a Prayer Book. In the evening he came down to fetch it, and to show me that he can read. I was very much pleased to see that they had taken my hint about nailing wooden slats across the windows of their poor huts, to prevent the constant ingress of the poultry. This in itself will produce an immense difference in the cleanliness and comfort of their wretched abodes. In one of the huts I found a broken looking glass; it was the only piece of furniture of the sort that I had yet seen among them. The woman who owned it was, I am sorry to say, peculiarly untidy and dirty, and so were her children; so that I felt rather inclined to scoff at the piece of civilized vanity, which I should otherwise have greeted as a promising sign.

I drove home, late in the afternoon, through the sweet-smelling woods, that are beginning to hum with the voice of thousands of insects. My troop of volunteer workmen is increased to five—five lads working for my wages after they have done their task-work; and this evening, to my no small amazement, driver Bran came down to join them for an hour, after working all day at Five Pound, which certainly shows zeal and energy.

Dear E[lizabeth], I have been riding through the woods all the morning with Jack, giving him directions about the clearings, which I have some faint hope may be allowed to continue after my departure. I went on an exploring expedition round some distant fields, and then home through the St. Annie's woods. They have almost stripped the trees and thickets along the swamp road since I first came here. I wonder what it is for; not fuel surely, nor to make grassland of, or otherwise cultivate the swamp. I do deplore these pitiless clearings; and as to this once pretty road, it looks "forlorn," as a worthy Pennsylvania farmer's wife once said to me of a pretty hillside from which her husband had ruthlessly felled a beautiful grove of trees.

I had another snake encounter in my ride this morning. Just as I had walked my horse through the swamp, and while contemplating ruefully its naked aspect, a huge black snake wriggled rapidly across the path, and I pulled my reins tight and opened my mouth wide with horror. These hideous-looking creatures are, I believe, not poisonous, but they grow to a monstrous size, and have tremendous *constrictive* power. I have heard stories that sound like the nightmare of their fighting desperately with those deadly creatures, rattlesnakes. I cannot conceive, if the black snakes are not poisonous, what chance they have against such antagonists, let their squeezing powers be what they will. How horrid it did look, *slithering* over the road! Perhaps the swamp has been cleared on account of its harboring these dreadful worms.

I rode home very fast, in spite of the exquisite fragrance of the wild cherry blossoms, the carpets and curtains of wild flowers, among which a sort of glorified dandelion glowed conspicuously—dandelions such as I should think grew in the garden of Eden, if there were any at all there. I passed the finest Magnolia that I have yet seen; it was magnificent, and I suppose had been spared for its beauty, for it grew in the very middle of a cotton field; it was as large as a fine forest tree, and its huge glittering leaves shone like plates of metal in the sun; what a spectacle that tree must be in blossom, and I should think its perfume must be smelled from one end of the plantation to the other. What a glorious creature! Which do you think ought to weigh most in the scale, the delight of such a vegetable, or the disgust of the black animal I had just met a few minutes before? Would you take the one with the other? Neither would I.

I have spent the whole afternoon at home; my "gang" is busily at work again. Sawney, one of them, came to join it nearly at sundown, not having got through his day's task before. In watching and listening to these lads, I was constantly struck with the insolent tyranny of their demeanor toward each other. This is almost a universal characteristic of the manner of the Negroes among themselves. They are diabolically cruel to animals too, and they seem to me, as a rule, hardly to know the difference between truth and falsehood. These detestable qualities, which I constantly hear attributed to them as innate and inherent in their race, appear to me the direct result of their condition. The individual exceptions among them are, I think, quite as many as would be found, under similar circumstances, among the same number of white people.

In considering the whole condition of the people on this plantation, it appears to me that the principal hardships fall to the lot of the women—that is, the principal physical hardships. The very young members of the community are of course idle and neglected; the very, very old, idle and neglected too; the middle-aged men do not appear to me overworked, and lead a mere animal existence, in itself not peculiarly cruel or distressing, but involving a constant element of fear and uncertainty, and the trifling evils of un-requited labor, ignorance the most profound (to which they are condemned by law), and the unutterable injustice which pre-cludes them from all the merits and all the benefits of voluntary exertion, and the progress that results from it. If they are ab-solutely unconscious of these evils, then they are not very ill-off brutes, always barring the chance of being given or sold away from their mates or their young—processes which even brutes do not always relish. I am very much struck with the vein of melancholy, which assumes almost a poetical tone in some of the things they say. Did I tell you of that poor old decrepit creature Dorcas, who came to beg some sugar of me the other day? saying, as she took up my watch from the table and looked at it: "Ah! I need not look at this; I have almost done with time!" Was not that striking from such a poor old ignorant crone?

XXIX

Christ Church

[April 5–7, 1839]

Dear E[lizabeth],

This is the fourth day that I have had a "gang" of lads working in the woods for me after their task hours for pay; you cannot think how zealous and energetic they are; I dare say the novelty of the process pleases them almost as much as the money they earn. I must say they quite deserve their small wages.

Last night I received a present from Mrs. F[raser] of a drum-fish, which animal I had never beheld before, and which seemed to me first cousin to the great Leviathan. It is to be eaten, and is certainly the biggest fish food I ever saw; however, everything is in proportion, and the prawns that came with it are upon a similarly extensive scale; this magnificent piscatorial bounty was accompanied by a profusion of Hamilton green peas, really a munificent supply.

I went out early after breakfast with Jack hunting for new paths; we rode all along the road by Jones's Creek, and most beautiful it was. We skirted the plantation burial ground, and a dismal place it looked; the cattle trampling over it in every direction, except where Mr. K[ing] had had an enclosure put up round the graves of two white men who had worked on the estate. They were strangers, and of course utterly indifferent to the people here; but by virtue of their white skins, their resting place was protected from the hoofs of the cattle, while the parents and children, wives, husbands, brothers and sisters, of the poor slaves, sleeping beside them, might see the graves of those they loved trampled upon and browsed over, desecrated and defiled, from morning till night. There is something intolerably cruel in this disdainful denial of a common humanity pursuing these wretches even when they are hid beneath the earth.

The day was exquisitely beautiful, and I explored a new wood path, and found it all strewed with a lovely wild flower not much unlike a primrose. I spent the afternoon at home. I dread going out twice a day now, on account of the heat and the sand flies. While I was sitting by the window, Abraham, our cook, went by with some most revolting-looking "raw material" (part, I think, of the interior of the monstrous drumfish of which I have told you). I asked him, with considerable disgust, what he was going to do with it; he replied: "Oh! we colored people eat it, missis."

Said I: "Why do you say we colored people?"

"Because, missis, white people won't touch what we too glad of."

"That," said I, "is because you are poor, and do not often have meat to eat, not because you are colored, Abraham; rich white folks will not touch what poor white folks are too glad of; it has nothing in the world to do with color; and if there were white people here worse off than you (amazing and inconceivable suggestion, I fear), they would be glad to eat what you perhaps would not touch."

Profound pause of meditation on the part of Abraham, wound up by a considerate: "Well, missis, I suppose so"; after which he departed with the horrid-looking offal.

Today—Saturday [April 6]—I took another ride of discovery round the fields by Jones's. I think I shall soon be able to survey this estate, I have ridden so carefully over it in every direction;

but my rides are drawing to a close, and even were I to remain here this must be the case, unless I got up and rode under the stars in the cool of the night. This afternoon I was obliged to drive up to St. Annie's: I had promised the people several times that I would do so. I went after dinner and as late as I could, and found very considerable improvement in the whole condition of the place; the houses had all been swept, and some of them actually scoured. The children were all quite tolerably clean; they had put slats across all their windows, and little chicken gates to the doors to keep out the poultry. There was a poor woman lying in one of the cabins in a wretched condition. She begged for a bandage, but I do not see of what great use that can be to her, as long as she has to hoe in the fields so many hours a day, which I cannot prevent.

Returning home, Israel undertook to pilot me across the cotton fields into the pineland; and a more excruciating process than being dragged over that very uneven surface in that wood wagon without springs I did never endure, mitigated and soothed though it was by the literally fascinating account my charioteer gave me of the rattlesnakes with which the place we drove through becomes infested as the heat increases. I cannot say that his description of them, though more demonstrative as far as regarded his own horror of them, was really worse than that which Mr. G[owen] was giving me of them yesterday. He said they were very numerous, and were found in every direction all over the plantation, but that they did not become really vicious until quite late in the summer; until then, it appears that they generally endeavor to make off if one meets them, but during the intense heats of the latter part of July and August they never think of escaping, but at any sight or sound which they may consider inimical they instantly coil themselves for a spring. The most intolerable proceeding on their part, however, that he described, was their getting up into the trees, and either coiling themselves in or depending from the branches. There is something too revolting in the idea of serpents looking down upon one from the shade of the trees to which one may betake one's self for shelter in the dreadful heat of the Southern midsummer; decidedly I do not think the dog days would be pleasant here. The moccasin snake, which is nearly as deadly as the rattlesnake, abounds all over the island.

In the evening I had a visit from Mr. C[ouper] and Mr. B[artow],[1] who officiates tomorrow at our small island church. The conversation I had with these gentlemen was sad enough. They seem good, and kind, and amiable men, and I have no doubt are conscientious in their capacity of slaveholders; but to one who has lived outside this dreadful atmosphere, the whole tone of their discourse has a morally muffled sound, which one must hear to be able to conceive. Mr. B[artow] told me that the people on this plantation not going to church was the result of a positive order from Mr. K[ing], who had peremptorily forbidden their doing so, and of course to have infringed that order would have been to incur severe corporal chastisement. Bishop B[owen],[2] it seems, had advised that there should be periodical preaching on the plantations, which, said Mr. B[artow], would have obviated any necessity for the people of different estates congregating at any given point at stated times, which might perhaps be objectionable, and at the same time would meet the reproach which was now beginning to be directed toward Southern planters as a class, of neglecting the eternal interest of their dependents. But Mr. K[ing] had equally objected to this. He seems to have held religious teaching a mighty dangerous thing—and how right he was! I have met with conventional cowardice of various shades and shapes in various societies that I have lived in, but anything like the pervading timidity of tone which I find here on all subjects, but, above all, on that of the condition of the slaves, I have never dreamed of. Truly slavery begets slavery, and the perpetual state of suspicion

[1] Rev. Theodore N. B. Bartow, married to Isabella Hamilton Couper, daughter of John Couper of Cannon's Point.

[2] Nathaniel Bowen, Bishop of South Carolina, and acting head of the diocese of Georgia.

and apprehension of the slaveholders is a very handsome offset, to say the least of it, against the fetters and the lash of the slaves. Poor people, one and all, but especially poor oppressors of the oppressed! The attitude of these men is really pitiable; they profess (perhaps some of them strive to do so indeed) to consult the best interests of their slaves, and yet shrink back terrified from the approach of the slightest intellectual or moral improvement which might modify their degraded and miserable existence. I do pity these deplorable servants of two masters more than any human beings I have ever seen—more than their own slaves a thousand times!

Today is Sunday [April 7], and I have been to the little church on the island. It is the second time since I came down to the South that I have been to a place of worship. A curious little incident prefaced my going thither this morning. I had desired Israel to get my horse ready and himself to accompany me, as I meant to ride to church; and you cannot imagine anything droller than his horror and dismay when he at length comprehended that my purpose was to attend divine service in my riding habit. I asked him what was the trouble; for, though I saw something was creating a dreadful convulsion in his mind, I had no idea what it was till he told me, adding that he had never seen such a thing on St. Simons in his life—as who should say, such a thing was never seen in Hyde Park or the Tuileries before. You may imagine my amusement; but presently I was destined to shock something much more serious than poor Israel's sense of *les convénances et bienséances,*[3] and it was not without something of an effort that I made up my mind to do so. I was standing at the open window speaking to him about the horses, and telling him to get ready to ride with me, when George, another of the men, went by with a shade or visor to his cap exactly the shape of the one I left behind at the North, and for want of which I have been suffering

[3] Good manners.

severely from the intense heat and glare of the sun for the last week. I asked him to hand me his cap, saying: "I want to take the pattern of that shade."

Israel exclaimed: "Oh, missis, not today; let him leave the cap with you tomorrow, but don't cut pattern on de Sabbath day!"

It seemed to me a much more serious matter to offend this scruple than the prejudice with regard to praying in a riding habit; still, it had to be done. "Do you think it wrong, Israel," said I, "to work on Sunday?"

"Yes, missis, parson tell we so."

"Then, Israel, be sure you never do it. Did your parson never tell you that your conscience was for yourself and not for your neighbors, Israel?"

"Oh yes, missis, he tell we that too."

"Then mind that too, Israel." The shade was cut out and stitched upon my cap, and protected my eyes from the fierce glare of the sun and sand as I rode to church.

On our way we came to a field where the young corn was coming up. The children were in the field—little living scarecrows—watching it, of course, as on a weekday, to keep off the birds. I made Israel observe this, who replied: "Oh, missis, if de people's corn left one whole day not watched, not one blade of it remain tomorrow; it must be watched, missis."

"What, on the Sabbath day, Israel?"

"Yes, missis, or else we lose it all."

I was not sorry to avail myself of this illustration of the nature of works of necessity, and proceeded to enlighten Israel with regard to what I conceive to be the genuine observance of the Sabbath.

You cannot imagine anything wilder or more beautiful than the situation of the little rustic temple in the woods where I went to worship today, with the magnificent live oaks standing round it and its picturesque burial ground. The disgracefully neglected state of the latter, its broken and ruinous enclosure, and its shaggy, weed-grown graves, tell a strange story of the residents of this island, who are content to leave the resting place of their dead in so shocking a condition. In the tiny little chamber of a church, the grand old Litany of the Episcopal Church of England was not a little shorn of its ceremonial stateliness; clerk there was none, nor choir, nor organ, and the clergyman did duty for all, giving out the hymn and then singing it himself, followed as best might be by the uncertain voices of his very small congregation, the smallest I think I ever saw gathered in a Christian place of worship, even counting a few of the Negroes who had ventured to place themselves standing at the back of the church—an infringement on their part upon the privileges of their betters, as Mr. B[artow] generally preaches a second sermon to them after the *white* service, to which, as a rule, they are not admitted.

On leaving the church, I could not but smile at the quaint and original costumes with which Israel had so much dreaded a comparison for my irreproachable London riding habit. However, the strangeness of it was what inspired him with terror; but, at that rate, I am afraid a Paris gown and bonnet might have been in equal danger of shocking his prejudices. There was quite as little affinity with the one as the other in the curious specimens of the "art of dressing" that gradually distributed themselves among the two or three indescribable machines (to use the appropriate Scotch title) drawn up under the beautiful oak trees, on which they departed in various directions to the several plantations on the island.

I mounted my horse, and resumed my ride and my conversation with Israel. He told me that Mr. K[ing]'s great objection to the people going to church was their meeting with the slaves from the other plantations; and one reason, he added, that he did not wish them to do that was, that they trafficked and bartered away the cooper's wares, tubs, piggins, etc., made on the estate. I think, however, from everything I hear of that gentleman [Mr. King], that the mere fact of the Hampton people coming in contact with

314 · *St. Simons Island*

the slaves of other plantations would be a thing he would have deprecated. As a severe disciplinarian, he was probably right.

In the course of our talk, a reference I made to the Bible, and Israel's answer that he could not read, made me ask him why his father had never taught any of his sons to read; old Jacob, I know, can read. What followed I shall never forget. He began by giving all sorts of childish unmeaning excuses and reasons for never having tried to learn—became confused and quite incoherent—and then, suddenly stopping, and pulling up his horse, said, with a look and manner that went to my very heart: "Missis, what for me learn to read? me have no prospect!" I rode on without venturing to speak to him again for a little while. When I had recovered from that remark of his, I explained to him that, though indeed "without prospect" in some respects, yet reading might avail him much to better his condition, moral, mental, and physical. He listened very attentively, and was silent for a minute; after which he said:

"All you say very true, missis, and me sorry now me let de time pass; but you know what de white man dat goberns de estate him seem to like and favor, dat de people find out bery soon and do it; now Massa K[ing], him neber favor our reading, him not like it; likely as not he lick you if he find you reading; or, if you wish to teach your children, him always say, 'Pooh! teach 'em to read—teach 'em to work.' According to dat, we neber paid much attention to it; but now it will be different; it was different in former times. De old folks of my father and mother's time could read more than we can, and I expect de people will dare to give some thought to it again now."

There's a precious sample of what one man's influence may do in his own sphere, dear E[lizabeth]! This man Israel is a remarkably fine fellow in every way, with a frank, open, and most intelligent countenance, which rises before me with its look of quiet sadness whenever I think of these words (and they haunt me), "I have no prospect."

On my arrival at home I found that a number of the people, not knowing I had gone to church, had come up to the house, hoping that I would read prayers to them, and had not gone back to their homes, but waited to see me. I could not bear to disappoint them, for many of them had come from the farthest settlements on the estate; and so, though my hot ride had tired me a good deal, and my talk with Israel troubled me profoundly, I took off my habit, and had them all in, and read the afternoon service to them. When it was over, two of the women—Venus and Tressa—asked if they might be permitted to go to the nursery and see the children. Their account of the former condition of the estate was a corroboration of Israel's. They said that the older slaves on the plantation had been far better off than the younger ones of the present day; that Major [Butler] was considerate and humane to his people; and that the women were especially carefully treated. But they said Mr. K[ing] had ruined all the young women with working them too soon after their confinements; and as for the older ones, he would kick them, curse them, turn their clothes over their heads, flog them unmercifully himself, and abuse them shamefully, no matter what condition they were in. They both ended with fervent thanks to God that he had left the estate, and rejoicing that we had come, and, above all, that we "had made young missis for them." Venus went down on her knees, exclaiming: "Oh, missis, I glad now; and when I am dead, I glad in my grave that you come to us and bring us little missis."

XXX

Rides and Visits

[April 8–12, 1839]

Dear E[lizabeth],

I still go on exploring, or rather surveying the estate, the aspect of which is changing every day with the unfolding of the leaves and the wonderful profusion of wild flowers. The cleared ground all round the new building is one sheet of blooming blue of various tints; it is perfectly exquisite. But in the midst of my delight at these new blossoms, I am most sorrowfully bidding adieu to that paragon of parasites, the yellow jasmine; I think I must have gathered the very last blossoms of it today. Nothing can be more lovely, nothing so exquisitely fragrant. I was surprised to recognize by their foliage today some fine mulberry trees by Jones's Creek; perhaps they are the remains of the silkworm experiment that Mr. C[ouper] persuaded Major [Butler] to try so ineffectually. While I was looking at some wild plum and cherry trees that were already swarming with blight in the shape of multitudinous caterpillars' nests, an ingenious Negro, by name Cudgie, asked me if I could explain to him why the trees blossomed out so fair, and then all "went off into a kind of dying." Having directed his vision and attention to the horrid white glistening webs, all lined with their brood of black devourers, I left him to draw his own conclusions.

The afternoon was rainy, in spite of which I drove to Busson Hill, and had a talk with Bran about the vile caterpillar blights on the wild plum trees, and asked him if it would not be possible to get some sweet grafts from Mr. C[ouper] for some of the wild fruit trees, of which there are such quantities. Perhaps, however, they are not worth grafting. Bran promised me that the people should not be allowed to encumber the paths and the front of their houses with unsightly and untidy heaps of oyster shells. He promised all sorts of things. I wonder how soon after I am gone they will all return into the condition of brutal filth and disorder in which I found them.

The men and women had done their work here by half past three. The chief labor in the cotton fields, however, is both earlier and later in the season. At present they have little to do but let the crop grow. In the evening I had a visit from the son of a very remarkable man, who had been one of the chief drivers on the estate in Major [Butler]'s time, and his son brought me a silver cup which Major [Butler] had given his father as a testimonial of approbation, with an inscription on it recording his fidelity and trustworthiness at the time of the invasion of the coast of Georgia by the English troops.[1] Was not that a curious reward for a slave who was supposed not to be able to read his own praises? And yet, from the honorable pride with which his son regarded this relic, I am sure the master did well so to reward his servant, though it seemed hard that the son of such a man should be a slave. Maurice himself came with his father's precious silver cup in his hand, to beg for a small pittance of sugar, and for a Prayer Book, and also to know if the privilege of a milch cow for the support of his

[1] Major Pierce Butler did indeed give Maurice (Morris) a silver cup, but the catastrophe in which the slave rendered such faithful service was the hurricane of 1804 and not, as Fanny has it, the War of 1812. The inscription on this cup reads: "To Morris from P. Butler, For his faithful, judicious, and spirited conduct in the hurricane of September 8, 1804, whereby the lives of more than 100 persons were, by Divine permission, saved." See Frances Leigh: *Ten Years on a Georgia Plantation Since the War* (London: 1883), 183–5.

family, which was among the favors Major [Butler] allowed his father, might not be continued to him. He told me he had ten children "working for massa," and I promised to mention his petition to Mr. [Butler].

On Sunday last I rode round the woods near St. Annie's, and met with a monstrous snake, which Jack called a chicken snake; but whether because it particularly affected poultry as its diet, or for what other reason, he could not tell me. Nearer home I encountered another gliding creature, that stopped a moment just in front of my horse's feet, as if it was too much afraid of being trampled upon to get out of the way: it was the only snake animal I ever saw that I did not think hideous. It was of a perfectly pure apple-green color, with a delicate line of black like a collar round its throat; it really was an exquisite worm, and Jack said it was harmless. I did not, however, think it expedient to bring it home in my bosom, though, if ever I have a pet snake, it shall be such a one.

In the afternoon I drove to Jones's with several supplies of flannel for the rheumatic women and old men. We have ridden over to Hamilton again, to pay another visit to the F[raser]s, and on our way passed an enormous rattlesnake hanging dead on the bough of a tree. Dead as it was, it turned me perfectly sick with horror, and I wished very much to come back to the North immediately, where these are not the sort of blackberries that grow on every bush. The evening air now, after the heat of the day, is exquisitely mild, and the nights dry and wholesome, the whole atmosphere indescribably fragrant with the perfume of flowers; and as I stood, before going to bed last night, watching the slow revolving light on Sapelo Island, that warns the ships from the dangerous bar at the river's mouth, and heard the measured pulse of the great Atlantic waters on the beach, I thought no more of rattlesnakes—no more, for one short while, of slavery. How still, and sweet, and solemn it was!

We have been paying more friendly and neighborly visits, or rather returning them; and the recipients of these civilized courtesies on our last calling expedition were the family one member of which was a party concerned in that barbarous challenge [2] I wrote you word about. Hitherto that very brutal and bloodthirsty cartel [3] appears to have had no result. You must not, on that account, imagine that it will have none. At the North, were it possible for a duel intended to be conducted on such savage terms to be matter of notoriety, the very horror of the thing would create a feeling of grotesqueness, and the antagonists in such a proposed encounter would simply incur an immense amount of ridicule and obloquy. But here nobody is astonished and nobody ashamed of such preliminaries to a mortal combat between two gentlemen, who propose firing at marks over each other's hearts, and cutting off each other's heads; and though this agreeable party of pleasure has not come off yet, there seems to be no reason why it should not at the first convenient season. Reflecting upon all which, I rode, not without trepidation, through Colonel H[azzard]'s grounds, and up to his house. Mr. W[ylly]'s head was not stuck upon a pole anywhere within sight, however, and as soon as I became pretty sure of this, I began to look about me, and saw instead a trellis tapestried with the most beautiful roses I ever beheld, another of these exquisite Southern flowers—the Cherokee rose. The blossom is very large, composed of four or five pure white petals, as white and as large as those of the finest Camellia, with a bright golden eye for a focus; the buds and leaves are long and elegantly slender, like those of some tea roses, and the green of the foliage is dark, and at the same time vivid and lustrous; it grew in masses so as to form almost a hedge, all starred with these wonderful white blossoms, which, unfortunately, have no perfume.

We rode home through the pineland to Jones's, looked at the new house which is coming on hideously, saw two beautiful kinds of trumpet honeysuckle already lighting up the woods in every

[2] The Butlers evidently paid a call upon Colonel William Hazzard, who resided at Pike's Bluff and was a near neighbor both of the Butlers and of his brother Thomas.

[3] Here used as a synonym for challenge.

direction with gleams of scarlet, and when we reached home found a splendid donation of vegetables, flowers, and mutton from our kind neighbor Mrs. F[raser], who is a perfect Lady Bountiful to us. This same mutton, however—my heart bleeds to say it—disappeared the day after it was sent to us. Abraham the cook declares that he locked the door of the safe upon it, which I think may be true, but I also think he unlocked it again. I am sorry; but, after all, it is very natural these people should steal a little of our meat from us occasionally, who steal almost all their bread from them habitually.

I rode yesterday to St. Annie's with Mr. [Butler]. We found a whole tract of marsh had been set on fire by the facetious Negro called Pun, who had helped me out of it some time ago. As he was set to work in it, perhaps it was with a view of making it less damp; at any rate, it was crackling, blazing, and smoking cheerily, and I should think would be insupportable for the snakes. While stopping to look at the conflagration, Mr. [Butler] was accosted by a three parts naked and one part tattered little she-slave—black as ebony, where her skin was discoverable through its perfect incrustation of dirt—with a thick mat of frizzly wool upon her skull, which made the sole request she preferred to him irresistibly ludicrous: "Massa, massa, you please to buy me a comb to tick in my head?" Mr. [Butler] promised her this necessary of life, and I promised myself to give her the luxury of one whole garment. Mrs. [Fraser] has sent me the best possible consolation for the lost mutton, some lovely flowers, and these will not be stolen.

XXXI

A Conversation with John Couper

[April 13, 1839]

Dear E[lizabeth],

I rode today through all my wood paths for the last time with Jack, and I think I should have felt quite melancholy at taking leave of them and him but for the apparition of a large black snake, which filled me with disgust and nipped my other sentiments in the bud. Not a day passes now that I do not encounter one or more of these hateful reptiles; it is curious how much more odious they are to me than the alligators that haunt the mud banks of the river round the rice plantation. It is true that there is something very dreadful in the thick shapeless mass, uniform in color almost to the black slime on which it lies basking, and which you hardly detect till it begins to move. But even those ungainly crocodiles never sickened me as those rapid, lithe, and sinuous serpents do. Did I ever tell you that the people at the rice plantation caught a young alligator and brought it to the house, and it was kept for some time in a tub of water? It was an ill-tempered little monster; it used to set up its back like a cat when it was angry, and open its long jaws in a most vicious manner.

After looking at my new path in the pineland, I crossed Pike Bluff, and, breaking my way all through the burned district, returned home by Jones's. In the afternoon we paid a long visit to Mr. C[ouper]. It is extremely interesting to me to talk with him about the Negroes; he has spent so much of his life among them, has managed them so humanely, and apparently so successfully, that his experience is worthy of all attention. And yet it seems to me that it is impossible, or rather, perhaps, for those very reasons it is impossible, for him ever to contemplate them in any condition but that of slavery. He thinks them very like the Irish, and instanced their subserviency, their flattering, their lying, and pilfering, as traits common to the characters of both peoples. But I cannot persuade myself that in both cases, and certainly in that of the Negroes, these qualities are not in great measure the result of their condition. He says that he considers the extremely low diet of the Negroes one reason for the absence of crimes of a savage nature among them; most of them do not touch meat the year round. But in this respect they certainly do not resemble the Irish, who contrive, upon about as low a national diet as civilization is acquainted with, to commit the bloodiest and most frequent outrages with which civilization has to deal. His statement that it is impossible to bribe the Negroes to work on their own account with any steadiness may be generally true, but admits of quite exceptions enough to throw doubt upon its being natural supineness in the race rather than the inevitable consequence of denying them the entire right to labor for their own profit. Their laziness seems to me the necessary result of their primary wants being supplied, and all progress denied them. Of course, if the natural spur to exertion, necessity, is removed, you do away with the will to work of a vast proportion of all who do work in the world. It is the law of progress that man's necessities grow with his exertions to satisfy them, and labor and improvement thus continually act and react upon each other to raise the scale of desire and achievement; and I do not believe that, in the majority of instances among any people on the face of the earth, the will to labor for small indulgences would survive the loss of freedom and the security of food enough to exist upon. Mr. [Couper] said that he had offered a bribe of twenty dollars apiece, and the use of a pair of oxen, for the clearing of a certain piece of land, to the men on his estate, and found the offer quite ineffectual to procure the desired result; the land was subsequently cleared as usual taskwork under the lash.

Now, certainly, we have among Mr. [Butler]'s people instances of men who have made very considerable sums of money by boatbuilding in their leisure hours, and the instances of almost lifelong, persevering, stringent labor, by which slaves have at length purchased their own freedom and that of their wives and children, are on record in numbers sufficient to prove that they are capable of severe sustained effort of the most patient and heroic kind for that great object, liberty. For my own part, I know no people who dote upon labor for its own sake; and it seems to me quite natural to any absolutely ignorant and nearly brutish man, if you say to him: "No effort of your own can make you free, but no absence of effort shall starve you," to decline to work for anything less than mastery over his whole life, and to take up with his mess of porridge as the alternative. One thing that Mr. [Couper] said seemed to me to prove rather too much. He declared that his son, objecting to the folks on his plantation going about bareheaded, had at one time offered a reward of a dollar to those who should habitually wear hats without being able to induce them to do so, which he attributed to sheer careless indolence; but I think it was merely the force of habit of going uncovered rather than absolute laziness. The universal testimony of all present at this conversation was in favor of the sweetness of temper and natural gentleness of disposition of the Negroes; but these characteristics they seemed to think less inherent than the result of diet and the other lowering influences of their condition; and it must not be forgotten that on the estate of this wise and kind master a formidable conspiracy was organized among his slaves.

We rowed home through a world of stars, the steadfast ones set in the still blue sky, and the flashing swathes of phosphoric light turned up by our oars and keel in the smooth blue water. It was lovely.

XXXII

A Fatal Encounter

[April 14, 1839]

My dear E[lizabeth],

That horrid tragedy with which we have been threatened, and of which I was writing to you almost jestingly a few days ago, has been accomplished, and apparently without exciting anything but the most passing and superficial sensation in this community. The duel between Dr. H[azzard] and Mr. W[ylly] did not take place, but an accidental encounter in the hotel at Brunswick did, and the former shot the latter dead on the spot. He has been brought home and buried here by the little church close to his mother's plantation; and the murderer, if he is even prosecuted, runs no risk of finding a jury in the whole length and breadth of Georgia who could convict him of anything. It is horrible.[1]

[1] The following account of the affray is taken from the Brunswick *Advocate,* December 6, 1838:

MELANCHOLY OCCURRENCE

It is with pain we lay before our readers an account of a fatal affray, which took place in this city on Monday last, between Mr. John A. Wylly and Dr. Thomas F. Hazzard, both of this county, which resulted in the death of the former. Most of our readers in this section are no doubt aware that a dispute has existed between these two gentlemen for some time past. It appears, however, that Dr. H[azzard] had recently addressed a letter to the mother of the deceased which was the immediate cause of the attack. They met on the piazza

I drove to church today in the wood wagon, with Jack and Aleck, Hector being our charioteer, in a gilt guard chain and pair of slippers to match as the Sabbatic part of his attire. The love of dirty finery is not a trait of the Irish in Ireland, but I think it crops out strongly when they come out here; and the proportion of their high wages put upon their backs by the young Irish maidservants in the North indicates a strong addiction to the female passion for dress. Here the tendency seems to exist in men and women alike; but I think all savage men rejoice, even more than their women, in personal ornamentation. The Negroes certainly show the same strong predilection for finery with their womenkind.

I stopped before going into church to look at the new grave that has taken its place among the defaced stones, all overgrown with briers, that lie round it. Poor young W[ylly]! poor widowed mother, of whom he was the only son! [2] What a savage horror! And no one seems to think anything of it, more than of a matter of course. My devotions were anything but satisfactory or refreshing

---

of the Oglethorpe House, and after exchanging a few words, Mr. W[ylly] struck Dr. H[azzard] with a cane. Judge [Charles S.] Henry, who was here holding a term of the Superior Court, and Col. [Henry] DuBignon happening to be present, immediately interfered and succeeded in separating them. A short time after, Mr. W[ylly] again met Dr. H[azzard] in the entry of the house and spat in his face, when the latter drew a pistol and fired, the ball of which passed directly through Mr. W[ylly]'s heart. He reeled a moment, at the same time striking at the doctor with his cane, then fell and expired instantly.
The case, as was natural, excited a great deal of local discussion, a lot

of which Fanny must have heard and participated in during her visits to neighboring homes, especially as she was on St. Simons Island as the time set for the trial—the April term of the Superior Court—drew near. For a further discussion of this incident and of its place in the *Journal,* see Margaret Davis Cate: "Mistakes in Fanny Kemble's Georgia Journal," *Georgia Historical Quarterly,* XLIV (March, 1960), 6–17, and the Editor's Introduction, pages lv-lvii.

[2] John Armstrong Wylly was not the only son of Margaret Armstrong and Alexander Campbell Wylly. An older son, Alexander William, had married Elizabeth, daughter of Thomas Spalding of Sapelo Island, and was living in 1839 on the mainland.

to me. My mind was dwelling incessantly upon the new grave under the great oaks outside, and the miserable mother in her home. The air of the church was perfectly thick with sand flies; and the disgraceful carelessness of the congregation in responding and singing the hymns, and the entire neglect of the Prayer Book regulations for kneeling, disturbed and displeased me even more than the last time I was at church; but I think that was because of the total absence of excitement or feeling among the whole population of St. Simons upon the subject of the bloody outrage with which my mind was full, which has given me a sensation of horror toward the whole community. Just imagine—only it is impossible to imagine—such a thing taking place in a New England village; the dismay, the grief, the shame, the indignation, that would fill the hearts of the whole population. I thought we should surely have some reference to the event from the pulpit, some lesson of Christian command over furious passions. Nothing—nobody looked or spoke as if anything unusual had occurred; and I left the church, rejoicing to think that I was going away from such a dreadful state of society. Mr. B[artow] remained to preach a second sermon to the Negroes—the duty of submission to masters who intermurder each other.

I had service at home in the afternoon, and my congregation was much more crowded than usual; for I believe there is no doubt at last that we shall leave Georgia this week. Having given way so much before when I thought I was praying with these poor people for the last time, I suppose I had, so to speak, expended my emotion, and I was much more composed and quiet than when I took leave of them before. But, to tell you the truth, this dreadful act of slaughter done in our neighborhood by one man of our acquaintance upon another, impresses me to such a degree that I can hardly turn my mind from it, and Mrs. W[ylly] and her poor young murdered son have taken almost complete possession of my thoughts.

After prayers I gave my poor people a parting admonition, and many charges to remember me and all I had tried to teach them during my stay. They promised with one voice to mind and do all that "missis tell we"; and with many a parting benediction, and entreaties to me to return, they went their way. I think I have done what I could for them—I think I have done as well as I could by them; but when the time comes for ending any human relation, who can be without their misgivings? Who can be bold to say, I could have done no more, I could have done no better?

In the afternoon I walked out, and passed many of the people, who are now beginning, whenever they see me, to say "Good-by, missis!" which is rather trying. Many of them were clean and tidy, and decent in their appearance to a degree that certainly bore strong witness to the temporary efficacy of my influence in this respect. There is, however, of course much individual difference even with reference to this, and some take much more kindly and readily to cleanliness, no doubt to godliness too, than some others. I met Abraham, and thought that, in a quiet tête-à-tête, and with the pathetic consideration of my near departure to assist me, I could get him to confess the truth about the disappearance of the mutton; but he persisted in the legend of its departure through the locked door; and as I was only heaping sins on his soul with every lie I caused him to add to the previous ones, I desisted from my inquiries. Dirt and lying are the natural tendencies of humanity, which are especially fostered by slavery. Slaves may be infinitely wrong, and yet it is very hard to blame them.

I returned home, finding the heat quite oppressive. Late in the evening, when the sun had gone down a long time, I thought I would try and breathe the fresh sea air, but the atmosphere was thick with sand flies, which drove me in at last from standing listening to the roar of the Atlantic on Little St. Simons Island, the wooded belt that fends off the ocean surges from the north side of Great St. Simons. It is a wild little sand heap, covered with thick forest growth, and belongs to Mr. [Butler]. I have long had a great desire to visit it. I hope yet to be able to do so before our departure.

I have just finished reading, with the utmost interest and admiration, J[ames Hamilton] C[ouper]'s narrative of his escape from the wreck of the *Pulaski:* what a brave, and gallant, and unselfish soul he must be! You never read anything more thrilling, in spite of the perfect modesty of this account of his. If I can obtain his permission, and squeeze out the time, I will surely copy it for you. The quiet, unassuming character of his usual manners and deportment adds greatly to his prestige as a hero. What a fine thing it must be to be such a man!

XXXIII

The Wreck of the Pulaski

[April 17, 1839]

Dear E[lizabeth],

We shall leave this place next Thursday or Friday [April 18 or 19], and there will be an end to this record; meantime I am fulfilling all sorts of last duties, and especially those of taking leave of my neighbors, by whom the neglect of a farewell visit would be taken much amiss.

On Sunday I rode to a place called Frederica to call on Mrs. A[bbott], who came to see me some time ago. I rode straight through the island by the main road that leads to the little church.

How can I describe to you the exquisite spring beauty that is now adorning these woods, the variety of the fresh, newborn foliage, the fragrance of the sweet, wild perfumes that fill the air? Honeysuckles twine round every tree; the ground is covered with a low, white-blossomed shrub more fragrant than lilies of the valley. The Acacias are swinging their silver censers under the green roof of these wood temples; every stump is like a classical altar to the sylvan gods, garlanded with flowers; every post, or stick, or slight stem, like a Bacchante's thyrsus,[1] twined with wreaths

---

[1] The thyrsus was a flowering staff attributed to Bacchus, god of wine, and to the crew of women—Bac- chae—who accompanied him and took part in his rituals.

of ivy and wild vine, waving in the tepid wind. Beautiful butter-flies flicker like flying flowers among the bushes, and gorgeous birds, like winged jewels, dart from the boughs, and—and—a huge ground snake slid like a dark ribbon across the path while I was stopping to enjoy all this deliciousness, and so I became less enthusiastic, and cantered on past the little deserted churchyard, with the new-made grave beneath its grove of noble oaks, and a little farther on reached Mrs. A[bbott]'s cottage, half-hidden in the midst of ruins and roses.

This Frederica is a very strange place; it was once a town—*the* town, the metropolis of the island. The English, when they landed on the coast of Georgia in the war, destroyed this tiny place, and it has never been built up again. Mrs. A[bbott]'s, and one other house, are the only dwellings that remain in this curious wilderness of dismantled crumbling gray walls compassionately cloaked with a thousand profuse and graceful creepers. These are the only ruins, properly so called, except those of Fort Putnam, that I have ever seen in this land of contemptuous youth. I hailed these picturesque groups and masses with the feelings of a European, to whom ruins are like a sort of relations. In my country, ruins are like a minor chord in music; here they are like a discord; they are not the relics of time, but the results of violence; they recall no valuable memories of a remote past, and are mere encumbrances to the busy present. Evidently they are out of place in America except on St. Simons Island, between this savage selvage of civilization and the great Atlantic deep. These heaps of rubbish and roses would have made the fortune of a sketcher; but I imagine the snakes have it all to themselves here, and are undisturbed by campstools, white umbrellas, and ejaculatory young ladies.

I sat for a long time with Mrs. A[bbott], and a friend of hers staying with her, a Mrs. A——, lately from Florida. The latter seemed to me a remarkable woman; her conversation was extremely interesting. She had been stopping at Brunswick, at the hotel where Dr. H[azzard] murdered young W[ylly], and said that the mingled ferocity and blackguardism of the men who frequented the house had induced her to cut short her stay there, and come on to her friend Mrs. A[bbott]'s. We spoke of that terrible crime which had occurred only the day after she left Brunswick, and both ladies agreed that there was not the slightest chance of Dr. H[azzard]'s being punished in any way for the murder he had committed; that shooting down a man who had offended you was part of the morals and manners of the Southern gentry, and that the circumstance was one of quite too frequent occurrence to cause any sensation, even in the small community where it obliterated one of the principal members of the society. If the accounts given by these ladies of the character of the planters in this part of the South may be believed, they must be as idle, arrogant, ignorant, dissolute, and ferocious as that medieval chivalry to which they are fond of comparing themselves; and these are Southern women, and should know the people among whom they live.

We had a long discussion on the subject of slavery, and they took, as usual, the old ground of justifying the system, *where* it was administered with kindness and indulgence. It is not surprising that women should regard the question from this point of view; they are very seldom *just,* and are generally treated with more indulgence than justice by men. They were very patient of my strong expressions of reprobation of the whole system, and Mrs. A[bbott], bidding me good-by, said that, for aught she could tell, I might be right, and might have been led down here by Providence to be the means of some great change in the condition of the poor colored people.

I rode home pondering on the strange fate that has brought me to this place so far from where I was born, this existence so different in all its elements from that of my early years and former associations. If I believed Mrs. A[bbott]'s parting words, I might perhaps verify them; perhaps I may yet verify, although I do not believe them. On my return home I found a most enchanting bundle of flowers, sent to me by Mrs. G[rant]; [2] pomegranate blossoms, roses, honeysuckle, everything that blooms two months later with us in Pennsylvania.

I told you I had a great desire to visit Little St. Simons, [3] and the day before yesterday I determined to make an exploring expedition thither. I took M[argery] and the children, little imagining what manner of day's work was before me. Six men rowed us in the *Lily,* and Israel brought the wood wagon after us in a flat. Our navigation was a very intricate one, all through sea swamps and marshes, mud banks and sandbanks, with great white shells and bleaching bones stuck upon sticks to mark the channel. We landed on this forest in the sea by Quash's house, the only human residence on the island. It was larger and better, and more substantial than the Negro huts in general, and he seemed proud and pleased to do the honors to us. Thence we set off, by my desire, in the wagon through the woods to the beach; road there was none, save the rough clearing that the men cut with their axes before us as we went slowly on. Presently we came to a deep dry ditch, over which there was no visible means of proceeding. Israel told me if we would sit still he would undertake to drive the wagon into and out of it; and so, indeed, he did, but how he did it is more than I can explain to you now, or could explain to myself then. A less powerful creature than Montreal could never have dragged us through; and when we presently came to a second rather worse edition of the same, I insisted upon getting out and crossing it on foot. I walked half a mile while the wagon was dragged up and down the deep gully, and lifted bodily over some huge trunks of fallen trees. The wood through which we now drove was all on fire, smoking, flaming, crackling, and burning round us. The sun glared upon us from the cloudless sky, and the air was one cloud of sandflies and

[2] Dr. and Mrs. Robert Grant, parents of the mainland planter Hugh Fraser Grant, lived at Oatlands and were near neighbors of the Butlers.

[3] Fanny's approximate course in the visit to Little St. Simons is charted on the map on page 335.

mosquitoes. I covered both my children's faces with veils and handkerchiefs, and repented not a little in my own breast of the rashness of my undertaking. The back of Israel's coat was covered so thick with mosquitoes that one could hardly see the cloth; and I felt as if we should be stifled if our way lay much longer through this terrible wood. Presently we came to another impassable place, and again got out of the wagon, leaving Israel to manage it as best he could. I walked with the baby in my arms a quarter of a mile, and then was so overcome with the heat that I sat down in the burning wood, on the floor of ashes, till the wagon came up again. I put the children and M[argery] into it, and continued to walk till we came to a ditch in a tract of salt marsh, over which Israel drove triumphantly, and I partly jumped and was partly hauled over, having declined the entreaties of several of the men to let them lie down and make a bridge with their bodies for me to walk over.

At length we reached the skirt of that tremendous wood, to my unspeakable relief, and came upon the white sand hillocks of the beach. The trees were all strained crooked, from the constant influence of the sea blast. The coast was a fearful-looking stretch of dismal, trackless sand, and the ocean lay boundless and awful beyond the wild and desolate beach, from which we were now only divided by a patch of low, coarse-looking bush, growing as thick and tangled as heather, and so stiff and compact that it was hardly possible to drive through it. Yet in spite of this, several lads who had joined our train rushed off into it in search of rabbits, though Israel called repeatedly to them, warning them of the danger of rattlesnakes. We drove at last down to the smooth sea sand; and here, outstripping our guides, [I] was barred farther progress by a deep gully, down which it was impossible to take the wagon. Israel, not knowing the beach well, was afraid to drive round the mouth of it; and so it was determined that from this point we should walk home under his guidance. I sat in the wagon while he constructed a rough footbridge of bits of wood and broken

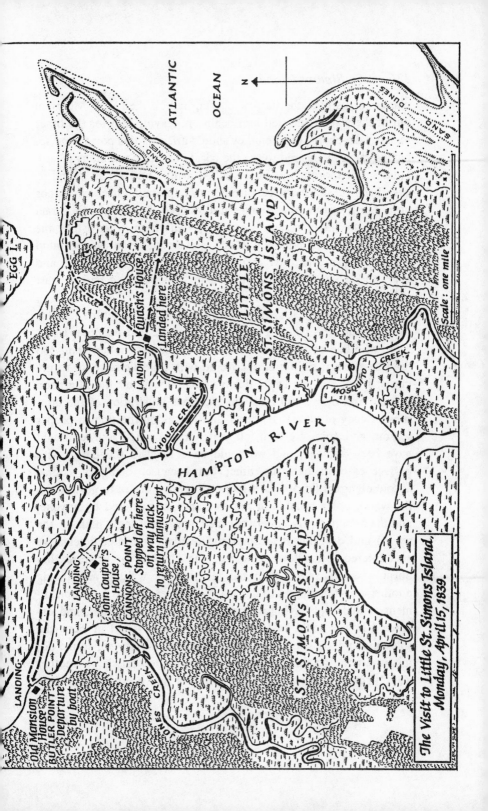

EGG I.

ATLANTIC

OCEAN

N

SAND DUNES

SAND DUNES

LITTLE ST. SIMONS ISLAND

SAND DUNES

Scale : one mile

LITTLE ST. SIMONS ISLAND

Quash's House

Landed here

LANDING

MOSQUITO CREEK

HOUSE CREEK

HAMPTON RIVER

ST. SIMONS ISLAND

LANDING

John Couper's House

CANNONS POINT

Stopped off here on way back to return manuscript.

JONES CREEK

LANDING

Old Mansion House

BUTLER POINT

Departure by boat

The Visit to Little St. Simons Island, Monday, April 15, 1839.

planks for us over the narrow chasm, and he then took Montreal out of the wagon and tied him behind it, leaving him for the other men to take charge of when they should arrive at this point. And so, having mightily desired to see the coast of Little St. Simons Island, I did see it thoroughly; for I walked a mile and a half round it, over beds of sharp shells, through swamps half knee-deep, poor little S[ally] stumping along with dogged heroism, and Israel carrying the baby, except at one deep *mal passo,* when I took the baby and he carried S[ally]; and so, through the wood round Quash's house, where we arrived almost fainting with fatigue and heat, and where we rested but a short time, for we had to start almost immediately to save the tide home.

I called at Mr. C[ouper]'s on my way back, to return him his son's manuscript, which I had in the boat for that purpose. I sent Jack, who had come to meet me with the horses, home, being too tired to attempt riding; and, covered with mud literally up to my knees, I was obliged to lie down ignominiously all the afternoon to rest. And now I will give you a curious illustration of the utter subserviency of slaves. It seems that by taking the tide in proper season, and going by boat, all that horrible wood journey might have been avoided, and we could have reached the beach with perfect ease in half the time; but because, being of course absolutely ignorant of this, I had expressed a desire to go through the wood, not a syllable of remonstrance was uttered by anyone; and the men not only underwent the labor of cutting a path for the wagon and dragging it through and over all the impediments we encountered, but allowed me and the children to traverse that burning wood, rather than tell me that by waiting and taking another way I could get to the sea. When I expressed my astonishment at their not having remonstrated against my order, and explained how I could best achieve the purpose I had in view, the sole answer I got even from Israel was: "Missis say so, so me do; missis say me go through the wood, me no tell missis go another way." You see, my dear E[lizabeth], one had need bethink one's self what orders one gives, when one has the misfortune to be despotic.

How sorry I am that I have been obliged to return that narrative of Mr. C[ouper]'s without asking permission to copy it, which I did not do because I should not have been able to find the time to do it! We go away the day after tomorrow. All the main incidents of the disaster [4] the newspapers have made you familiar with—the sudden and appalling loss of that fine vessel laden with the very flower of the South. There seems hardly to be a family in Georgia and South Carolina that had not some of its members on board that ill-fated ship. You know it was a sort of party of pleasure more than anything else; the usual annual trip to the North for change of air and scene, for the gaieties of Newport and Saratoga, that all the wealthy Southern people invariably take every summer.

The weather had been calm and lovely; and dancing, talking, and laughing, as if they were in their own drawing rooms, they had passed the time away till they all separated for the night. At the first sound of the exploding boiler Mr. C[ouper] jumped up, and in his shirt and trousers ran on deck. The scene was one of horrible confusion; women screaming, men swearing, the deck strewn with broken fragments of all descriptions, the vessel leaning frightfully to one side, and everybody running hither and thither in the dark-

[4] The steamship *Pulaski*, bound for Baltimore, left Savannah on June 13, 1838, with James Hamilton Couper and his party on board. The shipwreck occurred in the late evening of June 14, off the South Carolina coast, after the vessel had proceeded about one hundred and fifty miles from Charleston. Couper's account of the disaster, which cost the lives of seventy-seven passengers, was contained in a letter to his father written on June 16, the morning following his landing on the North Carolina shore. This letter, the original of which is in the Fraser-Couper Family Papers in the possession of the Georgia Historical Society, is reproduced in *Historical Collections of Georgia*, Rev. George White, ed. (New York: 1855), 353–64, and in Caroline Couper Lovell: *Golden Isles of Georgia*, 157–81. Fanny's account, evidently written from memory, does not differ in essentials from the original, though there is variation in minor detail. For another account of the disaster, see Mrs. Hugh Macleod: "The Loss of the Steamer Pulaski," *Georgia Historical Quarterly*, III (March, 1919), 63–95.

ness in horror and dismay. He had left Georgia with Mrs. F[raser]
and Mrs. N[ightingale], the two children, and one of the female
servants of these ladies under his charge. He went immediately to
the door of the ladies' cabin and called Mrs. F[raser]; they were
all there half-dressed; he bade them dress as quickly as possible,
and be ready to follow and obey him. He returned almost instantly,
and led them to the side of the vessel, where, into the boats, that
had already been lowered, desperate men and women were beginning to swarm, throwing themselves out of the sinking ship. He
bade Mrs. F[raser] jump down into one of these boats which was
only in the possession of two sailors; she instantly obeyed him, and
he threw her little boy to the men after her. He then ordered Mrs.
N[ightingale], with the Negro woman, to throw themselves off
the vessel into the boat, and, with Mrs. N[ightingale]'s baby in his
arms, sprang after them. His foot touched the gunwale of the boat,
and he fell into the water; but, recovering himself instantly, he
clambered into the boat, which he then peremptorily ordered
the men to set adrift, in spite of the shrieks, and cries, and com-
mands, and entreaties of the frantic crowds who were endeavoring
to get into it. The men obeyed him, and rowing while he steered,
they presently fell astern of the ship, in the midst of the darkness,
and tumult, and terror. Another boat laden with people was near
them. For some time they saw the heart-rending spectacle of the
sinking vessel, and the sea strewn with mattresses, seats, planks,
etc., to which people were clinging, floating, and shrieking for
succor, in the dark water all round them. But they gradually
pulled farther and farther out of the horrible chaos of despair,
and, with the other boat still consorting with them, rowed on. They
watched from a distance the piteous sight of the ill-fated streamer
settling down, the gray girdle of light that marked the line of her
beautiful saloons and cabins gradually sinking nearer and nearer
to the blackness, in which they were presently extinguished; and
the ship, with all its precious human freight engulfed—all but the

handful left in those two open boats, to brave the dangers of that terrible coast!

They were somewhere off the North Carolina shore, which, when the daylight dawned, they could distinctly see, with its ominous line of breakers and inhospitable perilous coast. The men had continued rowing all night, and as the summer sun rose flaming over their heads, the task of pulling the boat became dreadfully severe; still they followed the coast, Mr. C[ouper] looking out for any opening, creek, or small inlet that might give them a chance of landing in safety. The other boat rowed on at some little distance from them.

All the morning, and through the tremendous heat of the middle day, they toiled on without a mouthful of food—without a drop of water. At length, toward the afternoon, the men at the oars said they were utterly exhausted and could row no longer, and that Mr. C[ouper] must steer the boat ashore. With wonderful power of command, he prevailed on them to continue their afflicting labor. The terrible blazing sun pouring on all their unsheltered heads had almost annihilated them; but still there lay between them and the land those fearful foaming ridges, and the women and children, if not the men themselves, seemed doomed to inevitable death in the attempt to surmount them. Suddenly they perceived that the boat that had kept them company was about to adventure itself in the perilous experiment of landing. Mr. C[ouper] kept his boat's head steady, the men rested on their oars, and watched the result of the fearful risk they were themselves about to run. They saw the boat enter the breakers—they saw her whirled round and capsized, and then they watched, slowly emerging and dragging themselves out of the foaming sea, *some,* and only some, of the people that they knew the boat contained. Mr. C[ouper], fortified with this terrible illustration of the peril that awaited them, again besought them to row yet for a little while farther along the coast, in search of some possible place to take the boat safely to the beach, promising at sunset to give up the search, and again the poor men resumed their toil; but the line of leaping breakers stretched along the coast as far as eye could see, and at length the men declared they could labor no longer, and insisted that Mr. C[ouper] should steer them to shore. He then said that he would do so, but they must take some rest before encountering the peril which awaited them, and for which they might require whatever remaining strength they could command. He made the men leave the oars and lie down to sleep for a short time, and then, giving the helm to one of them, did the same himself. When they were thus a little refreshed with this short rest, he prepared to take the boat into the breakers.

He laid Mrs. N[ightingale]'s baby on her breast, and wrapped a shawl round and round her body so as to secure the child to it, and said, in the event of the boat capsizing, he would endeavor to save her and her child. Mrs. F[raser] and her boy he gave in charge to one of the sailors, and the colored woman who was with her to the other, and they promised solemnly, in case of misadventure to the boat, to do their best to save these helpless creatures;[5] and so they turned, as the sun was going down, the bows of the boat to the terrible shore. They rose two of the breakers safely, but then the oar of one of the men was struck from his hand, and in an instant the boat whirled round and turned over. Mr. C[ouper] instantly struck out to seize Mrs. N[ightingale], but she had sunk, and, though he dived twice, he could not see her; at last he felt her hair floating loose with his foot, and seizing hold of it, grasped her securely and swam with her to shore. While in the act of doing so, he saw the man who had promised to save the colored woman making alone for the beach; and even then, in that extremity, he had power of command enough left to drive the fellow back to seek her, which he did, and brought her safe to land.

[5] There is no mention, in Couper's original version, of this interesting detail about the Negro woman; as a matter of fact she had been transferred to the other lifeboat earlier in the day.

The other man kept his word of taking care of Mrs. F[raser], and the latter never released her grasp of her child's wrist, which bore the mark of her agony for weeks after their escape. They reached the sands, and Mrs. N[ightingale]'s shawl having been unwound, her child was found laughing on her bosom. But hardly had they had time to thank God for their deliverance when Mr. C[ouper] fell fainting on the beach; and Mrs. F[raser], who told me this, said that for one dreadful moment they thought that the preserver of all their lives had lost his own in the terrible exertion and anxiety that he had undergone. He revived, however, and crawling a little farther up the beach, they burrowed for warmth and shelter as well as they could in the sand, and lay there till the next morning, when they sought and found succor.

You cannot imagine, my dear E[lizabeth], how strikingly throughout this whole narrative the extraordinary power of Mr. C[ouper]'s character makes itself felt—the immediate obedience that he obtained from women whose terror might have made them unmanageable, and men whose selfishness might have defied his control; the wise though painful firmness which enabled him to order the boat away from the side of the perishing vessel, in spite of the pity that he felt for the many, in attempting to succor whom he could only have jeopardized the few whom he was bound to save; the wonderful influence he exercised over the poor oarsmen, whose long protracted labor postponed to the last possible moment the terrible risk of their landing. The firmness, courage, humanity, wisdom, and presence of mind of all his preparations for their final tremendous risk, and the authority which he was able to exercise, while struggling in the foaming water for his own life and that of the woman and child he was saving, over the man who was proving false to a similar sacred charge—all these admirable traits are most miserably transmitted to you by my imperfect account; and when I assure you that his own narrative, full as it necessarily was of the details of his own heroism, was as simple, modest, and unpretending as it was interesting and touching, I am sure you will agree with me that he must be a very rare man. When I spoke with enthusiasm to his old father of his son's noble conduct, and asked him if he was not proud of it, his sole reply was: "I am glad, madam, my son was not selfish."

Now, E[lizabeth], I have often spoken with you and written to you of the disastrous effect of slavery upon the character of the white men implicated in it; many among themselves feel and acknowledge it to the fullest extent, and no one more than myself can deplore that any human being I love should be subjected to such baneful influences; but the devil must have his due, and men brought up in habits of peremptory command over their fellow men, and under the constant apprehension of danger, and awful necessity of immediate readiness to meet it, acquire qualities precious to themselves and others in hours of supreme peril such as this man passed through, saving by their exercise himself and all committed to his charge. I know that the Southern men are apt to deny the fact that they do live under an habitual sense of danger; but a slave population, coerced into obedience, though unarmed and half-fed, *is* a threatening source of constant insecurity, and every Southern *woman* to whom I have spoken on the subject has admitted to me that they live in terror of their slaves. Happy are such of them as have protectors like J[ames Hamilton] C[ouper]. Such men will best avoid and best encounter the perils that may assail them from the abject subject, human element, in the control of which their noble faculties are sadly and unworthily employed.

I rode today [April 17], after breakfast, to Mrs. D[emere]'s, another of my neighbors, who lives full twelve miles off.[6] During the last two miles of my expedition I had the white sand hillocks and blue line of the Atlantic in view. The house at which I called was a tumble-down barrack of a dwelling in the woods, with a sort of poverty-stricken pretentious air about it, like sundry "proud planters' " dwellings that I have seen. I was received by the sons

---

[6] Fanny visited Mrs. Ann Demere, wife of Raymond Demere, at her Mulberry Grove home in the southeastern section of St. Simons Island.

as well as the lady of the house, and could not but admire the lordly rather than manly indifference with which these young gentlemen, in gay guard chains and fine attire, played the gallants to me, while filthy, barefooted, half-naked Negro women brought in refreshments, and stood all the while fanning the cake, and sweetmeats, and their young masters, as if they had been all the same sort of stuff. I felt ashamed for the lads. The conversation turned upon Dr. H[azzard]'s trial; for there has been a trial as a matter of form, and an acquittal as a matter of course; [7] and the gentlemen said, upon my expressing some surprise at the latter event, that there could not be found in all Georgia a jury who would convict him, which says but little for the moral sense of "all Georgia." From this most painful subject we fell into the Brunswick Canal, and thereafter I took my leave and rode home. I met my babies in the wood wagon, and took S[ally] up before me, and gave her a good gallop home. Having reached the house with the appetite of a twenty-four miles' ride, I found no preparation for dinner, and not so much as a boiled potato to eat, and the sole reply to my famished and disconsolate exclamations was: "Being that you order none, missis, I not know." I had forgotten to order my dinner, and my *slaves,* unauthorized, had not ventured to prepare any. Wouldn't a Yankee have said: "Wal, now, you went off so uncommon quick, I kinder guessed you forgot all about dinner," and have had it all ready for me? But my slaves durst not, and so I fasted till some tea could be got for me.

*   *   *   *

This was the last letter I wrote from the plantation, and I never returned there, nor ever saw again any of the poor people among whom I lived during this winter but Jack, once, under sad circumstances. The poor lad's health failed so completely that his owners

[7] At this time Dr. Hazzard had not yet been brought to trial for the manslaughter of John Armstrong Wylly. In point of fact he *was* later acquitted.

humanely brought him to the North, to try what benefit he might derive from the change; but this was before the passing of the Fugitive Slave Bill, when, touching the soil of the Northern states, a slave became free; and such was the apprehension felt lest Jack should be enlightened as to this fact by some philanthropic abolitionist, that he was kept shut up in a high upper room of a large empty house, where even I was not allowed to visit him. I heard at length of his being in Philadelphia; and upon my distinct statement that I considered freeing their slaves the business of the Messrs. [Butler] themselves, and not mine, I was at length permitted to see him. Poor fellow! coming to the North did not prove to him the delight his eager desire had so often anticipated from it; nor, under such circumstances, is it perhaps much to be wondered at that he benefited but little by the change—he died not long after.

I once heard a conversation between Mr. O—— and Mr. K[ing], the two overseers of the plantation on which I was living, upon the question of taking slaves, servants, necessary attendants, into the Northern states; Mr. O—— urged the danger of their being "got hold of," i.e., set free by the abolitionists, to which Mr. K[ing] very pertinently replied: "Oh, stuff and nonsense; I take care, when my wife goes North with the children, to send Lucy with her; *her children are down here, and I defy all the abolitionists in creation to get her to stay North.*" Mr. K[ing] was an extremely wise man.

APPENDIXES

APPENDIXES

APPENDIX A

A Letter to the Editor of the London Times

I wrote the following letter after reading several leading articles in the Times *newspaper, at the time of the great sensation occasioned by Mrs. Beecher Stowe's novel of* Uncle Tom's Cabin, *and after the antislavery protest which that book induced the women of England to address to those of America on the subject of the condition of the slaves in the Southern states.[1]*

My dear E[lizabeth],

I have read the articles in the. *Times* to which you refer on the subject of the inaccuracy of Mrs. Beecher Stowe's book as a picture of slavery in America, and have ascertained who they were

[1] *Uncle Tom's Cabin* was published in 1852 and at once became the most popular and the most hated book of the day. That same year a group of highborn English ladies met at Stafford House, the Duke of Sutherland's London palace, and drafted a document entitled *An Affectionate and Christian Address of Many Thousands of Women of Great Britain and Ireland to Their Sisters, the Women of the United States of America.* "We appeal to you," said the English ladies, "as sisters, wives, and as mothers, to raise your voices to your fellow citizens, and your prayers to God, for the removal of this affliction and disgrace [i.e. slavery] from the Christian world." Canvassers took this appeal to the country, and by the spring of 1853 had secured 500,-000 signatures in its support. Fanny Kemble did not feel free to add her voice to this appeal. She wrote, instead, a careful rebuttal of the proslavery apologetics of the London *Times,* and a defense of the essential veracity of Mrs. Stowe's book; and published this for the first time as an appendix to the 1863 edition of the *Journal.*

written by. Having done so, I do not think it worth while to send my letter for insertion, because, as that is the tone deliberately taken upon the subject by that paper, my counterstatement would not, I imagine, be admitted into its columns. I enclose it to you, as I should like you to see how far from true, according to my experience, the statements of the "*Times'* Correspondent" are. It is impossible, of course, to know why it erects itself into an advocate for slavery; and the most charitable conjecture I can form upon the subject is, that the Stafford House demonstration may have been thought likely to wound the sensitive national views of America upon this subject; and the statement put forward by the *Times,* contradicting Mrs. Stowe's picture, may be intended to soothe their irritation at the philanthropic zeal of our lady abolitionists. Believe me, dear E[lizabeth], yours always truly,

F. A. K.

Letter to the Editor of the London TIMES

SIR,

As it is not to be supposed that you consciously afford the support of your great influence to misstatements, I request your attention to some remarks I wish to make on an article on a book called "Uncle Tom's Cabin as It Is," contained in your paper of the 11th. In treating Mrs. Harriet Beecher Stowe's work as an exaggerated picture of the evils of slavery, I beg to assure you that you do her serious injustice: of the merits of her book as a work of art I have no desire to speak; to its power as a most interesting and pathetic story, all England and America can bear witness; but of its truth and moderation as a representation of the slave system in the United States, I can testify with the experience of an eye-witness, having been a resident in the Southern States, and had opportunities of observation such as no one who has not lived on a slave estate can have. It is very true that in reviving the altogether exploded fashion of making the hero of her novel "the perfect monster that the world ne'er saw," Mrs. Stowe has laid herself open to fair criticism, and must expect to meet with it from the very opposite taste of the present day; but the ideal excellence of her principal character is no argument at all against the general accuracy of her statements with regard to the evils of slavery; everything else in her book is not only possible, but probable, and not only probable, but a very faithful representation of the existing facts: faithful, and not, as you accuse it of being, exaggerated; for, with the exception of the horrible catastrophe, the flogging to death of poor Tom, she has portrayed none of the most revolting instances of crime produced by the slave system, with which she might have darkened her picture, without detracting from its perfect truth. Even with respect to the incident of Tom's death, it must not be said that if such an event is possible, it is hardly probable; for this is unfortunately not true. It is not true that the value of the slave as property infallibly protects his life from the passions of his master. It is no new thing for a man's passions to blind him to his most obvious and immediate temporal interests, as well as to his higher and everlasting ones—in various parts of the world and stages of civilization, various human passions assume successive prominence, and become developed, to the partial exclusion or deadening of others. In savage existence, and those states of civilization least removed from it, the animal passions predominate. In highly cultivated modern society, where the complicated machinery of human existence is at once a perpetually renewed cause and effect of certain legal and moral restraints, which, in the shape of government and public opinion, protect the congregated lives and interests of men from the worst outrages of open violence, the natural selfishness of mankind assumes a different development, and the love of power, of pleasure, or of pelf, exhibits different phenomena from those elicited from a savage under the influence of the same passions. The channel in which the energy and activity of modern society inclines more and more to pour itself is the peaceful one of the pursuit of gain. This is pre-eminently the case with the two great commercial nations of the earth, England and

America; and in either England or the Northern states of America, the prudential and practical views of life prevail so far, that instances of men sacrificing their money interests at the instigation of rage, revenge, and hatred will certainly not abound. But the Southern slaveholders are a very different race of men from either Manchester manufacturers or Massachusetts merchants; they are a remnant of barbarism and feudalism, maintaining itself with infinite difficulty and danger by the side of the latest and most powerful development of commercial civilization.

The inhabitants of Baltimore, Richmond, Charleston, Savannah, and New Orleans, whose estates lie, like the suburban retreats of our city magnates, in the near neighborhood of their respective cities, are not now the people I refer to. They are softened and enlightened by many influences—the action of city life itself, where human sympathy and human respect, stimulated by neighborhood, produce salutary social restraint as well as less salutary social cowardice. They travel to the Northern states and to Europe, and Europe and the Northern states travel to them, and, in spite of themselves, their peculiar conditions receive modifications from foreign intercourse. The influence, too, of commercial enterprise, which in these latter days is becoming the agent of civilization all over the earth, affects even the uncommercial residents of the Southern cities, and, however cordially they may dislike or despise the mercantile tendencies of Atlantic Americans or transatlantic Englishmen, their frequent contact with them breaks down some of the barriers of difference between them, and humanizes the slaveholder of the great cities into some relation with the spirit of his own times and country. But these men are but a most inconsiderable portion of the slaveholding population of the South—a nation, for as such they should be spoken of, of men whose organization and temperament is that of the southern European; living under the influence of a climate at once enervating and exciting; scattered over trackless wildernesses of arid sand and pestilential swamp; entrenched within their own boundaries; surrounded by creatures absolutely subject to their despotic will; delivered over by hard necessity to the lowest excitements of drinking, gambling, and debauchery for sole recreation; independent of all opinion; ignorant of all progress; isolated from all society—it is impossible to conceive a more savage existence within the pale of any modern civilization.

The South Carolinian gentry have been fond of styling themselves the chivalry of the South, and perhaps might not badly represent, in their relations with their dependents, the nobility of France before the purifying hurricane of the Revolution swept the rights of the suzerain and the wrongs of the serf together into one bloody abyss. The planters of the interior of the Southern and Southwestern states, with their furious feuds and slaughterous combats, their stabbings and pistolings, their gross sensuality, brutal ignorance, and despotic cruelty, resemble the chivalry of France before the horrors of the *Jacquerie* admonished them that there was a limit even to the endurance of slaves. With such men as these, human life, even when it can be bought or sold in the market for so many dollars, is but little protected by considerations of interest from the effects of any violent passion. There is yet, however, another aspect of the question, which is, that it is sometimes clearly *not* the interest of the owner to prolong the life of his slaves; as in the case of inferior or superannuated laborers, or the very notorious instance in which some of the owners of sugar plantations stated that they found it better worth their while to *work off* (i.e., kill with labor) a certain proportion of their force, and replace them by new hands every seven years, than work them less severely and maintain them in diminished efficiency for an indefinite length of time. Here you will observe a precise estimate of the planter's material interest led to a result which you argue passion itself can never be so blind as to adopt. This was a deliberate economical calculation, openly avowed some years ago by a number of sugar planters in Louisiana. If, instead of accusing Mrs. Stowe of exaggeration, you had brought the same charge against the author of the *White Slave,* I should not have been surprised; [2] for his book presents some of the most revolting instances of atrocity and crime that the miserable abuse of irresponsible power is capable of producing, and it is by no means written in the spirit of universal humanity which pervades Mrs. Stowe's volumes; but it is not liable to the charge of exaggeration any more than her less disgusting delineation. The scenes described in the *White Slave do* occur in the slave states of North America; and in two of the most appalling incidents of the book—the burning alive of the captured runaway, and the hanging without trial of the Vicksburg gamblers—the author of the *White Slave* has very simply related positive facts of notorious occurrence. To which he might have added, had he seen fit to do so, the instance of a slave who perished in the sea swamps, where he was left bound and naked, a prey to the torture inflicted upon him by the venomous mosquito swarms. My purpose, however, in addressing you was not to enter into a disquisition on either of these publications; but I am not sorry to take this opportunity of bearing witness to the truth of Mrs. Stowe's admirable book, and I have seen what few Englishmen can see—the working of the system in the midst of it.

In reply to your "Dispassionate Observer," who went to the South professedly with the purpose of seeing and judging of the state of things for himself, let me tell you that, little as he may be disposed to believe it, his testimony is worth less than nothing; for it is morally impossible for any Englishman going into the Southern states, except as a *resident,* to know anything whatever of the real condition of the slave population. This was the case some years ago, as I experienced, and it is now likely to be more the case than ever; for the institution is not *yet* approved divine to the perceptions of Englishmen, and the Southerners are as anxious to hide its uglier features from any note-making observer from this side of the wa-

[2] Richard Hildreth's *The Slave: or Memoirs of Archy Moore* (New York: 1836), enjoyed great popularity on both sides of the Atlantic as the first antislavery novel. It was published in London under the title *The White Slave, or Memoirs of a Fugitive.*

ter as to present to his admiration and approval such as can by any possibility be made to wear the most distant approach to comeliness.

The gentry of the Southern states are pre-eminent in their own country for that species of manner which, contrasted with the breeding of the Northerners, would be emphatically pronounced "good" by Englishmen. Born to inhabit landed property, they are not inevitably made clerks and countinghouse men of, but inherit with their estates some of the invariable characteristics of an aristocracy. The shop is not their element; and the eager spirit of speculation and the sordid spirit of gain do not infect their whole existence, even to their very demeanor and appearance, as they too manifestly do those of a large proportion of the inhabitants of the Northern states. Good manners have an undue value for Englishmen, generally speaking; and whatever departs from their peculiar standard of breeding is apt to prejudice them, as whatever approaches it prepossesses them, far more than is reasonable. The Southerners are infinitely better bred men, according to English notions, than the men of the Northern states. The habit of command gives them a certain self-possession, and the enjoyment of leisure a certain ease. Their temperament is impulsive and enthusiastic, and their manners have the grace and spirit which seldom belong to the deportment of a Northern people; but, upon more familiar acquaintance, the vices of the social system to which they belong will be found to have infected them with their own peculiar taint; and haughty, overbearing irritability, effeminate indolence, reckless extravagance, and a union of profligacy and cruelty, which is the immediate result of their irresponsible power over their dependents, are some of the less pleasing traits which acquaintance develops in a Southern character. In spite of all this, there is no manner of doubt that the "candid English observer" will, for the season of his sojourning among them, greatly prefer their intercourse to that of their Northern brethren. Moreover, without in the least suspecting it, he will be bribed insidiously and incessantly by the extreme desire and endeavor to please and prepossess him which the whole white population of the slave states will exhibit— as long as he goes only as a "candid observer," with a mind not *yet* made up upon the subject of slavery, and open to conviction as to its virtues. Every conciliating demonstration of courtesy and hospitable kindness will be extended to him, and, as I said before, if his observation is permitted (and it may even appear to be courted), it will be to a fairly bound, purified edition of the black book of slavery, in which, though the inherent viciousness of the whole story cannot be suppressed, the coarser and more offensive passages will be carefully expunged.

And now permit me to observe that the remarks of your traveler must derive much of their value from the scene of his inquiry. In Maryland, Kentucky, and Virginia, the outward aspect of slavery has ceased to wear its most deplorable features. The remaining vitality of the system no longer resides in the interests, but in the pride and prejudices of the planters. Their soil and climate are alike favorable to the labors of a white peasantry: the slave cultivation has had time to prove itself there the destructive pest which, in time, it will prove itself wherever it prevails. The vast estates and large fortunes that once maintained, and were maintained by, the serfdom of hundreds of Negroes, have dwindled in size and sunk in value, till the slaves have become so heavy a burden on the resources of the exhausted soil and impoverished owners of it, that they are made themselves objects of traffic in order to ward off the ruin that their increase would otherwise entail. Thus the plantations of the northern slave states now present to the traveler very few of the darker and more oppressive peculiarities of the system; and, provided he does not stray too near the precincts where the Negroes are sold, or come across gangs of them on their way to Georgia, Louisiana, or Alabama, he may, if he is a very superficial observer, conclude that the most prosperous slavery is not much worse than the most miserable freedom.

But of what value will be such conclusions applied to those numerous plantations where no white man ever sets foot without the express permission of the owner? not estates lying close to Baltimore and Charleston, or even Lexington and Savannah, but remote and savage wildernesses like Legree's estate in *Uncle Tom,* like all the plantations in the interior of Tennessee and Alabama, like the cotton fields and rice swamps of the great muddy rivers of Louisiana and Georgia, like the dreary pine barrens and endless woody wastes of North Carolina. These, especially the islands, are like so many fortresses, approachable for "observers" only at the owners' will. On most of the rice plantations in these pestilential regions, no white man can pass the night at certain seasons of the year without running the risk of his life; and during the day, the master and overseer are as much alone and irresponsible in their dominion over their black cattle, as Robinson Crusoe was over his small family of animals on his desert habitation. Who, on such estates as these, shall witness to any act of tyranny or barbarity, however atrocious? No black man's testimony is allowed against a white, and who, on the dismal swampy rice grounds of the Savannah, or the sugar brakes of the Mississippi and its tributaries, or the upcountry cotton lands of the Ocmulgee, shall go to perform the task of candid observation and benevolent inquiry?

I passed some time on two such estates—plantations where the Negroes esteemed themselves well off, and, compared with the slaves on several of the neighboring properties, might very well consider themselves so; and I will, with your permission, contrast some of the items of my observation with those of the traveler whose report you find so satisfactory on the subject of the "consolations" of slavery.

And, first, for the attachment which he affirms to subsist between the slave and master. I do not deny that certain manifestations on the part of the slave may suggest the idea of such a feeling; but whether, upon better examination, it will be found to deserve the name, I very much doubt. In the first place, on some of the great Southern estates, the owners are habitual absentees, utterly unknown to their serfs, and enjoying the proceeds of their labor in residences as far remote as possible from the sands and swamps where their rice and cotton grow, and their slaves bow themselves under the eye of the white overseer, and the lash of the black driver. Some of these Sybarites prefer living in Paris, that paradise of American republicans, some in the capitals of the Middle States of the Union, Philadelphia or New York.

The air of New England has a keen edge of liberty, which suits few Southern constitutions; and unkindly as abolition has found its native soil and native skies, that is its birthplace, and there it flourishes, in spite of all attempts to root it out and trample it down, and within any atmosphere poisoned by its influence no slaveholder can willingly draw breath. Some travel in Europe, and few, whose means permit the contrary, ever pass the entire year on their plantations. Great intervals of many years pass, and no master ever visits some of these properties: what species of attachment do you think the slave entertains for him? In other cases, the visits made will be of a few days in one of the winter months, the estate and its cultivators remaining for the rest of the year under the absolute control of the overseer, who, provided he contrives to get a good crop of rice or cotton into the market for his employers, is left to the arbitrary exercise of a will seldom uninfluenced for evil by the combined effects of the grossest ignorance and habitual intemperance. The temptation to the latter vice is almost irresistible to a white man in such a climate, and leading an existence of brutal isolation, among a parcel of human beings as like brutes as they can be made. But the owner who at these distant intervals of months or years revisits his estates, is looked upon as a returning providence by the poor Negroes. They have no experience of his character to destroy their hopes in his goodness, and all possible and impossible ameliorations of their condition are anticipated from his advent, less work, more food, fewer stripes, and some of that consideration which the slave hopes may spring from his positive money value to his owner—a fallacious dependence, as I have already attempted to show, but one which, if it has not always predominating weight with the master, never can have any with the overseer, who has not even the feeling of regard for his own property to mitigate his absolutism over the slaves of another man.

There is a very powerful cause which makes the prosperity and well-being (as far as life is concerned) of most masters a subject of solicitude with their slaves. The only stability of their condition, such as it is, hangs upon it. If the owner of a plantation dies, his estates may fall into the market, and his slaves be sold at public auction the next day; and whether this promises a better, or threatens a worse condition, the slaves cannot know, and no human being cares. One thing it inevitably brings, the uprooting of all old associations; the disruption of all the ties of fellowship in misery; the tearing asunder of all relations of blood and affection; the sale into separate and far-distant districts of fathers, mothers, husbands, wives, and children. If the estate does not lie in the extreme South, there is the vague dread of being driven thither from Virginia to Georgia, from Carolina to Alabama, or Louisiana, a change which, for reasons I have shown above, implies the passing from a higher into a lower circle of the infernal pit of slavery.

I once heard a slave on the plantation of an absentee express the most lively distress at hearing that his master was ill. Before, however, I had recovered from my surprise at this warm "attachment" to a distant and all but unknown proprietor, the man added: "Massa die, what become of all him people?"

On my arrival on the plantation where I resided, I was hailed with the most extravagant demonstrations of delight, and all but lifted off my feet in the arms of people who had never seen me before, but who, knowing me to be connected with their owners, expected from me some of the multitudinous benefits which they always hope to derive from masters. These, until they come to reside among them, are always believed to be sources of beneficence and fountains of redress by the poor people, who have known no rule but the delegated tyranny of the overseer. In these expectations, however, they very soon find themselves cruelly mistaken. Of course, if the absentee planter has received a satisfactory income from his estate, he is inclined to be satisfied with the manager of it; and as subordination to the only white man among hundreds of blacks must be maintained at any and every cost, the overseer is justified and upheld in his whole administration. If the wretched slave ever dared to prefer a complaint of ill-usage the most atrocious, the law which refuses the testimony of a black against a white is not only the law of the land, but of every man's private dealings; and lying being one of the natural results of slavery, and a tendency to shirk compelled and unrequited labor another, the overseer stands on excellent vantage ground when he refers to these undoubted characteristics of the system, if called upon to rebut any charge of cruelty or injustice. But pray consider for a moment the probability of any such charge being preferred by a poor creature who has been for years left to the absolute disposal of this man, and who knows very well that in a few days, or months at farthest, the master will again depart, leaving him again for months, perhaps for years, utterly at the mercy of the man against whom he has dared to prefer a complaint. On the estates which I visited, the owners had been habitually absent, and the "attachment" of slaves to such masters as these, you will allow, can hardly come under the denomination of a strong personal feeling.

Your authority next states that the infirm and superannuated slaves no longer capable of ministering to their masters' luxuries, on the estate that he visited, were ending their lives among all the comforts of home, with kindred and friends around them, in a condition which he contrasts, at least by implication, very favorably with the workhouse, the last refuge provided by the social humanity of England for the pauper laborer when he has reached that term when "unregarded age is in corners thrown." On the plantation where I lived the infirmary was a large room, the walls of which were simply mud and laths; the floor, the soil itself, damp with perpetual drippings from the holes in the roof; and the open space which served for a window was protected only by a broken shutter, which, in order to exclude the cold, was drawn so near as almost to exclude the light at the same time. Upon this earthen floor, with nothing but its hard, damp surface beneath him, no covering but a tattered shirt and trousers, and a few sticks under his head for a pillow, lay an old man of upward of seventy, dying. When I first looked at him I thought, by the glazed stare of his eyes, and the flies that had gathered round his half-open mouth, that he was dead; but on stooping nearer, I perceived that the last faint struggle of life was still going on, but even while I bent over him it ceased; and so, like a worn-out hound, with no creature to comfort or relieve his last agony, with neither Christian solace or human succor near him, with neither wife, nor child, nor even friendly fellow being to lift his head from the knotty sticks on which he had rested it, or drive away the insects that buzzed round his lips and nostrils like those of a fallen beast, died this poor old slave, whose life had been exhausted in unrequited labor, the fruits of which had gone to pamper the pride and feed the luxury of those who knew and cared neither for his life or death, and to whom, if they had heard of the latter, it would have been a matter of absolute though small gain, the saving of a daily pittance of meal, which served to prolong a life no longer available to them.

I proceed to the next item in your observer's record. All children below the age of twelve were unemployed, he says, on the estate he visited: this is perhaps a questionable benefit, when, no process of mental cultivation being permitted, the only employment for the leisure thus allowed is that of rolling, like dogs or cats, in the sand and the sun. On all the plantations I visited, and on those where I resided, the infants in arms were committed to the care of these juvenile slaves, who were denominated nurses, and whose sole employment was what they call to "mind baby." The poor little Negro sucklings were cared for (I leave to your own judgment how efficiently or how tenderly) by these half-savage slips of slavery—carried by them to the fields where their mothers were working under the lash, to receive their needful nourishment, and then carried back again to the "settlement," or collection of Negro huts, where they wallowed unheeded in utter filth and neglect until the time again returned for their being carried to their mother's breast. Such was the employment of the children of eight or nine years old, and the only supervision exercised over either babies or "baby minders" was that of the old woman left in charge of the infirmary, where she made her abode all day long, and bestowed such samples of her care and skill upon its inmates as I shall have occasion to mention presently. The practice of thus driving the mothers afield, even while their infants were still dependent upon them for their daily nourishment, is one of which the evil as well as the cruelty is abundantly apparent without comment.

The next note of admiration elicited from your "impartial observer" is bestowed upon the fact that the domestic servants (i.e., house slaves) on the plantation he visited were *allowed* to live away from the owner's residence, and to marry. But I never was on a Southern plantation, and I never heard of one, where any of the slaves were *allowed* to sleep under the same roof with their owner. With the exception of the women to whose care the children of the planter, if he had any, might be confided, and perhaps a little boy or girl slave, kept as a sort of pet animal, and allowed to pass the night on the floor of the sleeping apartment of some member of the family, the residence of *any* slaves belonging to a plantation night and day in their master's house, like Northern or European servants, is a thing I believe unknown throughout the Southern states. Of course I except the cities, and speak only of the estates, where the house servants are neither better housed or accommodated than the field hands. Their intolerably dirty habits and offensive persons would indeed render it a severe trial to any family accustomed to habits of decent cleanliness; and, moreover, considerations of safety, and that cautious vigilance which is a hard necessity of the planter's existence, in spite of the supposed attachment of his slaves, would never permit the near proximity, during the unprotected hours of the night, of those whose intimacy with the daily habits and knowledge of the nightly securities resorted to might prove terrible auxiliaries to any attack from without. The city guards, patrols, and night watches, together with their stringent rules about Negroes being abroad after night, and their well-fortified lockup houses for all detected without a pass, afford some security against these attached dependents; but on remote plantations, where the owner and his family, and perhaps a white overseer are alone, surrounded by slaves and separated from all succor against them, they do not sleep under the white man's roof, and for politic reasons, pass the night away from their master's abode.

The house servants have no other or better allowance of food than the field laborers, but have the advantage of eking it out by what is left from the master's table—if possible, with even less comfort in one respect, inasmuch as no time whatever is set apart for their meals, which they snatch at any hour and in any way that they can—generally, however, standing or squatting on their hams round the kitchen fire; the kitchen being a mere outhouse or barn with a fire in it. On the estate where I lived, as I have mentioned, they had no sleeping rooms in the house; but when their work was over, they retired like the rest to their hovels, the discomfort of which had to them all the additional disadvantage of comparison with their owner's mode of living. In all establishments whatever, of course some disparity exists between the accommodation of the drawing rooms and best bedrooms and the servants' kitchen and attics; but on a plantation it is no longer a matter of degree. The young women who performed the offices of waiting and housemaids, and the lads who attended upon the service of their master's table where I lived, had neither table to feed at nor chair to sit down upon themselves; the "boys" lay all night on the hearth by the kitchen fire, and the women upon the usual slave's bed—a frame of rough boards, strewed with a little moss off the trees, with the addition perhaps of a tattered and filthy blanket.

As for the so-called privilege of marrying—surely it is gross mockery to apply such a word to a bond which may be holy in God's sight, but which did not prevent the owner of a plantation where my observations were made from selling and buying men and their so-called wives and children into divided bondage, nor the white overseer from compelling the wife of one of the most excellent and exemplary of his master's slaves to live with him; nor the white wife of another overseer, in her husband's temporary absence from the estate, from barbarously flogging three *married* slaves within a month of their confinement, their condition being the result of the profligacy of the said overseer, and probably compelled by the very same lash by which it was punished. This is a very disgusting picture of married life on slave estates; but I have undertaken to reply to the statements of your informant, and I regret to be obliged to record the facts by which alone I can do so.

"Work," continues your authority, "began at six in the morning; at nine an hour's rest was allowed for breakfast, and by two or three o'clock the day's work was done." Certainly this was a pattern plantation, and I can only lament that my experience lay amid such far less favorable circumstances. The Negroes among whom I lived went to the fields at daybreak, carrying with them their allowance of food, which toward noon, and not till then, they ate, cooking it over a fire which they kindled as best they could where they were working; their *second* meal in the day was at night, after their labor was over, having worked at the *very least* six hours without rest or refreshment since their noonday meal— properly so called, indeed, for it was meal and nothing else, or a preparation something thicker than porridge, which they call hominy. Perhaps the candid observer, whose report of the estate he visited appeared to you so consolatory, would think that this diet contrasted favorably with that of potato- and buttermilk-fed Irish laborers. But a more just comparison surely would be with the mode of living of the laboring population of the United States, the peasantry of Ohio, Pennsylvania, and Massachusetts, or indeed with the condition of those very potato- and buttermilk-fed Irishmen when they have exchanged their native soil for the fields of Northern and Northwestern states, and when, as one of them once was heard to say, it was of no use writing home that he got meat three times a day, for nobody in Ireland would believe it.

The next item in the list of commendation is the hospital, which your informant also visited, and of which he gives the following account: "It consisted of three separate wards, all clean and well-ventilated: one was for lying-in women, who were invariably allowed a month's rest after their confinement." Permit me to place beside this picture that of a Southern infirmary, such as I saw it, and taken on the spot. In the first room that I entered I found only half of the windows, of which there were six, glazed; these were almost as much obscured with dirt as the other windowless ones were darkened by the dingy shutters which the shivering inmates had closed in order to protect themselves from the cold. In the enormous chimney glimmered the powerless embers of a few chips of wood, round which as many of the sick women as had strength to approach were cowering, some on wooden settles (there was not such a thing as a chair with a back in the whole establishment), most of them on the ground, excluding those who were too ill to rise; and these poor wretches lay prostrate on the earth, without bedstead, bed, mattress, or pillow, with no covering but the clothes they had on and some filthy rags of blanket in which they endeavored to wrap themselves as they lay literally strewing the floor, so that there was hardly room to pass between them. Here, in their hour of sickness and suffering, lay those whose health and strength had given way under unrequited labor—some of them, no later than the previous day, had been urged with the lash to their accustomed tasks—and their husbands, fathers, brothers, and sons were even at that hour sweating over the earth whose increase was to procure for others all the luxuries which health can enjoy, all the comforts which can alleviate sickness. Here lay women expecting every hour the terror and agonies of childbirth, others who had just brought their doomed offspring into the world, others who were groaning under the anguish and bitter disappointment of miscarriages—here lay some burning with fever, others chilled with cold and aching with rheumatism, upon the hard cold ground, the draughts and damp of the atmosphere increasing their sufferings, and dirt, noise, stench, and every aggravation of which sickness is capable combined in their condition. There had been among them one or two cases of prolonged and terribly hard labor; and the method adopted by the ignorant old Negress, who was the sole matron, midwife, nurse, physician, surgeon, and servant of the infirmary, to assist them in their extremity, was to tie a cloth tight round the throats of the agonized women, and by drawing it till she almost suffocated them she produced violent and spasmodic struggles, which she assured me she thought materially assisted the progress of the labor.

This was one of the Southern infirmaries with which I was acquainted; and I beg to conclude this chapter of contrasts to your informant's consolatory views of slavery by assuring you once more very emphatically that they have been one and all drawn from estates where the slaves esteemed themselves well-treated, were reputed generally to be so, and undoubtedly, as far as my observation went, were so, compared with those on several of the adjoining plantations.

With regard to the statement respecting the sums of money earned by industrious Negroes, there is no doubt that it is perfectly correct. I know of some slaves on a plantation in the extreme South who had received, at various times, large sums of money from a shopkeeper in the small town near their estate for the gray moss or lichen collected from the evergreen oaks of Carolina and Georgia, upon which it hangs in vast masses, and after some cleaning process becomes an excellent substitute for horsehair, for bed, chair, and sofa stuffing. On another estate, some of the slaves were expert boat makers, and had been allowed by their masters to retain the price (no inconsiderable one) for some that they had found time to manufacture after their day's labor was accomplished. These were undoubtedly privileges; but I confess it appears to me that the juster view of the matter would be this: if these men were industrious enough, out of their scanty leisure, to earn these sums of money, which a mere exercise of arbitrary will on the part of the master allowed them to keep, how much more of remuneration, of comfort, of improvement, physical and mental, might they not have achieved, had the due price of their daily labor merely been paid to them? It seems to me that this is the mode of putting the case to Englishmen, and all who have not agreed to consider uncertain favor an equivalent for common justice in the dealings of man with man. As the slaves are well known to toil for years sometimes to amass the means of rescuing themselves from bondage, the fact of their being able and sometimes allowed to earn considerable sums of money is notorious.

But now that I have answered one by one the instances you have produced, with others—I am sure as accurate, and I believe as common—of an entirely opposite description, permit me to ask you what this sort of testimony amounts to. I allow you full credit for yours, allow me full credit for mine, and the result is very simply a nullification of the one by the other statement, and a proof that there is as much good as evil in the details of slavery; but now, be pleased to throw into the scale this consideration, that the principle of the whole is unmitigated abominable evil, as by your own acknowledgment you hold it to be, and add, moreover, that the principle being invariably bad beyond the power of the best man acting under it to alter its execrable injustice, the goodness of the detail is a matter absolutely dependent upon the will of each individual slaveholder, so that though the best cannot make the system in the smallest particular better, the bad can make every practical detail of it as atrocious as the principle itself; and then tell me upon what ground you palliate a monstrous iniquity, which is the rule, because of the accidental exceptions which go to prove it. Moreover, if, as you have asserted, good preponderates over evil in the practice, though not in the theory of slavery, or it would not main-

tain its existence, why do you uphold to us, with so much complacency, the hope that it is surely, if not rapidly approaching its
abolishment? Why is the preponderating good, which has, as you
say, proved sufficient to uphold the institution hitherto, to become
(in spite of the spread of civilization and national progress, and the
gradual improvement of the slaves themselves) inadequate to its
perpetuation henceforward? Or why, if good really has prevailed
in it, do you rejoice that it is speedily to pass away? You say the
emancipation of the slaves is inevitable, and that through progres-
sive culture the Negro of the Southern states daily approaches
more nearly to the recovery of the rights of which he has been
robbed. But whence do you draw this happy augury, except from
the hope, which all Christian souls must cherish, that God will not
permit much longer so great a wickedness to darken the face of the
earth? Surely the increased stringency of the Southern slave laws,
the more than ever vigilant precautions against all attempts to enlighten or educate the Negroes, the severer restrictions on manumission, the thrusting forth out of certain states of all free persons
of color, the atrocious Fugitive Slave Bill, one of the latest achievements of Congress, and the piratical attempt upon Cuba, avowedly,
on the part of all Southerners, abetting or justifying it because it
will add slave territory and 600,000 slaves to their possessions—
surely these do not seem indications of the better state of things you
anticipate, except, indeed, as the straining of the chain beyond all
endurable tightness significantly suggests the probability of its giving way.

I do not believe the planters have any disposition to put an end
to slavery, nor is it perhaps much to be wondered at that they have
not. To do so is, in the opinion of the majority of them, to run the
risk of losing their property, perhaps their lives, for a benefit which
they profess to think doubtful to the slaves themselves. How far
they are right in anticipating ruin from the manumission of their
slaves I think questionable, but that they do so is certain, and self-
impoverishment for the sake of abstract principle is not a thing to

be reasonably expected from any large class of men. But, besides the natural fact that the slaveholders wish to retain their property, emancipation is, in their view of it, not only a risk of enormous pecuniary loss, and of their entire social status, but involves elements of personal danger, and, above all, disgust to inveterate prejudices, which they will assuredly never encounter. The question is not alone one of foregoing great wealth or the mere means of subsistence (in either case almost equally hard); it is not alone the unbinding the hands of those who have many a bloody debt of hatred and revenge to settle; it is not alone the consenting suddenly to see by their side, upon a footing of free social equality, creatures toward whom their predominant feeling is one of mingled terror and abhorrence, and who, during the whole of their national existence, have been, as the earth, trampled beneath their feet, yet ever threatening to gape and swallow them alive. It is not all this alone which makes it unlikely that the Southern planter should desire to free his slaves: freedom in America is not merely a personal right; it involves a political privilege. Freemen there are legislators. The rulers of the land are the majority of the people, and in many parts of the Southern states the black free citizens would become, if not at once, yet in process of time, inevitably voters, landholders, delegates to state legislatures, members of assembly—who knows?—senators, judges, aspirants to the presidency of the United States. You must be an American, or have lived long among them, to conceive the shout of derisive execration with which such an idea would be hailed from one end of the land to the other.

That the emancipation of the Negroes need not necessarily put them in possession of the franchise is of course obvious; but, as a general consequence, the one would follow from the other; and at present certainly the slaveholders are no more ready to grant the political privilege than the natural right of freedom. Under these circumstances, though the utmost commiseration is naturally excited by the slaves, I agree with you that some forbearance is due to the masters. It is difficult to conceive a more awful position than theirs: fettered by laws which impede every movement toward right and justice, and utterly without the desire to repeal them—dogged by the apprehension of nameless retributions—bound beneath a burden of responsibility for which, whether they acknowledge it or not, they are held accountable by God and men—goaded by the keen consciousness of the growing reprobation of all civilized Christian communities, their existence presents the miserable moral counterpart of the physical condition of their slaves; and it is one compared with which that of the wretchedest slave is, in my judgment, worthy of envy.

APPENDIX B

A Letter to C[harles] G[reville], Esq.[1]

Before entering upon my answer to your questions, let me state that I have no claim to be ranked as an abolitionist in the American acceptation of the word, for I have hitherto held the emancipation of the slaves to be exclusively the business and duty of their owners, whose highest moral interest I thought it was to rid themselves of such a responsibility, in spite of the manifold worldly interests almost inextricably bound up with it.

This has been my feeling hitherto with regard to the views of the abolitionists, which I now, however, heartily embrace, inasmuch as I think that from the moment the United States government assumed an attitude of coercion and supremacy toward the

[1] This letter was thrust unceremoniously in at the end of the 1863 edition of the *Journal*. It contains a number of signs of hasty preparation and could have been written any time between October 6, 1862, when the news of President Lincoln's preliminary Emancipation Proclamation reached England, where Fanny then was, and the spring of 1863. Lincoln's historic decision to free the slaves precipitated an effervescence in England that began in the second and third weeks of October 1862, subsided in November and December, and reached its climax in the first six months of 1863. During this period, probably between October 1862 and January 1863, Greville addressed to Fanny the questions which she here attempts to answer. Charles Greville and she were old acquaintances. The diarist disapproved of her acting, her divorce, and her politics. Here she gives a spirited defense of emancipation, which the British aristocracy was attacking in public and in private as the wildest of follies.

Southern states, it was bound, with its fleets and armies, to introduce its polity with respect to slavery, and wherever it planted the
standard of the Union, to proclaim the universal freedom which is
the recognized law of the Northern United States. That they have
not done so has been partly owing to a superstitious but honorable
veneration for the letter of their great charter, the Constitution, and
still more to the hope they have never ceased to entertain of bringing back the South to its allegiance under the former conditions of
the Union, an event which will be rendered impossible by any attempt to interfere with the existence of slavery.

The North, with the exception of an inconsiderable minority of
its inhabitants, has never been at all desirous of the emancipation
of the slaves. The Democratic party, which has ruled the United
States for many years past, has always been friendly to the slaveholders, who have, with few exceptions, all been members of it
(for, by a strange perversion both of words and ideas, some of
the most democratic states in the Union are Southern slave states,
and in the part of Georgia where the slave population is denser
than in any other part of the South, a county exists bearing the sa-
tirical title of *Liberty County*). And the support of the South has
been given to the Northern Democratic politicians upon the distinct understanding that their "domestic institution" was to be
guaranteed to them.

The condition of the free blacks in the Northern states has of
course been affected most unfavorably by the slavery of their race
throughout the other half of the Union; and, indeed, it would have
been a difficult matter for Northern citizens to maintain toward the
blacks an attitude of social and political equality as far as the borders of Delaware, while immediately beyond they were pledged to
consider them as the "chattels" of their owners, animals no more
noble or human than the cattle in their masters' fields.

How could peace have been maintained if the Southern slaveholders had been compelled to endure the sight of Negroes rising
to wealth and eminence in the Northern cities, or entering as fel-

low members with themselves the halls of that Legislature to which
all free-born citizens are eligible? They would very certainly have
declined with fierce scorn, not the fellowship of the blacks alone,
but of those white men who admitted the despised race of their
serfs to a footing of such impartial equality. It therefore was the
instinctive, and became the deliberate policy of the Northern people, once pledged to maintain slavery in the South, to make their
task easy by degrading the blacks in the Northern states to a condition contrasting as little as possible with that of the Southern
slaves. The Northern politicians struck hands with the Southern
slaveholders, and the great majority of the most enlightened citizens of the Northern states, absorbed in the pursuit of wealth and
the extension and consolidation of their admirable and wonderful
national prosperity, abandoned the government of their noble
country and the preservation of its nobler institutions to the slaveholding aristocracy of the South—to a mob of politicians by trade,
the vilest and most venal class of men that ever disgraced and
endangered a country—to foreign emigrants, whose brutish ignorance did not prevent the Democratic party from seizing upon them
as voters, and bestowing on the Irish and German boors just landed
on their shores the same political privileges as those possessed and
intelligently exercised by the farmers and mechanics of New England, the most enlightened men of their class to be found in the
world.

The gradual encroachment of the Southern politicians upon the
liberties of the North, by their unrelaxing influence in Congress
and over successive cabinets and presidents, was not without its
effect in stimulating some resistance on the part of Northern statesmen of sufficient intelligence to perceive the inevitable results toward which this preponderance in the national councils was steadily tending; and I need not remind you of the rapidity and force
with which General Jackson quelled an incipient rebellion in South
Carolina, when Mr. Calhoun made the tariff question the pretext
for a threatened secession in 1832, of the lifelong opposition to

Southern pretensions by John Quincy Adams, of the endeavor of Mr. Clay to stem the growing evil by the conditions of the Missouri Compromise, and all the occasional attempts of individuals of more conscientious convictions than their fellow citizens on the subject of the sin of slavery, from Dr. Channing's eloquent protest on the annexation of Texas,[2] to Mr. Charles Sumner's philippic against Mr. Brooks,[3] of South Carolina.

The disorganization of the Democratic party, after a cohesion of so many years, at length changed the aspect of affairs, and the North appeared to be about to arouse itself from its apathetic consent to Southern domination. The Republican party, headed by Colonel Fremont, who was known to be an antislavery man, nearly carried the presidential election six years ago, and then every preparation had been made in the South for the process of secession, which was only averted by the election of Mr. Buchanan, a proslavery Southern sympathizer, though born in Pennsylvania. Under his presidency, the Southern statesmen, resuming their attitude of apparent friendliness with the North, kept in abeyance, maturing and perfecting by every treasonable practice, for which their preponderating share in the cabinet afforded them facilities, the plan of the violent disruption of the Union, upon which they had determined whenever the Republican party should have acquired sufficient strength to elect a president with Northern views. Before, however, this event occurred, the war in Kansas rang a prophetic

---

[2] William Ellery Channing: *A Letter to the Honorable Henry Clay on the Annexation of Texas to the United States;* printed as a pamphlet (Boston: 1837).

[3] Charles Sumner delivered no philippic against Preston S. Brooks, who was representative to Congress from South Carolina. On May 19–20, 1856, the Senator from Massachusetts delivered in the Senate a hard-hitting indictment of the South entitled "The Crime against Kansas." This speech accused Southerners of a deliberately planned invasion of free soil; and it pilloried Senators Douglas of Illinois and Butler of South Carolina as respectively the Sancho Panza and the Don Quixote of this "crusade." Butler was Brooks's uncle, and Brooks responded to an attack that was both personal and political by making a savage physical assault on Senator Sumner on May 22.

peal of warning through the land; and the struggle there begun between New England emigrants bent on founding a free state, and Missouri border ruffians determined to make the new territory a slaveholding addition to the South, might have roused the whole North and West to the imminence of the peril by which the safety of the Union was threatened.

But neither the struggle in Kansas, nor the strange and piteous episode which grew out of it, of John Brown's attempt to excite an insurrection in Virginia, and his execution by the government of that state, did more than startle the North with a nine days' wonder out of its apathetic indifference. The Republican party, it is true, gained adherents, and acquired strength by degrees; and Mr. Buchanan's term of office approaching its expiration, it became apparent that the Democratic party was about to lose its supremacy, and the slaveholders their dominion; and no sooner was this evident than the latter threw off the mask, and renounced their allegiance to the Union. In a day—in an hour almost—those stood face to face as mortal enemies who were citizens of the same country, subjects of the same government, children of the same soil; and the North, incredulous and amazed, found itself suddenly summoned to retrieve its lost power and influence, and assert the dignity of the insulted Union against the rebellious attempt of the South to overthrow it.

But it was late for them to take that task in hand. For years the conduct of the government of the United States had been becoming a more desperate and degraded *jobbery,* one from which day by day the Northern gentlemen of intelligence, influence, and education withdrew themselves in greater disgust, devoting their energies to schemes of mere personal advantage, and leaving the commonweal with selfish and contemptuous indifference to the guidance of any hands less nice and less busy than their own.

Nor would the Southern planters—a prouder and more aristocratic race than the Northern merchants—have relished the companionship of their fellow politicians more than the latter, but *their* personal interests were at stake, and immediately concerned in their maintaining their predominant influence over the government; and while the Boston men wrote and talked transcendentalism, and became the most accomplished *ästhetische* cotton spinners and railroad speculators, and made the shoes and cowhides of the Southerners, the latter made their laws (I believe New Jersey is really the great cowhide factory); and the New York men, owners of the fastest horses and finest houses in the land, having made a sort of brummagem Paris of their city, were the bankers and brokers of the Southerners, while the latter were the legislators.

The grip the slaveholders had fastened on the helm of the state had been tightening for nearly half a century, till the government of the nation had become literally theirs, and the idea of their relinquishing it was one which the North did not contemplate, and they would not tolerate.

If I have said nothing of the grievances which the South has alleged against the North—its tariff, made chiefly in the interest of the Northeastern manufacturing states, or its inconsiderable but enthusiastic Massachusetts and Pennsylvania abolition party—it is because I do not believe these causes of complaint would have had the same effect upon any but a community of slaveholders, men made impatient (by the lifelong habit of despotism) not only of all control, but of any opposition. Thirty years ago Andrew Jackson— a man of keen sagacity as well as determined energy—wrote of them that they were bent upon destroying the Union, and that, whatever was the pretext of their discontent, that was their aim and purpose. "Today," he wrote, "it is the tariff, by-and-by it will be slavery." The event has proved how true a prophet he was. My own conviction is that the national character produced and fostered by slaveholding is incompatible with free institutions, and that the Southern aristocracy, thanks to the pernicious influences by which they are surrounded, are unfit to be members of a Christian republic. It is slavery that has made the Southerners rebels to their government, traitors to their country, and the originators of the bloodiest civil war that ever disgraced humanity and civilization. It is for their sinful complicity in slavery, and their shameful abandonment of all their duties as citizens, that the Northerners are paying in the blood of their men, the tears of their women, and the treasure which they have till now held more precious than their birthright. They must now not merely impose a wise restriction upon slavery, they must be prepared to extinguish it. They neglected and despised the task of moderating its conditions and checking its growth; they must now suddenly, in the midst of unparalleled difficulties and dangers, be ready to deal summarily with its entire existence. They have loved the pursuit of personal prosperity and pleasure more than their country; and now they must spend life and living to reconquer their great inheritance, and win back at the sword's point what Heaven had forbidden them to lose. Nor are we, here in England, without part in this tremendous sin and sorrow; we have persisted in feeding our looms, and the huge wealth they coin, with the produce of slavery. In vain our vast Indian territory has solicited the advantage of becoming our free cotton plantation; neither our manufacturers nor our government would venture, would wait, would spend or lose, for that purpose; the slave-grown harvest was ready, was abundant, was cheap—and now the thousand arms of our great national industry are folded in deplorable inactivity; the countless hands that wrought from morn till night the wealth that was a world's wonder are stretched unwillingly to beg their bread; and England has never seen a sadder sight than the enforced idleness of her poor operatives, or a nobler one than their patient and heroic endurance.

And now you ask me what plan, what scheme, what project the government of the United States has formed for the safe and successful emancipation of four millions of slaves, in the midst of a country distracted with all the horrors of war, and the male population of which is engaged in military service at a distance from their homes? Most assuredly none. Precipitated headlong from a state of apparent profound security and prosperity into a series of calamitous events which have brought the country to the verge of ruin, neither the nation or its governors have had leisure to prepare themselves for any of the disastrous circumstances they have had to encounter, least of all for the momentous change which the President's proclamation [4] announces as imminent: a measure of supreme importance, not deliberately adopted as the result of philanthropic conviction or farsighted policy, but (if not a mere feint of party politics) the last effort of the incensed spirit of endurance in the North—a punishment threatened against rebels, whom they cannot otherwise subdue, and which a year ago half the Northern population would have condemned upon principle, and more than half revolted from on instinct.

The country being in a state of war necessarily complicates everything, and renders the most plausible suggestions for the settlement of the question of emancipation futile, because from first to last now it will be one tremendous chapter of accidents, instead of a carefully considered and wisely prepared measure of government. But, supposing the war to have ceased, either by the success of the Northern arms or by the consent of both belligerents, the question of manumission in the Southern states when reduced to the condition of territories or restored to the sway of their own elected governors and legislatures, though difficult, is by no means one of insuperable difficulty; and I do not believe that a great nation of Englishmen, having once the will to rid itself of a danger and a disgrace, will fail to find a way. The thing, therefore, most to be desired now is, that Americans may unanimously embrace the purpose of emancipation, and, though they have been reluctantly driven by the irresistible force of circumstances to contem-

[4] This is very likely a reference to the Emancipation Proclamation of January 1, 1863. But it is quite possible that this letter was written before that date, and in that case the reference would be to the presidential Proclamation of September 22, 1862. This Proclamation announced the President's intention to free all persons held as slaves in states still in rebellion on January 1, 1863; the January 1 Proclamation gave practical expression to this statement of intent.

plate the measure, may henceforward never avert their eyes from it till it is accomplished.

When I was in the South many years ago I conversed frequently with two highly intelligent men, both of whom agreed in saying that the immense value of the slaves as property was the only real obstacle to their manumission, and that whenever the Southerners became convinced that it was their interest to free them they would very soon find the means to do it. In some respects the conditions are more favorable than those we had to encounter in freeing our West India slaves. Though the soil and climate of the Southern states are fertile and favorable, they are not tropical, and there is no profuse natural growth of fruits or vegetables to render subsistence possible without labor; the winter temperature is like that of the Roman states; and even as far south as Georgia and the borders of Florida, frosts severe enough to kill the orange trees are sometimes experienced. The inhabitants of the Southern states, throughout by far the largest portion of their extent, must labor to live, and will undoubtedly obey the beneficent law of necessity whenever they are made to feel that their existence depends upon their own exertions. The plan of a gradual emancipation, preceded by a limited apprenticeship of the Negroes to white masters, is of course often suggested as less dangerous than their entire and immediate enfranchisement. But when years ago I lived on a Southern plantation, and had opportunities of observing the miserable results of the system on everything connected with it—the souls, minds, bodies, and estates of both races of men, and the very soil on which they existed together—I came to the conclusion that immediate and entire emancipation was not only an act of imperative right, but would be the safest and most profitable course for the interests of both parties. The gradual and inevitable process of ruin which exhibits itself in the long run on every property involving slavery, naturally suggests some element of decay inherent in the system; the reckless habits of extravagance and prodigality in the masters, the ruinous wastefulness and ignorant incapacity of the slaves, the deterioration of the land under the exhausting and thriftless cultivation to which it is subjected, made it evident to me that there were but two means of maintaining a prosperous ownership in Southern plantations: either the possession of considerable capital wherewith to recruit the gradual waste of the energies of the soil, and supply by all the improved and costly methods of modern agriculture the means of profitable cultivation (a process demanding, as English farmers know, an enormous and incessant outlay of both money and skill), or an unlimited command of fresh soil, to which the slaves might be transferred as soon as that already under culture exhibited signs of exhaustion. Now the Southerners are for the most part men whose only wealth is in their land and laborers—a large force of slaves is their most profitable investment. The great capitalists and moneyed men of the country are Northern men; the planters are men of large estates but restricted means: many of them are deeply involved in debt, and there are very few who do not depend from year to year for their subsistence on the harvest of their fields and the chances of the cotton and rice crops of each season.

This makes it of vital importance to them to command an unrestricted extent of territory. The man who can move a "gang" of able-bodied Negroes to a tract of virgin soil is sure of an immense return of wealth; as sure as that he who is circumscribed in this respect, and limited to the cultivation of certain lands with cotton or tobacco by slaves, will in the course of a few years see his estate gradually exhausted and unproductive, refusing its increase, while its black population, propagating and multiplying, will compel him eventually, under penalty of starvation, to make *them* his crop, and substitute, as the Virginians have been constrained to do, a traffic in human cattle for the cultivation of vegetable harvests.

The steady decrease of the value of the cotton crop, even on the famous sea-island plantations of Georgia, often suggested to me the inevitable ruin of the owners within a certain calculable space of time, as the land became worn out, and the Negroes continued to increase in number; and had the estate on which I lived been mine, and the laws of Georgia not made such an experiment impossible, I would have emancipated the slaves on it immediately, and turned them into a free tenantry, as the first means of saving my property from impending destruction. I would have paid them wages, and they should have paid me rent. I would have relinquished the charge of feeding and clothing them, and the burden of their old, young, and infirm; in short, I would have put them at once upon the footing of free hired laborers. Of course such a process would have involved temporary loss, and for a year or two the income of the estate would, I dare say, have suffered considerably; but, in all such diversions of labor or capital from old into new channels and modes of operation, there must be an immediate sacrifice of present to future profit, and I do not doubt that the estate would have recovered from the momentary necessary interruption of its productiveness, to resume it with an upward instead of a downward tendency, and a vigorous impulse toward progress and improvement substituted for the present slow but sure drifting to stagnation and decay.

As I have told you, the land affords no spontaneous produce which will sustain life without labor. The Negroes, therefore, must work to eat; they are used to the soil and climate, and accustomed to the agriculture, and there is no reason at all to apprehend—as has been suggested—that a race of people singularly attached to the place of their birth and residence would abandon in any large numbers their own country, just as the conditions of their existence in it were made more favorable, to try the unknown and (to absolute ignorance) forbidding risks of emigration to the sterner climate and harder soil of the Northern states.

Of course, in freeing the slaves, it would be necessary to contemplate the possibility of their becoming eventual proprietors of the soil to some extent themselves. There is as little doubt that many of them would soon acquire the means of doing so (men who amass, during hours of daily extra labor, through years of unpaid toil, the means of buying themselves from their masters, would soon justify their freedom by the intelligent improvement of their condition), as that many of the present landholders would be ready and glad to alienate their impoverished estates by parcels, and sell the land which has become comparatively unprofitable to them, to its enfranchised cultivators. This, the future ownership of land by Negroes, as well as their admission to those rights of citizenship which everywhere in America such ownership involves, would necessarily be future subjects of legislation; and either or both privileges might be withheld temporarily, indefinitely, or permanently, as might seem expedient, and the progress in civilization which [took place] might justify such an extension of rights. These, and any other modifications of the state of the black population in the South, would require great wisdom to deal with, but their immediate transformation from bondsmen to free might, I think, be accomplished with little danger or difficulty, and with certain increase of prosperity to the Southern states.

On the other hand, it is not impossible that, left to the unimpeded action of the natural laws that govern the existence of various races, the black population, no longer directly preserved and propagated for the purposes of slavery, might gradually decrease and dwindle, as it does at the North, where, besides the unfavorable influence of a cold climate on a race originally African, it suffers from its admixture with the whites, and the amalgamation of the two races, as far as it goes, tends evidently to the destruction of the weaker. The Northern mulattoes are an unhealthy, feeble population, and it might yet appear that even under the more favorable influence of a Southern climate, whenever the direct stimulus afforded by slavery to the increase of the Negroes was removed, their gradual extinction or absorption by the predominant white race would follow in the course of time.

But the daily course of events appears to be rendering more and more unlikely the immediate effectual enfranchisement of the slaves: the President's proclamation will reach with but little efficacy beyond the mere borders of the Southern states. The war is assuming an aspect of indefinite duration; and it is difficult to conceive what will be the condition of the blacks, freed *de jure* but by no means *de facto,* in the vast interior regions of the Southern states, as long as the struggle raging all round their confines does not penetrate within them. Each of the combatants is far too busily absorbed in the furious strife to afford thought, leisure, or means either effectually to free the slaves or effectually to replace them in bondage; and, in the meantime, their condition is the worst possible for the future success of either operation. If the North succeeds in subjugating the South, its earliest business will be to make the freedom of the slaves real as well as nominal, and as little injurious to themselves as possible. If, on the other hand, the South makes good its pretensions to a separate national existence, no sooner will the disseverment of the Union be an established fact than the slaveholders will have to consolidate once more the system of their "peculiar institution," to reconstruct the prison which has half crumbled to the ground, and rivet afresh the chains which have been all but struck off. This will be difficult: the determination of the North to restrict the area of slavery by forbidding its ingress into future territories and states has been considered by the slaveholders a wrong, and a danger justifying a bloody civil war; inasmuch as, if under those circumstances they did not abolish slavery themselves in a given number of years, it would infallibly abolish them by the increase of the Negro population, hemmed with them into a restricted space by this *cordon sanitaire* drawn round them.

But, bad as this prospect has seemed to slaveholders (determined to continue such), and justifying—as it may be conceded that it does from their point of view—not a ferocious civil war, but a peaceable separation from states whose interests were declared absolutely irreconcilable with theirs, the position in which they will find themselves if the contest terminates in favor of secession will be undoubtedly more difficult and terrible than the one the mere anticipation of which has driven them to the dire resort of civil war.

All round the Southern coast, and all along the course of the great Mississippi, and all across the northern frontier of the slave states, the Negroes have already thrown off the trammels of slavery. Whatever their condition may be—and doubtless, in many respects, it is miserable enough—they are to all intents and purposes free. Vast numbers of them have joined the Northern invading armies, and considerable bodies of them have become organized as soldiers and laborers, under the supervision of Northern officers and employers; most of them have learned the use of arms, and possess them; all of them have exchanged the insufficient slave diet of grits and rice for the abundant supplies of animal food, which the poorest laborer in that favored land of cheap provisions and high wages indulges in to an extent unknown in any other country. None of these slaves of yesterday will be the same slaves tomorrow. Little essential difference as may yet have been effected by the President's proclamation in the interior of the South in the condition of the blacks, it is undoubtedly known to them, and they are waiting in ominous suspense its accomplishment or defeat by the fortune of the war; they are watching the issue of the contest of which they well know themselves to be the theme, and at its conclusion, end how it will, they must be emancipated or exterminated. With the North not only not friendly to slavery, but henceforward bitterly hostile to slaveholders, and no more to be reckoned upon as heretofore it might have been infallibly by the Southern white population in any difficulty with the blacks (a fact of which the Negroes will be as well aware as their former masters)—with an invisible boundary stretching from ocean to ocean, over which they may fly without fear of a master's claim following them a single inch; with the hope and expectation of liberty suddenly snatched from them at the moment it seemed within their grasp; with the door of their dungeon once more barred between them and the light into which they were in the act of emerging, is it to be conceived that these four millions of people, many thousands of whom are already free

and armed, will submit without a struggle to be again thrust down
into the hell of slavery?

Hitherto there has been no insurrection among the Negroes, and
observers friendly and inimical to them have alike drawn from
that fact conclusions unfavorable to their appreciation of the freedom apparently within their grasp; but they are waiting to see what
the North will really achieve for them. The liberty offered them is
hitherto anomalous, and uncertain enough in its conditions; they
probably trust it as little as they know it; but slavery they *do* know;
and when once they find themselves again delivered over to *that*
experience, there will not be ONE insurrection in the South—there
will be an insurrection in every state, in every county, on every
plantation—a struggle as fierce as it will be futile—a hopeless effort of hopeless men, which will baptize in blood the new American nation, and inaugurate its birth among the civilized societies
of the earth, not by the manumission, but the massacre of every
slave within its borders.

Perhaps, however, Mr. Jefferson Davis means to free the Negroes. Whenever that consummation is attained, the root of bitterness will have perished from the land; and when a few years shall
have passed, blunting the hatred which has been excited by this
fratricidal strife, the Americans of both the Northern and Southern states will perceive that the selfish policy of other nations
would not have so rejoiced over their division, had it not seemed,
to those who loved them not, the proof of past failure and the
prophecy of future weakness.

Admonished by its terrible experiences, I believe the nation will
reunite itself under one government, remodel its Constitution, and
again address itself to fulfill its glorious destiny. I believe that the
country sprung from ours—of all our just subjects of national pride
the greatest—will resume its career of prosperity and power, and
become the noblest as well as the mightiest that has existed among
the nations of the earth.

EDITOR'S APPENDIXES

APPENDIX C

A List of Persons Referred to in the Journal, with Biographical Notes[1]

ABBOTT, MARY (1792–1848). Wife of George Abbott and lived at Frederica, where Fanny Kemble visited her in April 1839.

ADAMS, JOHN QUINCY (1767–1848). Diplomat, diarist, son of John Adams who was the second President of the United States, and himself its sixth President, 1825–9. At the age of sixty-four, in 1831, he was elected to the House of Representatives and served there for seventeen years. In this period (1831–48) he rendered many public services, but in particular assumed the leadership, 1836–44, in the fight for the people's right to petition Congress on the matter of slavery.

ARMSTRONG, CAROLINE (d. 1855). This lady was the second wife of the St. Simons planter, William Armstrong, and occupied an estate directly adjoining the Butlers'.

[1] This list includes the names of all free persons mentioned in the *Journal* and in the Author's Appendices with the exception of one or two for whom positive identification could not be made. Where it has been judged helpful certain additional information has been provided: Mrs. Kemble's reference to Orallie Troup, e.g., makes necessary the listing of Dr. James McGillivray Troup; her reference to Sarah Spalding makes necessary the listing of Thomas Spalding, and so on.

The most valuable sources consulted in the preparation of these biographical notes are listed in the Bibliography. Almost all the material cited in that place yielded biographical data of significance.

BARRETT, JACOB. Rice planter who rented a portion of Champney's Island from Hugh Fraser Grant and who had his rice threshed at the Butler Island mill.

BARTOW, REV. THEO B. Rector of Christ Church, Frederica. He married Isabella Hamilton Couper, daughter of John Couper of Cannon's Point.

BOWEN, BISHOP NATHANIEL. Bishop of South Carolina, officiated as Bishop of the diocese of Georgia, which was organized in 1823, until the consecration of the first Bishop of Georgia, Stephen Elliott, on February 28, 1841.

BRAILSFORD, WILLIAM and MARIA. Came to Georgia in 1802 from South Carolina, buying Broughton Island and the adjacent mainland tract which they called New Hope. After the 1804 hurricane, which took the lives of many slaves, the decision was made to abandon Broughton—which was sold to Thomas Bryan (q.v.)—and to concentrate on New Hope, to which was later added the neighboring tract of Broadfield. William and Maria's daughter Camilla married Dr. James McGillivray Troup (q.v.) of Darien.

BROOKS, PRESTON (1819–57). Eldest son of Whitfield Brooks, plantation owner of Edgefield, South Carolina. Brooks was a representative to Congress from 1852 until his death. He delivered an attack on Senator Charles Sumner (q.v.) of Massachusetts on May 22, 1856, two days after Sumner, in his "Crime against Kansas" speech, had charged the South with aggression against free soil and had denounced Brooks's uncle, Senator A. P. Butler, for his part in this affair.

BRYAN, FLORIDA. See Troup, Florida.

BRYAN, THOMAS. Also known as Thomas Bryan Forman, was a rice planter who acquired Broughton Island from the Brailsfords (q.v.) in 1804. He married in 1835 Florida Troup (q.v.), whom Mrs. Kemble visited at Broughton in March 1839.

BUTLER, FRANCES KEMBLE (1838–1910). Younger daughter of Pierce Mease Butler and Frances Anne Kemble, "Fan" was born in the spring of 1838 and taken to Georgia with her parents as an infant-in-arms. Ideologically and emotionally closer to her father than to her mother, Fan struggled for ten years after the Civil War, first with her father, then after his death alone, and finally with her husband, to put the Altamaha estates back on a business footing. Not succeeding in this endeavor, she returned finally to England.

BUTLER, CAPTAIN JOHN (1806–47). Eldest son of Dr. James Mease and Sarah Butler of Philadelphia. Co-owner with his younger brother Pierce Mease Butler (q.v.) of the Hampton Point, Butler Island, and Woodville properties which the brothers inherited after the death of their grandfather Major Pierce Butler (q.v.) in 1822, and of their younger brother Thomas Mease in 1823.

BUTLER, MAJOR PIERCE (1744–1822). Of Irish origin, came to America in 1766 as a major in the British army, and married a South Carolina heiress, Polly Middleton, in 1771. Butler took the colonial side in the American Revolution, participated in the Constitutional Convention, and as a staunch Federalist was twice elected to the United States Senate. Between 1793 and 1800 he constituted the Hampton Point estate on St. Simons Island and purchased Butler Island. He planted sea-island cotton and made a fortune from it, part of which he invested in Philadelphia real estate and lands in western Pennsylvania. Butler had five children who survived him: four daughters, Sarah, Frances, Harriet, and Elizabeth; and a son, Thomas. Another son, Pierce Jr., died unmarried and without issue some time before 1800. Major Butler left the bulk of his wealth to Frances, who died unmarried and without issue, and to his grandchildren, among whom were Pierce and John Butler (q.v.). Thomas did not get much from his father's will; he had married a French woman, desired to live permanently in France, and bitterly resented his father's efforts to run his family affairs.

BUTLER, PIERCE MEASE (1810–67). Younger son of Dr. James

Mease and Sarah Butler of Philadelphia, and grandson of Major Pierce Butler (q.v.). Married Fanny Kemble in 1834 and came into possession of his grandfather's Georgia estates in 1836 at the death of his aunt Frances. Pierce Butler and his wife were divorced in 1849, and the father retained guardianship of the two children, Sarah and Frances (q.v.), until they should come of age. Butler was obliged to sell his slaves in 1859, but he retained ownership of the Georgia lands.

BUTLER, SARAH (1835–1908). Older daughter of Pierce Mease Butler and Fanny Kemble. As a child of three, was taken by her parents to the Georgia estate 1838–9. Sally married Dr. Owen Wister of Philadelphia, made her home in the United States, and became the mother of Owen Wister the novelist.

CHANNING, WILLIAM ELLERY (1780–1842). Minister of the Federal Street Church in Boston from 1803 until his death, architect of the Unitarian Association formed in 1825, and leader of the Unitarian movement, was one of the profoundest intellectual forces of his day, exercizing a deep influence on American theology and literature, and notably upon the transcendentalists. Channing was a champion of social change and liberal reform, which he believed could be accomplished by unleashing the "moral force" of the human soul. This position was expressed with matchless clarity in his little treatise *Slavery,* published in 1835, which helped to crystallize the thinking of Fanny Kemble prior to her visit to Georgia in 1838. As a man and a thinker Channing was the object of the actress's love and admiration. "After reading a sermon of his before going to bed the other night," she wrote in 1836 to Harriet St. Leger, "I dreamt toward morning that I was in Heaven. . . ."

CHAPMAN, DR. NATHANIEL (1780–1853). Born in Virginia, he studied medicine in Philadelphia under Benjamin Rush, and in Edinburgh. Was for half a century one of Philadelphia's most eminent physicians, and enjoyed the favor of an aristocratic clientele that included the Butler family.

CLAY, HENRY (1777–1852). From 1810 until the mid-century a major figure in American national politics and a leading spokesman for the National Republican and Whig Parties. Clay served in Congress as a Representative and then Senator from Kentucky with only short intervals from 1807 until his death. By 1839—when Fanny Kemble was "grinding her teeth" over his speech on slavery—Clay's early sympathies with the emancipation cause had given way to a conviction that abolitionism was a danger to the Union and to the efforts of reasonable men to find a *modus vivendi* between the North and the slaveowning South.

COUPER, ANN. See Fraser, Ann.

COUPER, JAMES HAMILTON (1794–1866). One of the leading planters of the Altamaha River estuary, was born at Sunbury, Georgia, the son of John Couper (q.v.) and Rebecca Maxwell. He graduated from Yale University in 1814, went to work for his father, and was given entire charge of the family's Hopeton plantation in 1816. By 1825 Hopeton, under his management, was considered the leading estate of the South and a showplace for visitors from other lands. In 1827, when John Couper sold the estate to his creditor and friend, James Hamilton, J. H. Couper acquired a half interest in it, together with 380 slaves, and became the manager of the property on yearly salary. In June 1838, he sailed on the *Pulaski* from Savannah in the company of Mrs. P. M. Nightingale (q.v.) and his sister, Ann Fraser (q.v.). He and his party were among the survivors when the ship blew up and foundered off the South Carolina coast with heavy loss of life. Retiring in 1852, Couper went to live at Altama, a portion of the Hopeton estate which he purchased from the Hamilton heirs. He married (1827) Caroline Georgia Wylly, daughter of Alexander Campbell Wylly (q.v.), and was the father of five sons and two daughters.

COUPER, JOHN (1759–1850). Was the owner of Cannon's Point, the estate adjacent to Pierce Butler's Hampton Point plantation at the northern extremity of St. Simons Island. The father, even as the son James Hamilton Couper (q.v.), was the object of Fanny Kemble's unstinted admiration. John Couper emigrated from Scotland in 1775, and on arriving in Georgia went into business with his friend, James Hamilton, after whom his son was named. In the 1790's Couper purchased large tracts of land in the Altamaha River estuary, acquired Cannon's Point, and built a permanent home on St. Simons Island some time after 1804. He retained possession of the mainland estate of Hopeton until 1827 when, on his own account, severe business reverses caused him to surrender the property to his chief creditor, Hamilton. But he continued to live in comfort on St. Simons Island. He corresponded with Thomas Jefferson and became renowned as a horticulturist and agricultural experimenter. He owned not only Cannon's Point but Long Island (now known as Sea Island), which he used as a cattle pasture. Many of his slaves were carried off by the British when they raided St. Simons in 1814.

DAVIS, JEFFERSON (1808–89). Mississippi planter, President of the Confederate States of America, 1861–5. Before the Civil War served as a United States Senator, and—1853–7—as Secretary for War.

DEMERE, ANN (1786–1847). Was the widow of Raymond Demere, grandson of Captain Raymond Demere who was one of the original settlers on St. Simons Island. The family owned two estates; Harrington Hall, in the center of the Island, and a mile to the south of German Village; and Mulberry Grove, near the southeastern extremity of the Island. It was at Mulberry Grove that Mrs. Kemble visited Ann Demere and her sons.

FRASER, ANN. Oldest child of John Couper of Cannon's Point and wife of Captain John Fraser (q.v.). When Mrs. Kemble visited St. Simons the Frasers were residing at Hamilton plantation, of which Captain Fraser was the manager. Mrs. Kemble, with whom Ann was evidently on good terms, described her as "a kindhearted, intelligent woman," and, for her gifts of flowers, fruit, fish, and meat from the Hamilton estate, "a perfect Lady Bountiful to us."

FRASER, CAPTAIN JOHN (d. 1839). Was a British officer who made the acquaintance of the Sea Islands during the War of 1812, met and fell in love with Ann Couper (q.v.), and decided to settle on St. Simons Island. He purchased Lawrence, a small estate about one mile south of Cannon's Point, but at the time of Mrs. Kemble's visit he and his wife were residing at Hamilton estate, of which he was the manager for the owner Agnes Rebecca Hamilton, daughter of James Hamilton (q.v.). It was Captain Fraser who conducted Basil and Margaret Hall (q.v.) around the Altamaha River plantations when the Halls visited Georgia in the spring of 1828. Fraser died at Hamilton shortly after Mrs. Kemble's visit in 1839.

FRASER, DR. WILLIAM. Brother of Captain John Fraser, settled on St. Simons Island in 1812 at the small estate of Sinclair. Married Frances, daughter of Alexander Campbell Wylly (q.v.) of German Village, and removed to Darien, where he was living at the time that Captain Basil and Mrs. Hall visited the area in 1828. William, like his brother a British officer, had been a navy surgeon.

GOWEN, MR. and MRS. Supervisors of the Hampton Point estate at the time of Fanny Kemble's residence there. Gowen resigned his position shortly after Pierce Mease Butler and his wife returned to Philadelphia.

GRANT, DR. ROBERT (1762–1843). An immigrant from Scotland, arrived in South Carolina sometime toward the end of the American Revolution and married Sarah Foxworth, a member of one of the state's leading families. Grant established his residence on St. Simons Island in the 1790's, and began to secure title to swamplands on the south bank of the Altamaha River. By 1825 he had consolidated 1500 acres into a plantation that he named Elizafield and that lay on the mainland directly to the south of Champney and Butler Islands. Grant retired in 1833 and returned to the small estate of Oatlands in the northeastern section of St. Simons Island; and he was in residence there at the time of Mrs. Kemble's visit. He had four sons, one of whom, Hugh Fraser Grant (q.v.), had a successful career as owner and manager of Elizafield. Dr. Grant was also a warden of Christ Church.

GRANT, MRS. SARAH. Wife of Dr. Robert Grant of Oatlands on St. Simons Island, and of Elizafield.

GRANT, HUGH FRASER (1811–73). Son of Dr. Robert Grant (q.v.). Inherited a portion of his father's Elizafield rice plantation on the south bank of the Altamaha River adjacent to Pierce Butler's Butler Island and Woodville. When Fanny Kemble visited Georgia in 1839, Hugh Fraser Grant was known as one of the leading rice producers of the Georgia coast.

GREVILLE, CHARLES CAVENDISH FULKE (1794–1865). English aristocrat, horse fancier, and political go-between, whose diaries for the years 1814–60 have been described as "the most important work of their kind of his generation." Greville saw a good deal of the Butlers when they visited England 1840–3. He expressed an acute disapproval of Fanny for pursuing her will-o'-the-wisp ideals and for neglecting to study and improve the character of her "weak, dawdling, ignorant, violent-tempered" husband. Greville's memoirs abounded with tart comments on everyone who was anyone, including royalty. An unexpurgated edition did not appear until 1938.

HALL, CAPTAIN BASIL (1788–1844). British naval officer and explorer, visited North America with his wife, Margaret, and his daughter, Eliza, in 1827–8, and published in 1829 a three-volume account of his experiences entitled *Travels in North America*. One volume of this work was devoted to the South. Hall visited Butler and St. Simons Island March 14 to 18 in the company of Captain John Fraser (q.v.), brother of his friend Dr. William Fraser (q.v.) of Darien.

HALL, MARGARET (1799–1876). Wife of Captain Basil Hall

(q.v.), accompanied him on his American trip in 1827–8 and made her own profound and interesting observations in a voluminous series of letters to her sister Jane. Only excerpts from these letters, which are in the possession of the Library of Congress, have been published.

HAMILTON, JAMES. Fell into the same category as John Couper, Major Pierce Butler, and Major William Page as one of the largest property owners on St. Simons Island. Hamilton established his estate on the southwestern shore of the island, at Gascoigne's Bluff, and was one of the first planters to grow sea-island cotton on the Georgia coast soon after the Revolution. He made a fortune from these operations, disposed of much of his coastal property, and moved to Philadelphia. Hamilton Plantation was thereafter administered by James Hamilton Couper on behalf of Hamilton's daughter, Agnes Rebecca.

HAZZARD, DR. THOMAS FULLER (1797–1857). Younger son of Major William Hazzard, who moved to St. Simons Island from South Carolina after the Revolution. Dr. Hazzard made his home at Pike's Bluff, a plantation more than a mile to the north of Fort Frederica, overlooking the Frederica River; and he was living there at the time of Mrs. Kemble's visit to St. Simons in 1839. A month before the actress's arrival in Georgia, Hazzard had met his neighbor, John Armstrong Wylly (q.v.), in Brunswick, and a quarrel ensued which resulted in Wylly's death.

HAZZARD, COLONEL WILLIAM WHIGG (1795–1862). Elder son of Major William Hazzard. Made his home at West Point Plantation, between Pike's Bluff and Fort Frederica on St. Simons Island, where he was residing at the time of Mrs. Kemble's visit. Hazzard was a principal in the group of associates who built the Brunswick-Altamaha Canal.

HILDRETH, RICHARD (1807–65). Massachusetts journalist, lawyer, polemicist, and historian, was the author of the very popular antislavery novel *The Slave: or Memoirs of Archy Moore*

(1836); a *History of the United States* (1849–52); and numerous pamphlets.

HOLMES, DR. JAMES. Darien physician and leading citizen, who attended the slaves on Pierce Mease Butler's Butler Island estate, and whose acquaintance Fanny Kemble made in January 1839.

JACKSON, ANDREW (1767–1845). Tennessee planter, hero of the War of 1812, seventh President of the United States, 1829–37. Under his administration popular participation in political, social, and reform movements reached its height in an era which is summarized by the label "Jacksonian Democracy." Jackson opposed the pretensions of South Carolina in the tariff conflict of 1832–3, championing the supremacy of Federal law over states' rights in a classic presidential message. The same President, Supreme Court decisions to the contrary notwithstanding, made no opposition to the confiscation of Creek and Cherokee lands by the State of Georgia and to the extension of slavery into the areas thus acquired.

KEMBLE, CHARLES (1775–1854). A noted Shakespearian actor, was the youngest son of Roger Kemble, a strolling player. In 1806 Charles married Marie Thérèse De Camp, herself from childhood a dancer and actress, and had five children, of whom Frances Anne was the third (the eldest, Philip, died in infancy). Kemble became manager of the Covent Garden Theatre in London in 1822 in the place of his brother John Philip, but did not make a business success of the venture. Financial pressure induced him to put his daughter on the stage as Juliet in 1829 and to undertake an American tour with her in 1832–4. Frances Anne, who may have been biased, but who had excellent dramatic judgment, said of him that "he was one of the best Romeos, and incomparably *the* best Mercutio, that ever trod the English stage."

KING, ANNA MATILDA (d. 1859). Daughter of Major William

Page, from whom she inherited Retreat Plantation, one of the largest St. Simons Island estates, located on the southernmost tip of the island. In 1823 she married Thomas Butler King (q.v.) of Hartford, Connecticut, and administered Retreat in his absence on state and national political activities. She has been called Georgia's "most noted woman agriculturist," and she developed a Retreat variety of sea-island cotton.

KING, ROSWELL, SR. (1763–1844). Born in Windsor, Connecticut, was the great-great-grandson of John King, one of the original settlers of Northampton, Massachusetts. King came to Georgia in 1788 and married in 1792 Catherine Barrington, member of a family that resided in the Darien locality. In 1803 King was employed by Thomas Spalding (q.v.) to build his South End home on Sapelo Island. The year previously he had become manager of Major Pierce Butler's estates and retained this position until his resignation in 1838. After Major Butler's death in 1822, King became a co-administrator of the Butler estate along with the Major's daughter Frances; from the latter he borrowed $10,000 in 1825 for the furthering of his local real estate transactions. A settlement of this debt was made only after a court action between King and Frances's heirs that lasted from 1838–44. After Major Butler's death, King left the main burden of management to his son Roswell, Jr. (q.v.), and concerned himself more with the advancement of his other interests. On leaving the Butlers' service he founded the town of Roswell, near Atlanta, where he and his son Barrington had acquired large tracts of land. King was a director of the Bank of Darien and one of that town's leading citizens.

KING, ROSWELL, JR. (1795– ?). The second son of Roswell King, Sr. and Catherine Barrington, grew up on the Butler estate, whose management in early manhood he shared with his father and the main burden of which he assumed after Major Butler's death in 1822. King resigned his position in 1838, shortly before the arrival in Georgia of Fanny Kemble and her husband; but sometime between 1839 and 1844 he resumed the position again and retained it at least until 1854.

KING, THOMAS BUTLER (1800–64). Originally from Palmer, Massachusetts, he studied law in Philadelphia and then settled in Georgia. Married, 1834, Anna Matilda, only daughter of Major William Page of St. Simons Island and owner of one of the Island's largest plantations, Retreat. King then embarked on a political career and became a figure in both state and national politics. He was a leading force in the promotion of the Brunswick and Altamaha Canal Project, and became President of the company in 1840.

LEWIS, MATTHEW GREGORY (1775–1818). Achieved a certain success as the writer of romantic novels, of which the most popular was *The Monk*. On his father's death in 1812 he inherited two estates, Cornwall and Hordley, in Jamaica, together with the slaves that toiled upon them. Being a man of conscience he was opposed to absenteeism and wished to see for himself how his property was being handled. He, therefore, paid Jamaica two visits and worked out a humane code for the treatment of his slaves, but died of yellow fever on returning from the West Indies in 1818. His most important legacy is the *Journal of a West India Proprietor* that deals with his experiences in the years 1815–18, and that was published in London in 1834 in time to serve as a model for Fanny Kemble.

LORRAIN, CLAUDE (1600–82). French painter renowned for his landscapes.

MCDUFFIE, GEORGE (1790–1851). Member of the House of Representatives from South Carolina 1821–34, and governor of the State of South Carolina 1834–8. A champion of states rights and also of slavery, he fired the opening gun in the South's counterattack against abolitionism with the setting forth of his "positive good" theory of slavery in his message to the South Carolina Assembly in 1835. "No human institution," said the

Governor, "in my opinion, is more manifestly consistent with the will of God, than domestic slavery. . . . That the African Negro is destined by Providence to occupy this condition of servile dependence, is not less manifest. It is marked on the face, stamped on the skin, and evinced by the intellectual inferiority and natural improvidence of this race."

MARTINEAU, HARRIET (1802–76). English story writer who became a literary lion in 1832. She was closely connected with the Philosophic Radicals of England, one of whose ideological spokesmen she was. Sailing to the United States in 1834, she made a tour of the South that winter and then visited other parts of the country before returning to England in the fall of 1836. She met Fanny Kemble in Philadelphia in 1834, but never really approved of the actress, though she tried her best to do so. Her impressions of America were published in 1837 in a two volume work, *Society in America.*

MEASE, BUTLER (1810–67). Youngest son of Sarah Butler and Dr. James Mease of Philadelphia. Changed his name after his grandfather's death in 1822 to Pierce Butler, in accordance with a provision in Major Pierce Butler's will. See Butler, Pierce Mease.

MEASE, JOHN (1806–47). Fourth child of Sarah Butler and Dr. James Mease of Philadelphia. Changed his name in 1836 to John Butler (q.v.).

MILLER, WILLIAM (1782–1849). Emerged in the 1830's as a revivalist leader in the United States, prophesying the second coming of Christ and the end of the world. His campaign reached its climax in 1842–4, when many people quit their jobs and left the crops unharvested in the expectation of an imminent day of judgment.

MILLOT, CLAUDE FRANÇOIS XAVIER (1726–85). Jesuit, historian, educator, and *philosophe,* of whom d'Alembert said: "You have my word for it that there's nothing clerical about him except the clothes." He wrote surveys of both French and English history, which a young student might have been pardoned for finding dull.

MOORE, ELY (1798–1860). Labor leader and from 1835 to 1839 Representative to Congress from New York City as a Tammany candidate then as a fusion candidate of Tammany and the Equal Rights party.

NIGHTINGALE, P. M. Georgia Sea-Island planter who lived at Dungeness on Cumberland Island. He appears in Fanny Kemble's *Journal* along with Hugh Fraser Grant as a contractor for the building of the Brunswick-Altamaha Canal.

NIGHTINGALE, MRS. P. M. Wife of P. M. Nightingale (q.v.), who made the trip on the *Pulaski* in 1838 with James Hamilton Couper, and was one of the survivors when the boat blew up and foundered off the coast of South Carolina.

O——, MR. Became the overseer of the Butler Island estate in 1838 with the departure of the Roswell Kings. His previous service had been on John Couper's estate on St. Simons Island.

O'BRIEN, MARGERY. Fanny Kemble's Irish nursemaid, who accompanied the Butler family on the trip to Georgia in 1838–9, and who was in charge of Sally and Fan Butler.

OGLETHORPE, JAMES EDWARD (1696–1785). Soldier, Jacobite, humanitarian, founder of the colony of Georgia. To this latter venture he gave all his energies in the years from 1733–43. He brought over Charles and John Wesley (q.v.) to serve the colony's spiritual needs, and in 1736 founded Frederica on St. Simons Island to serve as a military outpost against the threat of Spanish invasion from the South.

ST. LEGER, HARRIET. One of Fanny Kemble's intimate friends, with whom she carried on a lifelong correspondence. There is little reliable information about Harriet, except that she was a member of a "good" Irish family and lived her life out at Ardgillan Castle, on a hill near the Mourne mountains. Here from time to time Mrs. Kemble visited her. Fanny first met Harriet in 1825, and described her as ". . . the dearest friend I have ever known . . . . Tall and thin, her figure wanted roundness and grace, but it was as straight as a dart, and the vigorous, elastic, active movement of her limbs, and firm, fleet, springing step of her beautifully made feet and ankles, gave to her whole person and deportment a character like that of the fabled Atalanta, or the huntress Diana herself."

SEDGWICK, CATHARINE MARIA (1789–1867). Berkshire Hills novelist, daughter of Theodore Sedgwick, eminent Federalist and revolutionary leader, was born and lived for much of her life at Stockbridge, Massachusetts. Never marrying herself, she lavished her affection upon her married brothers and sisters and their children, passing many summers in the company of Charles and Elizabeth Sedgwick (q.v.) at their home in Lenox a few miles from Stockbridge. When Fanny Kemble came to America in 1832, Catharine Maria was already one of the most popular writers in the country and numbered many of the outstanding literary and intellectual figures of the day among her friends. It was she who, as a devotee of William Ellery Channing, introduced Mrs. Kemble to the great New England divine in 1833. Her novels, especially *Redwood, Clarence,* and *Hope Leslie,* may still be read with pleasure and instruction.

SEDGWICK, CATHARINE MARIA, JR. Born about 1820, "Kitty" was the oldest child of Elizabeth Dwight Sedgwick and the niece of Catharine Maria Sedgwick. Also a favorite of Fanny's, Kitty baby-sat for her and accompanied the actress in her rambles over the Berkshire hills.

SEDGWICK, ELIZABETH BUCKMINSTER DWIGHT (1801–64). The woman to whom Fanny Kemble's Georgia *Journal* was dedicated was born at Northampton, Massachusetts, the third child of Josiah Dwight, merchant and Hampshire County official, and Rhoda Edwards, the daughter of Colonel Timothy Edwards and the granddaughter of Jonathan Edwards. Elizabeth married, 1819, Charles, son of Theodore and brother of Catharine Maria Sedgwick (q.v.). Elizabeth and her husband became intimate friends of Mrs. Kemble, who visited them often in their Lenox home, carried on a correspondence with them for many years and, after her divorce in 1849, bought a cottage in Lenox and came to live during the summers near her friends. From 1828 until her death, Elizabeth conducted an elementary school in her own home, wrote a number of books for children, and came to be widely known as an educator. Of her five children, only three daughters, Elizabeth Dwight, Grace, and Catharine Maria, survived her. William was killed at Antietam and Charles died young.

SMITH, REVEREND. Conducted a Baptist Church at Darien for Negro slaves. This church was attended by slaves from the Butler estate and received a regular financial contribution from the latter.

SPALDING, SARAH LEAKE (1778–1843). Only daughter of Richard Leake, wealthy Georgia planter. Married Thomas Spalding (q.v.) in 1795, and bore him sixteen children, eleven of whom died in infancy or early youth. Was in residence at her home in Ashantilly, near Darien, where Fanny Kemble visited her in February 1839.

SPALDING, THOMAS (1774–1851). Son of James Spalding, a St. Simons Island planter who was a pioneer in the cultivation of sea-island cotton. In 1802 Thomas acquired huge land holdings on Sapelo Island and brought together a slave force from Charleston and from the West Indies. He became one of the wealthiest and most influential men in McIntosh County. Ashantilly near Darien was his home on the mainland.

STOWE, HARRIET BEECHER (1811–96). Author of *Uncle Tom's Cabin* (1852) and *Dred* (1856), antislavery novels, the first of which made her an international celebrity.

SUMNER, CHARLES (1811–74). United States Senator, lawyer, and orator from Boston, Massachusetts, who devoted his life to the struggle against slavery and to the emancipation of the slaves. From 1852–6 he became a dominant figure in the U.S.

Senate with his onslaughts upon proslavery bills, and was in these years one of the architects of the Republican party. In 1861 he was appointed Chairman of the Committee on Foreign Relations and became the acknowledged Senatorial leader of the radical republican group that demanded emancipation of the slaves, Congressional reconstruction of the South, and voting rights and freehold land for the emancipated slaves. He was an intimate of Fanny Kemble and, like her, a devotee of William Ellery Channing. Sumner first met the actress at Lenox in 1844. He was so entranced by her company that he made off with his host's horse, which he knew should not have been used on the Sabbath, in order to take a long Sunday ride with Fanny.

TROUP, FLORIDA. Daughter of George Michael Troup (q.v.), married Thomas Bryan of Broughton Island in 1835. Mrs. Kemble visited her there in 1839. Before her marriage, Florida and her sister Orallie (q.v.) lived for many years with their uncle, Dr. James McGillivray Troup (q.v.) at Darien; and it was from her uncle's house that Florida was married. She died young after bearing five children, one of whom, Georgia Bryan Conrad, later wrote the *Reminiscences* that have some value in the study of the history of the Sea Islands.

TROUP, GEORGE MICHAEL (1780–1856). Son of a wealthy Georgia merchant, grew up at his father's estate of Belleville, near Savannah. Governor of Georgia 1824–8, Democrat, and ardent champion of states rights and nullification during the tariff crisis of 1832–3. Served in the United States Senate 1829–33, retiring to devote himself to his numerous Georgia plantations. Troup ranked with Pierce Mease Butler as one of the wealthiest slave-owners in Georgia. Of his six children, two daughters and a son reached maturity.

TROUP, DR. JAMES McGILLIVRAY (d. 1849). Brother of George Michael Troup (q.v.), planter physician, and one of the most prominent men in McIntosh County. He resided at Troup House in Darien, and married Camilla Brailsford, daughter of William and Maria Brailsford (q.v.) of New Hope and Broadfield. The Troups had four daughters (Ophelia, Hannah, Clelia, and Matilda) and also served *in loco parentum* to Florida and Orallie Troup (q.v.), who lived with them at Darien for a number of years.

TROUP, ORALLIE. Daughter of George Michael Troup. Mrs. Kemble visited her at her uncle's home in Darien in 1839, and remarked upon her good looks. Orallie's cousin Ophelia recalled that she "was like a queen in her beauty . . . ." At her father's death she inherited her own plantation of Turkey Creek, near Rome, Georgia, but, it seems, did not marry.

TUNNO, DR. J. CHAMPNEY. Owner of Champney's Island, otherwise known as Tunno's Island, in the Altamaha River estuary adjacent to Butler Island. Though Tunno cultivated the island, it was owned by Hugh Fraser Grant at the time of Mrs. Kemble's visit. Transfer of ownership from Grant to Tunno took place in December 1839.

VAN BUREN, MARTIN (1782–1862). Eighth President of the United States, 1837–41. He had become the running mate of Andrew Jackson in the election of 1832, and it was upon his shoulders that the mantle of Jacksonian Democracy fell in 1836 with Jackson's retirement from active politics. For the following ten years Southerners may well have felt ambivalent about Van Buren, for he was a champion of states rights at the same time as an opponent of the extension of slavery to new soil. In 1848 he removed all doubts about his position on the slavery issue by accepting the nomination of the newly-formed Free Soil party as its presidential candidate.

WESLEY, JOHN (1703–91). Evangelical leader and founder of Methodism. Spent two years in the Southern colonies 1736–7, most of the time in Georgia, to which he was brought by James Oglethorpe (q.v.) to be the colony's spiritual adviser. Wesley visited Frederica a number of times and preached there. In later years he contributed through his sermons and writings to the growth of antislavery sentiment in England.

WHITLOCK, ELIZABETH (1761–1836). Sister of Charles Kemble (q.v.) and Fanny Kemble's aunt. As an actress she toured the United States in the early 1790's and was thought to have considerable talent. Fanny, with characteristic irreverence, dubbed her "a very worthy but exceedingly ridiculous woman, in whom the strong peculiarities of her family were so exaggerated that she really seemed like a living parody of all the Kembles."

WYLLY, ALEXANDER CAMPBELL (1759– ?). Georgia Tory, fled to the Bahamas at the end of the Revolution, married Margaret Armstrong, and moved back to Georgia in 1807, buying an estate at German Village on St. Simons Island. One son, Alexander William, married Elizabeth, daughter of Thomas Spalding (q.v.) of Sapelo. A daughter, Caroline Georgia, married James Hamilton Couper (q.v.), and another daughter, Frances, married Dr. William Fraser (q.v.).

WYLLY, JOHN ARMSTRONG (d. December 3, 1838). Younger son of Alexander Campbell Wylly (q.v.), was living with his widowed mother in 1838 on the family's German Village estate on St. Simons Island. In that year a feud broke out between Wylly and his neighbors the Hazzards (q.v.) over the boundary line dividing their respective estates. A chance encounter in Brunswick between Wylly and Dr. Thomas Hazzard led to a quarrel which resulted in Wylly's death on December 3, just four weeks before Fanny Kemble's arrival at Butler Island.

WYLLY, MARGARET ARMSTRONG (d. 1850). Wife of Alexander Campbell Wylly (q.v.), and mother of John Armstrong Wylly (q.v.). Mrs. Wylly was a member of the West Indian Armstrong family, and a noted beauty. At the time of Mrs. Kemble's visit to St. Simons Island she was widowed and living at German Village with her unmarried daughters.

APPENDIX D

Bibliographical Notes

This is a selected bibliography which includes the more important sources consulted in the preparation of this edition, but does not include all citations made in footnotes.

MAPS

The appropriate quadrangles of the 1:24,000 Geological Survey are Darien, Altamaha Sound, Brunswick East, and Sea Island. On the 1:62,500 scale only the Brunswick Quadrangle, which covers the southern part of St. Simons Island, is available. These maps may be obtained from the U.S. Geological Survey, Washington 25, D.C.

The charts of the U.S. Coast and Geodetic Survey are available on 1:40,000 and 1:80,000 scale, and are exceedingly useful for the study of the sea-island coast of Georgia and the Altamaha estuary. The appropriate quadrangles are Altamaha Sound and St. Simons Sound (1:40,000). Tybee Island to Doboy Sound, and Doboy Sound to Fernandina quadrangles (1:80,000), cover the entire Georgia coastline. These charts are obtainable from the Coast and Geodetic Survey, Washington 25, D.C.

The aerial survey maps of the Soil Conservation Service were of considerable value in the preparation of maps for this edition of the *Journal*. For St. Simons Island and Little St. Simons the appropriate sections are DSF-1L-125, 127, 206, DSF-2L-61, and DSF-8L-42; for Butler Island, the section showing the location of the old slave settlements is DSE-3L-72. These sheets are obtainable from the Reproduction Branch of the Division of Cartography, Soil Conservation Service, Beltsville, Maryland. These surveys may be supplemented by the appropriate section of the topographic survey made in 1869 by the U.S. Coast and Geodetic Survey. Register No. 1114 covers the northern part of St. Simons Island, Little St. Simons Island, and the western section of Butler Island. Photographic copies of No. 1114 are available from the Coast and Geodetic Survey, Washington 25, D.C.

A final map source used in the preparation of this edition was the manuscript "Butler Island, Altamaha River, Georgia, U.S.A.," dated January 1877, in the possession of Altamaha Waterfowl Management authorities on Butler Island. A photocopy of this map has been deposited with the Women's Archives of Radcliffe College, Cambridge, Massachusetts.

UNPUBLISHED SOURCE MATERIALS

The Folger Shakespeare Library, Washington, D.C. has over ninety autograph letters of Fanny Kemble's, many of them relating to the period before the Civil War, and a collection of sketches of the actress as Juliet made by John Hayter. One of the richest collections of Butler-Kemble manuscripts in the country is in the possession of the Historical Society of Pennsylvania. This material is not centralized in one place, but must be looked for under the following headings: Butler Papers, 1771–1900; H. E. Drayton Collection, boxes entitled Frances Butler Papers and Thomas Butler Estate; Cadwalader Collection, under Thomas, John, and George Cadwalader, and the McCall Legal Section; and the Simon Gratz Collection. Twenty-nine letters written by Mrs. Kemble to Mr. and Mrs. Charles B. Sedgwick, in the period from 1848 to 1868, are in the Columbia University Library. There are two autograph letters in the Fraser-Couper Family Papers of the Georgia Historical Society. Some Kemble correspondence is scattered among the Sedgwick Papers, in the possession of the Massachusetts Historical Society, but not yet catalogued. This collection, of course, is a fundamental source for the study of Mrs. Kemble's relationships with New England antislavery circles. It contains on deposit the manuscript journals of Catharine Maria Sedgwick. Many other institutions, including the Library of Congress (Cushman Correspondence), the Lenox and Stockbridge Library Associations, the New York Historical Society, and the Harvard College Library, have collections of Kemble materials. A very valuable collection at the time of writing (1960) is still in private hands, that of Mrs. Margaret Davis Cate of St. Simons Island. This collection includes records of the Butler Island estate, 1844–55, and probably the only surviving copy of the local newspaper, the Brunswick *Advocate,* for the period in which Mrs. Kemble was in Georgia.

Columbia University has, at the time of writing, made available a number of uncatalogued Kemble Mss., including a copy of Fanny's *Journal* (published in 1835) that contains her own manuscript notes and supplies a key to many of the blanks left in the text.

PUBLISHED WORKS AND CORRESPONDENCE OF F. A. KEMBLE

Much of Fanny Kemble's published writing is autobiographical. Almost all of it was of help in editing the *Journal.* The actress's autobiography is contained, in successive instalments, in: *Records of a Girlhood,* 3 vols., London: 1878–9, and New York: 1879; *Journal,* 2 vols., London and Philadelphia: 1835; *Records of Later Life,* 3 vols., London: 1882, and New York: 1882; *Journal of a Residence on a Georgian Plantation,* 1838–1839, London and New York: 1863; *A Year of Consolation,* London: 1847, and New York: 1849; and *Further Records,* 2 vols., London: 1890, and New York; 1891. Also of autobiographical value are *Notes upon Some of Shakespeare's Plays,* London: 1882, and collections of poems published at various times in London, Philadelphia, and Boston.

BIOGRAPHIES OF F. A. KEMBLE

Fanny Kemble awaits the biographer. Existing studies touch only aspects of her life, and none of them has tapped the rich manuscript material available in the United States. Dorothy Bobbé's *Fanny Kemble,* New York: 1931, is anecdotal. Leota Driver's study of the same title, Chapel Hill, N.C.: 1933, exalts outer fact at the expense of inner meaning. Margaret Armstrong's *Fanny Kemble, A Passionate Victorian,* New York: 1938, is a useful narrative, more readable than Driver, but suffering essentially from the same weaknesses. No focus is given to the actress's life, the Georgia experience is treated in a cursory and academic fashion, and the social context in which Fanny lived, moved, and had her being, is not made apparent. Henry Gibbs: *Affectionately Yours, Fanny,* London: 1946, concentrates on the earlier years of her life, in particular upon its theatrical aspects. Mme Auguste Craven: *La Jeunesse de Fanny Kemble,* Paris: 1880; translated as *Fanny Kemble,* Paris: 1888, deals primarily with Fanny's own *Records of a Girlhood.* Una Pope-Hennessy: *Three English Women in America,* London: 1929, is a sketch which is often inaccurate in detail, and of little value for Fanny's American experience. Of all the biographers, Henrietta Buckmaster alone grasps the centrality in Fanny's life of the moral conflict over slavery. Her study, *Fire in the Heart,* New York: 1948, deals with the early period, 1809–39, but, unfortunately, it is highly fictionalized. This is a pity since, in the case of Fanny Kemble, truth is much stranger than fiction and a good deal more interesting. Lacking a basis in solid study, Buckmaster's work has a thin and abstract quality doubly disappointing in the author of *Let My People Go.* Janet

Stevenson: *The Ardent Years,* New York: 1960, follows Buckmaster, and is subject to some of the same criticisms. As a novel it
shows some interesting insights, but Fanny Kemble is not brought
to life. A passionate, articulate, and essentially English genius does
not emerge from these pages. Part Four, or more than one quarter
of the whole book, is devoted to what is a rather pallid paraphrase
of the Georgia *Journal.* Mrs. Stevenson here repeats some of
Fanny's original errors, and adds not a few of her own.

F. A. KEMBLE: THE ANTISLAVERY BACKGROUND

For British abolitionist literature and its West Indian back-
ground, see Joseph Lowell Ragatz: *A Guide for the Study of British Caribbean History, 1763–1834, Including the Abolition and
Emancipation Movements,* Washington, D.C.: 1932, being vol.
III of the Annual Report of the American Historical Association,
1930. Helpful studies not included in this excellent bibliography
are J. H. Parry and P. M. Sherlock: *A Short History of the West
Indies,* London: 1956, and Eric Williams: *Capitalism and Slavery,*
Chapel Hill, N.C.: 1947.

For purposes of editing the Georgia *Journal,* study of Mrs. Kem-
ble's relationships with intellectual and antislavery circles in the
North was limited to her connections with W. E. Channing and the
Sedgwicks. For the former's life and writings, see the *Works of
William Ellery Channing,* Boston: 1886, and Arthur W. Brown:
*Always Young for Liberty: A Biography of William Ellery Chan-
ning,* Syracuse: 1956. For a touching introduction to Catharine
Maria Sedgwick upon whom, as the author points out, W. E.
Channing "had set the seal of his blessing," see Gladys Brooks:
Three Wise Virgins, New York: 1957. Catharine Maria's own
works must still be read in connection with the study of Fanny
Kemble, and they may be with enjoyment as well as profit, notably
A New England Tale, Redwood, Travellers, Hope Leslie, and
Clarence, New York: 1822, 1824, 1825, 1827, and 1830 respec-
tively. Indirectly of value for a study of the authoress is the essay

upon her father, Theodore, by H. D. Sedgwick: "The Sedgwicks of Berkshire," in vol. III of the Berkshire Historical and Scientific Society's *Collections,* Pittsfield, Mass.: 1900. *The Life and Letters of Catharine Maria Sedgwick,* Mary E. Dewey, ed., New York: 1871, is invaluable. Elizabeth Dwight Sedgwick's family relationships are made clear in Benjamin Dwight: *The History of the Descendants of John Dwight, of Dedham, Massachusetts,* New York: 1874. See also Elizabeth's own writings, in particular *A Talk with My Pupils,* New York: 1862.

There is unfortunately no published guide to the literature of the antislavery movement in the United States in the 1830's, in the context of which Mrs. Kemble must be seen and understood. But in connection with the Christian attitude toward slavery and the great debate over slavery, which are closely linked to a study of the *Journal,* the following are of especial use: Gilbert Hobbs Barnes: *The Antislavery Impulse 1830–44,* New York: 1933, reissued Gloucester, Mass.: 1957; Dwight Lowell Dumond: *Antislavery Origins of the Civil War,* Ann Arbor, Mich.: 1939, reissued as a paperback, 1959; Russel B. Nye: *Fettered Freedom: Civil Liberties and the Slavery Controversy,* East Lansing, Mich.: 1949; Jacobus tenBroek: *The Antislavery Origins of the Fourteenth Amendment,* Berkeley, Cal.: 1951; and William Sumner Jenkins: *ProSlavery Thought in the Old South,* Chapel Hill, N.C.: 1935.

F. A. KEMBLE: THE SOUTHERN EXPERIENCE

Burnette Vanstory: *Georgia's Land of the Golden Isles,* Athens, Ga.: 1956 and Caroline Couper Lovell: *The Golden Isles of Georgia,* Boston: 1932 combine an excellent introductory picture with a great deal of specific information on the families of the Altamaha River region. A number of memoirs focus upon the St. Simons Island region and the history of its leading families. Charles Spalding Wylly, related through both his mother and father to the leading families of St. Simons and Sapelo islands, wrote *Annals and Statistics of Glynn County, Georgia,* Georgia: 1897, and *The Seed*

That Was Sown in the Colony of Georgia: the Harvest and the Aftermath, 1740–1870, New York and Washington: 1910; Georgia Bryan Conrad, daughter of Thomas Bryan, owner of Broughton Island, wrote *Reminiscences of a Southern Woman,* Hampton, Va.: n.d.; Frances Butler Leigh, younger daughter of Pierce Butler and Fanny Kemble, wrote *Ten Years on a Georgia Plantation Since the War,* London: 1883. Of more recent works, Albert V. House: *Planter Management and Capitalism in Ante-Bellum Georgia: the Journal of Hugh Fraser Grant, Rice Grower,* New York: 1954, stands in a class by itself as a study in rice culture, as the publication of a significant plantation journal, and as a guide to sources. E. Merton Coulter: *Thomas Spalding of Sapelo,* University, La.: 1941, contains valuable information. Thomas P. Govan: "Was Plantation Slavery Profitable?" *Journal of Southern History,* VIII, (November, 1942), 513–35, embodies an excellent discussion of the Hopeton estate based upon the John Couper Mss. of the Southern Historical Collection of the University of North Carolina. Also of use for various aspects of ante-bellum life are Margaret Davis Cate: *Our Todays and Yesterdays,* Brunswick, Ga.: 1930; and—in collaboration with Orrin S. Wightman—*Early Days of Coastal Georgia,* St. Simons Island, Ga.: 1955.

Description of the Butler estates will be found in the writings of a number of visitors, notably in *The Correspondence of Aaron Burr, and His Daughter, Theodosia,* Mark Van Doren, ed., New York: 1929; Sir Charles Lyell: *A Second Visit to the United States, 1845–46,* 2 vols., London: 1849; and Basil Hall: *Travels in North America,* 3 vols., Edinburgh: 1829. A selection of the letters of Margaret Hall have been printed in *The Aristocratic Journey,* by Una Pope-Hennessy, ed., New York: 1931, but these are fragments. It is preferable to consult the originals in the Division of Manuscripts of the Library of Congress. Fredrika Bremer, who visited John Couper at Cannon's Point, has recorded her impressions in *The Homes of the New World,* 2 vols., New York: 1853. James Silk Buckingham visited the Savannah region while Fanny

Kemble was at St. Simons. His observations will be found in *The Slave States of America,* 2 vols., London: 1842. See also Jack K. Williams: "Georgia as Seen by Ante-Bellum British Travellers," *Georgia Historical Quarterly,* XXXII (September, 1948), 158–74, and XXXIII (September, 1949), 191–205.

A number of works on Georgian history were consulted. Documents relating to the history of Georgian slavery were found in *The Colonial Records of the State of Georgia,* Atlanta: 1904–15, compiled under the auspices of Allen D. Candler, and in *Tracts and Other Papers, Relating Principally to the Origin, Settlement, and Progress of the Colonies in North America,* Peter Force, ed., 4 vols., Washington, D.C.: 1836–46, reprinted New York: 1947. Other useful documents were found in the *Collections* of the Georgia Historical Society, 12 vols., Savannah, Ga.: 1840–1957. The general histories used were E. Merton Coulter: *Georgia, A Short History,* Chapel Hill, N.C.: rev. ed., 1947, and Walter G. Cooper: *The Story of Georgia,* 4 vols., New York: 1938. Especially useful was Ralph B. Flanders: *Plantation Slavery in Georgia,* Chapel Hill, N.C.: 1933, and two recent monographs, W. W. Abbott: *The Royal Governors of Georgia, 1754–75,* Chapel Hill, N.C.: 1959, and Kenneth Coleman: *The American Revolution in Georgia, 1763–89,* Athens, Ga.: 1958. Of the wider studies of Southern ante-bellum history, F. L. Olmsted: *The Cotton Kingdom,* New York: 1861, and 1953, and Lewis Cecil Gray: *History of Agriculture in the Southern United States to 1860,* Washington, D.C.: 1932, and Gloucester, Mass.: 1958, were indispensable.

F. A. KEMBLE: THE GEORGIA JOURNAL

The publication of Mrs. Kemble's *Journal* was an incident in the history of Anglo-American relations during the Civil War. Here Ephraim Douglass Adams's study *Great Britain and the American Civil War,* 2 vols., New York: n.d. was exceedingly helpful, notwithstanding the naïveté of the author's transformation of "Pam" from the fire-breathing dragon that he was into an olive-bearing dove. A reading of this work and Mrs. Kemble's own correspondence was supplemented with a study of the files of the London *Times*. Conflicting interpretations of the *Journal*'s contemporary influence were culled from sources already mentioned, from Medora Field Perkerson: *White Columns in Georgia*, New York: 1952, and from Mildred Lombard: "Contemporary Opinions of Mrs. Kemble's *Journal of a Residence on a Georgia Plantation*," *Georgia Historical Quarterly*, XIV (December, 1930), 335–43. Also of help was correspondence in the editor's files with the British and American publishers of the *Journal*. The pamphlet version of the latter that was issued in Philadelphia in 1863 is entitled *Views of Judge Woodward and Bishop Hopkins on Negro Slavery at the South*. Of the 1863 reviews the most useful were, for England, *The Spectator* (May 30), *The Athenæum* (June 6), and *The London Review of Politics, Society, Literature, Art, and Science* (June 6); and, for the United States, *Harper's Monthly Magazine* (August), *The North American Review* (October), and *The Atlantic Monthly* (August). Utilization of the *Journal* by the historical profession in the U.S. was studied in works previously cited and also in the following: for the South, Clement Eaton: *A History of the Old South*, New York: 1949; Ulrich B. Phillips: *Life and Labor in the Old South*, Boston: 1929; and William B. Hesseltine: *The South in American History*, New York: 1943. For the North, in addition to works already cited, James Ford Rhodes: *A History of the United States from the Compromise of 1850*, 4 vols., New York: 1893; John Hope Franklin: *The Militant South 1800–61*, Cambridge, Mass.: 1956; and Kenneth M. Stampp: *The Peculiar Institution: Slavery in the Ante-Bellum South*, New York: 1956.

F. A. KEMBLE: WORKS CITED IN THE GEORGIA JOURNAL

CHANNING, WILLIAM ELLERY: *A Letter to the Honorable Henry Clay on the Annexation of Texas to the United States*. Published as a pamphlet, Boston: 1837.

CLAY, HENRY: Speech on the Abolition of Slavery in Washington, D.C., delivered in the U.S. Senate, February 7, 1839. *Congressional Globe,* VII, 354–9.

DANTE ALIGHIERI: *Inferno.*

EDGEWORTH, MARIA: *Castle Rackrent.* Dublin: 1800.

HILDRETH, RICHARD: *The Slave: or Memoirs of Archy Moore.* New York: 1836. Issued as *The White Slave, or Memoirs of a Fugitive.* London: 1952.

LEWIS, MATTHEW GREGORY: *Journal of a West India Proprietor Kept during a Residence in the Island of Jamaica.* London: 1834.

McDUFFIE, GEORGE: Governor's Message to the Assembly of South Carolina. Delivered November 24–25, 1835, and printed in the *Journal* of the General Assembly of the State of South Carolina for the year 1835.

MARTINEAU, HARRIET: *Society in America.* 2 vols., London and New York: 1837.

MOORE, ELY: Speech on the Abolition of Slavery in Washington, D.C., delivered in the U.S. House of Representatives, February 4, 1839. *Congressional Globe,* VII, 237–41.

SCOTT, SIR WALTER: *The Bride of Lammermoor.* Edinburgh: 1830.

STAFFORD HOUSE ADDRESS. "An Affectionate and Christian Address of Many Thousands of Women of Great Britain and Ireland, to their Sisters, the Women of the United States of America." London: 1853.

STOWE, HARRIET BEECHER: *Uncle Tom's Cabin.* Boston: 1852.

———: *Dred, A Tale of the Great Dismal Swamp.* Boston: 1856.

SUMNER, CHARLES: "The Crime against Kansas." Speech delivered in the U.S. Senate, May 19–20, 1856. Boston: 1856.

INDEX

Abbott, Mary, visited by Fanny, 330–2
abolition movement: and British Empire, xxiv–xxviii; and Fanny Kemble, xlix–l, 369–70; denounced by Henry Clay, 209; home in New England, 356
Abraham: carpenter, 190, 194; and grandfather's purchase of freedom, 190–1; learns preparation of carcass, 236–7; conversation with Fanny, 308; and suspected theft, 320, 328
Acacia, 330
Adams, John Quincy: xv, 372; and conversation with Mrs. Kemble, 121
Aleck, house servant, 62; washes salad, 253; asks to be taught reading, 271; reading lessons, 302, 330; rides with Fanny, 326
alligators, 173, 321
Altamaha River: development of region of, xxxviii; described, 47, 49, 86–7, 118; softness of water, 189; encroachment of at Hampton Point, 232
Aristocracy, Southern, see Slaveholders, Southern
Armstrong, Caroline, 290
Ashantilly, home of Sarah Spalding, 182–3
Auber, aged slave, 235–6

Barrett, Jacob, and rice threshing, 117
Bartow, Rev. Theodore, 310, 326
bears, in the woods of Georgia, 173
Ben, son of Minda and R. King, Jr., 273–4, 282
Betty, wife of headman Frank, 91; petitions to be baptized, 175–6; as concubine of R. King, Jr., 176n, 249–50
birds: profusion of, 58–9, 109, 128–9, 168, 292, 331; songs of, 241; see also blackbirds, crane, eagle, duck, heron, mockingbirds, partridges, snipe, woodcocks
Bissett, Alexander, xxii
blackbirds, 84

Bowen, Bishop Nathaniel, acting head of Georgian diocese, 310
Brailsford, William, xli
Bran: Hampton Point driver, 201; relationship to R. King, Jr., 201; flogs Louisa, 215; works for wages, 303; talks with Fanny, 317
Branchtown, xxviii
Brooks, Preston S., 372
Broughton Island, Thomas Bryan's estate: xli; Butler's visit to, 278–80
Brown, John, 373
Brunswick: encounter of Wylly and Hazzard at, 325, 331–2
Brunswick *Advocate*, lvii, 104n, 325n
Brunswick Canal: project for digging of, 104, 122; use of slave and free labor on, 104–5, 122–5, 129; discussed, 279
Bryan, Thomas, owner of Broughton Island, xli, 117n, 278n
Buckingham, James Silk, lvn
Burr, Aaron, at Hampton Point, lvii
Busson Hill, slave settlement at, 268–9, 275, 298–9, 317–18
Butler, Elizabeth, xix, xxi
Butler, Frances, xviii, xix, xxi, xxiii
Butler, Frances (Fan), xxi, xxxvi, xlv, 195
Butler, Harriet, xix, xxi
Butler, John: heir to Georgia plantation, xviii–xix, xxii; family relationships, xx–xxi; mentioned, xxxvi; forbids Fanny to go South, xliv; and condition of estate infirmary, 71–2
Butler, Major Pierce: life and family of, xix–xxiii, 251; mentioned, xli, 274; feudal magnificence of, 220; owner of "Hampton," 228; discussed by John Couper, 265–7; as absentee owner, 283; and childbearing women, 293, 315; and Morris's silver cup, 317
Butler, Pierce Mease: courtship and marriage, xvi, xvii–iii; heir to Georgia plantation, xviii–xix, xxii; family re-

Hamilton, James, xli

Hamilton Plantation, at Gascoigne Bluff: xli, 220*n;* visited, 283–6, 318; fire in woods of, 284

Hammersmith, house on Woodville estate, 126

Hampton, slave settlement at, 199*n*

Hampton Point, Butler estate on St. Simons: xix, xxii; close to Frederica, xxxvii; shift in economic importance of, xxxviii–ix; Butlers' period of residence at, xli–ii; as refuge for Aaron Burr, lvii; and fattening of livestock, 82–3, 184; mentioned, 90, 131, 259, 278; invalids sent to, 146; overseer's house in course of erection, 199–200, 202, 218; high proportion of old people, 202, 203, 206; slave huts compared to Butler Island's, 219; great mansion of, described, 228–9; Altamaha's encroachments at, 232; Major Butler's acquisition of, 251; burial ground, 307–8, 243; *see also* Busson Hill, Hampton, Jones's Creek, St. Annie's

Hannah, Butler Island washerwoman, 94

Hannah, sister of House Molly, described, 227–8

Hannah, Jacob's daughter: 254–5; visited, 255

Harriet, sick slave woman: 72–3; is flogged, 74, 85–6

Hazzard, Dr. Thomas: quarrel with John Wylly, 292; encounter with Wylly, 325; chances of punishment, 332; trial of, and acquittal, 343; *see also* Wylly-Hazzard affair

Hazzard, Col. William: 291; visit to, 319

Hector, accompanies Fanny to Sinclair, 247

heron, blue, 89–90

Hildreth, Richard, author of *The White Slave,* 352*n*

Holmes, Dr. James: mentioned, lviii, 96; as plantation physician, 76; sent for, 90; discusses Darien society, 91–2; and slavery, 91–2; and Presidential candidates, 97; attitude to house servant, 102; on market value of slaves, 191

Hone, Philip, xv*n,* xlvi*n*

honeysuckle, 319–20, 330, 333

House Molly, Hampton house servant: 94; praised by R. King, Jr., 113; visits Butler Island, 174–5; retells story of Louisa, 203–4; and slave marriages, 207; and the quondam glories of Hampton, 228–9; confirms Renty's parentage, 250; tells of Major Butler, 250–1; visited in Jacob's hut, 254

house servants, Negro, in Butler Island household: 60–1, 62; meals and living conditions, 101, 361; degraded by favoritism, 102; not allowed to sleep in master's house, 360–1; *see also* Aleck, Abraham, Jack, John, House Molly, Hannah, Mary, Psyche

Huskisson, Charles, xxiii

Iago, 121

ilex, 184, 218, 242

Irish: discussed, 3–48, 129–30, 322; as laborers, 104–5, 122–5

Isaac, Sophy's son by driver Morris, 270

Israel: mentioned, 309; conversation with Fanny, 311–2; and literacy, 314; accompanies Fanny to Little St. Simons, 333, 334, 336

Ivy, on Butler Island, 56

Jack, Mrs. Kemble's personal slave: 84–5; and Altamaha shad, 146; fishes with Mrs. Kemble, 153–4, 159, 161–2, 172; conversation with, 174, 177; and use of spade in gardening, 191–2; mentioned, 234, 252, 263, 267; fear of snakes, 241, 244; conversation with Margery, 248; path-cutting with Fanny, 258, 292, 300, 303–4; tells of Glasgow's flogging, 275; rides with Fanny, 302, 321, 326; at the North, 343–4; *see also* Cripple Jack

Jackson, Andrew, xv, lvii, 371, 374

Jacob: mentioned, 171; father of Abraham, John, and Joe, 194; bids farewell to Fanny, 194; brother of House Molly, 254

Jaques, 58

jasmine, wild, 181, 192, 226, 261, 316

Jerome, Jennie, xliii

Joe, Psyche's husband: 194, 255; distress of, 136–7; Fanny pleads on behalf of, 137

John, Butler Island cook: 194; punished for theft of ham, 189–90

Jones's Creek: slave settlement at, 218, 275, 302–3, 316; mentioned, 234, 264, 282, 307, 308, 316, 322

jonquil, 195

Journal of a Residence on a Georgian Plantation: product of debate over slavery, ix, xxix; intense study of ante-bellum South, x; influence of Dante upon, xii; mentioned, xvi, xxxi, xxxvi; views of Channing as key to, xxxii–v; composition of, xli–xliv; publication of, xliv–l; English and U.S. editions of, xlix–l; contemporary impact of, l–liii; authenticity of, liii–lvii; picture of slavery in, lviii–lix; as part of American heritage, lix

A NOTE ON THE TYPE

THE TEXT OF THIS BOOK was set on the Linotype in a face called TIMES ROMAN, designed by Stanley Morison for *The Times* (London), and first introduced by that newspaper in 1932. Among typographers and designers of the twentieth century, Stanley Morison has been a strong forming influence, as typographical advisor to the English Monotype Corporation, as a director of two distinguished English publishing houses, and as a writer of sensibility, erudition, and keen practical sense.

Typography, decorations, and binding design by WARREN CHAPPELL.